LONDON CHARTISM
1838–1848

LONDON CHARTISM
1838-1848

DAVID GOODWAY

*Lecturer in the Department of Adult Education
and Extra-Mural Studies, University of Leeds*

CAMBRIDGE UNIVERSITY PRESS

Cambridge
London   New York   New Rochelle
Melbourne   Sydney

Published by the Press Syndicate of the University of Cambridge
The Pitt Building, Trumpington Street, Cambridge CB2 1RP
32 East 57th Street, New York, NY 10022, USA
296 Beaconsfield Parade, Middle Park, Melbourne 3206, Australia

First published 1982

Printed in the United States of America

Library of Congress catalogue card number: 81-12259

British Library Cataloguing in Publication Data
Goodway, David.
London Chartism, 1838–1848.
1. Chartism   2. Labor and laboring
classes – London – Political activity – History
I. Title
322.4′4′09421   HD8396
ISBN 0 521 23867 6

For
Eric and Raphael : Londoners

Contents

PART FOUR
THE TRADES

CONCLUSION   221

Tables

Illustrations

Preface

From the beginnings of scholarly interest in Chartism, effectively with Mark Hovell's *The Chartist Movement* (1918; Manchester, 2nd edn, 1925) and Julius West's *A History of the Chartist Movement* (1920), through G. D. H. Cole's *Chartist Portraits* (1941; 1965 edn) to A. R. Schoyen's *The Chartist Challenge: A Portrait of George Julian Harney* (1958) and Asa Briggs's 'The Local Background to Chartism',[1] the metropolitan origins of the movement and the course of events in the capital during 1838–9 received extensive consideration. Yet in 1960, in his inaugural address to the Society for the Study of Labour History, Asa Briggs rightly designated London Chartism as one of the 'open questions of labour history', as 'there is still . . . no account of Chartist activities in London'.[2] Since then London Chartism has found historians.

First came D. J. Rowe, whose thesis, 'Radicalism in London, 1829–1841: With Special Reference to its Middle- and Working-Class Components' (Southampton MA, 1965), supplied the material for a series of articles. His traditional preoccupation with the pre-history and initial phase of Chartism caused him to survey the years 1838–40, deduce, correctly, that the Spitalfields weavers and generally the metropolitan proletariat were then sluggish and apathetic, and erroneously assume that nothing changed throughout the 1840s.[3]

Iorwerth Prothero's work provided a valuable corrective, not merely to Rowe's contentions but to misconceptions concerning London Chartism that existed for half a century – and longer. His thesis, 'London Working-Class Movements, 1825–1848' (Cambridge PhD, 1967), which has given rise to two important articles,[4] is a detailed treatment of the continuity and diversity of all organized movements of the London working class in the two decades following the Repeal of the Combination Acts. He explicitly excludes 'mob activity and crowd psychology';[5] but his frame of reference provides no excuse for his almost total neglect of 1848 in London.[6]

Most recently David Large has done much to remedy this deficiency of Prothero's with 'London in the Year of Revolution, 1848',[7] an essay which, though often perceptive, fails, however, to do justice to either the rich incident of the year or the equally abundant primary materials.

This book is, then, the first full-length study to be devoted solely to Chartism in London. In Part One some leading characteristics of early-Victorian London, notably its economic and social structure, are considered. A short, introductory section, this concludes with a 'profile' of metropolitan Chartism, including the distribution of localities by year and area and an occupational analysis of Chartist militants. The principal section, Part Two, is a narrative account of London Chartism, correlating its development to fluctuations in the economy, from 1838 to 1848 and reveals that while 1842 saw the movement reach its peak in terms of conventional organization and agitation, 1848 marks the high-point of turbulence and revolutionary potential.[8] It is shown that the convergence, and eventual collaboration, of Chartism and Irish nationalism was of great significance in the upsurge of 1848.

Part Two finishes with the fullest attempt so far to extricate the insurrectionary plans of 1848, demonstrating that they cannot be dubbed as 'Cuffay's conspiracy'.[9] Attention too is paid to the riots of 1842 and 1848, but these, ignored by preceding historians other than F. C. Mather, Lisa Keller and Large,[10] are considered separately in Part Three where there is also a lengthy reappraisal of 10 April 1848, whose tag as a 'fiasco' is rejected. There follows an examination of the succeeding, but virtually unknown, crisis of 12 June 1848. These passages depend to a large extent on the Treasury Solicitor's Records and the printed *Sessions Papers,* the former, as far as is known, and the latter, without doubt, unused previously for a study of Chartism, as well as on one of the few systematic investigations of the Records of the Metropolitan Police Offices.

While there is considerable emphasis in Part Four on the trade societies, the attempt in this section is to write an economic history, albeit compressed, of the city in the Chartist decade, drawing on a variety of secondary and, predominantly, primary sources, and thereby to provide the socio-economic setting of the London movement (the political relationship between the trades and which, at each of its stages, is considered in Part Two).

It is argued that London's failure to rally to Chartism in 1838–9 was probably, despite all the other factors, in itself fatal to the movement's chances of success. Nevertheless the concentration of this book is necessarily on the events of the 1840s, which Prothero and Large alone have before treated in any depth. But whereas Prothero confined himself to organized Chartism and trade unionism, and Large almost exclusively to the former, here, in addition, crowd behaviour and the maintenance of order, and the background of changing economic organization and resultant tensions, are examined at length while the role of the Irish is also considered. And in contrast to Prothero's skimming over the Year of Revolutions, accepting the clichés of 120 years of historiography, the present writer, impressed by the scale of Chartist activity in 1848, particularly in London, undertakes a major reassessment: whose coverage is not only substantially more comprehensive than that of Large's essay but the conclusions of which differ significantly.

Acknowledgments

Acknowledgment should first be made to the principal institutions at which the research for this book has been conducted, whether the visits have been repeated frequently over the years, or, in one or two cases, consisted of single, rewarding ones. They are the Department of Printed Books, British Library; Department of Manuscripts, British Library; British Library Newspaper Library, Colindale; Public Record Office; British Library of Political and Economic Science, London School of Economics; University of London Library, especially the Goldsmiths' Library; University Library, Cambridge; Bodleian Library, Oxford; Guildhall Library; Bishopsgate Institute; Birmingham Reference Library; Manchester Central Library; Leeds Reference Library; Brotherton Library, University of Leeds.

The Royal Archives, Windsor Castle, were consulted (and are quoted from) with the gracious permission of Her Majesty the Queen.

The late James Klugmann directed me to the appropriate material in his Collection at the Library of the Communist Party of Great Britain.

This book started life as a doctoral thesis, which had an abnormally long gestation. That it was finally completed, and a book now appears, owes much to the generous encouragement and assistance I have received from many people. I have profited in various ways from conversations and correspondence with Dorothy Thompson, Iorwerth Prothero, Gareth Stedman Jones, George Pattison, Seán Hutton, Tom Kemnitz and Tony Donajgrodzki. I would like to thank my examiners, T. C. Barker and Asa Briggs, for their elatingly appreciative reception of the thesis and stimulating comments. Barrie Trinder very kindly provided me with a transcript of the relevant section of the Rev. W. T. Henderson's MS., 'Recollections of his Life'. In addition, material has been drawn to my attention by Nicholas Gould, George Hauger, George J. Billy (who also sent from New York photocopies of Robert Crowe's publications) and Neal Rigby (who then loaned me a volume which the British Library does not hold).

I am particularly indebted to Barrie Trinder, Dorothy Thompson, John Saville and the late J. E. Williams, who all invited me to address diverse groups and thereby ensured that sections of my research were written up. In this respect, though, the role of Raphael Samuel has been unparalleled. He has never lost confidence in me nor ceased to be enthusiastic about London Chartism and has been responsible for my giving no less than four papers connected with the subject at the Ruskin History Workshops.

I wish to express my immense gratitude to Eric Hobsbawm, the supervisor of the original thesis: for encouragement, criticism, extraordinary patience, and example. I owe more to him than I think he appreciates.

Most recently, John Saville has been selfless in his support of my work and its publication. His own book on the response of the British state in 1848, the culmination of more than thirty years' investigation and reflection, must be awaited by all students of Chartism and of the Victorian working class with eager anticipation.

For as long as Helen Goodway has lived with me she has lived with, off and on, London Chartism. Her belief in the value of this research seems to have been unfaltering; and it was she who converted a virtual palimpsest of a manuscript into a working typescript. All the same, she fully recognizes the justice of the dedication.

September 1980
Keighley

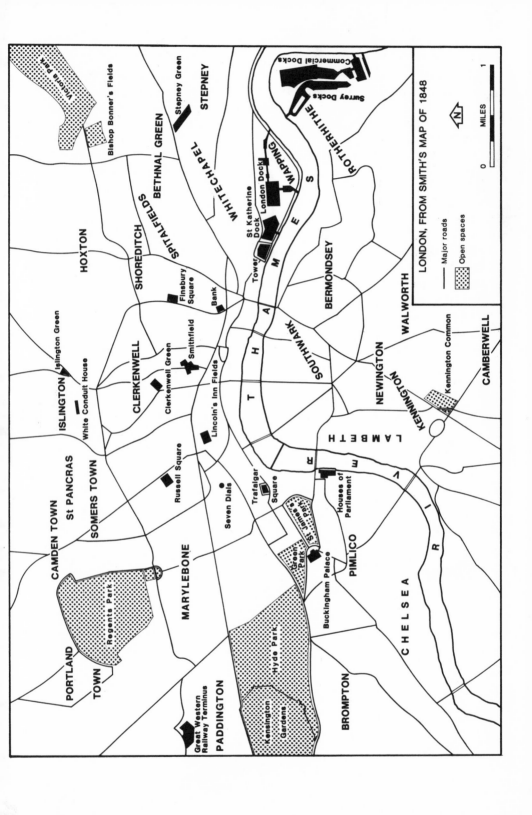

LONDON, FROM SMITH'S MAP OF 1848

— Major roads
⠿ Open spaces

N

0 ——— 1
MILES

VICTORIA PARK

Bishop Bonner's Fields

Stepney Green

STEPNEY

BETHNAL GREEN

SPITALFIELDS

WHITECHAPEL

SHOREDITCH

HOXTON

Finsbury Square

Bank

Smithfield

CLERKENWELL

Clerkenwell Green

Islington Green

ISLINGTON

White Conduit House

Lincoln's Inn Fields

Russell Square

Seven Dials

Trafalgar Square

St Katherine Dock

London Dock

WAPPING

Tower

Commercial Docks

Surrey Docks

ROTHERHITHE

THAMES

BERMONDSEY

SOUTHWARK

WALWORTH

NEWINGTON

KENNINGTON

Kennington Common

CAMBERWELL

LAMBETH

RIVER

Houses of Parliament

St James's Park

Green Park

Buckingham Palace

PIMLICO

CHELSEA

BROMPTON

Kensington Gardens

Hyde Park

PADDINGTON

Great Western Railway Terminus

Regents Park

PORTLAND TOWN

CAMDEN TOWN

St PANCRAS

SOMERS TOWN

MARYLEBONE

PART ONE

The character of
London and its Chartism

Some aspects of London in the
Chartist period

London was already a huge city, with populations of 1,873,676 and 2,362,236 in 1841 and 1851 respectively, easily the largest in Europe and, indeed, the world, far outstripping all rivals.[1] On the other hand, as a continuously built-up area, it remained remarkably compact. Concentrated urban development south of the Thames was very limited – principally to Lambeth, Southwark and Bermondsey, although Kennington, Newington, Walworth and Camberwell were being rapidly filled in – on account of the belated construction of bridges across the river. On the east, although the marshes of the Lea Valley were an impediment to expansion, the city still fell considerably short of them. To the north suburbs did not extend farther than Camden Town or Islington and to the west Kensington Gardens marked the boundary.[2]

In many significant ways London remained a pre-industrial city, exuberant, chaotic and semi-rural. For example, thousands of cows, pigs and sheep were kept in sheds and cellars in the central districts, even roaming the streets;[3] and twice or more a week the 'immense droves of cattle, besides herds and flocks of all kinds' collected at Smithfield spread 'disorder and confusion' throughout the capital.[4]

But, fundamentally, London life had been undergoing – and was continuing to experience – a radical transformation, becoming increasingly sober and orderly. Gas lighting made the streets incomparably safer by night. Pall Mall was illuminated as early as 1807; by 1841, it was claimed, 'the metropolis now burns gas in every square, street, alley, lane, passage, and court', and thereby 'half the work of prevention of crime was accomplished'.[5] With the establishment of the Metropolitan Police in 1829 the city, it is argued in Part Three, was, within a decade, subjected to an astonishingly far-reaching system of official regulation and restraint.[6] Beyond these two important innovations, centred on the 1820s and 1830s, lies a long-term alteration in the attitudes and behaviour of Londoners.[7]

The metropolitan populace had been notorious throughout the eighteenth century for its turbulence, insubordination, violence and brutishness – for Bartholomew Fair and 'Tyburn Fair'. In the 1750s it was remarked: 'In London amongst the lower class all is anarchy,

3

drunkenness and thievery.' Nevertheless M. Dorothy George convincingly discerns a vast difference between the second quarter and end of the century.[8] As is well known, Francis Place, born in 1771, dwelt obsessively on the improvements he considered had occurred by the 1820s since the years of his youth.[9] Although uncritical reliance on any part of Place's voluminous testimonies must be avoided[10] there is little reason to doubt his insistence on the change in metropolitan mores – for instance, not unfamiliar with East London, he was greatly struck by the progress that had taken place in Wapping and Rosemary Lane.[11] So, he wrote in 1834:

Forty years ago the working people with very few exceptions were to a great extent, drunken, dirty immoral and ignorant. He who was the best paid was then the most dissolute. This is not so now . . . Drunkenness among journeymen dirtiness, immorality and gross ignorance are not the prevailing vices. Their manners are greatly improved, their morals are mended their knowledge is considerably extended, and is constantly though slowly increasing. That these things are so will be affirmed by any one who has had the opportunity of observing the working people and has observed them during even the last twenty years. Proofs abound in every direction, in their dress their deportment their language in the reading rooms they frequent, in the book clubs and institutions of which they are members, and the books they possess as their own.[12]

These things *were* affirmed by others: by William Lovett, for one, as early as 1834 as well as in evidence to a Select Committee of 1849 and in his autobiography, who attributed the improvement to educational activities and the spread of coffee houses.[13] In short, Londoners by the Chartist decade were less intoxicated, brutal and debauched, more tractable, self-improving and self-disciplined. The alteration in mores had naturally not yet run its course. Executions continued to attract milling, gloating crowds;[14] and in 1869–70 John O'Neil and another 'Old Crispin' drew a stark contrast between the temper of that period and the drunkenness, pugilism, bull-baiting, dog-fighting and other vices of shoemakers forty to sixty years before.[15]

The metropolitan economy

We may trace the vastness of London, the varied character of its external features, and the wonderful diversity which its social aspects present, to three distinct causes. First, its official supremacy, as the residence of the sovereign, the seat of the government and legislature, and all the most important departments of the state; secondly, its manufacturing industry; and, thirdly, its commercial importance as a port. Any one of these elements would nourish a large amount of population; but without the two latter it would be kept within moderate limits, and it is chiefly in consequence of their influence that London is twice as large as Paris.[16]

The position – indeed dominance – which London possesses by virtue of capital city is too well appreciated by Britons for it to be elaborated upon, other than to stress that metropolitan Chartism's initial feebleness gravely undermined the entire movement's effectiveness.[17] The pre-eminence of the Port of London is less, but still widely, recognized: at mid-century a quarter of Britain's entire foreign trade was conducted on the Thames and, in addition, there was the extensive coasting trade.[18] Even so the link is rarely made between the raw materials imported or the goods exported[19] and their English destinations or origins. In both cases London itself was very often recipient or producer. And it is London's importance as a centre of 'manufacturing industry' that is generally overlooked for the entire nineteenth century – London was actually the country's *principal* centre of production.[20]

This fact was obscured from early in the century as it became assumed that: 'Our large manufacturing districts are, for obvious reasons, located in the vicinity of our coal-fields' and therefore 'London may be regarded as a vast trading and commercial, rather than a manufacturing town'.[21] Henceforward manufacturing industry was synonymous with textiles, metallurgical extraction and working, and steam-power; and the distinction was drawn between the products of the factory and 'mere handicrafts'.[22] It would, however, be manifestly absurd to deny the name of 'industry' to such prominent sections of the metropolitan (and national) economy as shoemaking, tailoring, hatting, building, silk-weaving, the working of copper, tin-plate and other metals, engineering, furniture-making, leather production, printing, watchmaking, shipbuilding, etc.[23] Further, it is necessary to

5

state categorically that, while many of these industries were either to collapse or to be drastically curtailed later in the century, before 1850 it was Spitalfields silk alone that was in decline (it had reached an advanced stage in its demise).[24]

Not only did symbiosis exist between the river and metropolitan industry: there was also considerable interdependence between many of the crafts. The hair and wool by-products of the leather trades provided the bodies for stuff hats, and the silk of their successors could come from Spitalfields.[25] Bermondsey leather met the demands of shoemakers, cabinet- and chair-makers, bookbinders, coachbuilders, etc. The coppersmiths produced boilers for London's sugar-refineries, breweries and distilleries as well as for engineers.[26]

Another prominent feature, much commented upon, was the extreme localization of several industries. Silk was overwhelmingly confined to 'Spitalfields', leather to Bermondsey, hatting to Southwark, watchmaking and jewellery to Clerkenwell, coachmaking around Long Acre and sugar-refineries 'in the neighbourhood of Goodman's Fields' (Whitechapel). This intense concentration of numerous producers in small, widely separated areas together with its opposite – the dispersal of other large industries throughout the vast city – may go some way to account for the impression of most contemporary observers that London was not the capital of 'manufacturing industry'.[27]

As Table 1 indicates the typical unit (of production and distribution) was a tiny shop with either a master working alone or employing one, two, three or four men; and although there were a considerable number of employers with between five and nineteen men, such concerns were still small-scale. On the other hand, there *were* 217 masters who employed more than fifty men and eighty masters with over 100.[28] In fact, an 1848 map of London displays an astonishingly large number of 'manufactories', etc.,[29] while, in 1841–2, George Dodd was able to publish a series of articles on 'days' at twenty-one *London* 'factories', stating:

There are many establishments in or near London, such as water-works, gas-works, ship-yards, tan-yards, brewhouses, distilleries, glass-works, &c., the extent of which would excite no little surprise in those who for the first time visited them. Indeed the densely packed masses of building forming the eastern districts of the metropolis, on both sides of the river, include individual establishments which, although they would appear like little towns if isolated, scarcely meet the eye of a passenger through the crowded streets.[30]

Whatever the size of the average unit, workers in the Chartist period had no doubts that large (or larger) employers, engrossing a disproportionate share of the market, had risen and were continuing

Table 1. *Number of men employed by London masters, 1851*

Number of men employed	Masters employing this number of men
0*	10,594
1	3,182
2	3,092
3	1,922
4	1,338
5	710
6	729
7	329
8	322
9	183
10–19	985
20–9	416
30–9	183
40–9	121
50–74	100
75–99	37
100–49	39
150–99	14
200–49	10
250–99	5
300–49	5
350+	7
TOTAL	24,323

*Or number not known.
Source: Population Tables, II, Ages, Civil Condition, Occupations, and Birth-Place of the People, 1852–3, LXXXVIII, Part 1, I [1691–I] [hereafter 1851 Census], p. 29.

to emerge from the shoal of small masters nor that a capitalist system was remodelling productive relationships.[31] The building trades were especially conscious of the operations of 'the devil-capitalists'.[32] Thus a carpenter wrote:

That the workman does not receive a price for his labour that will enable him to procure the necessaries and comforts of life for himself and family, and that the employer receives more than an equitable profit for the outlay of his capital, is evident . . . first look at the condition of the 'large employer'. You see men, the major part of whom have risen from the ranks of the journeymen, have accumulated large fortunes, and are now the worst enemies of the men, who spurn and revile you, and who often treat you worse than the dogs that prowl the streets of the metropolis. Why do they do so? . . . from a love of gain, that a few men may amass largely, while the mass of the men of the trade are reduced to a state of slavery, dependent on the caprice of these men for the food that sustains life. Then look at the condition of the 'small masters'. You see men, partly victims of the 'large masters', yet still more the victims of avarice and an aping disposition to follow the footsteps of the large employers; vieing with them in crushing labour to the earth.[33]

The Chartist locality of stonemasons, immediately before the furious strike of 1841–2, addressed the trade unionists of London:

Brothers in Bondage . . . We have been now engaged for a number of years in battling with a monster, which although we have at times rendered powerless, yet have we not been able to conquer. Fellow men, we adopted the system of Trades' Unions in the full hope that by that means we could defend ourselves against the ferocious monster CAPITAL, who is at all times eager to appease his greedy appetite upon the very miseries of the sons of industry.[34]

Another mason had similarly lambasted 'the determination of the capitalists to make tools of the operatives . . . whilst they themselves revel in luxury from the sweat of our brows'.[35] But throughout the London trades there was widespread recognition of the decisive influence of 'men of capital'.[36] The tailors particularly resented the new-found, excessive riches of their employers: 'The masters appeared to be increasing their wealth . . . that they now had their drawing rooms, counting houses, carriages, and, in some instances, their hunters and hounds, whilst the operatives, who produced all, were left to the miseries of a cold Poor Law bastile [sic].'[37] And, during the lock-out of 1838–9, the bookbinders castigated 'those unprincipled capitalists – and money-mongers' and 'the all-grasping capitalist'.[38] Even a Seven Dials broadside of 1853 could proclaim:

The monied men have had their way, large fortunes have they made,
For things could not be otherwise, with labour badly paid,
They roll along with splendour, and with a saucey [sic] tone,
As Cobbett says, they eat the meat, while the workmen [sic] gnaws the bone.[39]

Although substantial fortunes had been made from manufactures – but, above all, commerce – in the eighteenth century,[40] it is clear that a more pervasive, general process, a transformation, was occurring in the 1830s and 1840s and had got under way around the end of the Napoleonic Wars. One of the outstanding characteristics of London was the multitude of trades and occupations. Clapham, following the 1831 classification, settles for 'four hundred or so', but Dodd's conjecture of 1,300 to 1,400 is a more plausible estimate.[41] It is, however, erroneous to conclude from this that London's social structure was that of a pre-industrial city with a host of independent artisans or that, at most, a wage-earning labour force was only gradually appearing. While the majority of workers were hand craftsmen and many did not labour for wages but were paid by the piece (e.g. pair of boots, garment, item of furniture), there can be little doubt that the second quarter of the nineteenth century saw the making of a metropolitan proletariat.[42] Thus Bédarida, in his meticulous analysis of the 1851 Census data, can allocate four-fifths (80.5 per cent) of the total active population to the 'working class' – Classes III, IV and V of the classification by the twentieth-century Registrars-General – to which he has assigned employers of less than five men.[43]

Another essential aspect of the London economy was the existence of a luxury market serving not only its (more or less) permanent residents but the wealthy of the entire nation. Its presence ensured the continuance of quality production and highly skilled craftsmen, even if they worked increasingly within capitalist structures. On the other hand, there was a vast mass-market to be satisfied.[44] This was met, not by steam-power, mechanization and factory organization, but by simultaneously expanding the labour force, lowering wages and manufacturing an ample supply of underpriced goods – at their worst the produce of the intensively exploitative and uncontrollably expanding dishonourable trades. Slop production (i.e. sweating) and capitalism are impossible to separate, for in a handicraft economy their logic is identical. In relentless combination they moulded the working-class politics and trade unionism of the thirties and forties by the proletarianization of the metropolitan craftsmen, forging a common consciousness of disparate groups of workers.[45] The concomitant conflicts ensured that the class collaboration exemplified by cities like Birmingham and Sheffield could not flourish in London despite the superficial socio-economic similarity. This is not to say that no small employers were Chartists – a fair number, appreciating the thrust of contemporary developments, are known to have been – but in London there could be no significant, large-scale alliance between the bourgeoisie and the artisans.[46]

This two-pronged assault on the position of the artisan led to attempts to regain 'social independence', albeit in new, collective forms. First came the experiments in producers' co-operatives, designed to exclude middlemen between them and the consumers, of the late twenties and early thirties, culminating in the National Equitable Labour Exchange and United Trades' Association of 1832–4.[47] In 1832 the impressive Operative Builders' Union (OBU), based principally upon Manchester, Birmingham and London, emerged, uniting the building trades in seven sections. A trivial dispute in July 1834 concerning whose beer Cubitt's workmen would drink resulted in a lock-out by the London masters. The document was presented to the members of the Union, which rejected all forms of the contract system and demanded a uniform rate of wages and the dismissal of non-unionists. Virtual defeat in the autumn, following collapse in Lancashire and Birmingham, caused the break-up of the Builders' Union at the end of 1834.[48] The most spectacular – and mythologized – of the general unions was the (Grand National) Consolidated Trades Union (GNCTU) of 1834.

It is the Webbs who were, uncharacteristically, responsible for the exaggeration that: 'Within a few weeks the Union appears to have been joined by at least half a million members.'[49] Examination of balance sheets has convincingly indicated an approximate, but peak, national paying membership in April 1834 of little more than 16,000. Such a savage scaling-down of the Consolidated Union's countrywide support has, however, accentuated its importance for London, since, of that total, the capital contributed no fewer than 11,000 members. There were 4,600 tailors, 3,000 cordwainers, just over 1,000 silk-weavers and the remaining 2,500 or so were spread across twenty-one other occupations (of which the principal were the smiths, cabinet-makers, rope-makers, tanners, silk skein dyers, silk hatters and wood turners).[50]

No more is known of the weavers' involvement, save that their adherence had terminated by February 1835.[51] The tailors, who dominated the formation of the Consolidated Union in February 1834 – and had already been preparing to end the abuses in their trade – launched a major struggle against their employers in April demanding 'equalization' of wages, a fixed working day and no work except on the masters' premises. They had opened their houses of call to all and were seeking to abolish the division of their craft into 'honourable' and 'dishonourable' sections. The strike, which involved some 10,000 tailors, ended in complete capitulation and their secession from the Consolidated Union in June, when the cordwainers, confronting exactly the same problems and angry at the tailors' conflict taking precedence over their own grievances,[52] also withdrew. The defection of the two largest component groups ensured the Union's demise (though, renamed, it survived until the summer of 1835).[53]

The only success of 1834 was the massive meeting at Copenhagen Fields and procession to the Home Office on 21 April in protest at the transportation of the Dorchester labourers. As ever with popular demonstrations, estimates of the numbers involved varied according to political sympathies, but there is a reasonable consensus that 40,000 to 50,000 took part in the procession, while it would appear that more than 100,000 attended the preliminary meeting.[54]

The heady expectations and ensuing reverses of 1834 were a decisive influence on the politico-economic attitudes of Londoners in the Chartist years. In 1847, at a meeting to canvass support for the National Association of United Trades, a weaver declared:

he had been of opinion [sic] ever since the Builders' and Consolidated Union were broken up, that the working classes had been going downwards, for the want of an institution of the same magnitude, that these bodies were. The means at their disposal, at the present time, to resist the innovations of capital, were comparatively small, and were getting smaller: but the pence of the millions, with its moral power, will accomplish everything needed by the working classes, and rescue them from their present degraded state.[55]

On the other hand, many afterwards shied away from grandiose schemes of emancipation, especially if their trade societies were to be involved.[56]

A profile of London Chartism

The role of metropolitan Chartism in the national movement was inherently of major importance. The triumph or failure of Chartism, however formidable its provincial mobilizations, was ultimately dependent – to an extent probably not previously recognized – on the contribution that the capital made to the agitation. But any popular movement in the seat of government was inevitably subject to the most rigorous restrictions available; and from 1829 the authorities were equipped with an increasingly effective Metropolitan Police which in 1842 and 1848 was deployed to curb Chartist disturbances with impressive success. This second consideration, of the maintenance of public order, is treated in detail in Part Three; that of the indispensability of London's support runs throughout Part Two and is directly, albeit briefly, examined in the Conclusion.

Chartism in London, it will be emphasized, only emerged as a distinctive movement from 1840–1. During the 1840s metropolitan Chartist culture appears to have been much the same as that of the major centres of Chartist activity in other parts of the country: with one outstanding exception. The Londoners tended to be non-religious or actively anti-Christian.[57] Metropolitan rationalism was a deep-rooted characteristic both preceding and postdating Chartism.[58] Chartism inherited another metropolitan tradition dating from the 1790s, that of the insurrectionary conspiracy, with disastrous consequences in 1848.

Indeed, London Chartism was the natural extension, developing without discontinuity, of the previous half-century of artisan, Jacobin radicalism. The two principal, unrivalled influences on thought were William Cobbett and Thomas Paine. The birthday of the 'immortal Thomas Paine' was commemorated annually by suppers and speeches.[59] So, while the labour theory of value and class conflict were essential components of Chartist political theory, it was also intrinsically backward-looking: to the eighteenth century and beyond. It was not a confident, proletarian anticipation of socialism – at least, during the decade in which Chartism was a mass movement – and represents instead the mental endeavour to reassert artisan independence and an agrarian foundation of society in the new industrial world.

Table 2. *Number of Chartist localities per year and their distribution, 1838–49*

	1838	1839	1840	1841	1842	1843	1844	1845	1846	1847	1848	1849
Middlesex	1	4	1	2	3	3	2	2	2	0	1	0
Westminster	0	6	2	6	8	2	1	1	1	1	3	2
Marylebone	1	2	2	2	5	4	3	3	3	3	11	4
Finsbury	1	7	5	4	6	5	5	1	0	2	4	1
City	3	5	2	7	6	3	2	1	1	2	3	2
Tower Hamlets	2	13	4	10	13	10	8	3	3	8	25	8
Essex	0	1	0	0	0	1	1	1	0	1	1	0
Kent	0	2	0	2	3	2	2	2	1	1	2	1
Southwark	2	2	0	2	7	6	1	1	1	1	3	1
Lambeth	2	3	1	3	6	6	2	2	2	3	3	2
Surrey	1	6	1	1	6	1	0	0	0	1	1	0
TOTAL	13	51	18	39	63	43	27	17	14	23	57	21

Although in 1848 two, perhaps three, London localities were named after Ernest Jones, he was not yet the disciple of Marx and was honoured as martyr, poet and gentleman. The other localities which then took personal names were the Alfred Lodge,[60] Wat Tyler League and Wat Tyler Brigade, Wallace Brigade, William Tell Brigade,[61] Washington Brigade, Thomas Paine Locality and Emmett Brigade.[62]

While the Chartists were therefore linked with indissoluble bonds to their predecessors, their relationship to later metropolitan radicalism is utterly different. A profound hiatus exists around mid-century and although Chartism and former Chartists could not fail to influence developments in trade unionism and the renewed movement for parliamentary reform, the connections appear amazingly slight given the psychological hold, combined with the mass penetration, of Chartism in its heyday.[63] Intensive research on the three decades following 1850 could cause substantial revision of this view,[64] yet such an outcome seems unlikely. Only the tiny band of O'Brienites carried ideas of the 1840s into the 1860s and 1870s.[65]

Chartist life centred on the localities and Tables 2–5 show the total number of localities (more properly, for the earliest years, Chartist societies) which existed per year, 1838–49, and per month in the three peak years of agitation, for the entire metropolitan area. Localities are included which were experiencing periods of known disorganization and even whose existence is uncertain or conjectured. They are grouped according to the five parliamentary constituencies of Westminster, Marylebone, Finsbury, the City, Tower Hamlets, Southwark and Lambeth, and the adjoining counties of Middlesex, Essex, Kent and Surrey. This method is not ideal but does have the

Table 3. *Number of Chartist localities per month and their distribution, 1839*

	Jan.	Feb.	Mar.	Apr.	May	June	July	Aug.	Sept.	Oct.	Nov.	Dec.
Middlesex	1	1	2	2	1	1	1	1	0	0	0	0
Westminster	1	2	2	4	3	3	3	3	4	5	2	2
Marylebone	1	1	1	2	2	2	2	2	2	2	1	1
Finsbury	2	2	3	6	6	5	5	5	5	5	6	5
City	3	2	2	4	4	3	2	2	2	2	2	2
Tower Hamlets	4	4	8	10	6	7	6	5	6	6	4	3
Essex	0	0	0	1	1	0	0	0	0	0	0	0
Kent	1	0	0	0	1	1	1	0	0	0	0	0
Southwark	2	2	1	1	1	1	1	1	0	0	0	0
Lambeth	2	2	2	3	1	1	1	1	1	1	1	1
Surrey	3	3	3	5	5	2	2	1	1	1	1	1
TOTAL	20	19	24	38	31	26	24	21	21	22	17	15

Table 4. *Number of Chartist localities per month and their distribution, 1842*

	Jan.	Feb.	Mar.	Apr.	May	June	July	Aug.	Sept.	Oct.	Nov.	Dec.
Middlesex	2	2	3	3	3	3	3	3	3	2	2	2
Westminster	5	7	8	7	5	4	4	4	3	2	2	2
Marylebone	2	2	3	5	5	5	5	5	5	5	5	4
Finsbury	2	2	2	2	2	2	2	2	2	4	4	5
City	4	4	4	4	5	4	4	5	3	3	3	3
Tower Hamlets	7	8	9	10	8	8	9	8	7	8	8	8
Essex	0	0	0	0	0	0	0	0	0	0	0	0
Kent	2	2	2	2	2	1	1	1	1	2	2	2
Southwark	2	2	3	3	3	5	3	3	4	4	5	5
Lambeth	3	4	4	4	4	4	5	5	6	6	6	6
Surrey	2	2	2	2	3	3	3	1	1	2	3	3
TOTAL	31	35	40	42	40	39	39	37	35	38	40	40

considerable merit of employing geographical categories in terms of which Chartists themselves frequently thought.

The localities constituted organized Chartism and it is primarily its history that is traced in Part Two. In the excited years of 1842 and, above all, 1848 the course of Chartism also comprehended riotous outbreaks and great meetings. The Chartist crowd was an entity very different from the locality, not only in size but in social composition. Part Three is devoted to the crowd, its control by the police and the counter-demonstrations of 1848. The third dimension of metropolitan Chartism was the trades from which enrolled Chartists were overwhelmingly drawn and in whose affairs Chartists were prominent.

The occupations of all those Chartists (up to 1849 and including the members of the London Working Men's Association (LWMA),

Table 5. *Number of Chartist localities per month and their distribution, 1848*

	Jan.	Feb.	Mar.	Apr.	May	June	July	Aug.	Sept.	Oct.	Nov.	Dec.
Middlesex	0	0	0	0	0	0	0	1	0	0	0	0
Westminster	1	1	1	2	2	2	2	2	1	2	2	2
Marylebone	3	3	4	4	10	10	10	9	4	4	4	4
Finsbury	2	2	2	2	2	3	3	3	1	1	1	1
City	1	2	2	2	3	3	2	2	2	2	2	2
Tower Hamlets	7	7	7	9	17	16	14	12	9	9	7	5
Essex	1	1	1	1	0	0	0	0	0	0	0	0
Kent	1	1	1	2	2	2	2	2	1	1	1	0
Southwark	1	1	1	1	2	2	1	1	2	1	1	1
Lambeth	3	2	2	2	2	2	2	2	2	2	2	2
Surrey	1	1	1	1	1	1	0	0	0	0	0	0
TOTAL	21	21	22	26	41	41	36	34	22	22	20	17

1836–9) for whom information is available are analysed in Table 6. These figures seem in general to be reliable and to provide a serviceable indication of participation by individuals in the Chartist movement. An index greater than 1.00, of course, denotes a propensity to Chartism: but it is suggested that only trades with indices in excess of 2.00 can be designated as 'markedly Chartist' and those with indices over 4.00 as 'outstandingly Chartist'.

Several provisos must, however, be stated. If the leather finishers' locality of 1842–3 had had, like the coppersmiths and braziers or carvers and gilders, the names of its general council printed in the *Northern Star,* the number of leather dressers (and curriers) could have been increased by six or eight and the trade might then have appeared as 'outstandingly Chartist', which it undoubtedly was. In contrast the commitment of the printers and bookbinders, although Chartist crafts, is overstated. The numbers of both are approximately doubled by men who were members of the LWMA in 1836–9 but are not otherwise known as Chartists. The same reservation probably applies, less forcefully, to the cabinet-makers – certainly not to the other furniture trades – and only to the extent of relegating them from their tenuous position as 'markedly Chartist' to a Chartist propensity. Similarly, and of greatest deceptiveness, the total of clock and watchmakers, especially non-radical artisans, is inflated to twelve by the presence of eight LWMA members equally inactive after 1838.

Even allowing for these reservations the indices of Chartist participation are at odds with the schema advanced by Iorwerth Prothero: that it was the 'lower', weakly organized trades which were Chartist, while the 'upper' or 'aristocratic' trades held aloof.[66] Rather the engineers and millwrights were only marginally less radical than the

Table 6. *Chartist occupations*

Occupation	Number of Chartists	% of Chartists' occupations	Total in London, 1841	% of male population of economically active age, 1841	Index of Chartist participation (column 2/ column 4)
Boot and shoemakers	269	23.24	24,857	4.33	5.38
Tailors	98	8.46	20,265	3.53	2.40
Carpenters and joiners	91	7.86	18,238	3.18	2.48
Stonemasons	38	3.28	3,464	0.60	5.44
Bricklayers	17	1.47	6,719	1.17	1.26
Plasterers	12	1.04	2,586	0.45	2.30
Plumbers	7	0.60	3,607[a]	0.63	0.96
Painters and glaziers	22	1.90	7,820[a]	1.36	1.40
Other building trades (builders, paper-hangers, slaters)	7	0.60	2,677	0.47	1.30
Silk-weavers	57	4.92	7,720	1.34	3.66
Coppersmiths and braziers	11	0.95	1,029	0.18	5.30
Tin-plate workers	7	0.60	1,409	0.25	2.47
Boilermakers	1	0.09	452	0.08	1.10
Engineers and millwrights	23	1.99	4,977	0.87	2.29
Smiths (i.e. blacksmiths)	10	0.86	6,679	1.16	0.74
Other metal trades (brass-workers, whitesmiths, wire-workers)	12	1.04	3,109	0.54	1.91
Cabinet-makers	25	2.16	5,950[b]	1.04	2.08
Upholsterers	4	0.35	1,311[b]	0.23	1.51
Chair-makers	8	0.69	1,538	0.27	2.58
Turners	6	0.52	1,505	0.26	1.98
Carvers and gilders	18	1.55	1,975	0.34	4.52
Hatters	35	3.02	2,819	0.49	6.16
Tanners	1	0.09	894	0.16	0.55
Curriers and leather dressers	11	0.95	2,290	0.40	2.38
Other leather trades (fellmongers, leather-dyers)	2	0.17	304	0.05	3.26
Printers	44	3.80	6,553	1.14	3.33
Type-founders	2	0.17	449	0.08	2.21
Other printing trades (stereotype-founders, copper plate printers)	4	0.35	308	0.05	6.44

Table 6 (*cont.*)

Occupation	Number of Chartists	% of Chartists' occupations	Total in London, 1841	% of male population of economically active age, 1841	Index of Chartist participation (column 2/ column 4)
Bookbinders	15	1.30	2,184[c]	0.38	3.41
Booksellers and publishers	9	0.78	1,865[c]	0.32	2.39
Newsagents and newsmen	8	0.69	375	0.07	10.58
Newspaper editors and reporters; authors	6	0.52	321	0.06	9.27
Goldbeaters	0	—	371	0.06	—
Jewellers, goldsmiths and silversmiths	12	1.04	3,899	0.68	1.53
Other gold and silver workers	3	0.26	418	0.07	3.56
Clock and watchmakers	12	1.04	4,223	0.74	1.41
Ship and boat-builders	3	0.26	2,808	0.49	0.53
Rope-makers	1	0.09	1,162	0.20	0.43
Coopers	7	0.60	3,504	0.61	0.99
Sawyers	1	0.09	2,977	0.52	0.17
Bakers	13	1.12	8,791	1.53	0.73
Linen drapers	0	—	1,783	0.31	—
Drapers	1	0.09	2,762	0.48	0.18
Chemists and druggists	2	0.17	1,803	0.31	0.55
Clerks and accountants	20	1.73	21,463	3.74	0.46
Coal labourers (including whippers)	1	0.09	1,700	0.30	0.29
Labourers (employment unspecified)	21	1.81	49,456	8.61	0.21
Gardeners and nurserymen	11	0.95	4,861	0.85	1.12
Coffee-house keepers	7	0.60	562	0.10	6.18
Eating-house keepers	1	0.09	297	0.05	1.67
Publicans; beer-shop and innkeepers	9	0.78	5,274	0.92	0.85
Others	153	13.21	309,993	53.98	0.24
TOTAL	1,158	100.04	574,356	100.03	

[a] Separated according to the proportion returned in the 1831 Census (1841 Census, p. 46).

[b] Separated according to the proportion returned in the 1831 Census (1841 Census, pp. 46–7).

[c] Separated according to the proportion returned in the 1851 Census.

tailors and carpenters;[67] and hatting, with its powerful union, emerges (extraordinarily) as a more Chartist craft than shoemaking. A major argument of this book is that radicalism, political or industrial, was most closely correlated to the economic difficulties currently encountered by a given trade; that in the Chartist years the principal London industries were confronting massive innovation, whether purely technological or, for the majority, through the extension of capitalism and the process of proletarianization; and that this resulted in the temporary political unity of most London artisans. While the tailors, a former élite, were in the last throes of demotion, the metal trades were developing, but in conditions of stress, as the supreme aristocrats of mid-Victorian Britain. Such was the flux that the position of several trades in a hierarchy of status is unclear; and I suspect Prothero's certainty concerning the grading of occupations to be sometimes illegitimate in origin – that crafts regarded as Chartist are by definition not 'aristocratic', and that the non-Chartist crafts, notably the coopers, are, in turn, 'upper' trades.

Additional to the indices calculated in the above table, each craft's orientation to Chartism must be considered in conjunction with the trades' relationships with the movement in its three phases, in particular with the formation of trade localities in 1841–2 (pp. 34–5, 46–9, 69–71). In Part Four there is a full-scale examination of the economic position of the leading industries and summaries of the general attitudes of their trade societies.

PART TWO
The course of events

The political background to Chartism

The first of the metropolitan co-operative ventures of the late twenties gave rise, in 1829, to the British Association for Promoting Co-operative Knowledge, one of the working-class initiatives in Owenism that thrived during Owen's absence in America. This in turn spawned the National Union of the Working Classes and Others (NUWC) in 1831 and William Lovett, John Cleave, James Watson and Henry Hetherington were among those prominent in both bodies. The NUWC, of which Hetherington's *Poor Man's Guardian* was virtually the organ, advocated, in contradistinction to the moderate National Political Union (NPU), universal suffrage, the ballot, no property qualification and annual parliaments. After the passage of the First Reform Act the NUWC continued to agitate for its objectives, but the call for a National Convention in May 1833 was unsuccessful with the police breaking up the preparatory meeting at Coldbath Fields. One reason for the great importance of the NUWC is that it constitutes the primary political origin of the movement which was to develop into Chartism in London and, although Lovett resigned from the committee in 1832, Richard Carlile dubbed the NUWC of 1833 as 'Cleave's club', his only rival as leader having been William Benbow.[1]

In 1830 William Carpenter and Hetherington had begun the campaign for an unstamped press in which Cleave and Watson were also to play principal roles. Hundreds of newspapers appeared and hundreds of publishers and sellers were imprisoned in the ensuing struggle. The *Poor Man's Guardian* was declared legal in 1834, but the culmination, bitterly resented by the radicals, was the reduction of the stamp duty from 4d. to 1d. in 1836.[2]

The campaign brought close together some working-class and some middle-class radicals. A committee, of which Place and George Birkbeck were treasurers and Lovett joint-secretary, to pay off Cleave and Hetherington's remaining fines did so in May 1836. In 1835 Dr James Roberts Black, the American president of Place's Association for the Abolition of the Stamp Duty, had instigated for the working men assisting him with the Association's paperwork an informal educational scheme, developing into an Association of Working Men to Procure a Cheap and Honest Press, which issued an address, written

by Black, in April 1836. These activities overlapped and then coalesced. Lovett recalled: 'We found . . . that we had collected together
a goodly number of active and influential working men, persons who
had principally done the work of our late committee; and the question arose among us, whether we could form and maintain a union
formed exclusively of this class and of such men.'[3]

The answer was the foundation on 16 June 1836 of the Working
Men's Association, whose membership, costing 1s. per month, was
further restricted to 'persons of a good moral character among the
industrious classes', but honorary members could be elected from the
middle class.[4] There had therefore been a definite middle-class stim-
ulus to the formation of the London Working Men's Association
(LWMA), particularly in the person of Dr Black – though Place
insisted 'Under my direction' – and during the first year of its existence the working men heard lectures on and discussed orthodox
political economy receptively.[5]

In February 1837 the Working Men's Association held a public
meeting at the Crown and Anchor to petition Parliament for what
were to become known as the Six Points of the Charter. Meetings on
31 May and 7 June between the working men and 'the liberal members of Parliament' led to a committee of six from each group – and
then (probably in December) to Lovett and J. A. Roebuck alone –
being appointed to draw up a parliamentary bill incorporating the
Crown and Anchor petition. When Roebuck withdrew from the task
it was Place who provided the drafting expertise. The writing of the
Charter was thus the combined work of Lovett and Place, although
suggestions of the committee of twelve and of the LWMA resulted in
revisions to the original document.[6] The LWMA's exercise in collaboration between working and middle classes had always had ultra-
radical critics – O'Connor, O'Brien, Harney, etc. – yet, without significant exception, they became members.[7] Other bodies, however, continued to exist or were founded alongside the LWMA.

In September 1835 O'Connor had launched his Great Radical
Association at Marylebone and in December the remnants of the
NUWC amalgamated with the Marylebone Radical Association. At
least eight more Radical Associations were formed in various parts of
London during 1835–6. None markedly flourished for long and
O'Connor's attempt in June–July 1836 to form from them, as an
alternative to the LWMA, a Universal Suffrage Club was still-born.[8]
But the Great Radical Association was invested with immense per-
sonal significance for O'Connor, unseated as MP for County Cork in
June 1835 – who whenever he spoke in Marylebone in later years
rarely failed to mention it – for the Association marked the effective

beginning of his political career in England and provided the spring-board for his rapid emergence as a national leader[9] (and the Marylebone Radical Association seems to have developed, via the St Pancras Working Men's Association, into the West London Democratic Association of 1839 and hence the Marylebone Chartist locality of the forties).[10]

Leading figures in the Great Radical Association included Thomas Murphy, Dr Webb and John Savage, who were among the principal parochial reformers in Marylebone and St Pancras, boisterously dominating vestry politics for a decade from the late twenties and forming an important strand in metropolitan radicalism.[11]

The first real challenge to the LWMA came with J. B. Bernard's Central National Association, to which O'Brien, O'Connor and Murphy rallied, but this curious Tory–Democrat grouping, while occasioning Bronterre's denunciation of the Working Men's Association – as 'tools of the Malthusian sham-Radicals' – only lasted from March to August–September 1837.[12] Far more formidable, in the long term, was the East London Democratic Association, a Paineite club set up by George Julian Harney, Allen Davenport and Charles Hodgson Neesom in January 1837, though initially their attitude towards the LWMA appears to have been genuinely fraternal.[13]

It was when Daniel O'Connell's views on trade unions became public after the prosecution of the Glasgow cotton spinners[14] that the LWMA's compromised, equivocating stance provoked open war between its leaders and all their rivals. In a fury of mutual recrimination, Lovett attacked O'Connor as 'the great "I AM" of politics' and Harney, Neesom and Thomas Ireland, in March 1838, resigned from the Working Men's Association.[15] On 10 August the East London Democratic Association was formally reorganized as the London Democratic Association *tout court.*[16]

1838–1840: Apathetic London

The People's Charter was published by the London Working Men's Association on 8 May 1838; and in the same month the drafting of the National Petition was completed by the Birmingham Political Union. The juncture between London and Birmingham occurred at the great Glasgow demonstration of 21 May – Thomas Murphy being one of the LWMA's two representatives – at which Attwood proposed that a National Convention should be summoned. By the time that the Charter was officially launched at the Holloway Head meeting in Birmingham on 6 August, mass support for the new movement was already being mobilized, particularly in Lancashire and Yorkshire.[17]

In the late summer and early autumn of 1838 'monster' meetings were held throughout the country to adopt the Charter and elect delegates to sit in the forthcoming Convention. Gammage records that at Holloway Head 200,000 were present, at Bath 15,000, at the Western Counties demonstration on Trowle Common (between Trowbridge and Bradford-on-Avon) 30,000, at Sheffield 25,000, at Kersal Moor, Manchester, 300,000, and at the West Riding demonstration 250,000.[18] The number attending the London meeting of 17 September 1838 was estimated as a mere 15,000.[19]

The LWMA had been planning since May to submit the Charter, the product of their deliberations of more than a year – and later the National Petition – to the approval of the Londoners at 'a great public demonstration'. At the suggestion of the Birmingham Political Union, however, it was postponed until after the Birmingham meeting of 6 August. The meeting was intended to be, and in the event was, the epitome of respectability. It was convened, in consequence of a numerously signed requisition by inhabitants of Westminster, by the (Tory) High Bailiff of Westminster and, originally projected for Covent Garden Market, was ultimately able to be held in New Palace Yard after Parliament had risen.[20]

The LWMA remained in entire control of the proceedings, admitting ticket-holders only to the hustings, and the sole inconvenience suffered by Lovett and his colleagues came when 'O'Connor and Richardson (one of his disciples) marred the moral effect of our meeting by their physical force swagger.'[21] Their candidates – John Cleave, Henry Hetherington, William Lovett, Henry Vincent, Robert

Hartwell, Bronterre O'Brien, Richard Moore and George Rogers – were elected without dissent to represent London in the Convention. They had even hoped that Francis Place and J. A. Roebuck would accept nomination rather than the last two delegates.[22] The London Democratic Association (LDA), whose participation and alternative list were spurned by the LWMA,[23] had been outmanoeuvred and its leaders had thus to represent provincial towns in order to sit in the Convention. Harney was returned by Norwich, Derby and Newcastle, and Neesom by Bristol. A ninth delegate for London, who took his seat for Marylebone, William Cardo, a Somers Town shoemaker and advocate of physical force, was elected in December 1838 as the nominee of the society soon to call itself the West London Democratic Association.[24]

Despite the accuracy of the Home Office prediction that 'There is no Interest excited about it, and it will be a complete failure',[25] the Palace Yard meeting marks the zenith of London Chartism in 1838–40. None of the meetings held afterwards, when leadership passed into less scrupulous hands than those of the LWMA, exceeded it numerically. The obvious comparisons with the 'monster' Chartist demonstrations elsewhere at this time and the great gatherings of the metropolitan proletariat in the 1830s and 1840s[26] illustrate the relative insignificance of the Chartist agitation in London during the first phase of the movement.

While it provides a serviceable index of the level of early Chartist activity in London, the Palace Yard meeting was by no means typical of all the later developments, for the LWMA, whose dominant members had been the outstanding working-class leaders since the days of the NUWC (and even before), rapidly lost ground to the Chartist left and by 1839 the capital was firmly 'physical force'. Whereas Lovett's group had dominated events in Palace Yard in September, their moral-force policy was decisively rejected on 20 December at the Hall of Science, City Road. O'Connor was called to the chair and cheered, whereas Lovett, who declared 'If the people were to be called upon to arm – if they were to go on using violent expressions which must lead to mischief, he would have nothing to do with them', was hissed.[27]

In part, the position of the LWMA was undermined by dissension within. The contact of some of its members with the unrestrained mass movement in the country led them to advocate the establishment of a large agitating organization on the lines of the Political Unions and physical instead of moral force. Hartwell and Vincent were especially affected. Indeed Vincent was lost to both London and non-violence after his missionary tours and built up a following, unparalleled in its militancy, in the West of England and South Wales.[28] The

day before the Hall of Science meeting there had been another at the
Assembly Rooms, Theobalds Road, with Hetherington in the chair.
Hartwell stated that 'the meeting had been convened by himself and
others for the purpose of telling the working men of the metropolis
the state of feeling in the country . . . to hear from O'Connor, Vincent, and others what was the excited state of the country' and a
Committee of Agitation, including members of the LDA, was
formed.[29]

Although London Chartism moved to the left between September
1838 and the assembly of the Convention in February 1839, and the
LDA grew in size – in March it was claimed to have 'nearly three
thousand members'[30] – Harney and his 'Jacobins' failed to take over
the leadership which was slipping from the LWMA. The events of
April demonstrated the LDA's inability to gain widespread support.
For a meeting on 16 April at the Bell Inn, Old Bailey, to set up a
General Metropolitan Charter Association, as proposed by the Convention, each radical society in London had been asked to send two
delegates and almost all did. The LDA, on this occasion in alliance
with the West London Democratic Association, packed the meeting,
the *Charter,* which represented the standpoint of the LWMA, report-
ing that they came in a body of over fifty. The upshot was that a
resolution 'going to the effect of throwing the whole organization of
London into the hands of the "Democratic Association" ' was carried.
Yet a week later a further meeting was held at the Turk's Head, King
Street, Holborn, attended by members from fifteen London societies,
determined not to accept the decision of the Old Bailey meeting, and
the General Metropolitan Charter Association was established, with
Hartwell as secretary. An

attempt was made by about 20 or 30 members of the Democratic Association
to force their way into the room, this was resisted by the meeting, and the
chairman informed them that two of them could be admitted to take part in
the deliberations, but no more. They refused to accede to this, and after a
severe struggle, in which some blows passed, they left the place.[31]

Equally unsuccessful were the LDA's efforts to secure the return of
more delegates for the capital, to redress the inequitable selection of
the eight original members and reinforce the small group which was
urging the Convention to adopt extreme measures. On 22 April, at a
meeting on Kennington Common, Joseph Williams was declared delegate – despite the refusal of Henry Ross, the chairman and an ultra-
radical sympathizer of the LDA, to validate his election – for East
Surrey and Lambeth as opposed to Charles Westerton (whose candidature was proposed by Edmund Stallwood). The Wandsworth and
Putney Working Men's Associations and Wandsworth Female

Charter Association immediately protested at the interference in the proceedings by the LDA, 'very few of whose members reside in the district' – they had come from 'Finsbury, Marylebone, Kingsland, and elsewhere' *en masse*. The West London Democratic Association went so far as to request the *Charter* to state that they had not been involved in the incident. Williams was allowed to take a seat conditionally in the Convention, but was compelled to withdraw the following day.[32]

When the LDA attempted on 1 May to elect a member for the Tower Hamlets on Stepney Green, their adversaries were shown to have profited from their experiences of the methods of Harney and his comrades, and were so well organized that their amendment was carried by a vote of some three to one. Harney was 'received with hisses and groans' and 'three distinct rounds of applause were given for the London Delegates and the General Convention'. Neesom and Harney were sufficiently foolish to go ahead with their scheme and allege that William Drake had been returned from the Tower Hamlets. The Convention rejected Drake's claim to sit by a large majority.[33]

In 1839 metropolitan opinion undoubtedly favoured the advocates of 'physical force' in the movement, but, in shaking off the intellectual and political sway of the LWMA, the Londoners were not prepared to encamp on the far left of Chartism. Their resistance to the violent policies of the LDA was intensified when they were subjected to its opportunist tactics. London instead was becoming what it remained for many years: staunchly mainstream and 'O'Connorite'. Practically, in 1839, this meant that it supported the Convention and all its decisions, and believed it was necessary to make the Charter the law of the land 'peaceably if we can, forcibly if we must'.[34]

The National Convention had assembled in London on 4 February 1839. Of its first sitting Dr John Taylor wrote later in the year:

All the members with the exception of the London delegates, were ignorant of the state of political feeling of the metropolis, and even these delegates themselves were far from agreed upon it. It is certain that London had given no evidence of being alive to the importance of the move now made, its character was that of having sent more delegates worse paid, fewer signatures, less rent,[35] and held smaller meetings, in proportion than any district in England or Scotland, which returned a member to the Convention. It was of the utmost consequence that its real state of feeling should be known, as many thought that no movement could be effectual in which the capital did not take a most decided and active interest, if not a part.[36]

It is clear that many of the provincial delegates (in addition to Harney and his fellow 'Jacobins') had come to London in the anticipation that the metropolitan masses would play the same role – and sweep them to power – as the Parisian *sans-culottes* had in the French Revolution.

It was not long before they became aware of the true strength of the London movement and they did not conceal their shocked, and indignant, reaction.[37]

At first the coming of the Convention and its concerted attempt to agitate London raised false hopes. The *Charter* declared on 17 February:

The working men of London have given a decided refutation of the assertion that they are apathetic with regards to the PEOPLE'S CHARTER. The meeting at White Conduit House, and particularly the meeting held on Thursday evening, at Clerkenwell Green, have established the fact, beyond the possibility of denial, that they are the firm and steadfast friends of the great principles upon which the CHARTER is based.

There were 7,000 to 8,000 present on Clerkenwell Green[38] and J. C. Coombe, J. W. Parker, Henry Vincent, Dr Taylor and John Skevington all stressed, as the latter put it, that 'the meeting was a display which gave the lie to all those who said the men of London were apathetic'. The White Conduit House meeting was crowded to capacity and on the platform were assembled nearly all the delegates to the Convention as well as the leading members of both LWMA and LDA. The unassailable position which O'Connor had already created for himself, even in London, is apparent from his reception there. O'Connor enquired:

Suppose . . . that on the morrow the Convention, in the discharge of their sacred duty, were to be illegally arrested – for if they should be arrested it would be illegally – what would they (the meeting) do? – (Here the whole meeting . . . simultaneously shouted out 'We'd rise!' This was succeeded by tremendous shouting, which lasted for several minutes.) 'Now', said Mr. F. O'Connor, 'I'll stop: – I'm hard of hearing – let me hear it again.' And again the assembly vociferated, 'We'd rise – we'd rise! we'd fight'; and again they cheered.[39]

During the following week there were enthusiastic meetings at the Royal Standard, Waterloo Town, Bethnal Green, where an adjournment to the skittle-ground was necessary; the George and Dragon, Blackheath Hill, Greenwich; the Rockingham Assembly Rooms, New Kent Road; Wandsworth; the Duchess of Clarence, Vauxhall Road; Chesney's Rooms, Foley Street, Marylebone; and on Stepney Green, where there were 10,000.[40] On 25 February a meeting of the Tower Hamlets Rent Committee at the George, Commercial Road, was attended by some 7,000, the bulk of whom had to remain in the street while they were addressed from a window.[41] In reference to the series of meetings held the previous week the *Northern Star* demanded: 'Who shall despair after this? Who shall say that London is apathetic?'[42]

But this encouraging upthrust of activity was of short duration.

Although the members of the Convention and some, but by no means all, of the London leaders continued to exert themselves in the agitation of the metropolis, they did so without reward. The lack of response in the capital crippled the movement and ultimately, after it had disposed of the Petition on 7 May, the Convention withdrew to Birmingham to await further developments, possibly because its local authorities, among whom were the middle-class radicals who had been prominent supporters of Chartism earlier in the year, were expected to be sympathetic and lenient, and undoubtedly because it was closer to the mass of its support in the Midlands and North.[43] Unlike 1842, when a procession escorted the Petition to Parliament, and 1848, when a similar procession was intended, the Petition in 1839 was merely handed over to the two MPs who were to present it in the Commons. It was conveyed in a decorated van, followed by the delegates and a large crowd, to Fielden's house in Panton Street, where Attwood received it.[44]

On their realization of the actual situation in London some of the provincial delegates despaired, others were bitter. A meeting in Portland Town was 'so thinly attended' that W. G. Burns of Dundee and Richard Marsden from Preston 'spoke in a desponding tone of the apathy which the people of London had evinced, and their apparent want of feeling for the sufferings endured by the working classes in the manufacturing districts'.[45] At a Rotherhithe meeting of 'only about fifty or sixty' Lawrence Pitkeithly, a West Riding delegate, observed:

In the North he had only to call a meeting to discuss the charter [sic] and a room, six times as large as the one they now were in, would be so crowded that there would scarcely be room to stir, but to the shame of the working men of London the delegates often found the greatest difficulty in bringing them together in sufficient numbers to form a meeting.[46]

In the Convention, James Mills of Oldham demanded: 'in the name of freedom, what had London done? (Hear.) Nothing more than the poorest town in Scotland or England. (Hear.) Hardly a movement had been made until now, and whatever stir there was owed its rise entirely to the exertions of the delegates from the country.'[47] Some delegates went so far as to oppose the use of the national fund in paying for the expenses incurred in agitating London. They argued that London 'was, or ought to be from its position, the working people in it being better paid than in the country, therefore better able to contribute funds for that purpose than the impoverished districts of the north'.[48]

That Londoners were more highly paid than workers in other parts of Britain attracted the general attention of the members of the Convention and it was to this difference in wages that they unanimously ascribed the 'apathy' of the capital. As early as December 1838 O'Connor had stated the case, one which was endlessly repeated until London emerged from its lethargy in the second great phase of Chartism: 'The people of London were apathetic because they were better off than their brethren in the North.'[49] Burns concluded: 'If the people of the metropolis had equal afflictions with that of the people of the country they would have equal energy – an energy which was prompted by deep suffering' and, again:

the want of sympathy displayed by the working men of London was owing to the fact of the comparative high wages which they received for their labour, which made them perfectly contented with their own condition, for, as long as they could procure beef and porter, and enjoy their comforts, they appeared wholly to disregard the miseries and privations of their unhappy working brethren in the provinces.[50]

Peter Bussey of Bradford warned 'In London you have the extremes of wealth and poverty; and although the labour of your artizans may be better paid than in the provinces, the system will soon bring you down to our level.'[51] This reasoning was not lost upon the London activists. George Boggis declared: 'I think the majority of people in London are too well off: they get too much wages. I wish you were brought down to half what you now get – to a level with the men in the country.'[52] Even the *London Democrat,* which initially maintained that 'the mass of the working classes in the metropolis . . . are reduced to as wretched a state of degradation, as they are in any part of the country', soon conceded the commonplace explanation that 'the great majority of working men in London are too well fed and paid, to join as heartily in the cause as those who toil hard and get badly remunerated'.[53]

In spite of its perception of the hopeless state of affairs in London, the Convention persevered in its efforts to agitate the city throughout the spring of 1839. The attendance of delegates at metropolitan meetings was placed on a formal basis in late March when it was decided to ballot each Thursday for twelve members to attend meetings during the coming week. Those members who were hostile to the expenditure of monies from the National Rent on the London campaign were overborne by the majority who urged that 'no expense should be spared to produce a proper feeling in the minds of the people of London, whose apparent apathy could only be accounted for by their not having a rallying point around which they could rally'. O'Connor 'was in favour of expending large sums for the business of the agitation, especially of London. Metropolitan meetings gave a tone to the provinces.' The Convention agreed the establishment of trade and district associations in every part of the metropolis and its environs. They were to be known as 'Charter Associations', each member subscribing a penny per week, half of which was to go to the National Rent, half towards the general expenses of the association. A 'General Metropolitan Charter Association' was to be formed and its functions were to include the convening of meetings throughout London and the collection of funds.[54]

Having thwarted the attempt of the LDA to seize control of the new organization, fifteen Chartist bodies founded the General Metropolitan Charter Association on 23 April.[55] Its formation proved of little significance. It never played a prominent part in the agitation of London – though the Democratic Associations came to join it – and the Association was officially dissolved in November, when seventeen societies were requested to be represented.[56] In December 1839 the London Association of United Chartists made its appearance as an organization for concerting the efforts of the metropolitan Charter Associations.[57]

The tactics utilized by the LDA to arouse the Londoners were as ineffective as those of the Convention and the more moderate London leaders. Its attempts to make the Convention take a leftward turn had already proved unsuccessful. The LDA had no uncertainties about its task. As early as December 1838 Harney announced: 'Be assured that as the Gallic Convention of 1793 required a jacobin club to look after it, so will the British Convention of 1839 require the watchful support of the Democratic Association.'[58] Before trying to return further extremist delegates, it had endeavoured to bludgeon the existing members into action through 'extra-Conventional' pressure. At the Hall of Science, City Road, on 28 February, it was resolved 'that the People's Charter could be established as the law of the land, within one month from the present time, provided the people and their leaders do their duty, and . . . that it is essentially just, and indispensably necessary to meet all acts of oppression, with immediate resistance', and also 'that there be no delay . . . in the presentation of the National Petition, and we hold it to be the duty of the Convention, to impress upon the people the necessity of an immediate preparation for ulterior measures'. The presentation of the two resolutions to the Convention caused an uproar and the delegates who had attended the meeting – Harney (its chairman), Marsden and William Rider – were overwhelmingly censured.[59] On 16 March, however, at a crowded meeting at the Crown and Anchor, Harney was joined by, in particular, O'Connor, O'Brien, Dr Taylor and, most surprisingly, George Rogers, in his demand that the Convention should openly espouse the necessity for physical force and immediately prepare to take power.[60] The only movement achieved by this enterprising course was to cause the remaining middle-class radicals to resign from the Convention – which continued to proceed hesitantly and timidly.

For the city itself the LDA advocated 'measures of a bold nature', not an extension of the propaganda, to rouse the 'brown jackets' of London and engage their energies.[61] Its exertions to implement this policy were equally fruitless. Monday, 6 May, intended for the presentation of the National Petition, was chosen for an armed demonstration in Smithfield, designated 'the Great Day' and, presumably, for the beginning of an uprising in London, no attempt being made to disguise the purpose of the meeting.[62] Harney had shrieked in the *London Democrat*: 'THE SIXTH OF MAY is approaching. Prepare! Prepare!! Prepare!!! . . . In the two or three weeks you have remaining, let me exhort you to ARM . . . Your country, your posterity, your God demand of you to ARM! ARM!! ARM!!!'[63] In preparation for 6 May assemblies were held in Smithfield on 22 and 29 April. A certain amount of excitement and disturbance ensued, Lord Dungannon questioned Russell in the Commons, and eventually the Lord Mayor issued a proclamation banning the meeting announced for the 6th.[64] The LDA replied by marching, as soon as the presence of the City Police was perceived, from Smithfield to Islington Green where Harney addressed a sizeable gathering. 'Shouts of applause' greeted his statement that 'They would shortly be called upon to act . . . to resist oppression and assert their just rights.' But his call for those already armed to raise their hands was responded to by only 'about 20' and cries of 'oh! oh! that's going too far'.[65]

Undeterred, the LDA went ahead and convened meetings at Clerkenwell Green on the Tuesday – it being said: 'In London they would plant the Tree of Liberty and Bleed the veins of the Government to succour it' – Wednesday and Friday, on which day the Finsbury police superintendent considered the 'language if possible was stronger than it has hitherto been'. He discovered five pikes at a pub on the Green[66] and thereupon proceeded to raid the LDA's headquarters at Ship Yard, Temple Bar, where another pike, three banners and a 'mass of papers' were seized and also thirteen men – including Samuel Waddington, formerly an associate of Arthur Thistlewood – all later bound over to be of good behaviour for six months.[67] The failure of this week of action and their confrontation with the authorities sobered the LDA considerably.

London Chartism continued on its dreary, hopeless course throughout the summer of 1839. Even conservative estimates numbered the simultaneous meetings of Whitsun at Kersal Moor, Peep

Green, Glasgow and Newcastle in hundreds of thousands, and massive gatherings occurred all over Britain. The Chartist newspapers, in their reports of the assembly on Kennington Common, printed figures ranging from between 1,000 and 3,000 up to 8,000 to 10,000.[68] By August successful outdoor meetings were being held in several districts, notably by the West London Democratic Association at Harper's Fields, Paddington, and by the Southwark Democratic Association on ground close to London Road. But only 10,000 to 12,000 were present on Kennington Common on 12 August in support of the demonstrations called by the Convention in place of the National Holiday. William Carpenter felt it necessary to account for 'the comparative thinness of the meeting' by explaining that the metropolitan trades had declined to attend since they had not been given sufficient notice.[69]

By autumn the small London movement was collapsing and the news of the Newport Rising met with no response. Samuel Waddington produced and widely circulated the following handbill:

Men of London! assemble in Smithfield on Sunday, the 10th of November, at 3 o'clock in the afternoon. Wales is in a state of insurrection; justice calls aloud that the people's grievances should be redressed! Ye lovers of life, property, and religion, attend this great and solemn meeting, to petition the Queen to dismiss from her councils her present weak and wicked ministers, and save our country from a civil war! – Parents keep your children at home, and may God preside at the councils of the people!

The Londoners were unmoved by his appeal.[70] In contrast, the passing of the death sentence on Frost, Williams and Jones did stir the capital. Crowded meetings took place and 100,000 signatures to a petition were collected in three days.[71] This marked the beginning of a deep concern in London for the 'Welsh Martyrs', whose sentences were commuted to transportation for life; and throughout the 1840s well-attended gatherings pressed for their return to Britain.

London had experienced an insurrectionary flicker in January 1840. On Thursday, the 16th, police apprehended a dozen men – including Neesom and Joseph Williams – and a quantity of arms at the Trades' Hall, Abbey Street, Bethnal Green, where a meeting some 600 strong was in progress. For several days wild rumours had been circulating the city: that an uprising was imminent, selected individuals would be assassinated, churches, the docks, shipping, even the Thames, would be ignited, etc.; and extensive precautions were certainly taken, especially on the 14th, with the police fully mobilized and troops on stand-by.[72] The Chartists' actual intentions, though the fire-raising aspect was to reappear in 1848, are obscure, yet unquestionably connected with the national conspiracy of Sunday, 12 Janu-

ary, when Sheffield and Dewsbury attempted to rise, and also linked
to preparations dating from the time of Newport. Four anonymous
letters[73] and one signed of 15–18 November outline similarly incen-
diary plans, name Neesom and Williams, as well as Major Beniowski,
the Polish revolutionary, and mention meetings at the Trades' Hall,
Abbey Street (venue of the East London Democratic Association).[74]
(Beniowski was a known advocate of incendiarism as far back as July
1839. At a meeting on Clerkenwell Green 'he said it was understood
that the people of London were not prepared, but he could say that
they were, with the weapon he meant – He did not mean Guns,
Swords, Pistols, or Daggers, the weapon he meant had been spoken
of before – There was then a Cry from some of the people "You mean
Bon fires we suppose" '.[75])

The most plausible explanation of the events in London was
offered by the *Morning Herald*:

A meeting of Chartists took place last Saturday night, at which it was first
agreed to commence insurrectionary acts on the following (Sunday) morning,
but in consequence of a discovery having been made that spies were present
at that meeting, the original intentions were abandoned, and the meeting was
adjourned to Tuesday evening, when it was resolved, on account of the opposition of some influential members . . . to defer for the present any overt act
of riot or insurrection. There is to be a meeting of the Chartists to-night
(Thursday) at which, if not disturbed by the presence of what they call spies,
a final resolve . . . will be come to.[76]

The plot was, of course, terminated by the police, but had indeed
been exposed by spies.[77] The government ultimately regarded the
affair, at any rate in its metropolitan manifestation, to be sufficiently
trivial for the charges against the thirteen defendants (the initial
twelve had been joined in March by George Boggis) to be dropped.[78]

While the London trades did not come out in favour of the Charter
in the way that they were to do in, notably, 1841–2, but in 1848 too,
they were not uninterested in Chartism during 1838–9. From
November 1838 to June 1839 Bronterre O'Brien edited the *Operative,*
whose management committee consisted of trade unionists, including
the secretaries of the Friendly Society of Operative Carpenters and of
the compositors' and goldsmiths' societies.[79] In January 1839 a rival
newspaper, the *Charter*, also conducted by a committee of trade representatives, was launched with, as its first editor, William Carpenter,
who had proposed the venture to the London Trades' Combination
Committee.[80]

Some trade Charter Associations were even established in 1839.
The full title of the West London Radical Association, of whom Dr
Taylor reported 'A more enthusiastic set of men he had never seen',

appears to have been the West London Carpenters' Radical Association – it was they who donated to the Convention the machine for rolling up the Petition.[81] At the first meeting of the West London Boot and Shoemakers' Charter Association, held at the Crown, Broad Street, Golden Square, upwards of 400 enrolled.[82] In the autumn of 1839 the Metropolitan Tailors' Charter Association, of which William Cuffay was a member, was initiated, about eighty joining on the first night.[83] And a meeting at a lodge of the Friendly Society of Operative Carpenters, Bay Malton, Clipstone Street, Portland Road, formed the Regent's Park Charter Association.[84]

In addition, there were many instances of trade societies supporting the Chartists. As early as August 1838 the carvers and gilders, Stacey Street, 'approved' of the Charter.[85] When R. J. Richardson, the Manchester delegate, attended a carpenters' society at the Warwick Arms, Warwick Street, Golden Square, a resolution was carried to enter into a penny per week subscription to the National Rent.[86] 'The London Trade of Morocco Leather Finishers' made a donation of £7 to the Convention.[87] At a meeting convened by the London painters Chartist resolutions were passed unanimously.[88] Toasts were drunk to the *Charter* and the *Operative* newspapers and to the National Convention at the carpenters' annual festival in May at Highbury Barn.[89] The tin-plate workers in August expressed their solidarity with the Chartist prisoners, especially Lovett, and in January appointed a deputation to forward a petition to the Queen requesting her to spare the lives of Frost, Williams and Jones.[90] A hundred tailors meeting at the Bricklayers' Arms, King Street, undertook to pay a weekly sum during Lovett's imprisonment.[91] The stonemasons opened a subscription for the prisoners in October.[92]

Of the distribution of and the activity within localities themselves there is one noteworthy aspect. A disproportionate number of associations – and a greater degree of success was attained by these – were situated in the south-west of the city (Westminster, Pimlico, Chelsea, Knightsbridge, Kensington) and East Surrey (Wandsworth, Clapham, Mitcham, Putney). Westminster, Chelsea and Brompton were to become Chartist strongholds in the 1840s, but the Surrey villages, save for Wandsworth in 1841 (and that was a poor substitute for the one of 1839), never again formed flourishing localities. The Wandsworth and Clapham Working Men's Association held crowded meetings in the spring and summer of 1839, a female Charter Association was founded, and the *Northern Star* wrote of Wandsworth: 'All goes well in this spirited village, both as to signatures and rent.'[93] When the Mitcham Working Men's Association was formed in January: 'At least five hundred men were present, and numbers were congregated on the stairs and outside of the tavern who could not gain admission.'[94]

It was the Wandsworth and Clapham, Mitcham and Putney Working Men's Associations which decided in April 1839 to elect a member to the Convention for East Surrey. Protesting against the LDA's conduct and Williams's introduction into the Convention, Lovett explained:

> Mr. Westerton, a gentleman of talent and true patriotism, had, by great exertion, got up in the neighbourhood of Wandsworth, Kensington, Putney, and the surrounding districts, Associations for the purpose of carrying out the subjects of the Charter, – which associations had organised the tradesmen, principally dyers – had obtained many signatures to the petition, and proceeded to collect the rent with great success.[95]

Certainly it seems that the extension of the agitation into the Surrey countryside (associations were also set up at Croydon and Kingston[96]) – as well as its firm grip on south-west London – was due to the exertions of a small group of militants, none of them prominent Chartist leaders. In Mitcham, the *Operative* reported, 'the cause is progressing nobly under the auspices of as good a set of Radicals as the country can boast of'.[97]

Charles Westerton, Edmund Stallwood and John George were principally concerned with this intensive localized campaign. Westerton, a clerk from Knightsbridge, had joined the LWMA in January 1839 and later defected from Chartism proper to the National Association, becoming its secretary for several months.[98] Stallwood, who lived in Hammersmith, was to be in the 1840s one of the best-known metropolitan Chartists: delegate to the Convention of 1842 and London correspondent of the *Northern Star*.[99] 'Citizen' George, of Lambeth, was in his seventies and respected for his lengthy radical commitment, which had included membership of the London Corresponding Society.[100] Also active were James Mee, chairman at the Coldbath Fields meeting of 1833, and Captain Charles Ackerley (sometimes printed as Atcherley), a naval officer so eccentric that he was 'said to be deranged'.[101]

This handful of agitators were remarkable for their energetic application in spreading the propaganda, establishing new Chartist bodies and ensuring that they were not merely paper organizations.[102] They contrast markedly with the leaders, several of whom were national figures, of the LWMA, who rarely spoke at the weekly locality meetings, let alone embarked on a systematic campaign to create rank-and-file support for the Charter,[103] and for whose conspicuous inactivity the LDA's frenetic, opportunist programme and designs for an *émeute* provided no adequate substitute. Stallwood, Westerton and George are precursors of the cadre of second- and third-rank militants who only emerged throughout the city in the 1840s. In part, therefore, the failure of London Chartism in 1838–9 is to be ascribed to a failure in leadership.

Another reason for the capital's 'apathy' was indeed economic, although not a simple matter, as the members of the Convention concluded, of Londoners receiving higher earnings than elsewhere for, of course, the differential between metropolitan and country money wages was traditional.[104] Rather they did not suffer relative deprivation in 1837–9. There is no evidence of wage reductions and the level of employment was clearly maintained.[105]

Thirdly, in the North of England the fiery Anti-Poor Law Movement (itself fuelled by the Factory Movement of the early thirties) passed directly into and ignited emergent Chartism. In London, in the absence of acute hardship and of such an agitation – mass radicalism had been quiescent since the general unionism of 1834 (with the partial exception of the 'war of the unstamped', which lasted until 1836) – the new political movement had to begin entirely from cold.[106] Not until leaders of selfless application filled the void, economic conditions deteriorated and it had become an integral part of radical consciousness, could Chartism leap into flame in London.

1840–1842: The success of London Chartism

The London Association of United Chartists proved a feeble and short-lived body. Its successor, the Metropolitan Charter Union, formed after discussions spanning March and April 1840, and intended 'to unite the different associations in the metropolis in one union' so that 'There shall be no classes, divisions, or branches of this Union, but wherever the members may meet, it shall be a meeting of the Metropolitan Charter Union', is scarcely more noteworthy.[107] By August it was claiming to be holding weekly lectures in Clerkenwell, Shoreditch, Spitalfields and Lambeth.[108] While firm Chartist bases indeed existed in Clerkenwell and Lambeth, nothing more is heard of Spitalfields and Shoreditch for six and eighteen months respectively; and activity throughout London had reached an almost negligible level.

In July 1840 the new nationwide organization, the National Charter Association (NCA), was launched at a conference in Manchester. The Metropolitan Charter Union complacently resolved

that as the Chartists of the metropolis have decided, after the most mature deliberation, that the best plan of organization for the friends of liberty, is that recommended and adopted by the Metropolitan Charter Union ... it would be useless and impolitic to incur the expense of sending delegates to Manchester to reconsider what they, as a body, have already decided upon.[109]

All the same, London was represented belatedly and the Union, expressing its approval of the new plan of national organization, agreed to dissolve, reconstituting itself by September as the Metropolitan Division of the NCA.[110] A body representing and agitating the London societies was not a realistic proposition when there were so few in existence and so little interest in Chartism; and it was not until around the middle of 1841 that any mode of appropriate organization was achieved.[111] Even then Middlesex and Surrey County Councils were at work side by side, sometimes at such odds that Marylebone broke away from the Middlesex Council and collaborated with Surrey. It was only from July 1842 that satisfactory co-ordination of London was at last attained with their amalgamation as a single Metropolitan Delegate Meeting.[112]

The autumn of 1840 and the ensuing winter, however, saw the

38

beginnings of the real establishment of Chartism in London. With the formation of the NCA the remnants of the original Working Men's Associations, Democratic Associations, Radical Associations, Political Unions and Charter Associations were finally swept away and replaced by the uniformity of NCA branches. Existing bodies were reformed and consolidated, defunct societies were resurrected and, in some instances, branches sprang up in entirely new districts. By April 1841 there were thriving localities at Clerkenwell, Lambeth, Globe Fields (Bethnal Green), Marylebone, the City of London, Tower Hamlets, Westminster, Walworth and Camberwell, Bermondsey, Chelsea and St Pancras. All of these had lives extending for at least a couple of years and several continued, in one form or another, for the remainder of the decade.

It was in this period, of six months or so in 1840–1, that Chartism took effective root in London.[113] Before, despite the fact that the Charter had been formulated in the capital, Chartism, with its tenacity and passion, its several grievous weaknesses but with corresponding strengths and its maturity overshadowing them, above all with its intense class consciousness and thereby its inability to compromise or to co-operate with sympathetic middle-class radicals, had been, essentially, an alien import from the provinces. (As has been seen, the appeal of the indigenous product of 1838–9 – the Jacobinism of the LDA – was even smaller, except to an important minority of fervid adherents.) Afterwards, throughout the 1840s, London was a bastion of Chartism. As with its other strongholds – in the West Riding, Lancashire, the East and West Midlands, Scotland, and Northumberland and County Durham – Chartism had become inextinguishable in London. Sometimes the localities were reduced to a handful, but there would *always* be a significant number, however adverse the times to the Chartist cause. Sometimes it seems as if the activists only totalled several dozen, but though constantly changing in composition, there would *always* be sufficient dedicated Chartists to carry on the propaganda, open up new localities and around whom those who had fallen away could coalesce once again.

This irreversible implantation of Chartism in London was accompanied, in part effected, by the full emergence of a new group of activists, militants whose first commitment was to Chartism rather than any other cause (including trade unionism). At the same time the initial leadership, primarily that provided by the LWMA but to some extent also that from the LDA, fell away from the Chartist movement.

Many working-class radicals – for example, William Hoare, Robert Hartwell, John Simpson, Henry Vincent, John Skelton, Henry Ross,

Ruffy Ridley, perhaps John Cleave too[114] – had clearly joined the
LWMA in the late 1830s for the want of any better organization and
did not favour either its social exclusiveness or the inclination which
some of its principal members had to succumb to elements of bourgeois ideology. So, in 1839, Henry Ross observed:

I never could understand how men, ostensibly desirous of freeing their country from the fangs of an insatiable despotism, should waste their energies in
insulting harangues on the ignorance of the victims of oppression, and the
necessity for education as a preliminary step towards their emancipation,
when thousands of their unhappy brethren were suffering all the horrors of
the parish bastile [sic], and tens of thousands rapidly approximating to the
same dreadful alternative through want of employment, rascally remuneration when employed, and the cruel operation of the hellish Poor Laws as
amended by the Whigs; and although they appointed a committee to investi-
gate the same, more than two years and a half ago, they never could be
induced, though repeatedly called on to do so, to produce their report; this
circumstance and their close connexion with Roebuck, Leader, Hume, and
sundry other water gruel gentry, stamps them in my opinion as a set of comfortable, and respectable Malthusians; indeed, several of their members had
admitted themselves favourable to the doctrines of Malthus.[115]

The élitist and class-collaborationist position which had dominated
the LWMA's proceedings was exemplified in the person of William
Lovett.[116] During his imprisonment of 1839–40 he produced, with
John Collins of Birmingham, an account of his views published, after
his release, as *Chartism: A New Organization of the People.* In 1841 he
took steps to put his brand of educational Chartism – dubbed 'Knowledge Chartism' by his opponents – into practice and founded the
National Association for Promoting the Political and Social Improvement of the People. The scheme was denounced by the *Northern Star*
as a 'New Move', and all who wished to participate in it were compelled to isolate themselves from Chartism and align themselves
instead with Lovett, who had previously refused to join the NCA, as
he judged it illegal.[117]

This enforced separation scarcely, if at all, harmed metropolitan
Chartism. John Cleave maintained an ambivalent position, maybe
determined by his business interests, publishing for three years from
1841 an unstamped weekly, greatly praised by O'Connor, the *English
Chartist Circular,* in many respects the 'theoretical journal' of Chartism, although Cleave was, apparently, a member of the National
Association.[118] And Hetherington, who remained a staunch Owenite
to his death, but whose concern for political democracy was subordi-
nate to free-thought and the movement for the freedom of the press,
retained the respect of Chartists and very occasionally spoke at or
chaired their meetings.[119] For the rest there was no such halfway
house. Those who had been prominent in London working-class rad-

icalism and Chartism who joined the National Association included Vincent, James Watson,[120] Richard Moore, Neesom, Charles and James Savage, Charles Westerton, Arthur Dyson, Richard Spurr, James Hoppey and James Peat.[121]

The importance of Lovett, the LWMA and the National Association has been grossly overestimated by most writers on Chartism.[122] At this juncture it is merely necessary to state that the National Association was of no political significance, even in London. This is indubitably the case with respect to the working-class movement. However, in 1842 Dr M'Douall, analysing the attitudes of 'the middle classes in London', claimed that 'the great body of the liberal shopkeepers were in favour of Sturge's plan; another large body in favour of Lovett's plan'; and the National Association had attracted donations from prominent middle-class radicals. Financial support for the Association, though, was barely sufficient for it to open the National Hall in High Holborn in July 1842.[123] The Chartist localities all rejected the 'New Move' and there was never any tendency for them to lose strength to it.[124] It was, indeed, at this very time that London Chartism began to develop into a powerful force, up to fifteen new localities being formed in the summer and early autumn of 1841. W. J. Linton, himself a member, provided a damning assessment of the National Association and its progress: 'Lovett was impracticable; and his new association, after obtaining a few hundred members, dwindled into a debating club, and their hall became a dancing academy, let occasionally for unobjectionable public meetings.'[125]

The agitational record of the principal figures of the LWMA was remarkable. Hetherington, Cleave, Watson (an associate of Richard Carlile in the early 1820s) and Lovett were among those who had participated in the working-class experiments in Owenite co-operation, waged the war of the unstamped, and founded and directed the NUWC in the Reform Crisis. The Chartists had also played their part in these organizations, but their experiences tended to be of another, more embittered character. It was they who advocated the NUWC's calling a National Convention[126] and were attacked by the police at the Coldbath Fields demonstration, while Lovett and his *confrères* held aloof. They fought in the great trade struggles of 1834, when Lovett's group sought to persuade the GNCTU to pursue political rather than economic objectives, and were among the sufferers in the resulting defeats.[127] The tradition of the London Chartists was wracked by class conflict; and in the forties their crafts continued to be transformed by the growth of the dishonourable trades and other consequences of capitalist enterprise, so that a temporary alliance was forged between the highly skilled artisans of, predominantly, the West End and those

who were already in the grip of demotion. Their politics were altogether of a rougher texture than those of the ultra-respectable
LWMA and National Association tradition. They were neither
repelled by Feargus O'Connor's demagogic personality – so close to
that of the revered 'Orator' Hunt – nor shocked by the unrestrained
style of the *Northern Star*. Rather, the man and his newspaper were
advocates entirely suited to their attitudes and needs.[128]

Yet the differences between the Chartists of the 1840s and the men
of the LWMA and National Association must not be over-empha-
sized. The Chartists too were, for the most part, self-educating, earnest, sober and responsible. This fundamental similarity is well conveyed in the report of a meeting of the City of London locality at the
(Chartist) Political and Scientific Institute, Old Bailey. John Watkins,
a middle-class Chartist, in the summer of 1841 preached a sermon
calling for the assassination of Lovett and the other 'New Movers'.[129]
Afterwards, William Devonshire Saul, an Owenite, but a prosperous
wine-merchant and in every way associated with the other camp, lectured to the City Chartists. David Cater

begged leave to inform the Lecturer, as he had in his lecture made allusions
to what took place in the Hall of Science, the other evening, that that disturbance had its origin through a sermon preached in this room, which he (the
Speaker) considered disgraceful to the Chartist cause. He (Mr. C.) could
assure the Lecturer that the managing committee of the shareholders of this
Institute were wholly ignorant that the sermon would be of a personal nature;
that they do not encourage personal bickerings; and that he, as well as many
other members of the National Charter Association, were ready to forgive
and forget the opposing party, if they would cease their endeavours to stop
the progress of Chartism . . . The Lecturer . . . stated that when he came into
the room he expected to meet with much opposition, but it was pleasing to
him to have to say that he never attended a more orderly and rational assemblage of working men before.[130]

The new leaders of the London working class, then, were cast in a
mould fully compatible with the Chartism of the North and Midlands
– the reality of this is demonstrated by the complete interchangeabil-
ity during the forties of speakers and militants between capital and
country. The four outstanding activists to appear in 1841 and 1842 in
metropolitan Chartism were Edmund Stallwood, Ruffy Ridley,
Thomas Martin Wheeler and Philip M'Grath, all very much
O'Connorites, down to the preoccupation with the land and salvation
of the working class by means of financial companies. Stallwood, who
has already been mentioned for his contribution to the agitation of
1838–9, had been on the committees of the NUWC and GNCTU,
forming the latter's Lodge of Operative Gardeners. He took over in
1843 the post of London correspondent of the *Northern Star* from

1. Edmund Stallwood

Wheeler, in 1848 was allotted two acres at Charterville and was afterwards a member of the Chartist Executive.[131] Ridley and Stallwood, with M'Douall, were the London delegates at the Convention of 1842.[132] Ridley, another former member of the GNCTU's Central Committee, from 1843 ran the United Patriots' Benefit and Provident Insurance Society, later changing his name to Daniel William Ruffy.[133] Wheeler and M'Grath became right-hand men of O'Connor's and full-time officials of the NCA and Land Company. Appointed as the *Northern Star*'s metropolitan reporter in the autumn of 1841, Wheeler was obliged by O'Connor to relinquish his journalism after election as secretary of the NCA in 1843. He was secretary

to the Land Society too until he went in 1847 to cultivate a smallhold-
ing at O'Connorville. In 1850 he resumed his position on the *Star*,
replacing Stallwood.[134] M'Grath, an Irish tailor from Rosemary Lane,
rose meteorically from his first recorded appearance as a Chartist in
August 1841 to attaining the presidency of the NCA from September
1843. 'The working men's favourite agitator' was Georg Weerth's
description of M'Grath.[135] In the 1850s both Wheeler and M'Grath
turned for their livings to life assurance societies.[136]

At the beginning of October 1840 there were five Chartist localities
in London; by the end of April 1841 there were fifteen. During the
winter Chartism had at last become established in the metropolis. The
new strength of the Chartists was initially indicated by their ability to
carry any meeting to which they could obtain admission, official or
not. In January 1840 the moribund Anti-Corn Law body in London
had been reactivated.[137] As early as March 1840 the Chartists were
able to pass a universal suffrage amendment at a League meeting in
the Tower Hamlets,[138] but it was not until the spring of the following
year that they displayed an invincible superiority.

Place complained:

the interruption is made and sustained by from about 120 to 200 men, many
of them youths. They go from place to place where Anti-Corn-Law lectures
are given; they there make a disgraceful broil, which is reported in the *Northern Star* as 'a glorious victory'. These 150 men call themselves the *people,* and
their impudence and tyranny is without example.[139]

After the Chartist amendment had been carried at a meeting at the
Crown and Anchor in March 1841, the *Morning Herald* commented:

Chagrin and mortification were visibly depicted on the countenances of the
Chairman and those around him at the signal defeat they had sustained at
this the very commencement of their London campaign for 1841. It seems to
be clear that they have nothing else to expect at any future meeting they may
venture to hold in the metropolis; and therefore one would be inclined to
whisper in their ear, in a friendly way, 'discretion is the better part of val-
our'.[140]

Several weeks later Neesom drew an even stronger conclusion: 'As far
as London is concerned, the League is dead without the hope of a
resurrection.'[141]

The Chartists' opposition to the League was such that Sydney
Smith, secretary of the Metropolitan Anti-Corn Law Association – he
was to be secretary to the respective associations of London masters
in the lock-outs of the engineers in 1852 and of the building workers
in 1859[142] – was obliged to seek a magistrate's advice, as 'A number
of persons, calling themselves Chartists, follow me about from place
to place, and interrupt me so, that I am unable to go on, through

2. Philip M'Grath

their clamour.'[143] From early 1841 the Anti-Corn Law League in London was at the mercy of the Chartists. When it retreated and convened meetings to which admittance was by invitation only or held at times when working men could not be expected to attend, it could still suffer defeats. In 1842 four Chartists were even elected at Lambeth as delegates to the League's Conference (they were informed that it had been resolved not to recognize any delegates emanating from meetings where Chartist resolutions had been adopted).[144]

The unrelenting hostility manifested by the metropolitan Chartists towards the Anti-Corn Law League illustrates the gulf existing between them and the National Association. The Lovettites could never – at this stage, at least, in their political careers – have mounted such a persecution, often degenerating into the exchange of blows, of the League, including as it did radicals and potential allies like George Thompson, Colonel Perronet Thompson and P. A. Taylor junior. The spirit of the Chartists' intervention at the League's meetings and the class antagonism of their encounters emerge fully in the following account of Chartist participation at the Horns Tavern, Kennington, in 1843.

Mr. George White, of Birmingham, who attended the meeting at the request of the Lambeth Chartists, arose in the body of the Hall, and addressed the chair. Mr. Warburton asked the name of the individual who desired to address the meeting, and on Mr. White's name being announced, loud cheers were given by the Chartist party, responded to by hisses from the broad cloth gentry on the hustings. An indescribable scene of confusion followed this exhibition of feeling, and shouts of 'Go on the hustings White', arose from all parts of the crowded and spacious hall. Mr. White then proceeded towards the hustings, and Messrs. Ridley, Rouse, and other active Chartists moved forward at the same time. This was the signal for a general row. The Anti-Corn Law men on the platform rising in a body, clenching their fists, and placing themselves in a fighting attitude, headed by the parson, who had moved the first resolution. Mr. Ruffy Ridley being the first to ascend the hustings, was unceremoniously knocked off by the fighting parson, another of the gentry at the same time striking at Mr. White, but having missed his mark, Mr. White seized him by the collar and threw him into the body of the meeting, and the Chartist body proceeded at once to contest the platform, hand to hand, and in five seconds put the whole troop of well-fed middlemen to the rout.[145]

Francis Place was, of course, right to object to 150 men calling themselves 'the people'.[146] For while the Chartists' ability to pass their amendments at any (open) meeting they liked indicated that their numbers were sizeable, a popular movement is not content with swamping meetings called by other organizations. When in March 1842 O'Connor rejoiced, 'Have I now deceived you as to the position which the London Chartists have assumed? No New Move or blarney will stand for a single moment. With four hours' notice we can carry anything', his remarks, which would have been entirely in place a year previously, were by this date unintentionally uncomplimentary.[147]

In April 1841 there had been fifteen localities in London.[148] At the end of the year the number had almost doubled and there were twenty-eight localities.[149] By the time the Convention assembled in London in April 1842 the total had risen to forty-three.[150] Chartism was now not merely rooted in London. It had become the mass party. O'Connor went on to say: 'The Whigs are utterly paralysed, and the Tories are anything but comfortable, as it is now fully believed that the shopkeepers and trades will join in our movement.[151] The shopkeepers did not agitate for the Charter, but the most remarkable aspect of metropolitan Chartism in 1841–2 was the involvement of the trades.

The masons were the first to form their own Charter Association. In the *Northern Star* of 19 June 1841 there appeared an address from the eighteen masons who delivered a Chartist petition to the Commons after a special Petition Convention had met in May. Signed by 'The Eighteen Fustianed Petition Carriers being Stone Masons', it invited 'the several trades of England, Ireland, and Scotland to appoint a Charter Committee from their own body, and that when so much is accomplished a General Committee, consisting of a member from each trade, be appointed to act in connection with the associated body of Chartists, under legal rules and provisions for the attainment of our Charter of liberty'. Although this proposal was not taken up, the Masons' Charter Association was founded on 19 June and, when it met again on 26 June, more than fifty were enrolled.[152] By September O'Connor himself was addressing them at the masons' principal house of call, the Craven Head, Drury Lane.[153] Later in the month the masons entered into a tremendous struggle with the contractors Grissell and Peto, which lasted until May 1842.[154] The Masons' Charter Association was weakened by the struggle, yet it continued in active existence for over a year after its establishment, undergoing reorganization in November 1841.[155]

The coppersmiths and braziers entered the Chartist ranks (when visited by a deputation from the masons) in August 1841 after they had been on strike for over three months.[156] This locality did not last long. The following month it was reported to the Middlesex County Delegate Meeting (of the NCA) that because the coppersmiths' secretary had absconded with £35 belonging to the strikers the body was in a disorganized state.[157]

The formation of the other trade localities did not occur in conditions of open conflict; but all the trades which produced Chartist societies were experiencing significant – usually acute – economic difficulties, which are discussed in detail in Part Four. The bulk of the trade Charter Associations consisted of those of the tailors and boot and shoemakers, which each contributed five, and the industrial position of both crafts was deteriorating dramatically. In February 1842 the National Petition was adopted at a 'Great Public Meeting of the Tailors', convened by four of the tailor localities, with Cuffay in the chair and O'Connor, M'Grath and J. W. Parker among the speakers.[158]

It was the shoemakers, however, who went furthest as a trade to identify themselves with Chartism. A meeting of the West End Boot and Shoemakers, attended by more than 1,000, in August 1842, adopted the Charter with only five dissentients and resolved:

That we now declare ourselves ready to co-operate with all good men of every trade and class who feel desirous of introducing a better state of things, and that we do hereby agree to appoint a delegate from each of our divisions, in order that they may organize with the Trades, a system such as shall secure success to the cause for which we have met.

In another motion they had expressed the belief

that the great number of competitors in their trade, and the consequent struggle for subsistence, which have led to such a reduction in their prices, are to be attributed to the monopolies, restrictions, and overburthening taxation, which exclusive and corrupt legislation have engendered ... that though their trade union has to some extent been effective in protecting them against individual cupidity and injustice, they are satisfied that masters and men are alike the victims of those political causes which render nugatory all their efforts to maintain that remuneration for their labour which their industry merits.[159]

Within a month the City Men's Men agreed, with little opposition, to 'respond to the call of the Western Division, and immediately recognise the principles of the People's Charter ... we considering that to be the only remedy whereby the working classes can hope for salvation from their distressed and degraded condition'. By a very small majority it was decided: 'That the business of the trade be settled at a different time and place to Chartism.'[160] In October the West End and City Ladies' Shoemakers fell into line. The City Women's Men declared themselves, as a trade, in favour of the Charter by a majority of three to one. The West End Women's Men narrowly declined to make the Charter a trade question, but unanimously pledged themselves to assist in carrying out its principles, 'independent of trades' unions'. As this society of shoemakers was 'the most aristocratic' in the country, the *Northern Star* considered the outcome an important triumph, no one present opposing any Chartist tenet.[161]

Of the other trades to establish localities the silk-weavers formed two, the hatters one, possibly two, and the carpenters, leather finishers, and carvers and gilders one each. The pitiful and desperate situation of the Spitalfields weavers was notorious, and it is scarcely surprising to find one of their number stating 'the great body of the weavers were Chartists'. In February 1842 O'Connor addressed a meeting of some 300, called by the Broad Silk Weavers' Union, which adopted the Charter and National Petition.[162] Another assembly of 'the Silk Trade of Spitalfields and its vicinity', attended by John Campbell, secretary of the NCA, passed Chartist resolutions unanimously in August.[163] The leather finishers' locality was set up after a visit from Campbell, 'when the majority of the trade present declared themselves willing to join the National Charter Association'.[164] On the other hand, the Chartist carvers and gilders experienced such opposition that they abandoned the attempt to introduce the Charter as a trade measure and founded a locality independently.[165]

After the Convention had dissolved in May 1842 new localities continued to be formed in London. By the end of the year another sixteen had been added to the forty-three of April, although many of these were concurrently collapsing. No longer could London be described as 'apathetic'. In 1841–2 it took its place among the most militant Chartist areas in the country. London was now regularly included with those localities praised for their exertions and enthusiasm. In April 1842, for example, it was commended by John Campbell along with bastions, large and small, of Chartism of the order of Todmorden, Sowerby, Halifax, Ripponden, Bradford, Nottingham, the Potteries, Manchester, Hyde, Ashton and Bury.[166] In his original, and very important, calculation of local Chartist strengths, James A. Epstein estimates that a total of around 8,000 membership cards were taken out in London during the two years up to the autumn of 1842 compared with, for example, Leicester's 3,100, Manchester's 2,800, Sheffield's 2,000, Bradford's 1,500–1,900, Nottingham's 1,650, the Hanley district's 1,000, and a national aggregate exceeding 70,000.[167]

Stallwood reported to the Convention that metropolitan Chartism 'was in a healthy state'. M'Douall and Ridley, however, were less sanguine. M'Douall considered

the position of Middlesex, and more especially London, was better than it had been at any former period; still many improvements might be effected in its organization.[168] He was averse to giving a flattering report, but from his own experience, it was in a better position now than at the last Convention,[169] and much better than at the first Convention.

Yet he went on to say: 'They had a large body of the trades, and they had the great majority of the working classes' and Ridley regarded Chartism as occupying 'a proud and prominent position' in London.[170] London easily headed the list for signatures collected for the 1842 Petition and, with respect to monies received by the Convention, only took second place to Yorkshire.[171]

As has been seen, the foundation for the upsurge of 1841–2 was laid in the winter of 1840–1. The depression of 1841–2, unlike that of 1837(–9), then hit the capital with considerable intensity and obviously stimulated the mobilization of mass support for Chartism. Stallwood told the Convention that 'distress prevailed amongst the working classes to an unprecedented extent. In the Spitalfields district distress was equally prevalent as in those districts spoken of by Mr. Beesley.[172] The tailors, printers,[173] shoe-makers, and other bodies had never before experienced such a state of total destitution.'[174] In December 1841 J. W. Parker, prominent Chartist and tailor, said he had been out of work for seven months and that three-fifths of the journeymen tailors in London were unemployed with the remainder only partially employed.[175] It was stated in July 1842 that thousands were starving in Bermondsey and half the shops were to let or entirely closed.[176] Bronterre O'Brien, referring to the lowering of wages in the country, explained: 'In London, you have not experienced this reduction of wages, but you are equally suffering from dearth of employment.'[177]

The climax of the Chartist agitation in London during 1841–2 was the presentation of the National Petition on 2 May 1842. *Le National* of Paris called 'the attention of our readers to the petition presented to the House of Commons by the English Chartists. It is not the first time that the formidable association of operatives in that country addressed their grievances to Parliament; but at present this proceeding has been of so serious a character, that all London was affected by it.'[178] The Petition was accompanied to the Commons by an enormous crowd. O'Connor, always excitable on such occasions, enthused:

Our procession took one hour and ten minutes to pass one spot. Procession did I say! we had no procession! it was a dense mass of streets full!! Procession means a number of persons marshalled four or five a-breast, but our numbers could not have been marshalled. The 'Times' allow us 50,000. Now you may safely multiply that by 10. It was acknowledged by all that it was the largest, the very largest gathering of people that ever was seen in London.[179]

It does not, in fact, appear to be unreasonable to estimate that 100,000 to 150,000 participated in the demonstration.

In the arrangements for the day the metropolitan localities were grouped into four divisions, each to arrive at Lincoln's Inn Fields at 10.00 a.m.[180] At about 1.30 p.m. the procession set off for Westminster with the Petition, placed in a frame attached to two poles thirty feet long, borne by relays of thirty men drawn from the London trades. The route taken was via Holborn, Great Russell Street, Oxford Street, Regent Street, Waterloo Place and Charing Cross, thoroughfares packed with cheering spectators. 'Omnibuses and cabs sported the tricolour; and all seemed to be aware of the respect due to such a demonstration of the party of the people.' The line extended for more than one and a half miles and when the front portion arrived at the Commons, the rear had yet to leave Oxford Street. It 'was allowed by all parties to be larger and more splendid than the procession of the Trades' Unionists for release of the Dorchester labourers'. The *Northern Star* was triumphant:

though the heat was intense and the dust very inconvenient, yet to the honour of the men of London be it said, that not a single instance of drunkenness occurred during the whole route. If it had been a procession of teetotallers they could not have acted in a more sober or orderly manner; indeed their conduct on this day will show that the foul charge of ignorance, violence, &c., so often brought against them is a base and calumnious falsehood.[181]

Three months later the London populace were in a very different mood; and, if anything had been gained by the pacific display on 2 May, it was certainly forfeited in the turmoil of August, when, for ten days, the capital was gripped by disorders prompted by sympathy with those paralysing other parts of the country. From 13 August detachments of troops were dispatched from their barracks to the North and Midlands and *en route* to Euston and outside the station were surrounded by milling, taunting crowds. Lord FitzRoy Somerset (the future Lord Raglan) reported that the 3rd Battalion the Grenadier Guards was 'assailed with groans and abuse, such as "Bloody Butchers &c" '. On several occasions the order was given to fix bayonets and at Euston Square itself the military required the assistance of the police, who were positioned at Chalk Farm, to foil any attempt to rip up the railway line. By 20 August Wellington, only reappointed as Commander-in-Chief of the forces from the 17th, was advocating to the Home Secretary the desirability of the return of the Battalion of Guards to London where the government feared a serious outbreak the following week.[182]

Large meetings were held on Clerkenwell Green on 15 and 16 August in solidarity with 'the men of the North'.[183] Another was called for the 16th on Stepney Green and, although the police acted vigorously against the display of posters advertising it, there was a crowd of 10,000 to 20,000 on the evening, 'all the papers allowing it to be the largest meeting ever held in the neighbourhood; the road being completely blocked up'. At the conclusion hundreds of those seeking to enrol as Chartists were unable to gain access to 'a spacious bowling-green set apart for that purpose'.[184] A third great assembly took place at Clerkenwell Green on Wednesday, 17 August; and despite the use of 'language of a very determined description' and the fact that 'an extraordinary degree of excitement prevailed throughout the neighbourhood',[185] it was not until after the events on the night of the 18th that Chartist meetings were proscribed.

Early on the Thursday evening there was an attendance on Islington Green which *The Times* acknowledged as 'immense'. After an hour the gathering dispersed quietly; but before long an assembly was being held on Clerkenwell Green and the crowd then moved in procession through the City to Lincoln's Inn Fields, where, after 10.00 p.m., they were addressed by O'Connor and Duncombe. From Lincoln's Inn there was a surge back to the east and it was not until the small hours that it petered out in Bethnal Green. These movements had taken place contrary to police instructions. Sir James Graham apologized to the Queen that he 'had given positive orders to the Police not to allow any Mob, as Night approached, to enter London'[186] and informed Wellington:

The accounts on the whole continue favorable [sic] from the North; but in London the excitement is increasing; and we have been determined not to allow an adjourned meeting to assemble this Evening at Islington, in consequence of the proceedings of this same assemblage of Persons last night; who paraded the town in procession till one in the morning, and listened to speeches of a most atrocious and treasonable character.[187]

Thus on Friday, 19 August, the police guarded all approaches to Clerkenwell Green and the two sitting magistrates walked to and fro clutching copies of the Riot Act. Such numbers eventually collected that many were able to break through the police cordons and remained in possession of the Green until a late hour, as they 'kept moving about in sulky knots, defying the power of the authorities to remove them' and cheering for the Charter. All the same no public meeting was held there and instead, around 10.00 p.m., speeches were delivered in Lincoln's Inn Fields. This gathering was dispersed by the police with the result that a column set off for Covent Garden and it was in the area of Bow Street that the most serious clashes of the night occurred. After several constables had been beaten to the ground by brickbats and stones, the crowd drifted away; there were no further disturbances and 'the peace of the Metropolis was preserved'.[188]

The climax – and abrupt culmination – of the disorder came on Monday, 22 August, for which evening the Chartists had announced simultaneous demonstrations at Kennington Common and Paddington. The weekend was completely calm, but the police were retained on a full alert and elaborate preparations were made for the 22nd. 'Every wall, public building, &c. is thickly studded with Proclamations, Cautions, &c. emanating from the various authorities, strictly prohibiting public meetings, &c. . . . London may be said to be under police, if not under military law.'[189]

Throughout Monday afternoon crowds, 'very numerous, very gay', assembled on Kennington Common: 'The whole appearance of the scene was rather of a gay and festive kind, and quite different from that which the gatherings of the fierce democracy at Islington, Clerkenwell, and Stepney exhibited.'[190] O'Connor arrived, intending to speak if that was thought advisable (for he was bound over), and since 'the committee very prudently determined that he had much better not be present, as no doubt the intention was to nab him', departed from the vicinity. Fifteen minutes later, as the meeting was beginning, the police swarmed on to the Common with a mounted squadron, led by Richard Mayne himself, in the van. The gathering scattered in all directions 'and in an inconceivably short time the common was wholly in possession of the force'. The demonstrators could not, however, be dislodged from the approach roads and continued to mill there, skirmishing with the police, throughout the evening. Graham, in relief, wrote to Wellington that 'The Police have dispersed a Chartist meeting on Kennington Common without the aid of the military: there were some broken heads but no serious resistance.' In contrast, the police battled for more than three hours to clear the area around the Great Western Railway terminus; and a third, unannounced, assembly on Clerkenwell Green proved more than the exhausted local constabulary could deal with.[191]

It seems probable that the tide was now turning for the Londoners in their confrontation with the police, but after 22 August there were no further disturbances in the capital. A meeting on the 23rd, addressed by O'Connor and Duncombe, was held indoors at the White Conduit House (although it had to adjourn to the gardens on account of its great size); while by the 29th the Chartists had complied with the continuing proscription of open-air evening assemblies and instead met at noon outside the Pin Factory in the Borough Road.[192]

Nor had any strike movement developed in London, though it was reported that 600 of Cubitt's men had struck,[193] but the 'general strike' of the coal-whippers from 24 August had no political component.[194]

1843–1847: Difficult years

After 1842 London Chartism drastically contracted; and until the revival of 1847–8 there were never more than some ten active localities. Still, the branches tended to be spread evenly over the city and, should one become silent or go out of existence, the likelihood was that another would be stirring itself once more. The tenacity with which working-class radicals held their beliefs ensured that a great many men remained adamant advocates of Chartism, but by no means would they automatically be Chartist militants when the prospects for agitation were poor. Other pursuits, often entirely compatible with Chartism – in particular, trade unionism – might claim them, partially or wholly, temporarily or permanently.

The basis of the movement's continuing coherence was the community and comradeship which membership of a locality afforded, with non-political interests and pastimes fused in the struggle for social emancipation. Nowhere was the satisfaction of these needs more requisite than in the 'great metropolis' of two million inhabitants. Chartism became a way of life, a solace in the brutal world of early-Victorian London, for the fortunate few. 'In the midst of the Harmony' of a ball and concert in support of the Political and Scientific Institute, Old Bailey, in 1841,

Mr. Andrew Hogg . . . claimed the indulgence of the numerous and highly respectable company, to announce good news from York Castle; the company instantly became as silent as death, and the evening 'Sun' was read, announcing the liberation of their unflinching champion, Feargus O'Connor, from the tyrant's claws. The company instantly rose and uncovered simultaneously; they burst forth their feelings of loud and protracted cheering, to the alarm and consternation of the 'Blue Devils' that nightly prowl the street, the astonishment of the poor wretches in the gloomy cells of Newgate, and the chagrin and envy of the sycophants and apostates.[195]

During this period of five years Chartist hopes and energies were sustained by a variety of issues subsidiary to the primary purpose of the attainment of the Charter. In the mid-forties there was a comparative increase in trade union activities. The summer of 1844 saw massive solidarity for the striking miners of Northumberland and Durham.[196] Earlier in the same year there had been a short, intense campaign against a Masters and Servants' Bill then before Parlia-

54

ment.[197] This was defeated when an amendment of Duncombe's was adopted by the Commons. A Duncombe Testimonial Committee was established by the London trades and Chartists to raise a fund for a presentation to Duncombe in gratitude for his services in general to the working class, but especially for his opposition to the Masters and Servants' Bill. The proposal was initially taken up enthusiastically in London and throughout the country. (The Committee's anticipations, however, were disappointed and the testimonial, costing £620 – a representation in silver of 'the spirit of British Liberty . . . rewarding her champion' – was finally presented informally to Duncombe in April 1846.)[198]

The impetus derived from the success of April–May 1844 and from the formation of the Testimonial Committee contributed to the foundation in 1845 of the National Association of United Trades (NAUT), with Duncombe as president. The idea of 'a General Confederation of Trades' Delegates', or 'a Trades Parliament', was recommended by an editorial in the *Northern Star*. It was taken up by the Sheffield trades in a correspondence with Duncombe. The Central Association of London Trades convened a preliminary delegate meeting of the metropolitan trades and a joint committee of the Londoners then called a conference for Easter 1845, when the National Association of United Trades for the Protection of Labour was inaugurated at the Parthenium, St Martin's Lane.[199]

The National Association of United Trades for the Protection of Industry was not a general union but a federation of trade societies. Its aims, in addition to building collective solidarity – 'mutual assistance and protection' – were to keep watch over, as well as to initiate, legislative developments and to provide conciliation and arbitration in disputes. At its second conference, in July 1845, the Association launched a companion organization, the National Association of United Trades for the Employment of Labour – 'in Agriculture and Manufactures'. The second part of this scheme may appear to be an anachronistic return to the enthusiasms of the early thirties, but, as will be seen below,[200] artisans in the 1840s retained an ineradicable yearning for self-employment (although the Association never had more than handfuls of men working under its aegis).[201] Settlement on the land by the National Association of United Trades failed to materialize at all, yet the announcement of this intention, coming only a few months after the initiation of the Chartist Land Plan, was also very much in tune with contemporary aspirations.[202]

Chartists, in fact, much approved of the National Association of United Trades and their influence in it was strong. Many of its officers and activists were Chartists and, in London at least, there is a rough equation between the trades which affiliated and those whose orientation was Chartist. Its president, Duncombe, was, in effect, a Chartist MP, Peel describing him as 'the organ of the Chartist Party'.[203] Joshua Hobson, the editor of the *Northern Star*, was a member of the provisional Central Committee,[204] the *Northern Star* beginning, from 1846, to devote several columns each week to reports of the Association's affairs. And when Duncombe finally resigned the presidency in 1852, he was succeeded by G. A. Fleming, the current editor of the *Star*.[205] Indeed it is not unreasonable to view the NAUT as Chartism's contribution to trade unionism; but George Howell, in claiming that the Association 'became the centre of a great movement', was most probably guilty of considerable exaggeration.[206]

From August 1848, for ten months, the Association issued its own weekly journal, the *Labour League,* preceded by ten 'monthly reports'.[207] It is this period, however, which seems to mark the irreversible decline of the organization, though it certainly remained active in the early fifties.[208] According to Howell, it was only in 1860 – or 1867 – that the Association expired.[209]

Early in 1846 the government proposed a Militia Bill and there were popular fears of a war with the United States over the Oregon territory. The London Chartists proclaimed 'No Vote! No Musket!!' and, to protect themselves if drawn for the militia, joined a National Anti-Militia Association.[210] An essential element in their protest was radical sympathy with republican and democratic America. A more complete internationalism was pioneered by the Fraternal Democrats, the London society (with country members) of Chartists and European exiles, which Harney built up during 1845–6.[211] The London Democratic Association tradition transmuted into the revolutionary internationalism of the Fraternal Democrats exercised a far broader appeal – attracting such men as M'Grath, Ridley, Stallwood, John Shaw and John Arnott – than had the Jacobinism of 1838–9, but this remained, it must be stressed, a coterie rather than a majority interest among Chartists. The new tendency reached a larger public in the expression of support for Poland following the insurrection of 1846. The Fraternal Democrats and London Chartists together convened a great meeting at the Crown and Anchor in March, with even O'Connor speaking, at which the Democratic Committee for Poland's Regeneration was set up.[212]

Ideal means for consolidating the diminished movement in these difficult years of the 1840s were achieved when the Land Company was established. The launching of the Land Plan succeeded the Chartist Convention of April 1845.[213] O'Connor touched a deep longing in the English people, the scheme being immediately acclaimed by

Chartists throughout the country, and monetary contributions began to pour in. O'Connor himself was staggered by the response.[214] The industrial towns and the agricultural districts, for the first time responding significantly to Chartism, were equally enthusiastic; and London was no less forthcoming than the provinces. Most leading London Chartists became eager converts and lectures on 'the Land' displaced every topic in popularity.

After the first colony had been opened at Herringsgate (O'Connorville), near Rickmansworth, in May 1847 – and even before – there were frequent expeditions by the metropolitan localities to admire it and mass gatherings, of Londoners predominantly, on special occasions.[215] By the end of June 1845, when the Land Company was not yet two months old, there were already nine London branches: at Lambeth, City of London, Westminster (St Martin's Lane), Somers Town, Spitalfields, Marylebone (Lisson Grove), Camberwell, Bethnal Green and Greenwich.[216] A year later the number had only increased by three: the Spitalfields branch had disappeared and the four new branches were at Marylebone (Circus Street, New Road), Kensington, Limehouse and Hammersmith.[217] But within the next six months the total was raised to twenty with another eight branches being formed: at Gray's Inn Road, Cripplegate, Mile End, Chelsea, Whitechapel, Shoreditch and two at Walworth.[218] 'Chartist Pork!' from 'Fat Pigs' fed by Stallwood at Charterville was on sale in Little Windmill Street for Christmas 1848.[219] At the trial of William Cuffay, joint auditor of the Land Company, the prosecution produced a blue banner, discovered in his garret, bearing the insurrectionary slogan 'Westminster District' – it had originally been carried during a celebration at O'Connorville.[220]

Once the inevitable split between the group around Lovett's National Association and the NCA had occurred in 1841, the quarrels of the principal Chartist personalities, which were continually thrashed out for all to see, scarcely disturbed London. The capital continued firmly in the main camp of Chartism – that is to say, O'Connorite. The argumentative and, it would appear, unbalanced John Watkins, who came to London from the North Riding in the winter of 1840–1, followed the normal pattern of first worshipping O'Connor and the *Northern Star* (it was he who had gone to the extreme of recommending the assassination of the 'New Movers') and then surging away violently, attempting to form an opposition, and letting forth a torrent of invective. In 1843 O'Connor wrote that Watkins, 'a man to whom I have never afforded the slightest pretext, has perambulated the metropolis upon a tour of denunciation; but thanks to the honest men of London he has been routed and discomfitted'.

Watkins's campaign against O'Connor indeed collected no support and the *London Chartist Monthly Magazine* which he had begun to edit was a failure.[221]

It is more remarkable that Thomas Cooper was unable to secure a permanent following in London. He reached the capital in May 1845 after his release from prison, was warmly welcomed and at once began to play a prominent part in the metropolitan movement. In August he commenced the first of two series of twelve lectures at the City Chartist Hall on world history and culture, each delivered to packed audiences. In September he was elected secretary to both the Veteran Patriots' Fund and the Exiles' Widows and Children's Fund, national offices of some authority. His reputation (and the respect of the Londoners) was augmented in the autumn by the publication of his long poem, *The Purgatory of Suicides: A Prison-Rhyme.*[222]

At the beginning of 1846 Cooper attended meetings, principally those which were protesting 'No Vote! No Musket!!', and tried to carry his own pacifist petition declaring that 'all wars and fightings are wrong', rejecting 'even the doctrine of the right of war in self-defence, as a delusion and an error'. This amendment, on the occasions when it could find a seconder, was defeated by large majorities, even at a meeting organized by the National Association.[223] The unpopularity of Cooper's pacifism (in working-class circles)[224] meant that it could be treated as the harmless eccentricity of a very talented man. In April the City locality elected him as their delegate to the forthcoming Chartist Convention and O'Connor spoke in May at a 'soirée' to commemorate the anniversary of Cooper's liberation from Stafford prison.[225] Cooper unwisely proceeded from the advocacy of non-violence to criticism of the Land Plan and thereby ensured his ostracism from the Chartist body. O'Connor answered his accusations in the *Northern Star* and the rank-and-file resoundingly 'denounced the denouncer'.[226] When the Convention assembled in August Cooper was expelled on a resolution moved by Ernest Jones, delegate for Limehouse, a recent recruit to Chartism.[227] Support for Cooper's policies had existed in the City of London, the locality he was representing, but on the day before the Convention met in Leeds he and one other were ejected by an overwhelming vote. With this Cooper's influence in London ceased.[228]

The co-ordination of the movement in London and the maintenance of an acceptable level of agitation there proved perpetual problems. In March 1843 the Lambeth and Southwark localities, followed in April by Marylebone, withdrew from the weekly Metropolitan Delegate Meeting. Not until November, when the Metropolitan District Council was convened under the new plan of organization adopted by the Chartist Conference of September 1843, did the secession cease.[229] The Convention of April 1844 amended the constitution of the NCA and so a new Metropolitan Delegate Council was initiated in May.[230] By the summer the Council was experiencing such difficulty that it requested the Chartist Executive to recommend a plan for the reorganization of London. The outcome was the inauguration of a Metropolitan District Council in October 1844;[231] but the Council's work was at so low an ebb twelve months afterwards that it began to meet fortnightly.[232]

Only at the Chartist Convention of August 1846 was the basis of organization in London debated. Thomas Clark, with whom M'Grath concurred entirely, moved that all localities should be recommended to discontinue meeting in pubs:

He intended this resolution to apply more particularly to London. He had seen the evils at meetings held in public houses in London; they had halls if they would only unite and support them, instead of meeting in public houses, where they sat and smoked their pipes and drank their ale. This system generated local and sectional feelings, and caused Chartism in the metropolis, instead of setting a tone to the country, to be an injury to it: if they would unite into one or two good localities, they could have a second Conciliation Hall in London, where such men as Duncombe, Wakley, Ernest Jones, and others of that class would attend; by so doing they would effect great good, and get rid of the evil of each man looking for his own crochets being carried out in his locality.

Wheeler justly countered this argument:

he had always been opposed to public house meetings, but he thought it unfair that the men of London should alone be singled out for complaint; they were peculiarly situated in the metropolis, their district was very extensive, and the building of halls more expensive than in the country; and it was well known to some of the London Delegates, that had it not been for their meeting in a public house, some of their localities would have been entirely broken up.[233]

It is indeed a striking feature of London Chartism that the localities met predominantly in pubs rather than coffee houses or halls. Such was the extent of this that it became commonplace for a locality to become known not by its district but by the sign of the hostelry at which it met: the Whittington and Cat locality, King of Prussia, Brassfounders' Arms, Globe and Friends, and so on.[234]

London's position as a major Chartist centre was recognized, and further enhanced, by the move there of the Chartist Executive from Manchester after the Conference of September 1843 (initially a provisional arrangement, it was made permanent in April 1844) and the *Northern Star* from Leeds in November 1844. There were various reasons for the changes. Primarily, they were necessitated by the need of the Executive to direct the agitation from the country's seat of government and for the *Northern Star* to be published in the capital if it were to maintain its status as a national newspaper (for it had soon ceased to be a local or, even, regional journal) and hence its circulation.[235] (O'Connor had previously engaged in the interesting, but scarcely known, venture of running a daily paper in London, the *Evening Star*, acquiring the editorship and management in August 1842, but which he was compelled to relinquish on 31 January 1843, its American publisher and proprietor George Frederick Pardon having sustained a loss of £2,500 to £3,500.[236]) Still, these removals would have been inconceivable in 1838–40. If London had not been the metropolis the changes would not have occurred; on the other hand, a basic requirement for the headquarters of Chartism was the existence of a strong local movement to support the leadership and its organization. The shift from Lancashire and Yorkshire to London affirmed that not only had Chartism been established there, but it was a potentially powerful force.

The Irish

The Irish Repeal movement had originated in the campaign for Catholic relief, Daniel O'Connell creating a mass organization in the 1820s with the Catholic Association and remaining undisputed Irish national leader for some twenty years. When Catholic emancipation was obtained in 1829 O'Connell immediately turned to the question of Repeal; then came the struggle for Parliamentary Reform and it was temporarily dropped. After the successful outcome of 1832, O'Connell broke with the Whigs but when their majority was slashed at the general election of 1835, the Repealers, in the Lichfield House Compact, exchanged parliamentary aid for measures of reform for Ireland from the Whig ministry.[237] Feargus O'Connor, an Irish MP from 1832 to 1835, when he was unseated for lack of property qualification, had already, in 1833, headed an opposition to O'Connell's cautious approach. One result of the Repealers' alliance with the Whigs was, by late 1836, O'Connor's complete rupture with O'Connell, the transference of his energies to English working-class politics, and a permanent, unremitting enmity between the two men.[238]

Daniel O'Connell, regarding it 'a dismal prospect to have the insolent Tories again in power',[239] founded in 1840 the Loyal National Repeal Association; and with Peel's victory at the 1841 election the Repeal agitation was recommenced. A huge organization was built up, with local branches throughout Ireland and among the Irish immigrants in England, and hundreds of pounds of Repeal Rent poured into Dublin each week.[240] In 1843 O'Connell addressed a series of enormous demonstrations and the government banned the final meeting, to be held at Clontarf, where in 1014 the forces of Brian Boru had swept the Vikings into the sea. O'Connell, who unquestionably – in spite of Clontarf's violent association – was a believer in the employment of peaceful means, and eight others were charged with conspiracy to alter the constitution by force and found guilty, but on appeal the sentence was quashed. This marked O'Connell's last great triumph, for his leadership was shortly to be challenged by the Young Irelanders.[241]

O'Connell was no revolutionary and was always careful to keep the popular movement within bounds and under his personal control. He was among the MPs who attended the meetings of the LWMA that led to the publication of the Charter. Like the others he was a middle-class radical and had no objection to utilizing working-class energies as long as they remained under middle-class domination.[242] O'Connell particularly must have found the independence of the English working men hard to stomach – his alternative plan for reform was rejected at the British Coffee House on 7 June 1837[243] – but, even after the furore caused within the ranks of nascent Chartism by the exhibition of his virulent hostility towards trade unionism,[244] he remained a member of the committee of twelve which finally approved the Charter in the spring of 1838.[245] He then quickly changed tack, launching in August 1838 the Precursor Society, forerunner of the Repeal Association, having an exclusively Irish programme and rigorously isolating itself from the Chartists. As he explained, 'Ireland is so discontented . . . that it is impossible to keep the people quiet. They would agitate *with* the Radicals of England if I did not throw their exertions into another and better channel.'[246]

O'Connell considered 'the sanguinary and misguided Chartists seek to overthrow the groundworks of the social state', which he defined as 'the protection of property and the institutions of the country'; and it was natural he should hold Chartism – quasi-revolutionary and almost wholly proletarian as it was – in extreme abhorrence.[247] In August 1839 the Chartist Convention appointed Robert Lowery to visit Dublin as its emissary. O'Connell's followers broke up the meeting of welcome and Lowery was fortunate to escape uninjured. O'Connell wrote proudly of 'this loyal demonstration' that had 'rejected and defeated the missionaries who had come to Ireland to preach Chartist violence and insurrection'.[248]

O'Connell was especially anxious that Irishmen in England should not join the NCA. In September 1841, Ray, Secretary of the Repeal Association, instructed all the British branches to avoid any contacts with Chartists. O'Connell was able to implement his policy of total separation from Chartism inflexibly. When Dublin was informed in May 1843 that O'Connor, O'Brien and other Chartists had been admitted to Repeal Wards in London (and elsewhere), he ordered that their money be refunded, and Ray wrote a letter stressing that Repealers should shun the Chartists if they wished to 'act with us and under the guidance of our august leader'. The response was reassuring, for the following week Ray was able to announce that replies had been received from various parts of England confirming unswerving support for O'Connell. Buckley's Repeal Ward, Boswell's Court, Fetter Lane, which had accepted O'Connor as a member, returned their subscriptions to him and eight other Chartists. The same course was taken by Repeal Wards in Chelsea and other districts of London.[249]

But a fringe of the Repeal movement continued to associate with the Chartists. It was only with great reluctance that Buckley's Repeal Ward excluded O'Connor; and a week later Dennis Dwaine, who had proposed his membership (and had himself belonged to the NUWC), stated that, although as Repealers they were bound to abide by orders from Dublin and not admit Chartists, instructions had not yet been issued preventing them from attending and co-operating at meetings organized by Chartists.[250] (In this, of course, he was mistaken.) And if the official attitude of the Repealers was one of animosity, that of Chartism was the reverse. In addition to the natural sympathy of Chartists for Ireland's cause, Feargus O'Connor always had ambitions towards the leadership of Irish nationalism[251] and after 1842, with Chartism waning and the Repeal Association expanding rapidly, there were efforts to create an Irish–Chartist alliance. In July 1843, at a large meeting convened by the middle-class radicals at Hall's Riding School, Albany Street, to protest against the Tories' Arms Bill, a Chartist addition for the Repeal of the Union was overwhelmingly carried. The London Repeal Wards had refused to collaborate with the radicals and O'Connor savoured 'the glorious and memorable victory achieved in Marylebone, by the united body of English Chartists and Irish Repealers'.[252] The following year a 'Monster Meeting in [sic] Behalf of Ould Ireland', attended by 10,000 to 20,000, in Covent Garden Market demanded the release of O'Connell and 'his brother martyrs', imprisoned after Clontarf. Three cheers were given for Feargus O'Connor and three for Repeal and the Charter.[253] The *Northern Star* devoted much space in 1843 and 1844 to accounts of the Repeal agitation and for a period reported the meetings of the metropolitan Repeal Wards.[254] When the newspaper was transferred from Leeds to London in November 1844, it remarked that its connection with the Repealers would no doubt be increased and printed a list of the forty Wards in and about London to enable those Chartists who so wished to visit them.[255]

The 1841 Census recorded 73,133 persons and the 1851 Census 108,548 of Irish *birth* living in London.[256] Yet the total metropolitan Irish population was such that in 1844 the number of enrolled Repealers was put at more than 80,000.[257] The majority of the men were labourers of one kind or another, but almost 20 per cent of the Irish born (compared with around 40 per cent of all Londoners) had crafts, principally confined to shoemaking, tailoring and the building trades.[258] The impression that the Repeal Wards (and, later, Confederate Clubs) convey is of predominantly artisan societies[259] –

undoubtedly bodies whose leadership was drawn from skilled workers and the tiny metropolitan Irish middle class.[260]

But how did the Irish artisan, long settled or raised in England,
decide which he was to be: Repealer or Chartist? Philip M'Grath, a
tailor from Rosemary Lane, at the heart of the Irish settlement in East
London, an Irishman who spoke with an Irish brogue, was otherwise
thoroughly English and president of the NCA for many years. Others
moved between Chartism and Repeal, according to the political fortunes of the two movements. Daniel and Charles M'Carthy were stal-
warts of the Chartist trade locality of the City Boot and Shoemakers
in 1842. With the rise of the Repeal Association they deserted Chartism and eventually became Wardens.[261] By 1848 they were once
more in the Chartist camp and Charles M'Carthy was delegate to both
the National Convention and National Assembly. Robert Crowe, one
of the political prisoners of 1848, when he was a member of the Irish
Confederation, recalled that by 1843 'my spare time was divided
between ... the temperance movement under Father Mathew, the
repeal movement under Daniel O'Connell, and the Chartist or
English movement under Fergus [sic] O'Connor' and that he continued to take 'an active part' in Chartism until his prosecution.[262] There
must have been many other Irish who considered themselves Chartists as well as Repealers, even if most – on account of loyalty to Erin
or of the anger of the Liberator – effectively were only Repealers.
O'Connor often lectured in London on Irish topics and he was always
said to draw large numbers of appreciative, admiring fellow-country-
men.[263]

In the mid-forties O'Connell for the first time began to face serious
opposition within the Irish national movement with the emergence of
the Young Ireland group. The *Nation* was founded in 1842 by
Thomas Davis, John Blake Dillon and Charles Gavan Duffy and gradually the Young Irelanders formulated a conception of nationality,
similar to that held by other European nationalists, with a romantic,
vague glorification of an ultimate recourse to violence.[264] The defeat
of Peel in June 1846 caused the withdrawal from the Repeal Association of the Young Irelanders, who rejected the idea of any understanding with the Whigs. The onset of the Famine, and the ensuing
discontent created by the failure of the Repeal Association, provided
the dissidents with a following and in January 1847 the Irish Confederation was launched.[265]

Young Ireland was at first no more inclined to collaborate with the
Chartists than was O'Connell. An appeal by the Chartist Convention
of 1846 for union was haughtily repudiated: 'Between us and them
there is a gulf fixed; we desire not to bridge it over, but to make it

wider and more complete.'[266] The exception among the Young Ire-landers was Thomas Davis who, as early as 1842–3, recognized the Chartists as 'a growing power with no interest hostile to ours, and which might become our ally'.[267] Davis, however, had died, much mourned, in 1845. During 1845 W. J. Linton met Duffy, Thomas Francis Meagher and Smith O'Brien in London. He had already writ-ten for the *Nation* and afterwards contributed some prose and much poetry. But Linton was not an O'Connorite, had close contacts with the 'moderate reformers', and was still too radical for Young Ire-land.[268] The Confederation's attitude towards Chartism was changed through the stress of the Famine and the February Revolution[269] – and, in general, by the realization that the Irish struggle could not be won without external aid.[270] O'Connor's forthright conduct on Irish affairs in the Commons, after his election in August 1847, also helped. It contrasted strongly with that of the Repeal MPs and led Meagher to announce in November: 'I am no Chartist but the leader of the Chartists deserved the gratitude of this country.'[271]

Still, Irish–Chartist collaboration was only reluctantly achieved. In February 1848 John Mitchel, the leader of the group not only being impelled towards the acceptance of agrarian revolution but also advo-cating co-operation with the Chartists, seceded from the Confedera-tion, founding his own newspaper, the *United Irishman,* which reported Chartist meetings in each issue.[272] It was under Mitchel's patronage that the first meeting of Chartists and Confederates had occurred in Dublin on 12 January 1848. James Leach of Manchester represented the Chartists and one of the two delegates from the Irish Confederates of Britain was Thomas Daly of London. The conserva-tive elements in the Confederation followed in Mitchel's wake, and an invitation to attend a joint meeting in Manchester on St Patrick's Day was accepted by members of the Confederation's Council, Smith O'Brien being assured that 'the Chartists have promised not to intro-duce their doctrines'. By 10 April the Irish–Chartist union was com-plete and O'Brien spoke defiantly in the Commons, accepting 'the aid which the Chartists are universally prepared to give'.[273]

It was not until the autumn of 1847 that the Confederation began to make an impact in London, although relations between the met-ropolitan Repealers and Dublin had become so strained in 1845 that the Repeal Association dissolved the Wardenmote, the body of the London Repeal Wardens. This led to a massive exodus of Repealers from the London Wards – by September 1846 the Repeal Rent sent to Dublin weekly had dwindled from a maximum of £50 at the height of the agitation to less than £2. By 1847 scarcely one Repeal Ward was meeting.[274]

The first branch of the Confederation in London was opened in March 1847 at Cartwright's Coffee House, Redcross Street. This was actually a group of Chartist Repealers (closely linked with the Cripplegate branch of the Land Company) and soon came into conflict with the Council of the Confederation when it adopted an address stating:

seeing that all political leaders of our countrymen have from time to time declared in favour of the people's enfranchisement, we trust it is not too much to expect from the Council of the Irish Confederation a similar pledge of good faith ... we contend that every man of sound mind of twenty-one years of age, and unconvicted of crime, should be entitled to vote at the general election.

In September the connection of the branch with the Confederation ceased and it renamed itself 'The Irish Democratic Confederation of London', with O'Connor as president.[275] Its membership included such men as Dennis Dwaine and Charles M'Carthy, who had moved between Chartists and Repealers for several years; L. T. Clancy, secretary of the Dublin Chartist Association in 1839 and who had emigrated to England in 1840;[276] and John James Bezer, who was to be imprisoned for two years in 1848.

The real start to the formation of Confederate Clubs was made much later, in August 1847, and during September the Davis Club, which became the principal London Club, opened in Dean Street, Soho.[277] Two of its secretaries, Francis Looney and William Dowling, were defended the following year by the Club's president, Edward Kenealy, then a young barrister and who clashed with the Attorney General over his personal political involvement.[278] In the 1870s Kenealy, as leading counsel for the Tichborne Claimant, launched the *Englishman* and Magna Charta Association, appealing to working people to call themselves Magna Chartists.[279] The decision to begin a determined Confederate campaign at first was countered by the resistance of parties of 'Old Irelanders',[280] but this enmity was swept away in the following months with the radicalization of most sections of the Irish national movement. By April 1848 there were also Confederate Clubs in Berwick Street, Soho (the Curran Club); Carteret Street, Broadway, Westminster (Honest Jack Lawless Club); Newenham Street, Edgware Road (Daniel O'Connell Club); Greenwich; Orchard Place, Portman Square (United Irish Club); Wapping; and Vere Street, Lincoln's Inn Fields.[281] The policy of the London Confederates was militant and they proceeded to acquire firearms. Thomas Daly, the leading London Confederate (and Cripplegate furrier), insisted early in 1848 that it was right for Irishmen in England to arm; and, if Charles M'Carthy's announcement to the Chartist Convention in April was exaggerated, its spirit was accurate enough: 'the Confederalists were determined to achieve their liberties; and they had their rifle clubs, showing at once their determination to fight for their liberties, if necessary . . . and should a single shot be fired in Ireland, forty thousand Irishmen, in London, were ready to avenge their brethren'.[282]

Union with the London Chartists was achieved in step with the changing outlook of the Confederate leaders in Dublin and by 10 April the alliance had been cemented. (On the other hand, some close contacts between the Confederates and Chartists in London had previously existed. For example, the Davis Club in September 1847 took rooms, which had been occupied until then by the Land Company, at the Chartist Assembly Rooms, Dean Street; and Daly, a member of the Council of the Confederation, publicly professed his admiration for O'Connor and was a shareholder of the Land Company.)[283] On 2 April a Chartist deputation attended the Curran Club at the Green Man, Berwick Street, and asked that delegates be sent to the Metropolitan Delegate Committee to make arrangements for the Kennington Common demonstration – two representatives were appointed. The next evening the Davis Club elected two men to attend the Delegate Committee and two more were appointed at a meeting of the Westminster Confederates, addressed by William Dixon of the Chartist Executive. On 4 April Daly seconded the adoption of the National Petition at a gathering convened by the Fraternal Democrats, with Ernest Jones in the chair and several delegates to the Convention among the speakers.[284]

At Kennington Common on 10 April there was a contingent consisting of thousands of Irishmen. Their main banner was 'formed of green silk, fringed with orange. An ancient Irish harp was emblazoned in gold, and underneath the words "Let every man have his own country".' The *Nation* reported: 'When it appeared there were cries of Erin go Bragh – Ireland for ever.'[285] The numbers on the Common were so great that speeches were delivered at different points within the crowd; and the Confederates were separately addressed by Daly, Reynolds, John West (of Macclesfield, but a native of Dublin)[286] and Harney from a balcony overlooking the demonstration.[287]

1848: Turbulent London

It was in 1848 that the English ruling class regarded Chartism as a serious threat for the first time. The upper- and middle-class public, in general, feared that the February Revolution and consequent unheavals on the Continent would have repercussions in Britain. Inside the government a more specific danger was anticipated: insurrection in Ireland and a juncture between Irish nationalists and Chartists.[288] *The Times* went so far as to conclude: 'The Chartists, in fact, are but tools in the hands of a gang of desperadoes. The true character of the present movement is a ramification of the Irish conspiracy. The Repealers wish to make as great a hell of this island as they have made of their own.'[289] Irish–Chartist collaboration, as has been shown in the preceding chapter, was attained in London by April 1848. This was of decisive importance in the fourth, most turbulent phase of metropolitan Chartism.[290]

During the winter of 1847–8 there had been increasing Chartist activity,[291] but the revival was not major until details reached England at the end of February of the Revolution in Paris. The movement immediately surged into life and arrangements were made for the holding of the Convention and the presentation on 10 April of the new Petition.[292] London was second to none in its response to the news. When it was learned on 25 February that the proclamation of a republic was intended, 'the greatest excitement prevailed in the metropolis. Several men on horseback rode up some of the leading thoroughfares shouting, "The Republic for ever." They were followed by a large concourse of people, reiterating the cry with enthusiasm . . . The French Revolution seems to exercise a powerful influence on all minds.'[293] Several days later the pit and gallery at Sadler's Wells 'unanimously called for the Marseillaise Hymn which was played and received with enthusiastic plaudits'.[294] On 2 March, in 'the Great Circus' of the National Baths, Westminster Road, some 10,000 assembled – in 1850 it was still judged to have been 'the largest indoor meeting ever seen in London' – and appointed Harney, Ernest Jones and M'Grath to visit Paris to deliver a congratulatory address.[295]

The Revolution occurred during (and prolonged and deepened)

the last acute economic depression of the Chartist decade.[296] There can be no question that this time London was severely affected – considerably more than in 1841–2.[297] The *Northern Star* stated that the winter of 1847–8 had been rendered 'remarkable' by the 'extreme prevalence' of the fatal diseases influenza, bronchitis, pneumonia, typhus, measles and scarlatina. Smallpox was also widespread. In December, January and February the weekly aggregate of deaths regularly exceeded average seasonal mortality (of around 1,100) by 257 to 553.[298] The 'great distress' of 'the bad years of 1847–9' exhausted the funds of the Running Horse Society of Carpenters and Joiners, founded in 1800, and led to its breaking into two.[299] Mayhew was informed in 1850: 'Two winters ago the shoemakers were literally starving.'[300] In December 1848 'nearly 80,000 persons . . . are at present receiving parochial aid, being 7,000 more than on last Christmas day'.[301] A drastic decline in the demand for luxury goods was experienced:

The falling off in the glass-cutting trade is to be ascribed, first to the terrible railway losses amongst the upper classes two years ago: followed up by the commercial panic, and tremendous losses occasioned by the excessive importation of foreign corn. Rich cut glass is an article of luxury, and when the means of the consumers of luxuries are crippled they must cease to purchase. They are obliged to suffer their houses to go unpainted another year, make no alterations or additions to their buildings, change no old furniture for new, buy no new jewellery, make their apparel last twice the usual time, and economize in their number of balls and entertainments.[302]

Henry Reeve's 1847 diary ended: 'Remarkable depression in the last months of this year in society; general illness; great mortality; innumerable failures; funds down to 76; want of money; no society at all' and he commented: 'A curious presage of the impending storm!'[303]

On 1 March 1848 a meeting convened by the unemployed members of the Upholsterers' Institute resolved to call a Trades' Delegate Meeting to discuss the alarming conditions and adopt relevant measures: 'There is nothing speculative nor equivocal in the statement, that the depression of trade during the last twelve months has been of an appalling character; nor that it has now assumed a greatness which threatens to pauperize the already too-much dependent situation of the workman.' Besides upholsterers, the delegates at the preliminary meeting were carpenters, coachmakers, chair-makers, cabinet-makers, compositors, masons, shoemakers, tailors and weavers. Members of the following additional trades were present at the succeeding March meetings: type-founders, tin-plate workers, plumbers, carvers and gilders, painters, silk-dyers, pressmen, goldbeaters, farriers and paper-stainers.

There were over 100 representatives of the metropolitan trades at the first session of the Trades' Delegate Meeting. It was stated that more than two-thirds of the weavers were out of work (many had cut up their looms in order to cover their children), half of the City men's shoemakers and half of the plumbers; and a figure of 60,000[304] for the total of the metropolitan unemployed was given. A committee was appointed, which later reported that, of London's 200,000 craftsmen, in March 1848 one-third were employed (although often receiving 'greatly reduced wages'), one-third were half-employed and the remaining one-third were entirely unemployed ('and have been so for several months past').[305]

The committee also recommended a series of measures that combined the traditional preoccupations of English trade unionists and Chartists with the strong influence of the 'Right to Labour' programme of the Provisional Government in France:[306] self-supporting home colonies to employ surplus labour; a 'Labour-Protecting Board', elected by the working class, and whose members should sit in the Commons and the president of which be a member of the Cabinet; universal suffrage; a graduated property tax in place of all other taxes; a currency based on the nation's credit and real wealth instead of the fixed price of gold; protection against unfair foreign competition; and the legal implementation of a fair day's pay for a fair day's labour in each trade. When the Trades' Delegate Meeting adopted its committee's address at the end of April, an amendment inserting the other five points of the Charter and the Repeal of Union was carried by a very large majority.[307]

(These demands were formulated in a petition, presented to the Commons by Ashley. Later in 1848, after the political excitement had subsided, steps were taken to constitute the Metropolitan Trades' Delegates as a permanent body;[308] and it was ambitiously projected concurrently to create a 'National Organization of Trades, for the Industrial, Social, and Political Emancipation of Labour'.[309] During 1849, while the notion of the 'National Organization of Trades' was not dropped, the Metropolitan Trades' Delegate Meeting was consolidated as a permanent institution, with the Chartist silk-weaver A. E. Delaforce as secretary, and another Chartist, Alfred A. Walton, a mason, exceptionally prominent, and a parliamentary bill was discussed seeking the twin objectives of home colonies and local boards of trade (for the regulation of wages).[310]'

The decision of the Trades' Delegate Meeting to come out for the Charter was representative of the current attitude of the London proletariat; only there was, during 1848, minimal formation of trade localities. It was mentioned by the *Northern Star* that the Masons' Charter Association had been reorganized, though nothing further is heard of it; the Washington Brigade, meeting at the King and Queen, Foley Place, was a locality of ladies' shoemakers; and in July a trade society of boot and shoemakers opened a locality at the Orange Tree, Orange Street, Red Lion Square.[311]

A protest against the income tax, convened for 6 March by Charles Cochrane, a middle-class reformer,[312] was banned by the Commissioners of Police and abandoned by its organizer. Between 10,000 and 15,000 people –'the great mass of them apparently out of employment', *The Times* reported – gathered in Trafalgar Square at 1.00 p.m., called G. W. M. Reynolds to the chair in place of Cochrane (the occasion marked Reynolds's *début* as a Chartist)[313] and proceeded to pass a resolution calling on the Ministry to effect the immediate repeal of income tax 'or to resign the reins of power into other hands', even though a police inspector estimated that not more than one out of every 200 present paid the tax and, according to *The Times*, probably not a dozen altogether. The crowd gave, moreover, 'thundering cheers for the brave Parisians, and the People's Charter'. The inspector reported that Joseph Williams had

made a very violent speech and in speaking of the Government said that sooner or later the villains would repent. He said he had been asked what he would do with Louis Philip if he had him in his Grasp? would he kill him? No! He would turn him to better advantage, he would put him into Woombel's[314] Menagerie and exhibit him for sixpence per head.

The meeting concluded, Reynolds was accompanied up the Strand to his house in Wellington Street, where he spoke again from the balcony. Meanwhile in Trafalgar Square a brawl developed, which led to police intervention and an immense escalation of the disturbance. Protracted fighting ensued in and around the Square. In the evening the disorder was carried to other parts of central London and several bread shops were entered. During the following two days, rioting, based on Trafalgar Square, was resumed and not until 9 March was London calm again.[315]

A week after the meeting in Trafalgar Square another[316] was held under the auspices of Reynolds. On this occasion the venue was Kennington Common, and while again neither Executive nor Metropolitan Delegate Committee had any responsibility for calling it, in addition to the maverick militant Joseph Williams the Chartist leadership was now well represented by Clark, Dixon, M'Grath and Ernest Jones, the latter two newly returned from Paris. By noon on the 13th 20,000 were assembled; and a massive police presence failed to prevent an immediate breakaway by 400 to 500 proceeding to neighbouring Camberwell and looting shops.[317] The riots of 6–8 March and the announcement by Reynolds of a 'Grand Meeting' on Kennington

Common had initiated the enrolment of special constables;[318] and this process was justified by the outbreak on the 13th. It was in a situation of accelerating bourgeois alarm that the Chartist intentions were publicized:

The Executive Committee have resolved that the National Petition, as the will of the sovereign people, shall be presented on the 10th of April, and that such petition shall be accompanied to the door of the House of Commons, by an immense concourse of the people of this metropolis, who will form an excellent guard of the National Register. The Executive Committee wish to convert the presentation of the petition into a demonstration of national sympathy, and with such view it is their intention to spare no pains to make such a display of strength as will make the cause respected.[319]

In their speeches at Kennington Common on 13 March Ernest Jones had envisaged the massing of 200,000 and M'Grath a quarter of a million Chartists; by the end of the month the address of the Trades' Demonstration Committee contemplated half a million.[320]

The panic of 10 April, therefore, originated in the events of 6–13 March.[321] It was during that week that the formation of a special constabulary was begun, London having experienced, within a fortnight of the February Revolution, disturbances more acute and more spontaneous than those of 1842 and in which the Metropolitan Police were at their least effective. The ministry remained calm (Russell remembered that his 'first notion' had been to allow the procession to cross Westminster Bridge and deliver the Petition 'at the doors of Parliament')[322] and it was not until April that it acted. The London magistrates were instructed on the 3rd to swear in constables and on the 6th a proclamation was issued banning not only the proposed procession but also the assembly on the Common.[323] Grey had 'every hope' on the 3rd that the government would 'get quietly over the 10th'.[324] By the day of the demonstration even the coolest of aristocrats had succumbed to a hysteria which infected – and united – all the propertied classes. Palmerston worried that at Osborne the Queen would be in 'rather an unprotected Situation, and the Solent Sea is not impassable'; and, on 10 April, requested that armed police should relieve the clerks of the exposed Foreign Office at nightfall.[325] It would appear that Grey alone remained 'unmoved when all London was in terror.'[326]

The government's preparations for 10 April have not been exaggerated by previous writers. More than 4,000 police were positioned at the Thames bridges and in Kennington and Westminster. Twelve guns were brought up from Woolwich. Troops numbering 3,202 were moved into the capital from Woolwich, Hounslow, Windsor, Chatham, Dover and Chichester and the central garrison thereby almost doubled. A total of 7,122 soldiers were concentrated in the

3. The Bank of England in a state of defence on 10 April 1848

capital. At the very last moment, on the morning of the 10th, 450 infantrymen and two additional guns with 37 of the marines were dispatched from Gosport.[327] In addition, 1,231 pensioners were mobilized.[328] On the 8th the Queen had travelled with the Court to Osborne.[329] Public buildings were barricaded and manned by their clerks and porters who had been enrolled as specials: 'everybody who had a character or position to lose was expected to join', recalled the son of a minor official at the Inland Revenue.[330] At the General Post Office between 1,200 and 1,300 employees had been sworn in and the request was made for fifty hand grenades for the defence of its 'weak side'.[331] The British Museum was provided with fifty muskets and one hundred cutlasses and weapons were also issued for the defence of prisons.[332] Over the gates of Somerset House and the Custom House *chevaux-de-frise* were erected. Sand bags were used to fortify the General Post Office, East India House, Guildhall and even the Tower of London. 'The most active exertions' centred on the Bank of England:

A breastwork of sandbags, with loopholes for muskets and small guns, had been thrown up along the parapet wall of this establishment . . . at each corner of the building, musket batteries, bullet-proof, were raised, having loopholes for small carronades.

The line of road from the Strand to the new Houses of Parliament has all the appearance of a thoroughfare in a besieged capital ... Notices from the Police Commissioners, that no carts, vans, or omnibuses are to be allowed upon the road from Abingdon-street to Cockspur-street after eleven o'clock, and that no delay is to be permitted in the other streets, agitate the public, and the appearance of patrols of mounted police, and of single files of soldiers in the usually quiet street, is ominous and alarming.[333]

The authorities had learned from the events in Paris. They were resolute that no buildings should be occupied by demonstrators. The Chartists might have the streets; but there was determination that they should not gain a control which could serve as a focus for prolonged disturbance and potential insurrection. The obsession (which, otherwise, seems so extraordinary) with the defence of public buildings on the 10th was therefore rational and is entirely explicable.[334]

On the other hand, the number of special constables amounted to no more than (the still very considerable figure of) some 85,000.[335] And few of these were volunteers from the working class, although the services of thousands of artisans and labourers had been impressed.[336] The significance of this enrolment – and indeed of 10 April itself – lies in its decisive indication that the middle classes were now prepared to ally themselves unreservedly with the ruling class against the threat of proletarian revolt.[337] It was the *Nonconformist* which, on 12 April, wrote most aptly of the 'counter-demonstration on the part of the middle classes'. A magistrate who swore in 800 constables at Brixton and Clapham reckoned 'quite a third of them *Gentlemen* in Business'.[338] Not only were 200 staves required for the students of King's College but 'the 200 young gentlemen' of University College constituted 'a corps ready for any thing of the *active* kind'.[339]

In contrast, most from Stepney College (for Baptist ministers) donned their worst clothes and joined the crowd[340] along with others from a tiny dissident and probably primarily youthful section of the middle classes. Millais and Holman Hunt, for example, accompanied the contingent from Russell Square, although at the Common they were careful to remain outside the enclosing rails.[341]

The Chartists never intended 10 April to be anything but a peaceable mass demonstration. Delegates waited upon the Home Secretary on 7 April to assure him that: 'the National Convention never has advised and utterly repudiates the idea of an armed Assembly being called or an armed Procession taking place ... we shall entirely discountenance any attempt that may be made on Monday next to create disorder or break the public peace'.[342] As in 1839, the resort to physical force was to come months after the rejection of the Petition. On the other hand, London was more tumultuous on the 10th than has

CHARTIST
DEMONSTRATION!!

"PEACE and ORDER" is our MOTTO!

TO THE WORKING MEN OF LONDON.

Fellow Men, —The Press having misrepresented and villified us and our intentions, the Demonstration Committee therefore consider it to be their duty to state that the grievances of us (the Working Classes) are deep and our demands just. We and our families are pining in misery, want, and starvation! We demand a fair day's wages for a fair day's work! We are the slaves of capital —we demand protection to our labour. We are political serfs—we demand to be free. We therefore invite all well disposed to join in our peaceful procession on

MONDAY NEXT, April 10,

As it is for the good of all that we seek to remove the evils under which we groan.

The following are the places of Meeting of THE CHARTISTS, THE TRADES, THE IRISH CONFEDERATE & REPEAL BODIES:

East Division on Stepney Green at 8 o'clock; City and Finsbury Division on Clerkenwell Green at 9 o'clock; West Division in Russell Square at 9 o'clock; and the South Division in Peckham Fields at 9 o'clock, and proceed from thence to Kennington Common.

Signed on behalf of the Committee, JOHN ARNOTT, *Sec.*

4. Poster for the demonstration of 10 April 1848

been appreciated. The Honourable Artillery Company marched from their ground at 9.00 a.m. to occupy the Guildhall and the surgeon recorded in his journal: '*What* a mob filled the street! It was as much as we could possibly do to make our way, and a perfect roar of hooting and cursing attended us. At one time matters looked serious, and the mob began to pelt us.'[343] A 'strong' shoemaker declared: 'I hate physical force and revolutions, but I went to Kennington-common on the 10th of April, knowing or caring nothing what might happen.'[344] Also, some did attend with rudimentary weapons – 'but that was quite against the instructions', a rank-and-file Chartist confirmed[345] – and they comprised a small proportion of the total of 150,000. Among these were members of the Communist League, George Eccarius armed with his tailors' scissors;[346] and indeed the authorities were especially concerned about the contribution that foreign radicals might make.[347]

On the 7th the Convention informed Grey of their resolve that the Petition would be borne to the House of Commons by the demonstrators from Kennington.[348] Over the weekend they climbed down and attempted to negotiate with the Commissioners of Police a route whereby the procession would cross Blackfriars Bridge and move along Holborn and Oxford Street to Edgware Road, with the Petition being dispatched to Westminster, unaccompanied by the crowd, from Regent's Circus. Mayne's refusal of the proposal was conveyed to M'Grath at 8.30 a.m. on the 10th. When the Convention sat at 9.00 a.m., while O'Connor urged a quiet dispersal in the event of the ground being occupied in advance and the abandonment of any procession, the other delegates disputed on the course of action to pursue.[349] The authorities were determined that no bodies of Chartists in formation should progress to the north bank of the river – and if any had attempted to do so that day there would have been a blood-bath.[350] What they were prepared to concede was the right of public assembly;[351] and the thousands who, in defiance of the government's proscription, streamed over to the Surrey side, mainly in processions emanating from Russell Square, Clerkenwell Green/Finsbury Square and Stepney Green, assembled on the Common *en masse*. It is argued below that 150,000 is a not unreasonable estimate of the support.[352]

At 11.45 Mayne reported:

I have seen Mr O'Connor & communicated to him that the petition would be allowed to pass & every facility given for that, & its reaching the House of Commons. but no procession or assemblage of people would be permitted to cross the Bridges.

Mr O'Connor gave me his word that the procession would not attempt to cross the Bridges. he added that the Petition should be sent in Cabs.[353] I had sent Mr Malalieu [sic] to ask Mr O'Connor & two or three of the leaders to come to me to receive such a communication. there was considerable excitement amongst the people as Mr O'Connor came to me. it was evidently supposed that he was taken into custody. I never saw a man more frightened than he was, & he would I am sure have promised me anything. he had some difficulty in keeping the people about us on the road quiet, & got on the top of a Cab to tell them he had received a friendly communication on which he was resolved to act.[354]

O'Connor met Grey in the Home Office at 1.00 p.m. and informed him that 'the meeting at Kennington Common had come to an unanimous Resolution to give up the Procession & to disperse quietly'.[355]

Most of the vast crowd on the Common did dissolve peaceably. Frustration at the turn of events led many, including Cuffay, to advocate a confrontation with the military but Vernon's challenge to Cuffay, 'Come – we will lead if you will follow, come weal, come woe', remained unanswered.[356] The only collisions occurred at the bridges as the demonstrators struck north and were merely allowed to trickle across. The most vicious confrontation was at the approaches to Blackfriars Bridge, where the police barred the way for over an hour before their line was broken. Many of the crowd were forced into the streets leading off Blackfriars Road, and there some banded together and fighting erupted.[357] As early as 1.45 Wellington wrote: 'There is now a considerable Body in Palace Yard, and a Mob coming over Westminster Bridge.'[358] By 3.00 rain was falling[359] and some observers considered it contributed markedly to clearing the streets of demonstrators.[360] Wellington had, at 1.45, considered 'the heart of the *Affair* broken, and I am already proceeding to have the orders made out to send the troops to their Barracks'.[361] At the Stock Exchange news of the abandonment of the procession led to the national anthem being sung – and consols immediately rose a point.[362] At 4.00 Grey could request the nine magistrates allocated to the detachments of the troops to assemble at the Home Office, since the neighbourhoods of their stations were reported quiet; and by 6.00 he was able to release those in attendance at the Police Courts.[363]

This account of 10 April 1848, sustained by the argument of pp. 129–42, is very different from the traditional version, accepted by historians for over a hundred years. Like the blanket dismissal of the Petition of 1848 as largely worthless, full of forged and fictitious names, the description of the demonstration of 10 April as a 'fiasco' is 'a piece of non-knowledge with a blatant class function'.[364] The contemptuous cliché is not founded upon historical fact; it results from the curious, complicated psychological reflex in the immediate aftermath. If there was a 'fiasco' on the 10th it lay not in the Chartists' holding their meeting, although abandoning the intended procession, but in the massive over-reaction of their opponents.[365] Yet it is the ludicrously elaborate and unnecessary preparations that have been proudly recounted, to the extent of doubling the size of the special constabulary. The legend of 10 April celebrates the spirit which the English display in an emergency.[366] In this it is akin to the middle-class view of the General Strike; but it goes beyond 1926 with the insistence upon the inter-class composition of the specials and the presentation of an image of all sections of English society rallying against extremists, preserving Britain as that unusual entity: a nation which holds no truck with insurrectionaries, a polity that does not experience revolutions. 'The dangerous assemblage was put down, not by the troops, nor even by the police, but *by the people* themselves – by the zealous and almost unanimous determination of all classes that such proceedings should not be permitted.'[367] Hence, in addition to exaggerating the voluntary, non-partisan mobilization against the Chartists, it was imperative, at the same time, to diminish the turn-out of demonstrators to insignificance. The result is a caricature of the whole affair into self-congratulatory farce in which an elephant of order crushes a mouse of rebellion. 'It could not be said that the majority were rising against the tyranny of a small minority. A minority was demonstrating against the overwhelming majority of the nation.'[368]

It is remarkable that the stuff of the myth was presented before the event – on the morning of 10 April by *The Times* with vehement, denunciatory assurance – and repeated by the morning papers on the 11th,[369] although the contention that *Alton Locke* was seminal in developing its ramifications is convincing.[370] Relief that the 10th had passed without incident was succeeded by the passage of the original fear into oblivion – panic could only be justified by Chartist strength and that had been judged as negligible – perhaps speeded there by a sense of foolishness. Henry Vizetelly recalled 'how the very people who had been almost prostrated with terror in the morning plucked up courage and laughed at what they described as their neighbours' fears; pretending that they themselves had never for a moment believed there was reason for apprehending the faintest danger'.[371] On the 9th Greville had commented 'it is either very sublime or very ridiculous'.[372] The *Daily News* was honest enough to admit that 'we, loyal Londoners, cut a very foolish figure yesterday evening, and he is a bold man who, even this morning, can look at his neighbour without a blush or a smile'.[373] (As has been suggested, the ironist can detect a fiasco beyond that of the familiar assessment.) Preoccupation with the peculiarities of their own society has prevented English historians from postulating a connection between the events of 10 April and the determined treatment by the Provisional Government of the workers' demonstration in Paris on 16 April.[374]

Propertied Londoners also neglected to remember in later years that their alarm was renewed in May and June and that 12 June was in many ways a repetition of 10 April. The events of the summer of 1848, however, foundered almost entirely without trace, while Kennington Common passed into the national ideology.[375] Politicians soon began to revel in the lesson of 10 April which could teach so much to their unfortunate counterparts on the Continent, but for another four months or so remained apprehensive of a major rising. Although Palmerston wrote of the 'Waterloo of peace and order' as early as the 11th, he more realistically informed Clarendon, Lord-Lieutenant of Ireland: 'Things passed off beautifully here yesterday, but the Snake is scotched not killed, & we must continue on our guard. It would be folly to be lulled into security by the temporary quiet of the Tiger who has missed his first spring.'[376] Outside the government Sir James Graham commented lugubriously: 'I cannot shut my eyes to the certainty that the establishment of a Republic in France will give immense activity to the democratic movement in this country; and a rebellion in Ireland may be the signal for a servile insurrection which would spread far and wide.'[377]

While Chartists themselves did later come to view 10 April 1848 as a decisive turning-point for their movement,[378] at the time they were not dispirited by the events of that day – drawing the strictly practical conclusion never again to meet south of the Thames and thereby allow themselves to be trapped should the authorities choose to seize the bridges[379] – and exertions towards the attainment of the Charter were increased.[380]

The Chartist agitation was spread with particular vigour in East London, where, during April, May and June, thirteen new localities were opened in Hoxton, Shoreditch, Spitalfields and Bethnal Green.[381] The formation of these branches was both stimulated and supplemented by open-air gatherings. By April 'monster meetings' were regularly held in Bishop Bonner's Fields and in May Nova Scotia Gardens, Bethnal Green, began to be used weekly.[382] It seems probable that this extraordinary level of activity in a relatively small district is attributable to the energies of one man, H. Mander May (later ably assisted by John Shaw and Alexander Sharp), who makes his first appearance on 7 March at a Bethnal Green meeting in support of the revolution in Paris, when 'three hearty cheers were . . . given for the French Republic; three groans for Louis Philippe; and three cheers for Mr May'.[383]

May's agitational achievements were paralleled to a lesser extent by the Somers Town locality. A weekly assembly was held in St Pancras Fields from April to June[384] and seven localities initiated.[385] A third

area in which there were outdoor meetings was Paddington, where
the Emmett Brigade organized several at Irongate Wharf, Praed
Street.[386]

The adoption by the National Assembly – at which London's delegates were John Shaw and Alexander Sharp (Tower Hamlets), W. J.
Vernon[387] and Henry Child (West London), James Bassett and T. M.
Wheeler (South London) and Charles M'Carthy and Churchill (City
of London and Finsbury) – of the New Plan of Organization in May
provided an additional impetus. The basic units were now to be the
class of ten men and ward of ten classes, each locality being divided
into the appropriate number of wards.[388] Organization in classes and
wards was ideally suited to secret communication and conspiratorial
preparations; and the evidence suggests that substantial reconstruc-
tion of existing localities occurred as well as arming on a significant
scale.[389]

Already, in April, the Chartists and Confederates of Greenwich
had combined to form a joint association.[390] In June the Maze Club
was founded at the Bull's Head, Tooley Street, and the John Mitchel
Club at the South London Chartist Hall, Blackfriars Road, both Irish–
Chartist bodies.[391] The Chartists of the Wallace Brigade, Strutton
Ground, amalgamated with the Confederates of their district.[392] To
these four clubs, explicitly stated to be formed of both Confederates
and Chartists, may be added another Irish–Chartist body: the Theobald Wolfe Tone Club, later the Felon Club, which, first held at the
Temperance Hall, Cock Lane, Snow Hill, transferred to Cartwright's
Coffee House, Redcross Street, an old meeting ground of Chartists
and Repealers.[393]

In London, then, Chartist organization merged at several points
with that of the Confederation. On the other hand, formal (certainly,
public) contacts were not developed between Dublin and the joint
London movement. Whereas Michael Doheny represented Salford at
the National Assembly, Captain William Bryan, from the Confederates in Dublin, explained that his lawyer had advised him against taking a seat for an Irish constituency. The best way for the Chartists
and Confederates to assist one another was by each agitating for their
common objectives – beyond that they could not go.[394] Thomas Frost
comments, however: 'Communications passed at this time between
plotters of revolution on both sides of St. George's Channel';[395] and
Thomas Daly, for one, travelled between London and Dublin during
these weeks.[396]

The political potential of these developments – the implementation
of the New Plan of Organization and the further consolidation of the
Irish–Chartist alliance – was exhibited to the full when the news

reached London that Mitchel had been sentenced to fourteen years' transportation. He was found guilty on 26 May and sentenced the following day. During the trial, on 25 and 26 May, fiery meetings in his support were held on Clerkenwell Green, for their part in which Sharp and Williams were later charged. On Sunday, 28 May, a large group of Irishmen marched four abreast from the Theobald Wolfe Tone Club, Cock Lane, via Holborn and Oxford Street to Marylebone High Street, where they were joined by several thousand others. Francis Looney was among those who then addressed an outdoor gathering, said to have been attended by 10,000 to 12,000 people.[397]

On the evening of 29 May several thousand assembled on Clerkenwell Green and listened to the 'very violent and inflammatory' speeches from John Fussell, Joseph Williams and Daniel M'Carthy. Williams announced:

My Friends, the bloody aristocracy has done its work at last . . . When I give you the signal I want you to fall into marching order four abreast and to follow me where I will lead you I will then take you to a place where you will meet ten times as many people as are here and then you will be advised what to do.

Therefore the crowd quit the Green at 7.45 and proceeded by way of Old Street and City Road to Finsbury Square, which they perambulated for half or three-quarters of an hour waiting for a gathering from Stepney Green, numbering another 3,000 or so (and which had been addressed by Ernest Jones, M'Crae, M'Douall, Mander May and Charles M'Carthy), to join forces with them. Not until around 9.00, Russell informed the Queen (in response to her indignant enquiry the next day), did the Home Secretary learn that 'great numbers of people were collected in Finsbury Square & were coming towards the West End of the Town'.

The combined procession, headed by Williams, Fussell and one or two others, marched along Chiswell Street and Long Lane to Smithfield, through Holborn and Seven Dials to Leicester Square and then via Dean Street, Oxford Street, Regent Street and Pall Mall to Trafalgar Square. As the demonstration progressed from the City to the West End it attracted numerous adherents: 'the general cry was – "The Chartists are out" '. The eventual size of the crowd was huge: 'it was increased by large numbers at every street – the party said, "Fall in", and the people did fall in, as they went along'. Thus testified Frederick Town Fowler, a free-lance reporter for *The Times* and other newspapers, who was principal government witness at the ensuing trials: 'it was almost impossible to say the number at the last, you could not see then', but, he said, 'there might be 50,000 or 60,000'. Fowler was, actually, fairly confident of this estimate, repeating it on several occasions, although he also thought the total could have eventually reached 80,000 or 90,000.[398] In Regent Street 'the Mob hissed and yelled at the Carriages as they drove past', and, as the alarmed shop-keepers began to shut up early, they were assumed 'don't close your shops we're only Chartists'. In fact, 'a great many respectable people' appear to have participated in the procession, 'respectable tradesmen and householders following' as well as 'gazing on'. At about 10.30 the column passed in orderly fashion through Trafalgar Square and then proceeded along the Strand (where the Marseillaise and 'some words about the Charter' to the tune of 'Rule Britannia' were sung), Fleet Street, Farringdon Street and Smithfield until Finsbury Square was again reached, by which time the great majority who participated in this massively imposing display had dispersed. The conclusion of the *Northern Star* was: 'Let my Lord John beware in time that the working classes – ay, and a good portion of the middle classes too – sympathize with John Mitchel, and demand in unmistakable terms, both the Charter and Repeal.'[399]

Not all of the crowd dissolved peaceably on the night of the 29th. Outside Cartwright's Coffee House in Redcross Street between 3,000 and 4,000 people collected and were addressed by Williams, Vernon and Charles M'Carthy. Williams asked: 'Do you think that Mitchell [sic] had a fair trial?' 'No' came the answer. 'Do you think it necessary that we should have a Republican government?' 'Yes' was the cry. When the police attempted to clear the street, they encountered, for an hour or two, considerable resistance. All types of sharp and heavy objects were hurled and even hot water was thrown from windows.[400]

Next day the Commissioners of Police issued a proclamation ban-ning all assemblages and processions, as those of the preceding night had been 'under circumstances calculated to excite terror and alarm'. In the evening Chartists and Confederates again gathered at Clerken-well Green, where Williams, Sharp and Daly spoke to them. The organizers left the Green at 9.00 and when the numbers had thinned a strong force of police attempted to disperse the remainder; but the police were not dismissed until after midnight.[401]

On 31 May the government stationed two detachments of soldiers in the proximity of Clerkenwell (with a third off Mile End Road) and two troops of the Horse Guards hard by the Green, and prepared for a major encounter with the populace. Thousands reassembled on the Green, but the only speech was delivered by an eccentric socialist, James Elmzlie Duncan, 'The Mad Scotchman', who 'clung to the top of the lamp-post in the middle of the Green'.[402] After 9.00 lines of police swept on to the Green achieving considerable success in dis-persing the crowd there but experiencing more determined opposition in the neighbouring streets. By midnight the rioting had petered out without any very considerable conflict or alarm for the authorities. The following night saw a renewed gathering at Clerkenwell and concomitant battle with the police force, but this marked the end of the disorder in the quarter.[403] Greville noted: 'The Government are now getting seriously uneasy about the Chartist manifestations ... especially in London, and at the repeated assemblings and marchings of great bodies of men.'[404] *The Times* on 2 June, echoing Palmerston's private observation of 11 April, concluded: 'Chartism is neither dead nor sleeping. The snake was scotched not killed on the 10th of April. The advancing spring has brought with it warmth, vigour, and renovation.' The previous day it had written of 'a serpent, toothless perhaps, but long, slimy, insidious, and unaccountable'.

The series of meetings and disturbances provoked by the conviction and sentencing of John Mitchel culminated on Sunday, 4 June, in rioting in Bethnal Green by police as well as people. Late on Saturday night information had been received from a former police constable that a Chartist meeting was to be held on Bishop Bonner's Fields at 5.00 a.m. the following morning and that at the same time ' a Pike drill' would be taking place in Victoria Park. 'A Rank of Men' were accordingly surprised whom Superintendent Johnston of N Division 'fancied ... were probably at Pike Exercise'. Nearby, 300 to 400 men 'sprang over the Hedges and dispersed in all directions', when a party from N Division marched upon them; and then London Fields, Hackney, were occupied to forestall gatherings. Over 500 police were involved in this early morning mobilization and apparently remained on duty throughout the day. Their growing fatigue combined with the expectation that many Chartists would be armed at the announced meetings probably account in great measure for an ill-judged intervention at Nova Scotia Gardens and their uncontrolled outbreak after the Bonner's Fields meeting in the evening.[405] The suppression of the meeting called in Nova Scotia Gardens for 10.00 a.m. resulted in the neighbourhood venting for three hours its hatred of all constables, regular or special: 'many of the persons were dressed alike, in old coats and fustian jackets'. Such cries were recalled as 'Down with the b—y police! give the b—rs the brickbats!'; 'Come on, give it to the b—y special'; and 'Three cheers for the Chartists!'[406]

In the afternoon a meeting, largely Confederate, was held at 3.00 in Bonner's Fields and it was succeeded by another there at 5.00, addressed by an excited Ernest Jones, who was leaving that night for the West Riding, and Alexander Sharp. When the meeting concluded after 6.30 p.m. popular attention was directed towards the church which stood in the centre of the Fields and which had sheltered police throughout the afternoon – indeed a service had been conducted while some sat there 'with their staves in their pockets' and more marched in. Windows were now smashed, an inspector assaulted and the adjoining area cleared by a rush of the officers from their concealment. Chartists and Confederates formed only one element among the diverse crowd on the common and the ensuing onslaught by the police was on political and non-political alike as they made frenzied attacks upon not only those still in the Fields but the inhabitants of a considerable area around – within, it was claimed, a radius of almost a mile. The Broad-Silk Handloom Weavers' Union of Bethnal Green was unanimous in its denunciation of 'a wanton and cruel outrage upon the rights and liberties of a harmless and defenceless people'.[407]

During the succeeding week some of the leading Chartist exponents of physical force in London were arrested for their parts in the disorders triggered off by Mitchel's sentence. And in July the following were each imprisoned for two years: Joseph Williams (for Clerkenwell Green on 25, 26 and 29 May), Alexander Sharp (Clerkenwell Green, 26 May, and Bonner's Fields, 4 June), William John Vernon (a seditious speech at Dean Street, 28 May, and Clerkenwell Green, 29 May), John Fussell (Clerkenwell Green, 29 May) and Ernest Jones (Bonner's Fields, 4 June).[408] Fussell briefly attained infamy for his speech advocating 'private assassination':[409]

What made the Emperor of Austria fly from his country? why, the fear of assassination, and it was by that means our rulers would fly. I have five sons, and I do declare that I would disown one that would refuse to assassinate any one who may be instrumental in banishing me from my country for such an offence as John Mitchel was found guilty.[410]

At the same time the government struck at the Confederates with the indictment of Francis Looney, secretary of the Davis Club, for delivering seditious speeches on 5 June at Dean Street and the South London Chartist Hall. He too was sentenced to two years' imprisonment.[411]

It was the Queen's pressure which instigated the prosecution of the six men. On 31 May, obviously shocked by the press reports of Fussell's views, she asked: 'Does not Lord John think some of the Speeches held outragiously [sic] violent & seditious? Could nothing be done to take up some of these people?' Russell explained: 'In order to prosecute for seditious words, a reporter of the govt must be present, & unless notice is received of the meeting this is not [seldom] the case' and on 4 June Grey elaborated:

In the case of the speech attributed to Mr Fussell, the Commissioners of Police have been endeavouring to obtain such evidence as would enable proceedings to be taken against him, but in the absence of any Reporter expressly engaged for the purpose of taking down the speeches made at such meetings there is considerable difficulty in obtaining the sworn information on which alone any proceedings could be successfully instituted.[412]

The difficulty was overcome by resorting to the evidence of the newspaper reporters (and engaging shorthand writers to cover the meetings of 4 and 5 June). Warrants for the arrest of the six were issued on 6 June; by the 8th five were in custody and warrants were also out for May and Daly. This marked the beginning of the numerous arrests throughout the country in the summer of 1848.[413]

The Chartists reacted bitterly to the prime minister's declaration in Parliament that he considered that the English people did not desire the Charter and they called for nationwide demonstrations on Whit Monday, 12 June. The Executive of the NCA informed Russell: 'We have accordingly made arrangements to convince you, on Whit-Monday, that your supposition is utterly unfounded'; while the Home Secretary was given notice that the metropolitan meeting would be held on Bonner's Fields at 2.30 p.m., for 'the discussion of grievances, the receiving of a report regarding the presentation of memorials to the Queen, the adoption of an address to Lord John Russell, and of a petition to Parliament for the release of Political Offenders, and the enactment of the People's Charter'.[414]

The government's response was to ban all assemblies in London[415] and to amass forces on a scale comparable with that of 10 April. The troops in the city totalled 4,576 officers and men, of whom 949 had been drawn from Woolwich, Windsor and Chichester. A further 727 were held in readiness at Hounslow and Windsor. (But the 17th and 63rd Foot were not moved up from Dover and Chatham respectively, as they had been on 10 April.) Six guns were brought in from Woolwich with three troops of the Royal Horse Artillery. There were 400 pensioners mobilized and positioned in the Workhouse at Bonner's Fields. Additional payments were received by 4,343 of the police for duties performed on 12 June – 1,100 were concentrated, together with 28 mounted men, at the Fields, while 350 more were to proceed there if necessary. Alarm over the expiry of the warrants of those special constables sworn during March and April for a period of two months led to instructions for their re-enrolment.[416]

Official Chartist expectations for 12 June, in contrast to those on 10 April, are opaque. The Executive issued an address, which counselled: 'Respect property. Be not aggressors. Let not our cause be disgraced by riots, nor thrown back for years by partial outbreaks. Defend your liberties and lives like men, and whilst you keep the law on your side, do not allow it to be broken over your heads.'[417] In

Greenwich this was interpreted as: 'We expect it will be a peaceable demonstration; but, at all events, be prepared for the Worst – We leave it to your own discretion to come up in what Manner you please, Knowing you to be Sensible Men – and we expect every Man will do his duty.'[418] It was not until the afternoon of the 12th that M'Douall and twenty-four others initiated the first conspiracy of 1848; but rumours of an outbreak were rife.[419] At the South London Chartist Hall James Bassett, who was to become a leading insurrectionary, 'called on them to attend the meeting to be held on Bonner's Fields tomorrow (Cries of we will) and stand firm and if a Blow is struck be prepared to avenge it, he then said are you armed (Cries of yes) will you stand firm (Cries of we will) then attend the meeting'.[420] The Chartist leadership would probably have welcomed the Bonner's Fields demonstration developing into a rising.

It was against this background that the authorities regarded the proposed mass meeting on 12 June as offering a challenge of an altogether more threatening kind than had the riots of 29 May to 4 June. Indeed, they viewed it as commensurate with the confrontation of 10 April.[421] Public buildings were again strongly defended. Cutlasses were issued to the police. The guard at Buckingham Palace was doubled and the Gentlemen at Arms were called for duty at St James's Palace. Magistrates, prepared to read the Riot Act, were stationed with the troops in seven positions: Bishop Bonner's Fields; Bethnal Green Workhouse; Gardiner's Barn (at the south-east corner of Victoria Park); Eastern Counties Goods Station, Spitalfields; Leather Lane, Holborn; Albany Street Barracks, Regent's Park; and the Royal Hospital, Chelsea. Special constables were still being sworn in on the morning of the 12th; but of East London M'Douall commented: 'The number of Specials I . . . ascertained to be unusually limited in number, the loyal steam having evaporated from the empty tills.'[422] The *Morning Herald* judged on the Whit Monday morning: 'From the formidable arrangements made by the authorities, nothing in the shape of a popular commotion need be anticipated, and it would be worse than madness for any parties to offer the least resistance at Bonner's Fields.'[423] Several Whit Monday meetings had initially been proposed for London. Wanstead Flats had been named – and a detachment numbering sixty-three were accordingly drafted for the protection of the Enfield Small Arms Factory and Waltham Abbey Powder Mills – as had Blackheath, Clerkenwell Green and Cumberland Market. These were ultimately abandoned for a single gathering at Bonner's Fields.[424]

Some time after 1.00 p.m. M'Douall, who of the Chartist Executive of five alone remained in London, arrived at Bonner's Fields in a cab from Perry's Coffee House where the committee organizing the demonstration met. 'Perceiving the immense mass of police armed with cutlasses' on the Fields' perimeter, he proceeded to the Workhouse, where he took cognizance of the pensioners, and spoke with Arnold, the acting magistrate. M'Douall enquired whether indeed the government proposed to suppress the demonstration. The reply was that 'the proposed meeting was illegal and would be prevented'. M'Douall told Arnold that, this being the case, 'he should prevent all men under his control from attending on the ground'.[425] He reported in the *Northern Star:* 'I found all prepared outside during the brief parley, and the forces in line. I walked down the police line, and made my observations, accompanied by a great crowd, who, however, speedily dispersed, when informed of our intentions, and the intention of the Government.'[426] M'Douall and the committee thereupon quit the scene. A drizzling rain, followed at about 4.00 by 'a tremendous thunder storm', drove away those of the people who had lingered, described by *The Times* leader as: 'ill-favoured and ill-satisfied weavers; larking youngsters and sombre adults; brawny Confederates in breeches, worsted stockings, frieze coats, and straw hats; ginger-beer men, orange women, children, and that invariable ingredient of an English assemblage, women with children in their arms'. M'Douall remained in the neighbourhood until 8.00 and observed no incidents – 'except dreadful hooting and groaning at the mounted police'.[427] At 5.00 the special courts were informed that they need no longer remain assembled; Arnold remained on duty to 9.30 and the magistrates at the police courts were not dismissed until 10.00.[428]

Remembrance by the upper and middle classes of the renewed alarm of June 1848 slipped away almost entirely. Only Thomas Hughes recounted that: 'again in June, the Bank, the Mint, the Custom House and other public offices were filled with troops, and the Houses of Parliament were not only garrisoned but provisioned as if for a siege'.[429]

M'Douall did indeed stay in the neighbourhood of Bonner's Fields on 12 June for it was he who took the chair at a meeting in the afternoon at the Albion beershop, Bethnal Green Road, at which conspiratorial preparations for an insurrection were set in motion.[430] There had been a previous meeting at the Windsor Castle, Holborn, on 6 June, but, M'Douall said, 'their proceedings now were assuming the shape of conspiracy – and they must go on with it'. It was resolved 'to appoint a Committee of four delegates, besides three of the executive, two Confederates, and two members of the trades union – to sit at a place to be named hereafter – and appoint the day and hour when the final struggle is to take place'. The police received two reports of this meeting, one from George Davis of Greenwich, who attended as a delegate in June and again in July and August, the other from Thomas Riordain Reading, the *Northern Star*'s correspondent for the affairs of the London Irish.[431] The revolutionaries met the following evening at the Windsor Castle, when the four who constituted 'the Secret Committee of delegates, were appointed to concoct plans for overthrowing the Government, and taking possession of London – to be laid before the general Committee of twenty four for approval'. The four members of 'the Secret Committee' were Henshaw (for East London), Pitt (West London), Honeybold (North London) and Percy (South London).[432]

In the morning (of 14 June) at the John Street Institution:

A map of London was produced, and different plans of attack formed – One was to construct Barricades near the New Church in the Strand. (Temple Bar would form a serviceable one) up Ludgate Hill; one at the end of Cheapside across to Newgate Street, to extend down to S^t. Martin's le Grand as far as the Barbican, and then down Aldersgate Street across to Clerkenwell – across Saffron Hill up the back streets to Hatton Garden. (where plenty of old materials might be found of houses that have been pulled down) then as far as S^t. Giles' Church – from thence to Drury Lane. Russell S^t. Covent Garden and so back to the Strand. The Churches, Theatres and other public buildings to be set fire to – & pawnbrokers gunsmiths etc. to be plundered of their arms. Barricades might be carried across Waterloo Bridge to the Kent Road – the Police Station there attacked and the March of the Artillery towards Town intercepted, and their guns spiked and ammunition seized.

M'Douall adjourned the meeting until 8.00 the same evening at the Lord Denman, Great Suffolk Street,

when they would then take into consideration the sending of two Delegates to Manchester & other parts to warn them of the intended outbreak (which ought to take place on Friday or Sunday night at farthest–) –

At 8.30 p.m. there were seven gathered at the Southwark beershop,

when a Delegate from the South London District, brought a message from M^r M^c. Douall stating that he had had an interview with M^r M^c.Crae – and that he was deputed by him to inform the Delegates that they were dissolved by order of the Executive. Upon being questioned, the Messenger said he had asked M^c.Douall why they were dissolved, and he said, something had transpired since the morning that had caused this – He also denied all knowledge of his former plans, or even that the Delegates had been assembled for any specific purpose.

It is scarcely surprising that: 'This announcement caused great consternation ... The Delegates present express'd their intention of going to their different localities and telling the members how they had been treated by M^r. M^c.Douall – and advise them to have nothing more to do with the Chartist Cause.'[433]

Definite arrangements, then, were being made for an uprising which would probably have taken place during the weekend 16–18 June, but on 14 June 'the general Committee of twenty four' was disbanded by the Chartist Executive. The Executive was not merely aware of the parallel existence of the revolutionary committee. M'Douall was a member of both; and the authority of the insurrectionaries derived entirely from that of the Chartist Executive. What had transpired to alarm M'Douall and M'Crae so greatly is not known, but most probably the presence of further spies had been discovered. Already, at the Albion on 12 June, M'Douall had announced that informers had attended the meeting of 6 June. On 13 June they were named as H. Mander May and Plume.[434]

Whatever its cause, the shock M'Douall and M'Crae received was not sufficient to prevent them talking wildly in public. William Taylor, a Paddington teetotaller, complained that, only a week later, on 21 June, before a meeting numbering 400 or 500 in Carlisle Street, Portman Market, they 'spoke most violently agst: Lord John Russell & Sir Geo: Grey – I recollect that *McDowell said* a secret plot shoᵈ. be formed to assinate Lord John Russell . . . MᶜCrea was very violent in his language. he said Lord John Russells days were numbered, but I do not know whether he meant "in Office" or "personally".[435]

For five or six weeks the excitement in London subsided. Then, on Tuesday, 25 July, the bill to suspend Habeas Corpus in Ireland, introduced in Parliament by Russell on 22 July, received royal assent. On Monday the police had dispersed a crowd of several hundred which gathered on Clerkenwell Green and arrested the speaker, John Sayer Orr, not a known Chartist or Confederate.[436] On Tuesday, Wednesday, Thursday and Friday, amidst renewed ferment – and morning newspapers reported on the 27th that the long-awaited insurrection in Ireland had at last broken out – overflowing meetings of Chartists and Confederates were held at the Milton Street Theatre, Cripplegate, and the John Street Institute. Clearly an *émeute* was anticipated by the authorities, particularly one based on Milton Street, for large detachments of police, many armed with cutlasses, were detailed to the Cripplegate and Tottenham Court Road areas and the whole city kept on the alert.[437]

In the following weeks the government proceeded with a further wave of arrests and the defendants were prosecuted for delivering seditious speeches – all of which had stressed solidarity with the Irish people and urged positive support by Londoners. Five were each imprisoned for two years: John Shaw and John James Bezer (sedition committed at the Milton Street Theatre, 28 July), George Shell and James Maxwell Bryson (South London Hall, 28 July), and Robert

Crowe (Dean Street, 31 July). Warrants were issued for the arrest of Joseph Rooney and William (or John?) Wilson for offences on 28 July at the South London Hall and Milton Street respectively, but they were never brought to trial.[438]

Meetings of the insurrectionaries had been resumed on 10 July at the George, Old Bailey. This was the day of Ernest Jones's trial and the intention was to attempt a rescue as the Chartist prisoners were removed from Newgate to Coldbath Fields Prison. It was said

That it was a shame that the prisoners should go to Gaol without one struggle to release them . . . that the route the prisoners would take to go to Cold Bath Fields would be through Cow Cross from Newgate and that would be the best place to attack them – that they would find a friend there who would lead the Irish out from the Localities . . . to assist them.

At the trial of Cuffay, Lacey and Fay, Davis stated that he understood the 'friend' to be Thomas Daly, the revolutionary leader of the London Irish; but Daly wrote from the safety of Paris denying any knowledge of the plan, stressing that he had been in France since 17 June.[439] In any case it does not seem that the discussion at the George prompted any preparations for the release of Jones and the others, but arrangements for a rising were begun again in earnest.[440]

This time the committee of delegates existed independently of the Chartist Executive. George Davis, who was in constant communication with police, was now joined by Thomas Powell (alias Johnson) from the Cripplegate locality, each unaware that the other was a spy. While both acted as *agents provocateurs* in their localities (Davis much less than Powell), they were fairly passive at the delegate meetings. It was Powell who was principal witness for the prosecution at the ensuing trials and whose demonstrable mendacity, unsavoury background and acts of provocation were exposed with relish by the defence. In writing an account of the conspiracy what is important is that Powell's evidence was corroborated by Davis's[441] – although only four of the reports which they gave the police immediately after the meetings have survived.[442]

Between 20 July and the day eventually fixed for the intended outbreak, 16 August, there were some sixteen meetings, normally of between twenty and forty men, in various parts of central London. Their exact locations with known attendance will be found in Appendix II.

At the Black Jack, Portsmouth Street, on 20 July, a smaller, secret committee was appointed which, as before, was to draw up plans for the rising. The sub-committee, called the 'plotting committee' or 'Ulterior Committee', consisted of five men, each to prepare a plan:

Rose (secretary), Payne (chairman), Mullins (vice-chairman and trea-surer), Dowling and Brewster.[443] Payne, on the 23rd, declared, 'Gentlemen, our object is to destroy the power of the Queen, and, if possible, to establish a republic', to which 'there was a general acqui-escence'.[444] On 26 July, as on the 20th,[445] 'reports were given in from the Delegates as to the feeling prevalent among the members of their locality and the numbers of men that could be depended upon as ready to fight', a duty which at subsequent meetings all new delegates were expected to perform.

At the meeting on 30 July the sub-committee resigned, for it was thought necessary to increase the number to nine – and there was some talk of Rose and Mullins being spies. The same five were re-elected with the exception of Brewster who was replaced by Bassett; and the delegates decided to elect four others at the next meeting. Thus on 1 August Fay, Thompson, Lynch and Donovan, all of whom were Irish, were added to the 'Ulterior Committee', where they joined a fifth Irishman, Dowling.

At Cartwright's Coffee House, on 4 August, either Mullins or Bas-sett announced to the delegates 'that he had seen Mr Kydd[446] on that day, and that he (Mr Kydd) had received a circular from Manchester, and in the circular was a request and a desire to know, how soon they would dispatch a person to Manchester?' The delegates agreed to send William Lacey. Mullins, as treasurer, gave money for the expenses to Bassett, who immediately left to inform Lacey of his mis-sion. On the following morning Lacey departed for Manchester.[447]

At Denny's Coffee House, Seven Dials, on 7 August the entire sub-committee of nine resigned. This was partly due to news from Ireland that Smith O'Brien had been arrested and the insurrection put down. A division had also developed between the Chartist and Irish mem-bers of the committee – although possibly Dowling sided with the four Chartists against the other four Confederates. Each group com-plained that the other was preparing plans independently without even showing them. (The four Confederates had originally been elected to the 'Ulterior Committee' on 1 August because 'There was a feeling of jealousy existed & the whole of the 4 [had] spoken that evening and they stated that there was not a sufficient number of Irishmen on the Committee.') A new committee of five was appointed, consisting of Payne, Mullins, Rose, Brewster and Bassett.[448] Bassett, who received the lowest number of votes, was to withdraw from membership of the sub-committee when 'the provi-sionary President', called 'the Visionary President' by Thomas Powell (sceptical perhaps), took up his seat. Mullins gave the delegates to understand that the president was to be a man called Churchill,[449] then living in France. Churchill remains a most shadowy figure, but he had been in May a member of the National Assembly – where he had felt obliged to defend himself as a 'new Chartist' – and his name is strongly linked to the revolutionary movement of 1848.[450] A letter from Lacey in Manchester was read by Payne and the news that 'Trade was very good and you would soon receive a good order' was 'received with satisfaction' by the meeting.

At 8.00 on the morning of 11 August the house of John Rose, secretary of the 'plotting committee', was searched and papers seized by the police. As a result the delegate meeting which was to have been held in Shoreditch that evening was cancelled, but meetings were resumed on Sunday, 13 August.[451] Not many attended in the morning at Hopkinson's Coffee House, Saffron Hill, and the delegates were invited upstairs to a meeting of the Finsbury locality. 'Then there was a Motion made whether the District of Clerkenwell should turn out for physical force or not, and it was put to the vote and carried that they should turn out', the Finsbury Chartists pledging themselves 'to abide by any ultimate measures the Sub Committee might agree upon in a day or two'. The delegates adjourned to 3.00 in the afternoon at Breedon's Beershop, Shouldham Street, Marylebone. Cuffay was now appointed secretary, in place of Rose, and Warry was also elected to the 'Ulterior Committee'. Another letter from Lacey in Manchester (the third) was read. Written on Saturday, 12 August, it stated:

'he expected to see D^r. M^c.Douall on Sunday – that trade was very brisk – he had to go to Birmingham, Loughborough, Leicester, and Nottingham – that he wished them to send him that large order he mentioned, by the last train on Monday night –' (understood to mean that Manchester was to rise on Monday night) 'and that he should probably be in Town on Monday Morning'.

It was agreed that the sub-committee would sit throughout Monday and that should an insurrection take place in Manchester at night so would one in London.[452]

But Lacey did not return to London on Monday and although the delegates sat until 10.00 p.m. at the Orange Tree, Orange Street, Red Lion Square, waiting for him, they were compelled to adjourn to the Lord Denman, Great Suffolk Street, the following evening.[453] Lacey arrived in the capital on Tuesday and, shaking off the police, attended the meeting at the Lord Denman. He informed the delegates that elsewhere the rising was fixed for that night and then withdrew with the members of the 'plotting committee' to the Temperance Coffee House in the same street.

After three-quarters of an hour the committee came back to the beershop – without Lacey. Mullins took the chair and addressed the meeting:

Gentlemen as you are aware the Committee have retired and come to certain resolutions and decisions. They have requested me to give you the following instructions. Our friend Mr Lacey has informed us that the men of Birmingham and Manchester are up and doing or would be doing that night . . . and we have no reason to doubt the correctness of his statement. Therefore Gentlemen tomorrow night you must come out to fight and strike the blow. It is necessary you should speak out honestly and boldly for there must be no flinching in the matter.

Mullins then asked each delegate in turn: 'Will you come out to fight?' All save two replied they would. Final preparations were then made for the insurrection to take place on the evening of Wednesday, 16 August. The localities were to meet at 8.00 and be at their respective stations at 9.20 precisely. 'Almost the last words' Powell heard Mullins speak before the meeting dispersed were 'May God's bitterest curse hang upon the Soul of that man who shall betray us.'[454]

Linked with the capital in the conspiracy were Manchester and the surrounding towns, Liverpool, Leicester and Loughborough, Nottingham, Birmingham – and perhaps Bradford.[455] In London, of course, the plot had been doubly penetrated for weeks. At 6.00 p.m. on the 16th eleven men were seized at the Orange Tree, Orange Street, Red Lion Square – these were the 'luminaries' who, under the direction of Joseph Ritchie, *soi-disant* 'Red Republican' and returned from France but two or three weeks before,[456] were to have set London ablaze not merely to cause confusion but to act as a general signal.[457] Later, at about 9.00, an armed group of thirteen were arrested at the Angel, Webber Street, Southwark. Around 9.30 a sizeable crowd was dispersed at Seven Dials. That night and during the next four days other arrests were made, and 'combustible balls' and weapons discovered in the prisoners' homes and elsewhere.[458]

No account of the strategy to have been employed in the proposed rising exists; yet undoubtedly the final intentions were very similar to the plan produced during the June conspiracy.[459] The four stations from which the outbreak was to be attempted were Seven Dials (to be directed by Mullins), Strutton Ground, Westminster (by Bassett), Clerkenwell Green (by Brewster) and Tower Hamlets (by Payne). The entire Western District of Marylebone, Paddington, Somers Town and Chelsea was to proceed to Seven Dials and the Dean Street and several South London localities were to assemble at Strutton Ground.[460]

The outcome was the transportation for life in September of Joseph Ritchie, William Lacey, Thomas Fay, William Cuffay and Wil-

liam Dowling (a portrait painter who had succeeded Looney as secretary of the Davis Club)[461] and in November of George Bridge Mullins.[462] Twelve others were imprisoned for two years and three for
eighteen months.[463] Their arrests and consequent sentences –
regarded as savage, given Powell's part as *agent provocateur*[464] – struck
gravely at London Chartism, already in decline by August. But while
there was initially stern dissociation from most of the insurrectionaries, the contracting movement was partially sustained in the mobilization of aid for the numerous metropolitan victims of 1848.

The conspiracy of 1848 was not only the last of the revolutionary
attempts which originated in the 1790s; it was also the one based on
the greatest degree of support in London. The commonest miscon-
ception concerning the insurrectionary movement is its attribution to
William Cuffay, the negro tailor, under five feet tall,[465] who had been
active in London Chartism since 1839. In part this was due to the
middle-class press, especially *Punch* which had eagerly utilized him as
a figure of derision from as early as April 1848, when he had been a
member of the Convention.[466] Even Holyoake recalled him as 'a small
black man bearing the absurd name of Cuffy [sic]' (though recognizing him as 'an honest, well-conducted man').[467] The unjustifiable
emphasis on Cuffay is also a product of Thomas Frost's *Forty Years'
Recollections,* which names him as 'president of the committee' and
apparent 'concoctor of the conspiracy'.[468]

Although Cuffay was, on 16 August, secretary of the 'Ulterior
Committee' he had only occupied that position since the 13th; and his
first appearance as a delegate was, according to Powell, and implicitly
confirmed by Davis,[469] on 4 August. The true leaders and originators
of the revolutionary attempt should rather be identified as Payne,
Mullins, John Rose, Brewster and James Bassett. Payne was chairman
at every meeting, except the last at the Lord Denman, but it is Mullins,
a surgeon's apprentice aged twenty-two,[470] who seems, increasingly,
to have been the dominant insurrectionary.[471]

Unlike that of June, the second conspiracy was entirely independent of the Chartist Executive. On 26 July Ferdinando complained
that 'it was not sanctioned by the executive'.[472] All the same the Chartist leadership came to know that plans for a rising had been renewed
and some undoubtedly gave the revolutionaries their support. It was
Kydd who had opened up the communication between London and
Manchester; and on 13 August Lacey had expected to see M'Douall.
Powell gave evidence that: 'Mullins stated he had seen Mr. Kydd that
day, 1st Aug., and that Mr. Kydd had said, if the people came out for
physical force, he would not be backward in heading them; but that

5. William Cuffay

he, Kydd, had entered on the executive as a moral-force man, and had taken the office only on that ground.'[473]

The conspiracy had far greater backing in London than has been supposed. The claim on the 14th that 'there were nearly 5000 fighting men of the Chartists alone' and 'about the same number' of Confederates, although clearly intended to boost morale, does not appear unduly extravagant.[474] Besides Cuffay and Rose, the following delegates were all well-known Chartists, most of long-standing: Shell,

Bligh, Allnutt, Ferdinando, Fuzzen, Pedley, Salmon, Ford. These were men usually engaged patiently in the pedestrian, but demanding, work of locality or trade society, not in revolutionary plottings. Still, it is scarcely surprising that the conspiracy of 1848 struck deep roots among the political militants of the metropolis, for one of the most important traditions to which London Chartists were heirs was conspiratorial insurrection, the outstanding example being that of Thistlewood and his associates, of whom both Thomas Preston and Samuel Waddington survived to become Chartists – and teachers of Chartists.[475]

PART THREE
Disturbance and the maintenance of order

Metropolis and police[1]

A fundamental difference between London and the provinces during the Chartist period – most markedly at the outset – was the existence of the Metropolitan Police; and this was a factor of great significance in the containment of Chartism in the capital, so that once it had grown into a mass movement, in the 1840s, its manifestations were checked from developing into either a 'challenge' of 1838–9 dimensions or, even in 1842, a riotous movement of the order which then affected a large region in the North and Midlands.[2]

The force was founded in 1829 with Lieutenant-Colonel Charles Rowan and Richard Mayne as Commissioners, a joint command that lasted until Rowan's retirement in 1850.[3] A remarkable new figure now made his appearance in the street. In the words of one of the constables:

The Metropolitan policeman of the 'forties was a strange-looking individual. I wore a swallow-tailed coat with bright buttons, and a tall hat. The hat was a fine protection for the head, and saved me from damage from many a Chartist's bludgeon. It had a rim of stout leather round the top, and a strip of covered steel on each side. Then I had a truncheon, a weapon that was capable of doing a lot of execution, and gave a good account of itself in those rough and dangerous times.[4]

The original Metropolitan Police district had a radius of between four and seven miles from Charing Cross. Only ten years later the Metropolitan Police Act of 1839 increased it enormously: 'The Police District extends over the whole County of Middlesex, and 15 miles round Charing Cross, (excepting the City of London). – The circumference is about 90 Miles, and comprises an Area of 700 square miles.' Such was the prescience with which the vast district was formed that it corresponded roughly to the Registrar-General's 'Greater London' of the 1870s and 1881, of which only the 'inner' ring became the County of London in 1888. Its population in 1848 was almost 2,400,000.[5]

Police numbers were, in contrast, meagre but growing. An initial establishment of 909 had been raised to 3,283 by January 1831 and 3,444 by January 1839. (The former Bow Street (Mounted) Horse Patrol had been absorbed, as the seventy-three mounted police, in

1836.)[6] The incorporation of the Thames Police[7] and over 500 recruited to cope with the extension of the district in 1839 resulted in a total of 4,271 by January 1840. In January 1848 the establishment stood at 4,887; by the end of the year, largely as a result of the alarms of the spring and summer, it had been increased to 5,490, including a Reserve Force of 336 instituted to act in emergencies.[8]

The force consisted of seventeen divisions in the Chartist years:[9]

Division A : Whitehall	L : Lambeth
B : Westminster	M : Southwark
C : St James's	N : Islington
D : Marylebone	P : Camberwell
E : Holborn	R : Greenwich
F : Covent Garden	S : Hampstead
G : Finsbury	T : Kensington
H : Whitechapel	V : Wandsworth
K : Stepney	

The outer divisions – K, N, P, R, S, T and V – comprised the huge area between central London and the circumference of the Police District and it was to these that the mounted men were overwhelmingly attached.[10] By 1841, 337 buildings, in total, had been acquired as premises for 'Station and Section Houses' and stabling.[11]

The principal novelty of the Metropolitan Police – and its general importance – resided in its being a uniformed and disciplined but unarmed (save for a baton), non-military force, subject to legal constraints and public scrutiny.[12] The title of only one of its ranks was drawn from the army.[13] From 1839, in addition to the two Commissioners, there were an Inspecting Superintendent (Captain William Hay), 17 Superintendents (each in charge of a division), 77 Inspectors, 354 Sergeants and some 3,000 Constables (divided into three classes approximately equal in number). Pay was extraordinarily low. From 1839 Superintendents earned £250 per annum and Inspectors £118 6s., Sergeants 21s. 6d. per week and Constables on average 19s.[14] These rates are startlingly poor when compared with the (best) artisan earnings discussed in Part Four. On the other hand, each policeman was ensured of fifty-two weeks' employment in the year.[15]

There was indeed no shortage of recruits during the harsh economic decades of the thirties and forties – men would join for the temporary refuge of a secure post. This posed one problem for the Commissioners. The other was the intrinsic unsuitability of so many entrants to a force with the highest standards. To deter either type of applicant the tripartite classification of constables was introduced in 1839, with the 1st Class earning 21s. weekly, the 2nd Class 19s. and the 3rd Class only 17s.; although in the same year a superannuation scheme was inaugurated. 'The Commissioners have good reason to believe that the proposed arrangement will not diminish the candi-

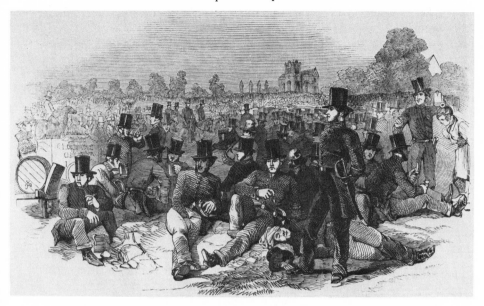

6. The police at Bishop Bonner's Fields on 12 June 1848

dates so as to deprive them of any men who intend to make the Police a permanent occupation and are likely to become valuable Constables' for, they argued:

one of the greatest difficulties the Commissioners have always had to contend with arises from men who had learned their duties, gained experience and were useful Constables, leaving the Service. The number of changes has been upwards of 1000 every year, and probably 600 of those were from men resigning whom it would have been desirable to retain. The proposed increase of pay,[16] and the ultimate provision by the Superannuation Fund now established, will it is hoped, prevent good men from leaving the Service . . . Such advantages will it is hoped give a great additional encouragement to good conduct in all.[17]

For the first six years of the force's existence a total of 3,603 men resigned but, in addition, no less than 3,858 were dismissed for improper conduct.[18] Discipline within the force was severe; and the stream of Police Orders, often reiterated, relating to conduct, save for the resolve from the outset to eliminate drunkenness on duty,[19] is austere. 'The most perfect civility at all times . . . to the public, of whatever class' and 'a perfect command of temper' were constantly counselled.[20]

Four examples alone must suffice.

The Superintendents will call the particular attention of the Police Constables to the order . . . respecting their loitering or gossiping with Servant Girls and other females any Constable found disobeying this order in future will be brought before the Commissioners.[21]

On Public occasions the Police on duty in the Streets are not to stand idling or talking to each other or to persons around them their whole attention is to be given to the duty for which they are placed there . . .[22]

Superintendents cautioned that the Police when taking Parties to the Station for Misdemeanours are not to use unnecessary violence but had better not lay hands upon them at all, unless it appears that they will not go quietly along without it. Laying hold of people by the arm or by the collar is most likely to produce irritation and violence and had better be avoided when it is possible to do so without risk of losing a Prisoner.[23]

The Constables on beats are to keep the right hand of the foot way unless when in passing persons it is from any circumstances more convenient to go to the left hand; they are to keep in mind that the object of this order is to give the greatest facility for persons to pass without interruption.[24]

An unlikely member of the Metropolitan Police in the 1830s, Thomas Ainge Devyr, soon to become a leader of physical-force Chartism on Tyneside, recalled that 'to use the club, except in the most extreme necessity, brings, and very properly, instant dismissal . . .'.[25]

Such instructions, together with punitive penalties for their infraction, were demanded for the creation of 'an entirely new system', a highly ordered, civilian force, with appointment and promotion dependent on merit, not political patronage, in daily contact with all categories of the London populace. They were also essential in a purely defensive way in view of 'strong opposition, and a very general public feeling hostile to any Police Establishment'. This was how in 1850 Mayne described the original situation; but as early as 1839 he and Rowan could write of the 'success and popularity' of the Metropolitan Police and even around 1835 Mayne noted among 'Proofs of success': 'Public opinion, shewn by Newspapers at first now changed./ very many letters & testimonials.' These appraisals of the metamorphosis of attitudes towards the new police are to a large extent justified and, as the Commissioners considered, it found expression in the Metropolitan Police Act of 1839 (and, also, they could have justly claimed, in the County Police and City of London Police Acts of the same year, the latter instituting a force entirely distinct from – and independent of – the Metropolitan Police).[26] Already, in *Sketches by Boz*, written between 1833 and 1837, the efficient, if listless, 'policeman at the street-corner' is an accepted, omnipresent figure.[27]

Yet immense antagonism towards the police remained and was actually reinforced by the measures of 1839. Middle-class radical suspicion, indeed antipathy, is overt in the early volumes of *Punch*, which even in 1848 offered harsh criticism[28] and did not begin to present its 'traditional' image of the dependable 'Bobby' until the 1850s.[29]

Among Chartists the hatred was virulent and united moral- and physical-force men. 'A constant reader' of the *Northern Star* and member of the Land Company, although a Metropolitan Policeman, complained of 'the rancour against the police . . . We are styled "bludgeon men", "government minions", "brutal police", and anything else but good men.'[30] He might also have mentioned such abusive epithets as 'the blue bottles', and 'raw lobster force', 'the unboiled'[31] and 'these skull-cracking ruffians, these kitchen spies and pimps'.[32] Examples of 'brutal assaults' and 'outrages' by the police were continuously reported.[33] From the most popular level of all comes the broadside, 'The Irish New Policeman', with a savage woodcut, accusation of dishonesty and chorus of

> Ranting, rolliking, Irish joys,
> Always wrangling; never at peace, man;
> Kissing the girls, wolloping boys:
> Whack! rioting new policeman.[34]

Chartists condemned the County Police Bill for the extension of an un-English 'spy system' – a *gendarmerie* in fact[35] – from the capital to the rest of the country and the Metropolitan Police Bill for its creation of 'twenty *new crimes*'. The new police were denounced, in general, for their military and centralizing character, undermining local and individual liberty, and, now and then, for their anti-Chartist capacities. In the view of the moderate *Chartist*:

The centralization which is so prevailing a Whig mania, is nothing more than another word for despotism . . . The New Poor Law is an egregious instance of what it is likely to effect. The London Police Bill is to be followed by a Rural Police Bill, and that is to be followed by other schemes all of the same tendency, each calling into being several thousand of Government spies.

From Chartist Convention to Shoreditch vestry strongly worded resolutions were carried against the Bills of 1839.[36]

For the argument of this book two aspects of the Metropolitan Police are of prime importance: the ability to control crowds, to be discussed in the succeeding pages, and the extent to which they were empowered to impose on Londoners a far-reaching system of social control, that was indeed rapidly implemented.[37] While the Metropolitan Police Act of 1829 equipped the police with wide powers 'to apprehend all loose, idle, and disorderly Persons',[38] during the next ten years, although the Commissioners were still combating indiscipline within their own ranks, significant incursions were made into the city's easy-going ways. Beggars were arrested.[39] Devyr sought promotion 'by petty and mean acts . . . I had so far sank my manhood as to open and search little bundles belonging to people'.[40] Children were detained overnight in the stations for playing games on Sunday afternoons. Such severity did lead to a rebuke from the Commissioners, but they *had* issued an order to prevent the nuisance of the dangerous 'practice of Boys flying Kites in the Streets or on the roads in the Parks'.[41] A constable brought a successful charge against 'Two persons of genteel appearance' for plucking ears of wheat, to the value of one penny, while they were strolling in Battersea Fields.[42]

It was, however, the Act of 1839 that authorized the police to act against an extraordinary range of high-spirited, quasi-rural behaviour, often of an innocuous variety. Fairs[43] and coffee houses and other places of non-alcoholic refreshment were cracked down on. Public-houses were to be closed on Sunday mornings; and unlicensed theatres, premises used for bear-baiting, cock-fighting, etc., and gaming houses were subjected to police raids. Most significant was the itemization of twenty-five types of nuisance, each liable to a penalty not exceeding 40s. Among these were: driving furiously or without holding the reins; rolling or carrying 'any Cask, Tub, Hoop, or Wheel, or any Ladder, Plank, Pole, Showboard, or Placard, upon any Footway'; bill-posting or writing on walls without the owner's permission; the playing of games in any public place 'to the Annoyance of the Inhabitants or Passengers'; bell-ringing and door-knocking (by pranksters); beating or shaking carpets or rugs ('except Door Mats before the Hour of Eight in the Morning') or throwing 'any Dirt, Litter, or Ashes, or any Carrion, Fish, Offal, or Rubbish' in a thoroughfare; and not keeping 'sufficiently swept or cleansed all Footways and Watercourses' adjoining commercial or domestic premises.[44]

In the eighteenth century social control had in many cases been maintained by the citizenry informally – by such 'summary chastisement' as thrashing a young thief or dowsing a pickpocket under a pump.[45] With the establishment of a police most offenders eventually passed into their hands;[46] and a great mass of previously non-criminal activity became unlawful and was regulated, with amazing success, by the force. Street-sellers became 'a *proscribed class* . . . bandied about at the will of a police-officer', command to 'move on' so as not to cause an obstruction.[47] It was prohibited in 1839 to blow horns or 'any other noisy Instrument' to call people together or announce entertainments and in hawking, collecting or begging. As early as 1841 this legislation had been so completely enforced as 'to have banished from our streets all those uncommon noises which did something to relieve the monotony of the one endless roar of the tread of feet and the rush of wheels': 'the horn that proclaimed extraordinary news', 'the bell of the dustman' and 'the tinkle of the muffin-man'.[48] Throughout the 1840s the Commissioners conducted a campaign against boys trundling hoops in the streets and parks – the iron hoops were confiscated

– but in this instance without apparent victory for repeated orders to the Superintendents were followed by renewed complaints of an increase in the nuisance.[49]

Londoners made little serious opposition to this intervention, which affected the minutiae of their lives as much, if not considerably more, as the crises. Not only were the police instructed to remove orange peel from the pavements[50] but:

The Superintendents will call the attention of the Constables to the circumstance of obscene words being written or chalked on the Walls of Buildings, Gates of Houses and Palings &c – the Men on beats will in such cases deface these words quietly in the Night time when it is possible to do so. Any party committing the offence may be apprehended & charged.[51]

Despite frequent assaults on and 'collisions' with the police – and even the murder of several – the new, stringent system of social control was accepted, physically, with comparative docility.[52] An incredulous Frenchman wrote in 1845 of his experience in the Princess's Theatre of 'your very efficient police in the presence of a free English public':

From the first the gallery was rather full, all the seats being occupied, and some people standing behind; yet all was quiet orderly [sic] until the half-price rushed in in crowds, forcing their way onwards behind the seats over the opposite side, encouraged by the police, who, I imagine, had promised some friends of theirs to find room for them, Now, the space between the seats and the wall was filled with a thick mass, which it was quite impossible to pierce; and the stout invaders struggling onwards with all their strength, we were obliged to make all possible efforts to avoid being overturned over the ladies, screaming on their seats at the alarming impending danger of being crushed by our fall; but, unmoved by any pity, the policemen urged on till they became at last convinced of the utter impossibility of going through. Now, the free public, who were put to such a trial, did not offer any other resistance than that of an inert mass – they did not venture to make any complaint – they allowed the police to do with them what they pleased . . . Had it been possible to pass through (not between) their bodies, they would have, I think, raised no objection. I called a policeman who took the most prominent part in the affray . . . to cease such a scandal. No attention was paid to the voice of A SLAVE CITIZEN OF FRANCE.[53]

This account illustrates admirably both the degree to which the bullying of the new police was received with passivity and their capacity to manage crowds.[54]

Riot

═══════════

The testing of the Metropolitan Police by severe disturbances in London did not occur – to its good fortune – until thirteen years after its foundation, for in neither 1830–2 nor 1839 was there a prolonged or dispersed challenge to public order.[55] It was only in August 1842 that, for almost a week and a half, daily meetings, processions and fighting with the police erupted, moving from one quarter of the city to another and sometimes taking place in several concurrently.

From 13 August contingents of troops began to leave London for deployment in the areas seized by the Plug Riots. On the first evening, the 3rd Battalion the Grenadier Guards marched from St George's Barracks, Charing Cross, to Euston.

They were followed by a large crowd of persons, which continued during their progress to increase by accumulations of women and boys, until their arrival at the railway station. By the time they reached the Quadrant . . . murmurs of groans and hisses burst from the crowd, which continued to increase as they advanced up Regent-street, mingled with exclamations of 'Remember you are brothers' . . . about the middle of Regent-street, the crowd pressing so closely on the band, the officer in command directed the band to strike playing, and at the same time ordered the soldiers to 'fix bayonets' . . . That, however, did not silence the groans and hisses, which were uttered by the crowd until the battalion reached the terminus.[56]

The Guards had been preceded by a detachment of the Royal Artillery at Euston where the crowd was so large and threatening that it was necessary for police to clear the gates and expedite the departure of the military. Similar scenes were repeated during the next day, while on the 15th the soldiers were, according to the *Northern Star*, 'compelled to charge the people at the point of the bayonet' several times 'before they could effect an entrance to the Railway Station'.[57]

The first major meeting called by the Chartists was at Stepney Green on Tuesday, 16 August, 'to take into consideration "the massacre of an unarmed Populace, and to show sympathy with the Brethren in the North" '. The police tore down posters, arrested boardmen, prosecuted shopkeepers for displaying the placards and attempted to intimidate the organizers. Sir James Graham wrote to Wellington:

7. Departure of the troops at Euston, August 1842

'Some symptoms of a feverish kind are beginning to shew themselves in this Metropolis'; and he had provided accordingly for a cavalry regiment to be 'at our disposal'. Nevertheless there was no intention of suppressing the Stepney assembly – which proved both sizeable and orderly – and the police were merely instructed 'to take immediate steps to preserve the Public Peace if any appearance of disturbance from the Meeting . . . should arise'.[58]

Similar orders were issued to the police on the Thursday for which a meeting had been advertised to take place on Islington Green. Despite further suppression of Chartist publicity thousands gathered and listened to speeches for an hour or so. They dissolved peaceably, and since it appeared to the police that Chartist activity had concluded for the evening, the command was given that: 'The day duty men now in reserve will be dismissed, and every thing go on as usual.' On leaving Islington, however, the Chartists proceeded to hold at Clerkenwell Green a second assembly which later traversed the City to hear more speeches between 10.00 and 11.00 p.m. in Lincoln's Inn Fields. The police had been expressly required to forestall any movement from Islington Green into the centre of the city and Mayne, who had heard nothing after the report of the dispersal at Islington until the appearance of a 'multitude' at Lincoln's Inn, was obliged to account for the blunder to the Home Secretary. (Peel and Graham, interrupted by the news while at dinner, went to the Home Office, where they remained until the early hours of the morning.) Other than the deceptive termination of the proceedings at Islington and the failure of the Superintendent of G Division (Finsbury) to report that they had been renewed on Clerkenwell Green, Mayne pleaded the difficulties inherent in the separate jurisdiction of the City of London. The parade from Clerkenwell was by way of Smithfield and hence after 400 yards was inside the boundaries of the City, and remained so until within 400 yards of Lincoln's Inn. After a final assembly there a procession, singing 'the "Marsellaise Hymn", and other revolutionary airs', departed for Bethnal Green (where at about 1.00 a.m. Mayne in person ordered the disruption of the remnant) and was therefore soon in the City again, passing through at midnight. Thus, as Mayne wrote to the Home Office, 'for a Considerable portion of the whole way they were not under the control nor observation of the Metropolitan Police'.[59]

In the morning proclamations were 'issued by the Government in conjunction with the Lord Mayor' banning all meetings. 'The heat throughout the day was most intense, the thermometer standing at noon at 92 degrees.' As the Chartists had named Clerkenwell Green for an assembly on the evening of the 19th, well before the announced time of 7.00, 130 policemen mustered on the Green, with 100 more in the vicinity and another 1,200 in readiness over most of the divisions. Initially the police had little difficulty in manning the several entrances to the Green, thereby causing, *The Times* reported, 'Much sullen displeasure . . . when it was found that there was no admission to the square . . . some were heard to say that, be the consequences what they might, a meeting should be held in the Green that night.' Meanwhile a small group marched away to Smithfield, intending to rally the crowd which had collected there. On their return, with several hundred, no sooner had they recrossed the City boundary than one of the two banner-carriers was seized along with their flags, a large Union Jack and 'a small blue and white printed silk, having on it the words, "Reform in Church and State" ' and surmounted by a crimson Cap of Liberty. Their following retreated to the safety of Smithfield whither 'it was not deemed prudent to pursue them any further' by the police. A total of nearly fifty were arrested in Clerkenwell during the course of the evening.[60]

In time the press around the Green became so great that large numbers broke the police lines and were able to hold the area until late at night, although there was no attempt to begin the desired meeting.[61] Instead, at about 10.00, an assembly took place and speeches were heard in Lincoln's Inn Fields where thousands had been milling all evening. The police intervened, causing a procession to depart along Great Queen Street, and thereby provoked the most serious disturbances of the day in which several constables were badly used. Large and excited crowds had also filled the streets of St Giles, 'shouting and yelling most vehemently'. Thomas Buckley urged them to 'Assert your rights, boys, assert your rights; agitate boldly, but peaceably' and, after he had been cautioned, 'Don't molest the police; assert your rights – assert your rights; down with the rich and up with the poor.' But Buckley's 'very violent' oratory prompted the solitary policeman to arrest him in Monmouth Street, 'upon which the mob immediately set up a most hideous yelling and groaning, and stones and other missiles were thrown in every direction'. PC F15 led Buckley towards Bow Street pursued by stones and the angry populace who, in Long Acre, mingled with those streaming out of Great Queen Street. Only a handful of policemen were on duty in Bow Street – they were struck by fists, stones, brickbats and a hedge stake and one constable was seriously injured. Yet they succeeded in conveying Buckley and three other prisoners to the station-house; and when this had been effected, the crowd, large and menacing though it was, evaporated.[62]

The following two days were uneventful. This was not anticipated by the authorities; the police were issued with rigorous instructions and kept at the ready, and plans laid to disperse simultaneous meetings called for Monday, 22 August. The Horse Guards moved a squadron of cavalry from Hounslow to Kensington and a battery of four guns from Woolwich was stationed on Clapham Common. Wellington reiterated the advisability of returning the Battalion of Guards to the capital: 'I think that it will be very desireable [?] to bring the Guards back from Manchester as soon as it may be possible. It will have a good appearance which is not unimportant in these Revolutionary Warfares'; but success in the maintenance of public order in August 1842 was, in part, dependent on not only the lack of resort to direct military aid but also keeping the troops mobilized for duty in London out of sight of the demonstrators.[63]

Throughout the afternoon of the 22nd very large numbers (estimated by the Chartists as not less than 40,000) collected on Kennington Common. A phrenologist lectured; cricket was played; and, although 'the congregation consisted chiefly of working men, with a great number of the white jackets', there were also women, wearing their best dresses, and many children. 'At six o'clock the Common had the appearance of a fair ... everybody seemed in search of amusement rather than the discussion of politics.' At 6.30 the meeting was commenced, and as the police had determined to suppress any

assembly held after 6.00 p.m. they immediately intervened. A Chartist named Anderson was moving the first resolution and

proceeding to condemn the conduct of 'the Bluebottles' . . . when a loud cry
was raised of 'the Peelers, the Peelers!' On turning round, it was discovered,
that about a dozen of the horse patrol, armed with heavy cutlasses, and
backed by several divisions of police, were rapidly advancing upon the crowd.
In another moment the horse patrol galloped into the assemblage, knocking
down several persons, some of whom were severely injured. The vast multitude was then seen flying in all directions, pursued by the horse patrol and
the other police . . . From all parts of the Common, men were seen coming
away with the blood streaming from their heads.[64]

The Times complimented the police on their 'masterly style' and lack
of 'unnecessary violence', but the Home Secretary acknowledged privately the 'broken heads' and the *Northern Star* protested that: 'The
Common was literally strewed with persons who had been either rode
or knocked down' and that 300 to 400 were in some way injured. The
Evening Star, which only passed to O'Connor's control on the 23rd,
was outraged by the police conduct: 'There was no warning given,
and the staffs of the constables were used without mercy. Men,
women, and children were driven like beasts of prey, before their
pursuers, and even those who showed their willingness to escape,
were followed, receiving the most cruel treatment.' The police's success in expelling the people from the Common was countered by their
inability to clear the surrounding streets and alleys. These remained
packed all evening; and the crowds were here able to revenge themselves on the invaders by pelting them with missiles.[65]

The simultaneous demonstration at Paddington attracted only a
quarter of the Kennington numbers – *The Times* estimating that over
10,000 were present – yet the police, who again moved to suppress
the meeting when it began at 6.30, were fought for more than three
hours before they could clear the area around the terminus of the
Great Western Railway:[66] 'stones and brickbats were thrown at the
police by the mob, who hissed and yelled at them repeatedly . . . until
late in the evening the police repeatedly charged the mob, dispersing
them in all directions'. Meanwhile the organizing committee had
adjourned the assembly and headed a procession to Portland Place,
expecting to join forces with a procession formed by those at Kennington Common.[67] It was this intention of the Chartists which
caused the authorities most alarm, led to precise co-ordination
between the City of London and the rest of the capital's police, and
meant that the Commissioners preferred to hold the bridges in force
at the expense of committing their reserves to the restitution of order
in Kennington and Paddington.[68]

A third, spontaneous,[69] gathering took place later in the evening on Clerkenwell Green. After 8.00 Chartists proceeded to open a public meeting and, as before, the speakers retired when a police reinforcement arrived at the Green. Not so their audience, which instead grew in size over the next hour or two. *The Times* observed: 'The mob continued to augment, and were evidently determined on harassing the police, who seemed perfectly worn out with incessant duty, by their continuing up to a late hour . . . to move about in small detached parties.'[70]

Four years later Henry Ross, a veteran radical who had fled Scotland in 1819, was ranking Kennington Common and 'the Paddington terminus' with Coldbath Fields and the Birmingham Bull Ring as recognized – and notorious – examples of the brutality of the Metropolitan Police. Another participant was also haunted by the memory of 1842. Speaking in the debate on the Corn Laws Graham, on 10 February 1846, recalled: 'We had in this metropolis, at midnight, Chartist meetings assembled in Lincoln's Inn Fields. Almost for nearly three weeks there were assembled in all the environs of this metropolis, immense masses of people, greatly discontented, and acting in a spirit dangerous to the public peace.'[71]

There were at least eighty arrests – and probably considerably more – on 19 and 22 August (nearly fifty at Clerkenwell Green on the 19th and eighteen at Paddington and fourteen at Kennington Common on the 22nd);[72] but details of the arrested men are scanty. The names of twenty-two are known and, of these, the occupations of seventeen: three shoemakers (one unemployed), three carpenters (one earning 30s. a week), two tailors, a surgical-instrument maker, bricklayer, plasterer (who had 'the appearance of an agricultural labourer', since he wore 'a shiny cap and smock-frock'), journeyman coachmaker, paper-stainer, sawyer, journeyman printer, porter and 'a common informer'. Three men were drunk and three were recognized Chartists (including two members of the Marylebone locality). A boot and shoemaker was aged forty, a tailor thirty-two, the plasterer thirty-nine, the sawyer sixty, and one of the carpenters was 'a very respectable looking elderly man'.[73]

TRAFALGAR SQUARE, 6–8 MARCH 1848

Charles Cochrane had called one of the first rallies in (the still unfinished) Trafalgar Square against 'the present odious income tax'. The Police Commissioners intervened, invoking the prohibition of assemblies within one mile of Parliament when in session, and Cochrane reluctantly agreed to withdraw.[74] On Monday, 6 March, it was G. W. M. Reynolds who took the chair at 1.00 p.m. and an orderly

8. The beginning of the Trafalgar Square riots, 6 March 1848

political meeting was held, addresses being delivered 'congratulatory of the French people – against the Income Tax – denunciatory of the present system of taxation – in favour of the People's Charter'. Two hours later the crowd of more than 10,000 was dissolving quietly when, according to the *Northern Star*, 'some sleek well-fed man asserted that the people assembled were lazy, and would not work – that they could get work if they wanted it, which caused an indignant feeling, and he was reprimanded for his libellous language on the suffering sons of toil'.

At this a fight broke out, causing the police to make a clumsy, ill-judged incursion, presumably stimulated by the illegality of the gathering. Truncheons were wielded freely and provocative acts were in large measure responsible for the ensuing full-scale riot. Matthew Arnold, who was among the crowd during the riots as a quite sympathetic, but non-participant, observer – he was secretary to Lansdowne, Lord President of the Council – criticized the police who 'are always, I think, needlessly rough in *manner*'.[75] Considerable reinforcements were brought up and by 4.00 the police were in command of the

Square, but M. H. Molyneux, a working man, objected to the Commissioners that

the conduct of your officers Was quite Sufficient to create instead of quelling a disturbance . . . for example at 10 minutes Past 4 o clock, Policeman 105 F Threatened to Knock some Respectable men ass over Head, for no offence, at 4 o clock Policeman 131 F Said (by way of Bravado) there is plenty of us left to Kill 4 or 500 more. at 23 minutes past 4. 147 D was amusing himself By Pushing a little Boy off the curb amongst the cabs, as was 158 D at ½ Past 4 Pushing a Boy off the Steps of St Martin's Church at 25 minutes to 5 at least 30 of your officers made a Rush towards the Strand & took a man Prisoner Surely Gentlemen there was enough officers to take 1 Prisoner without Splitting his head open.[76]

Around 6.00 p.m. the police withdrew from Trafalgar Square. The crowd surged back, ripped apart the hoarding surrounding Nelson's Column, arming themselves with the pieces of wood – broken granite from the newly macadamized roads formed a useful source of ready missiles[77] – and fighting in and about the Square continued until late at night.

In the course of the evening a detachment of several hundred broke away from the *mêlée* and rushed along Pall Mall to St James's Park, headed by John White, an eighteen-year-old wearing epaulettes, smashing windows (including those of the Reform Club) and shattering and extinguishing the gas-lamps on the way. The cry of 'To the Palace' was raised. Outside Buckingham Palace 'two or three of the fine large lamps were demolished; but here the guard had been promptly turned out' and the crowd, many 'carrying large bludgeons, clothes-props, and other heavy weapons', moved into James Street and York Street. Here bread shops were broken into and the bakers obliged to distribute their loaves. The rioters continued their progress through Westminster via Strutton Ground, the Broad Sanctuary – where, opposite the Sessions House, Charles Tothill, a clerk aged twenty, second only to White as leader, called 'Halt! To arms! Let's have arms' – and Parliament Street to rejoin their fellows at Trafalgar Square. By midnight the Square and its immediate neighbourhood were fairly quiet, although a thousand or so moved into the Haymarket and at 12.15 a.m. the police were still confronting 'a mob of disorderly persons', by whom they were 'sorely maltreated', in Grosvenor Place. Not until 1.00 could Grey write to Russell that Mayne had reported that all at last was tranquil. The slogans of the evening had been various: 'Free trade!'; 'Down with the crushers'; 'Come on my boys, death or glory'; and 'Occasionally a cheer for a republic was got up'.

By 9.00 a.m. (on Tuesday, 7 March) the disturbance had been renewed, the boards at the base of Nelson's Column further dismantled and a barricade erected in Charing Cross alongside the statue of Charles I. Large numbers of police were moved in and for the remainder of the day the conflict was renewed around Trafalgar Square. At dusk a large crowd proceeded along Whitehall and Parliament Street, but the rampage of the previous evening was not repeated.

The continuing gravity of the riots is indicated by the Commissioners' instructions on the 7th for the security of supplies of firearms in their District, while the following day the Home Secretary requested the withdrawal of twenty-one men from guard duty at the Enfield Small Arms Factory and Waltham Abbey Powder Mills: 'As he wishes for all the disposable force he can have in London'.[78] Whereas only 1,189 police had been on duty or in reserve on the 6th, 2,842 were mobilized on the 7th and 2,460 on the 8th.

On Wednesday, 8 March, though there was still great excitement, it now began to subside, the police regaining control. Early in the afternoon, a band of some 700 set off for the City, entering by Temple Bar and Chancery Lane, smashing the lamps and windows as they went, led by a tailor, William Spencer, who carried for the purpose 'a tall board with which he broke windows on each side', and returning by way of Fetter Lane and Fleet Street. In the evening, after the termination of a Chartist meeting on Stepney Green, there were several incidents in Whitechapel Road; and a crowd proceeded through the City, breaking glass on Ludgate Hill. 'The Cochrane Mob' – as it was remembered in June[79] – also 'smashed some of the handsome plate glass windows in Swan and Edgar's shop' and other leading Regent Street establishments. By the Friday, however, *The Times* could report: 'Yesterday scarcely any traces were to be met with of the excitement and tumult which, to a greater or less extent, prevailed at Charing-cross and in other parts of the metropolis on the three preceding days.'[80]

The names and ages of 127 of the rioters arrested over the three days are known and the striking feature, as indicated in Table 7 (and greatly stressed at the time),[81] is the youth of those detained – sixty-one were less than twenty years old.

CAMBERWELL, 13 MARCH 1848

A week after the Trafalgar Square meeting Reynolds convened another on Kennington Common and this time was joined on the platform by a number of the Chartist leaders. The authorities had taken extensive precautions and troops were under orders to be called out, if necessary, with General Brotherton in command, and

Table 7. *Numbers of arrested rioters by age, 6–8 March 1848*

Age	Number	Age	Number	Age	Number
12	2	20	7	28	2
13	0	21	13	29	2
14	0	22	9	30–39	6
15	5	23	5	40–49	4
16	12	24	5	50–59	1
17	14	25	5		
18	15	26	5		
19	13	27	2		
				TOTAL	127

Source: MEPO 2/64, Police Returns

the mobilization of police totalled an extraordinary 3,881:[82] 2,111, including eighty mounted men and one hundred in plain clothes, in the vicinity of the Common; 1,141 on the Surrey side of the bridges; and the remainder in reserve.[83]

In the event, no obstruction was offered to 400 or 500 men who about noon – for which time the commencement of the proceedings was announced – departed, so the Camberwell Division of Police later reported, on a signal being given 'by raising a Pole'. The band took

in their Route the most retired and unfrequented byeways supposed for the purpose of avoiding the observations of the Police and Special Constables until they reached Bowyer Lane where they commenced an attack upon the small Shop Keepers by breaking their Windows and in some cases forcing down the Shutters and carrying away a quantity of their Goods.

The shops rifled in Camberwell consisted of a pawnbroker's, three boot and shoemaker's, a tailor's, a clothes shop, a confectioner's, baker's, broker's and three general dealer's. The looters were armed with 'staves of barrels, and sticks of all descriptions', including palings. One of the shoemakers told them: ' "I am a poor man; if you want something, don't come to me" – I said I was no maker of laws, I had nothing to lose, and begged them not to distress me.' He persuaded fifty or sixty to pass on, but when the main body came up they beat in his shop-front and removed 162 pairs of boots and shoes, worth £35 16s. The principal target was the premises of a pawnbroker and silversmith. His shutters and doors were attacked with 'Hatchets Hammers Shovels and other offensive and dangerous weapons' to cries of 'Hurrah for Liberty' and 'Come on, my brave boys, we'll have our liberty';[84] and 'watches were thrown into the street over the heads of the people'. He estimated his loss at upwards of £900, including as it did 200 watches and 170 rings.

The entire episode occurred within the space of an hour and only nine arrests were made (by a party of mounted police, assisted by special constables) at the time, but since a number of the rioters had been recognized by the locals twenty-five were brought to trial in April. Several witnesses identified among the leaders Charles Lee, a gipsy (not apprehended until a year later), and David Anthony Duffy, a 'man of colour' and unemployed seaman, known to the police as a beggar in the Mint, where he went about 'without shirt, shoe, or stocking'. (Benjamin Prophett, known as 'Black Ben', was another 'man of colour' and seaman.)[85] Eighteen men, of whom four had previous convictions, were sentenced to from seven to fourteen years' transportation and three to one year's imprisonment. The ages of all twenty-six (including Lee) are known: only ten were aged twenty or over (Prophett at twenty-nine was the eldest) and the youngest were three thirteen-year-olds. The Camberwell police superintendent dismissed the offenders as: 'All Labourers and Costermongers'; yet of the twenty-five tried in 1848 a substantial number had trades, even though most of them were still in their teens. The occupations were: four labourers, three seamen, one fishmonger, costermonger, hawk boy, errand boy, brickmaker, ginger beer maker, bonnet box maker, baker, carpenter, bricklayer, sealing wax maker, glass blower, printer, tailor, currier, shoemaker, twine spinner (rope-maker), and brushmaker (and seller of brooms and brushes).[86] Although the Camberwell riot was of short duration it was intense and also of historical importance, for it contributed to the hysterical prelude to 10 April 1848 in London[87] and it was upon 8 and 10 April that the minatory sentences were imposed upon the rioters. It has, however, been overlooked by virtually all historians – and others. The *Northern Star* did not carry a report of either the riot or the resultant trials. Mayhew mentions the pillaging of a pawnbroker's shop but assumes that it took place on 10 April (while his collaborator John Binny transcribed the autobiographical narrative of Charles Lee after his return from transportation for life).[88]

CLERKENWELL, 29 MAY–1 JUNE 1848

On Monday, 29 May, two days after London learned of Mitchel's sentence, 3,000 or 4,000 gathered on Clerkenwell Green to listen to speeches from the Chartist left. The crowd was variously, although unflatteringly, depicted:

There were some working men; the others I hardly know how to describe, the lower orders I suppose; they were very dirty and very ragged composed of working men, costermongers, and some very low sort of characters – there were a great many Irishmen

the majority was composed for Boys of from eighteen to twenty and from the appearance of their faces I should say they were pickpockets – There were some labouring men.

After 'there were three curses given either for the b—y Aristocracy or the b—y Whigs', the assembly at Clerkenwell Green combined at Finsbury Square with another originating from Stepney Green and the resultant procession marched into the West End, accumulating vast numbers in its progress.[89] After passing through Trafalgar Square the demonstration returned via the Strand and Fleet Street to Finsbury Square. Outside the office of the *Weekly Dispatch* it had 'hooted and groaned a very great deal', and 'several cried out Let's break in or smash in' followed by the call: 'Let's go to the Times Office', but the bulk separated after considerable orderliness had been exhibited *en route* despite 'a great noise and disturbance throughout the whole of the way'.[90]

Back in the City several thousand repaired to Redcross Street and were there addressed from the balcony of Cartwright's Coffee House. Williams declared

he was the getter up of the meeting to shew Finality Jack whether they wanted Reform or no – that he would not allow them to have a meeting on the 10th April last they [had] now had one without his leave and would continue to have meetings on Clerkenwell Green and Stepney Green every night until they heard such news from Ireland as our damnable press would not give us. I mean when our Irish brethren will require us to assist them.

Some in the street shouted to Vernon: 'come down among us and lead us and we will do it to night'. Charles M'Carthy replied: 'no not to night but tomorrow night and bring your Guns and pikes with you'. The City police, with the aid of the Finsbury Division, then moved after 11.00 to disperse the crowd, 'the great majority' consisting 'of Irish, and boys and women'. Although most did not resist in Redcross Street but instead ran through to Golden Lane, the police met there with vicious retaliation.[91] An enormous variety of missiles were hurled: stones, bricks, pieces of coal and coke, glass-bottles, two or three earthenware jugs and an iron pot were all mentioned by constables in their evidence at the Old Bailey. Hot water, too, was poured on to them from the windows above.[92] At 11.30 Rowan had received a report that 'some few men have been seen carrying pikes with handles about 6 feet long'. It took sixty to ninety minutes for the streets to clear and a party of police was stationed in the locality until 6.00 a.m.[93]

On the evening of the 30th a police proscription of all meetings and processions was defied by some 4,000 who collected on Clerkenwell Green and were addressed by Williams, Sharp and Daly, who all, despite fighting talk, recommended their audience to disperse without trouble at the culmination of the proceedings. The speakers departed around 9.00 p.m. and as the crowd diminished a large detachment of police, accompanied by some mounted men, swept across the Green. John Bedford Leno, a novice to such encounters, stood his ground 'discussing the Irish question', with the result that 'a disguised policeman . . . commenced to belabour me with a truncheon . . . till the blood fairly poured down my face'. The alternative attraction of a major fire in Whitechapel supplemented the work of the police by drawing many, including Leno; while another party appear to have made a foray into the City. It was not until 12.30 a.m. that Rowan announced to Grey that the metropolis was 'all quiet'.[94]

On Wednesday, 31 May, the authorities publicized a further version of their proclamation[95] and took measures appropriate for the suppression of a projected *émeute*. Special constables were mustered to act in the Divisions from which the police were withdrawn. Squadrons of Life Guards were stationed in three positions – the Old King Harry close to the Jews' Hospital, Mile End Road (with Stepney Green nearby); Dyer's Livery Stables, Finsbury Place, Finsbury Square; and the stables, 81 Leather Lane. The Chief Magistrate of the Metropolitan Police District was instructed by the Home Secretary to have a magistrate in communication with each commanding officer (that is, provision was made for the reading of the Riot Act). At 7.30 two troops of the Horse Guards rode slowly through the crowd and were quartered in St John Street. These precautions were unnecessary for again the sole intervention of the police was effective, although, as customary, a long drawn out process. The centre of confrontation was once more Clerkenwell Green; and while none of the Chartist or Irish orators spoke, by 9.00 it was densely crowded, as were the surrounding streets. Shortly afterwards, from the east, 'an immense body of constables on foot suddenly emerged from their places, and began to clear the ground'. Superintendent Johnston of N Division described the opening of the operation:

the G Division was the first that marched upon Clerkenwell Green, I immediately followed and formed 4 lines across, marching with two and leaving the other two in my rear; I marched about 6 paces in front of my lines and at this time I saw no blow struck whatever by any of my men . . . None of the men of this Division went to the Church, that part of the Green being protected by the G Division.

The crowd's initial response, as on the previous two nights, was to scamper in full flight from the police advance. This was followed by resistance, when there was ready resort to the truncheon, and the relative ease with which the police were able to clear the Green itself was succeeded by the almost impossible task of controlling the immediate neighbourhood to the west. By 10.00 Saffron Hill and some adjoining streets had been pacified and within an hour attempted demonstrations in Finsbury Square, Smithfield and elsewhere prevented. At Stepney Green the superintendent of K Division was stabbed in the leg whilst dispersing an assemblage.[96] The Chartists' last resistance came about midnight when they violently – yet unsuccessfully – counter-attacked in the approaches to Clerkenwell Green and Finsbury Square.[97]

The series of disturbances in Clerkenwell concluded on Thursday, 1 June, 'after a somewhat severe conflict' at the Green. *The Times* reported:

a man nobody appeared to know, dressed in a brown holland blouse ... began his harangue by upbraiding the people for their cowardice in not resisting the police the previous night. (Cries of 'We did.') 'Yes, but how did you do it? ... you suffered them to knock down your friends in the same manner the horses are slaughtered in Sharp's-alley. You are not fit to be called Chartists or Repealers.' ... (Cries of 'What do you want us to do?') 'Why, go to work at once, and pull up the pavement. You could do that before the police got there [sic] if you liked; you have done nothing yet. Where are your broken bottles and old mantel-pieces that Mitchell [sic] had recommended?'

After 8.00 an excited crowd was cleared from the Green within a mere thirty minutes by the police, though 'To drive the mob back from the bye streets was a work of considerable difficulty.'[98]

One of the policemen in his old age recalled of May 1848:

the police were nearly run off their legs in trying to keep order ... where, in these days, many arrests would be made, we, in the 'forties, used to brush the mobs off the streets, and out of the way. The chief thing was to get rid of them ... The weapons that were mostly used in the beginning were bludgeons and stones and bricks. There was plenty of ammunition going, because the streets were not what they are now, and there were heaps of rubbish at hand. As for the Chartists' bludgeons, they got them easily enough from trees and fences ... in Clerkenwell the police were always coming into conflict with the mob. At first it was a general sort of skirmishing. Men would assemble to go for us, and we went for them ... A famous battle ground was Clerkenwell Green, and another place I remember well was Cowcross Street. There was plenty of open space on the Green for fighting, and many houses in which the Chartists could hide and throw things at us ... Day after day we came into collision with them.[99]

BETHNAL GREEN, 4 JUNE 1848

While Clerkenwell lapsed into calm, the agitation in protest against Mitchel's transportation continued and on Sunday, 4 June, Bethnal

Green was seized by disorder, which, however, marked the finale of the major riots of the Chartist decade. A 'monster meeting' called for 10.00 a.m. in Nova Scotia Gardens attracted only several hundred persons, yet the police decision to disrupt proceedings roused the adjoining neighbourhood of Bird Cage Walk, Virginia Row and Gibraltar Walk (between Hackney Road and the eastern half of the modern Bethnal Green Road).[100] A party of forty constables, six sergeants and one inspector, supported by eight or ten on horseback with drawn swords, and an unknown number of specials, were mobbed by thousands, who taunted and stoned them – and, in two instances, produced a knife and a pike as weapons – under a rain of objects from the upper storeys, until 1.00. Alfred Andrews, 'An artisan and a Special Constable' from Hackney (who in court gave his occupation as compositor and reporter), wrote to the Commissioners:

At eleven o'clock Nova Scotia Gardens contained about 900 or 1000 persons of the lowest and most abandoned class, who had met to listen to a speech from a well-known inciter of the people. The first attempts to disperse this dangerous mob proved only partially successful; the mounted patrol arrived; a cowardly attack was instantly made upon them and the constables by a shower of stones; and after a severe conflict some of the aggressors were captured. On attempting to repulse a mob in a street in Gibraltar-walk, the scene became of a most alarming nature. Every tenement furnished a number of persons who threw missiles at the officers, and yelled and hooted at them in terms of the most appalling execration. The Queen, her progeny, the present Government, with that of the late Premier's, the constitution of the country, the representatives of Parliament, and the Lords Spiritual and Temporal, were denounced as accursed, and loud complaints were made of the necessity for a complete social revolution by an equal distribution of the wealth of the country. A feeling of insatiable revenge was repeatedly uttered against the Special constables, as standing in the way of the growing desire for a revolution in England . . . I heard large numbers of the misguided mob express a determination to conquer the police force at a forthcoming suitable opportunity.[101]

Throughout the afternoon, while political assemblies were held on Bishop Bonner's Fields, more than forty police were concealed in the Church of St James the Less, 'so as not to excite, but to be present in Case of Need'. At the termination of the second meeting, after 6.30 p.m., the crowd of 6,000 or 7,000 began to break up. A crowd of as many hundreds clustered around the church, and began to throw stones at the windows; but it was when the inspector in charge of the force returned that tempers erupted: 'the Mob raised a Shout of Execration against him saying there goes the b— Inspector give it him upon which a Volley of Stones were thrown at Him'. Inspector Waller, K Division, ordered his men out and, his request for a peaceable dispersal being met by a further discharge of stones, to clear the immediate area. The crowd stood their ground and then the resort to truncheons shifted them within a few minutes from the vicinity of the church. Meanwhile detachments from other divisions and from the horse patrol were engaged in other parts of the spacious Fields, where religious and other Sabbath activities, including promenading, had been taking place, and it was these – and not the populace – who now ran amok. They moved into the surrounding streets of Bethnal Green pursuing fugitives from the Fields, bursting into houses and assaulting churchgoers in their indiscriminate attacks. There was widespread opinion that the police were drunk. An extensively signed protest to the Home Secretary was to claim that 'an indiscriminate, wanton, unhuman, and brutal attack was made upon Men, Women and Children by the Police not only in the Field where the Meeting was held but in all the various Localities for near a Mile around, breaking into Houses destroying the property and draging [sic] your Memorialists into the Streets'. Among the individual statements collected were the following:

Left my home about six o'clock, was sitting in a garden when the wall was scaled by Police, others breaking through a doorway. An avenue was formed by about 20 policemen through which I was compelled to pass and in doing so received at least 20 blows from their staves. I have no hesitation in saying that ¾ths of the number were in a beastly state of intoxication.

(William Service, aged fifty-seven)

I likewise saw many persons beaten as they were entering their own houses in some cases being followed in-doors by the policemen. Several were also cruelly used in my presence and one of the mounted Policemen called out distinctly in my hearing 'Kill the Buggers!' (John Fearne)

I saw a large body of policemen demand admittance to the Greyhound public house I saw them beat the door and break the window with their truncheons, while some forced their way into the skittle ground to drive out the people others stood at the door & knocked them down as fast as they made their appearance till there had accumulated a heap of bodies at the door.

(Joseph Leserf)

A former sergeant of artillery and veteran of the French wars surrendered his special constable's staff in protest, as he had 'in the moments of the severest Hostile Strife never witnessed more Ferosity [sic] than he saw exerted upon the defenceless and Unresisting on this occasion'. The 'police riot' is a well-attested phenomenon and there can be little doubt, though there were official denials of anything untoward, that one took place in Bethnal Green on the evening of 4 June. Such was local fury at the behaviour of the police that the jury at the inquest on a twenty-six-year-old Chartist weaver, who had been injured during the rioting *in the morning,* refused to accept the coroner's instructions that he had died a natural death on 17 June from fever, and returned a verdict of death caused by blows received on the 4th.[102]

Riot: The maintenance of order

London's experience in the Chartist decade of rioting proper was therefore limited to three short periods: 19–22 August 1842, 6–13 March 1848 and 29 May–4 June 1848. That the outbreaks were contained in both duration and intensity was in large measure the achievement of the Metropolitan Police. Inexperienced in the control of London mobs, the new police indeed blundered – in its alarm it could intervene clumsily or even unnecessarily – and on occasion the rank and file engaged in punitive retaliation against stray individuals or the local populace. Yet overall the pioneering strategy of unprovocative action and minimal violence contributed to a record of extraordinary success.[103] The 'great end' to which 'every effort' of the Metropolitan Police was to be directed was specified in 1829 as *'the Prevention of Crime'*.[104] One of the most striking aspects of the next two or three decades was the virtual elimination of riot. In 1856 a commentator could contend: 'There seems to be no fear a London mob will ever prove a serious thing in the face of our present corps of policemen. A repetition of the Lord George Gordon riots would be an impossibility.'[105]

Certain prophylactic measures were possible in riotous situations. An intended meeting place could be occupied in advance (although the assembly at Clerkenwell Green on 19 August 1842 proved immune to this treatment).[106] The main body of police (and the military) would be stationed nearby but concealed from the crowd and not antagonizing it by their observed presence. Knowledge of the course of proceedings could be communicated by means of plain clothes men planted in a gathering.[107] In 1842 particularly there was the resort to the arrest of speakers (i.e., leaders) thereby prematurely terminating a meeting.[108] In a fully policed city, as was London in the 1840s, possible recognition by a constable might deter a potential rioter – that is, a man might already be known or, otherwise, spotted in the streets after participation in a riot.[109]

Nor was the costly mistake of 1833 repeated when, at Coldbath Fields, not only was a peaceable, albeit prohibited, assembly assailed and broken up, but the 3,000 or 4,000 present had also been surrounded by the police, not allowing adequate exits for dispersal. The results – the stabbing to death of Constable Culley and the verdict by the coroner's jury of justifiable homicide – are well-known.[110]

To disperse a crowd the prescribed procedure was first to warn the participants to depart and if this was ignored for a police line to compel them to move in the desired direction, principally through the pressure of its own advance but resorting to blows from the truncheon on those who chose to resist. Thus on 4 June 1848 (in the confrontation *immediately outside* St James's Church), Inspector Waller preceded his men and requested: 'Now disperse quietly to your homes, will you?' One of his constables testified: 'I did not hit one man – I was in the front rank – some of the people ran away, some would not – those who would not run were pushed on'. Waller explained in court: 'orders to disperse means to strike, if the people do not disperse; but I gave an order not to aim at the head unless it was imperative'.[111] In Redcross Street on 29 May 1848 a City constable recounted: 'At first we endeavoured to disperse the Mob quietly without drawing our Truncheons but this proved ineffectual – We then drew out Truncheons and proceeded to disperse the mob.'[112] Whilst the mounted men were, as horsemen, equipped with swords, the issue of cutlasses to the foot police occurred only in June–August 1848, after the riots had ceased, and when insurrection in London was anticipated as imminent.[113]

Once, however, a crowd had made a stand, truncheons would be wielded viciously and police discipline could triumph over popular spontaneity despite gross inequality of numbers. 'It was our trained strength against their wild, unorganized rushes, and our heavy truncheons against their sticks and stones and fists.'[114] (Innocuous as the weapons of Chartist rioters – and Chartist conspirators – may appear they were identical to those of contemporary London criminals: brickbats and bludgeons, knives at worst and rarely firearms.)[115] Such innocents as were caught up in street-fighting received no courteous caution but instead were liable to suffer broken heads or limbs – an occupational hazard for the plain clothes men during riots.[116] For the police to go further than battling with pugnacious adversaries and to run amok, as they did on 4 June 1848, was, even in the formative years of the Metropolitan Police, exceptional. Still James Cornish remembered that in one instance: 'Our blood was up, and those of us who were not too damaged to spring and skip about dashed into the houses and fought our way into the bedrooms and to the roofs . . . We cleared the streets and roofs and houses at last, leaving many an aching bone and sore head.'[117]

Surveillance and disruption by the police were essential in the diminution of the Chartist riots to sporadic and fairly harmless outbursts.

The ineffectiveness of crowd action is, however, also to be attributed to the nature of Chartism itself. Highly specific in its demand for the Six Points, its ends were otherwise ill-defined and diffuse; and neither the programme for parliamentary reform nor the desired social changes readily provided physical objectives for assault. There were not machines to be smashed, factories to be occupied, land to be seized, or legal documents to be destroyed[118] – at least, with any measure of significance in the metropolitan situation. None of the London prisons in the mid-nineteenth century enjoyed the odium of a Bastille. The Tower of London or Bank of England failed to attract the Chartist crowd as symbols of aristocratic oppression or bourgeois exploitation. Westminster, Whitehall and Buckingham Palace were relatively protected in their geographical location to the centres of proletarian habitation and gathering; and it was rare for the crowd to mass in their proximity.[119] The principal exception, the Trafalgar Square riots, are notable for their *élan* and uncontrollability. In March 1848 contributory to these characteristics was perhaps a second element: the attacks on the smart retailers of the West End and the looting of foodshops.[120] At Camberwell on the 13th it was undoubtedly the precise objective of ransacking the local shops that determined the furious success of the riot. As for human targets, the military were mobbed in 1842 and hooted in 1848 and the rich suffered no worse treatment – their houses remained unscathed (safeguarded, mostly, by segregation in separate quarters), although their persons were at times taunted. Only when the bourgeois appeared as special constable was he in danger of assault. But overwhelmingly it was the Metropolitan Police as the everyday instruments of authority who aroused popular venom. In the 1840s the policeman had displaced all other objects as the symbol – indeed agent – of oppression and the Londoner's hatred for him helps to explain the single-minded concentration on battling with the force which typified the Chartist riot.

Chartism's tragic predicament as a political movement was its historical placement between pre-industrial and industrial modes of action. In the streets this resulted in an uneasy (and unquestionably unsuccessful) hybrid of the spontaneous violence of the eighteenth-century riot and the pacific, disciplined strength of a labour movement.[121] Whereas the Chartist leadership welcomed rioting as expression of working-class misery (and hence as a means of political pressure) it was embarrassed by the indication of irrationality and irresponsibility. In the confrontation with government and police in London its prime concern was maintaining the rights of public assembly. From this insistence riots were generated, but the Chartist objectives, ceasing to be abstract, were clear: the ability to hold meetings, to pass resolutions and to move in procession. Thus in the contests of 1842 and 1848 Chartists sought primarily for their orators to speak rather than to lead in revolutionary action. For the latter the precondition was seen as conspiratorial instigation, not the random acts of a Clerkenwell *mêlée*.

Chartism provided the occasion for disorder, although very few of those arrested were members of Chartist localities. Some women usually appear to have been in the crowd.[122] Middle-class participation was negligible – at Bonner's Fields a man 'in respectable attire', carrying an umbrella, was especially marked by the police.[123] Outdoor assemblies were a spectacle and many attended them as a source of entertainment. During the Trafalgar Square riots *The Times* castigated 'that silly crowd which flocks to scenes of mischief simply to see what is going on. It is they who make the crowd. They are the body of the mob, and thus give encouragement and security to a few dozen ruffians and rogues.'[124] It is noteworthy that almost all the riotous outbreaks occurred at sites where political meetings had been regularly held for several (up to as many as nine or ten) weeks. The local population became familiarized and excited by the repeated event; and were eventually drawn in to the developing disturbance:

my whife said to me, come and let us see the police in Clerkenwell-green. We went accordin, an we saw a great body of police . . . but there were not many people, no not more than there have been on any future occasion. I meets a friend in the green, who was there like myself hout of idle curiosity . . . Hi was took up by the police as speedily as nothing momentary.[125]

Most reports stress the important role played by 'boys' in the disorder of 1842 and 1848. They are confirmed by analysis of the ages of 127 arrested during 6–8 March 1848 (48 per cent aged nineteen or under) and the twenty-six accused of participating on 13 March 1848 (62 per cent aged nineteen or under).[126] Comparable information only exists for the twenty-three arrested in Bethnal Green on 4 June 1848; and though, in contrast, of these only 26 per cent were in their teens[127] there is no reason to doubt the significance of the contribution by young and very young men – and even boys – to the genesis of disorder.[128]

Some of the boys would have been the pickpockets observed at all, not just Chartist, open-air gatherings. Yet criminals, street-folk and labourers were drawn to Chartism as such, in particular for its riotous possibilities. While the locality in no way impinged on their world, the Chartist crowd was much to their liking and largely influenced by their presence. Those charged with strictly political offences in 1848, the conspirator Thomas Fay the youngest at twenty and the eldest forty-five with only the sixty-year-old Cuffay falling outside this age

Table 8. *Educational attainment of persons charged with indictable offences: Chartist and Irish Confederate speakers and insurrectionaries compared with rioters, 1848*

'Degree of instruction'	POLITICAL OFFENCES (Sedition; unlawful assembly; conspiracy to levy war against the Queen; etc.)		RIOTOUS OFFENCES (Riotous assembly; house-breaking and larceny; assaulting police; etc.)	
	Number charged	%	Number charged	%
Sup(erior)	1*	2.3	0	—
Well	18	41.9	6	11.1
Imp(erfect)	24	55.8	33	61.1
N(one)	0	—	15	27.8
TOTAL	43	100.0	54**	100.0

*Ernest Jones
**Comprised of: the seven leading Trafalgar Square rioters; the twenty-five tried in 1848 for the Camberwell riot; twenty-two of the twenty-three arrested in Bethnal Green on 4 June.
Sources: HO 26/54; HO 27/86

range, also contrasted with the rioters in terms of literacy, as is shown in Table 8. There was widespread concurrence as to the preponderance of 'idle rascals and swarms of vagabond boys',*'canaille,* thieves, pickpockets, and ragamuffins', and 'dirty boys' in the Trafalgar Square riots, dubbed 'The Ragged Riot' by a broadside.[129] 'Stand together, and we will soon have a rumpus', one man urged his fellows on Clerkenwell Green[130] where in 1848 *The Times* remarked on 'The low population of the neighbourhood, attracted to the spot partly by curiosity and partly to have the excitement of a row with the police'.[131] Vagrants streamed into London for several days prior to the demonstration of 10 April 1848.[132] The participation of the dangerous classes heightened Chartist ambivalence towards action in the streets.[133] The assailants of a supposed special were castigated: 'Don't act as brutes, if you are Chartists, don't act as brutes.'[134] At the National Assembly Samuel Kydd announced that he 'was opposed to demonstrations in London . . . in London there was a little world of thieves who would always take advantage of any demonstration to steal, break windows, rob houses, and injure their neighbours, and all that would not help the Chartists'.[135]

Given the participation of such stalwart combatants the pusillanimity of the Chartist crowd is all the more surprising. On Clerkenwell Green, where experience of street-fighting was greatest, the onrush of police would cause the majority to scamper like so many rabbits. 'The people were terrified and fled', Leno recalled simply of 30 May 1848.[136] That evening the force had been sighted while Daly was speaking – when 'a large proportion of the meeting began to move off' – and he 'denounced them as cowards, and inquired how they meant to fight for their liberties if they were afraid of such a handful of men?'[137] The cry of 'Police', even if false alarm, would produce 'a general rush'.[138] But police control of London had cut so deep that a single constable could thwart the populace of Seven Dials and arrest, with relative impunity, an orator in Monmouth Street.[139]

The great meetings of 1848

The Trafalgar Square riots, following hard on the February Revolution and accompanied during the same three days by serious disturbances in Glasgow, initiated the panic which turned the heads of the middle classes until the events of 10 April were concluded and which by that day they had fully communicated to their patrician rulers.[140] Already a Finsbury resident wrote to the Home Secretary, on 11 March: 'I can assure You the lower orders are going around with Staves and Stones, and it rests with You to deliver London from anarchy, Bloodshed and Pillage.'[141] On the 13th a breakaway from the Chartist demonstration on Kennington Common looted shops in Camberwell; while at the meeting M'Grath announced that at least 250,000 men would deliver to Parliament the new Petition from the Common. That week the Executive named 10 April to the country as the day of presentation.[142]

On 9 March, 'large bodies' of the parishioners of St Martin in the Fields and St James Westminster having volunteered as special constables, Sir George Grey requested the magistrates at Bow Street, Great Marlborough Street and Westminster Police Courts 'to swear in such respectable persons as present themselves'.[143] During the following two days, in response to the registered coal-whippers of Wapping and some inhabitants of Poplar, instructions to enrol special constables on the riverside were issued. In preparation for the Kennington meeting of 13 March the Lambeth and Southwark magistrates were requested on the 11th, also, to recruit respectable volunteers as constables. W. F. Beadon of Wandsworth Police Court acted, without any direction from the Home Office, on the 13th and swore in, among others, 300 at Nine Elms Station; while two Surrey JPs similarly appointed 168 constables for St Mary Newington.[144] Other than these figures and a total of 1,557 whippers, there is no official indication of the numbers in which specials were enrolled during the second week of March 1848, but *The Times* claimed on the 13th 'about 20,000 special constables . . . for the protection of the peace in Middlesex alone', while the *Northern Star* referred sarcastically to their

Table 9. *Total of special constables enrolled for*
10 April 1848

(i)	For service in the parishes		28,168
(ii)	Reserve for general service		3,157
(iii)	Sworn in at the Police Courts		9,632
(iv)	City of London		22,653
(v)	Additions	approx.	18,000
	TOTAL		81,610

having been sworn in 'in all directions' for that day's
demonstration.[145] By 15 March, with a Chartist meeting announced
for Blackheath that day, constables had been appointed for six
months' service in the two Deptford parishes, Greenwich, Charlton,
Woolwich, Plumstead, Lewisham, Lee and Eltham.[146]

It was not until 3 April that Grey issued a general directive respecting special constables;[147] yet it is clear that for the preceding three
weeks jittery magistrates had continued to enrol on their own initiative under bourgeois pressure. By 25 March 225 had been sworn in
at the Marylebone Police Court and 200 at Hackney; and on 7 April
Worship Street Police Court reported that 750 had been appointed
there within the 'last few weeks'.[148]

Several deep-rooted myths surround the drama of 10 April 1848.
The first concerns the number of special constables who acted on the
day, thereby averting proletarian revolution. The number generally
accepted is 170,000 – *for London alone.*[149] This total is derived from
Hovell, the magisterial Halévy and, ultimately, their own source: the
Annual Register.[150] An aggregate of this order has no surer basis than
that of partisan assertion. Both the *Express* and the *Northern Star*
reported that 'upwards of 70,000' specials had been sworn merely for
the City of London, while the *Globe* and the *London Telegraph* gave
20,000 to 30,000 (which, as will be seen, is extraordinarily accurate)
and a total for all London of 130,000. The *Standard* and the *Sun*
agreed with the *Morning Chronicle* that there were 250,000. And on
the morning of 10 April *The Times* had proclaimed a figure of
'upwards of 150,000', its exaggeration being compounded by the
deduction that, with police and military, 'a force of about 200,000
men will be available for the protection of public order and the maintenance of the law'.[151] It is, instead, possible – in Table 9 – to calculate
a total authoritative in its dependence on official figures, although on
17 April Grey said he 'had not been able to ascertain the precise number of special constables'.[152]

An undated 'Return of Special Constables in the Metropolitan

Police District' provides the numbers included in (i) and (ii)[153] and their general reliability is indicated by the many letters received by the Home Secretary after 10 April and which contained definitive totals for certain parishes, factories, etc.[154] The source for (iii) is the 'List of Special Constables sworn in at Police Courts on 7th & 8th April 1848, who are not entered in Return of Constables by Parishes',[155] a document which indicates the late date of the 'Return' (it should be remembered that 9 April was a Sunday) and accounts, this writer suggests, for the enrolment of government employees (as well as some workmen who were to man their masters' establishments) who were not available for service in the parishes. To answer a question the Home Secretary sought, and received, from the Lord Mayor 'A Return of the number of Special Constables sworn in at the Mansion House and in the several Wards of the City of London. April 1848', which aggregate is given as (iv).[156] On 17 April Grey stated in the Commons: 'In the city of London there were about 23,000, and from some other parishes he had obtained returns; but a great number of working men were sworn in upon the premises of their employers, and no accurate list has been kept of those, though the number of them certainly amounted to several thousands.'[157] The additions of (v) consist of not only the certain and probable, but also possible, increases, and this category almost definitely involves some double-counting. Its components are derived from annotations to the 'Return of Special Constables in the Metropolitan Police District' and from the letters already mentioned (some written after Grey's statement containing important information); and they include parishes omitted from that return (such outer metropolitan districts as Notting Hill, Chiswick, Ealing and Hounslow) and the workforces at the docks, Cubitt's and elsewhere. (These additions amount, in fact, to just under 18,000.) The summation of special constables thus obtained is 81,610 and to allow for further omissions it is considered that an approximate figure, both realistic and authoritative, would be 85,000. Any total much in excess of 85,000 is extremely unlikely. One above 100,000 (or even, perhaps, 90,000) is to be completely discounted.

A second fallacy concerns the social composition of this special constabulary. Historians have accepted the retrospective view of contemporaries that considerable numbers of working men enrolled as specials.[158] It is undoubtedly correct that a substantial proportion of the 85,000 were workers. What is to be disputed is that a significant number of these volunteered for duty because they opposed Chartist objectives and feared the possibility of revolution – that, as *The Times* put it, there was a 'great demonstration of the lower classes against

Chartism'.[159] The coal-whippers did, of course, offer their services to the government – as early as 9 March [160] – but evidence of the voluntary appointment of either labourers or artisans as specials is otherwise scanty. The great majority of working-class special constables were required to enrol by their employers – or lose their jobs. The distinction was made, for example, between those at Marylebone Police Court who had freely tendered their services and those who were servants of the London and North Western Railway Company.[161] Many workers agreed to be sworn whilst declining to act as constables beyond their workplaces. Both Christy's, the hatters, and Bevington's, the leather dressers, 'were very desirous that a large portion of their men should serve in the neighbourhood but the men would only take charge of their Masters' premises'.[162] As a tin-plate worker, discharged for his refusal to be sworn in, observed: 'although I am not a Chartist by enrolment, I am one from conviction; and there are very few working men who are not Chartists in that sense of the word.'[163] P. Bingham attended from Great Marlborough Street

at the Geological Museum in Piccadilly for the purpose of swearing in as special Constables the numerous body of workmen employed on that building: I am sorry to have to apprize that the feeling exhibited by them was anything but satisfactory: Some refused to be sworn, and those who consented, insisted on limiting their services to the inside of the Building: I willingly assented to this under the circumstances I have stated, considering they might otherwise be on Kennington Common:

I was then desired to attend at Lord Ellesmeres, where a very large body of workmen is employed: The Foreman informed me that the whole of them, with the exception of three, refused to be sworn, but that they had promised to defend the building in case of attack.

After this, I thought it better to abstain from going farther.[164]

It was indeed the truculence and Chartism of all sections of the proletariat, rather than their 'good spirit', that was most remarked by their social superiors prior to 10 April.[165] The Marquess of Salisbury recounted that he had sent two magistrates (one of them, presumably, Bingham)

to different establishments of workmen for the purpose of swearing them in as special constables.

The reports I have received from these gentlemen are not at all satisfactory as to the feeling of that class of persons They almost to a man refused to be sworn in except for the protection of their masters property Some have refused to be sworn in at all and have avowed themselves to be Chartists. Under these circumstances and also from the reports I have received from one or two other localities it is my duty to inform you that in my opinion no reliance can be placed upon the cooperation of the Artizans who are all Unionists if the police should receive a check but that where they had the opportunity they would rather turn against them.[166]

Table 10. *Police arrangements for 10 April 1848*

Positions at 10.00 a.m.	Number of all ranks
Palace Yard	545
Great George Street	445
Trafalgar Square	690
Patrols from Trafalgar Square to the House of Commons	101
Ball's Livery Stables, Kennington Cross	500
Vauxhall Bridge	200
Westminster Bridge	500
Hungerford Bridge	50
Waterloo Bridge	500
Blackfriars Bridge (including 40 mounted men)	500
Princes' Mews (mounted men)	40
Thames Police (7 boats at the Bridges)	42
TOTAL	4,113

Sources: MEPO 7/12; WO 30/111

Russell informed Prince Albert, who had protested against the reduction in public works: 'The masons, especially the hodmen, are generally infected with repeal or chartism – & employment has not prevented many of them from having refused to be sworn in as special constables, because the oath *contained the Queen's name*.'[167] Many were obviously of Bingham's opinion that it was better for a potential troublemaker to be sworn in so there would be one less at Kennington Common. 'A lover of order and a Shopkeeper' argued thus since with the closure on the 10th of 'the places of business . . . all the men in them with no bad intentions will go out and swell the crowd this was very much the case at the disturbances in Trafalgar Square'[168] while in Lambeth 'Mr Maudsley Engineer has 1000 for his own premises most of whom are thus secured from taking the wrong side as they are on ill terms with Police.' As for the wretched whippers, of the 1,557 enrolled: 'only 800 can be depended upon – they are disposable on any point'.[169] On 10 April itself at least one who had been sworn in as a special 'not through choice, but compulsion' was among the Chartist demonstrators on the Common, and in the Kingsland Road 'Many Special Constables neglected to attend muster'.[170]

The special constables acted either within their own parishes or at their places of work – some 3,000 only were available for general service in the capital. Their function was to support the police, who were withdrawn from their normal duties and concentrated strategically

Table 11. *Military arrangements for 10 April 1848*

Corps	Field officers	Captains	Sub-alterns	Staff	Sergeants	Trumpeters and drummers	Rank and file	Horses	Station from which ordered up	Station occupied at 6.00 a.m.
Cavalry										
1st Life Guards	2	5	11	5	41	9	339	230	Regents Park	2 squadrons: Horse Guards duty; 2 squadrons: Rose Inn, Farringdon Street
2nd Life Guards	2	7	14	5	42	9	335	239	Hyde Park	2 squadrons: Bethlehem Hospital: *with* 4 guns; 2 squadrons: Hyde Park Barracks
Royal Horse Guards	2	7	11	2	32	4	206	210	Windsor	1 squadron: Somerset House; 1 squadron: Berkeley House and Stafford House; 1 squadron: Millbank Prison; 1 squadron: Hyde Park Barracks
12th Lancers	2	6	9	3	17	6	210	211	Hounslow	Hyde Park Barracks
Artillery										
6 Six-pounders 2 Twelve-pound Howitzers	0	3	5	0	2	4*	99	84	Woolwich	4 guns: Bethlehem Hospital: *with* 2nd Life Guards; 4 guns: Royal Mews, Pimlico
3 Six-pounders 1 Twelve-pound Howitzer	1	1	3	2	4	4*	54	52	Woolwich	4 guns: Carlton House Stables

Infantry									Home station	Duty station
Grenadier Guards 1st Batt.	2	7	17	4	31	0	655	–	Wellington Barracks	Wellington Barracks
2nd Batt.	1	5	4	2	0	0	520	–	Chichester	Somerset House
3rd Batt.	1	8	16	4	27	0	507	–	St John's Wood	On duty at the Palaces and in occupation of the Magazine, Hyde Park
Coldstream Guards 1st Batt.	1	7	12	4	19	0	517	–	Tower of London	Bridewell, Bridge Street, Blackfriars; leaving detachments at Mint and Bank of England
2nd Batt.	3	8	13	3	30	17	620	–	Windsor	Royal Mews, Pimlico
Scots Fusilier 1st Batt.	1	8	16	4	28	0	481	–	St George's Barracks	St George's Barracks
2nd Batt.	2	8	15	4	27	0	479	–	Portman Street Barracks	Portman Street Barracks
17th Foot	3	9	14	5	42	15	693	–	Dover	Millbank Prison
63rd Foot	3	8	14	3	33	17	600	1026	Chatham	Tower of London
SUB-TOTAL	26	97	174	50	375	85	6315	1026		
Pensioners London Division	4	7	6	0	72	0	1142	–		Various stations (as in Table 12)
TOTAL	30	104	180	50	447	85	7457	1026		
PLUS										
Marine artillery 2 light guns	2**						35		Gosport (on morning of 10 April)	
Infantry 12th Foot							450		Gosport (on morning of 10 April)	Nine Elms Station

*Artificers **Officers

Sources: WO 30/81; also WO 30/111 and MEPO 2/65.

Table 12. *Distribution of pensioners on 10 April 1848*

Woolwich Division	
400 men	In Greenwich ready to be brought up at a moment's notice by train
Northern Division	
200 men	100 in reserve at Tower of London
	100 at the Bank of England and the Mint
Eastern Division	
250 men	100 at the Bank of England and the Mint
	150 in reserve at the Tower of London
Southern Division	
140 men	70 at Peto's works, near Vauxhall Bridge
	70 in reserve at Chelsea[a]
Western Division	
300 men	100 at the Pantechnicon
	100 at Battersea Bridge
	100 in reserve at Chelsea[a]

Source: MEPO 2/65   [a] See n.171

along the river and in Westminster and Whitehall, as in Table 10. These figures do not include the City of London force and underestimate the actual police commitment of 4,099 constables alone (including eleven pensioners and only thirty-four mounted men) to whom extra pay for duty on the 10th was allowed.[172]

The military mobilization and deployment can be detailed with the unfaltering exactitude of Table 11. This indicates that 1,231 pensioners[173] participated in the military arrangements. The distribution (with rounded figures) originally intended is given in Table 12.

The military and police commitments are, therefore, known precisely; and it can be accepted with confidence that there were approximately 85,000 special constables. No such summation of the final, essential component – the assembly of Chartists on Kennington Common – can be provided, although it is on this aggregate that the legend of 10 April so heavily depends.

The morning newspapers, with the honourable exception of the *Morning Post,* printed figures ranging from 10,000 to 30,000 (although *The Times* did give sceptical mention to 'the most liberal estimate' of 50,000) (see Table 13) and most subsequent accounts have given a total of this order.[174] At the other extreme the Convention and the *Northern Star* maintained there were not less than 250,000, while O'Connor variously claimed the attendance was 'rather under than over 400,000' and between 400,000 and 500,000.[175] Thomas Frost concurred with James Watson, the experienced and moderate Chartist, that there were 150,000 and Gammage

Table 13. *Newspaper reports of the number present on 10 April 1848*

	Issue of 10 April	Issue of 11 April
Evening papers		
Evening Sun	150,000	*
Express	100,000	15,000
Globe	*	*
London Telegraph	80,000 to 100,000	*
Shipping and Mercantile Gazette	100,000	50,000
Standard	9,000 to 10,000	10,000
Morning papers		
Daily News		15,000
Morning Advertiser		*
Morning Chronicle		20,000 to 25,000
Morning Herald		25,000 to 30,000
Morning Post		120,000; 80,000 to 150,000
The Times	20,000 (3rd edn)	10,000 to 20,000 (editorial); 20,000 to 50,000 (report)
Radical weeklies	Published on 15/16 April	
Lloyd's Weekly London Newspaper	100,000 (report); 200,000 to 300,000 (editorial)	
Nonconformist	150,000	
Northern Star	250,000	
Weekly Dispatch	50,000 to 200,000	

*Not reported

also settled for 150,000 to 170,000.[176] It is a crowd of this intermediate magnitude for which there is persuasive evidence, and the cluster of extraordinarily small estimates from conservative sources[177] are to be rejected with the inflated claims of the Chartists, who had committed themselves in advance to an unattainable turn-out.

F. T. Fowler, free-lance reporter for *The Times* and other newspapers, engaged for 10 April by the *Express,* informed O'Connor he was confident there were 'upwards of 200,000' and that 'The Commissioners of Police on Monday evening last, sent round to the papers a document marked *private,* requesting them to state that there were only 15,000 persons present at the meeting.'[178] The assertion is correct, as several newspapers made fairly explicit, though (other than the *Daily News*) the morning papers of 11 April could not commit themselves fully to a figure quite so low as 15,000. The estimates of the evening papers on the 10th therefore become the most significant data. The Third Edition of *The Times* announced that the demonstration had not exceeded 20,000, while the 'country party's' *Standard* insisted on half that number.[179] The other four, in contrast, made estimates ranging from 80,000 to ('at least') 150,000. The *Express* in its issue of the 11th disavowed its judgment of the previous day:

> The numbers ... have been variously estimated at from 200,000 to 50,000 ... We have since learned that a careful estimate was formed by several military persons of great experience in making such computations, and they, on comparing their different calculations, agreed that no more than 15,000 persons were present, as spectators and as forming part of the procession.

At the weekend the radical papers reverted to aggregates of 100,000, 200,000 or 300,000.[180]

Mayne *was* of the opinion that there were only 15,000 demonstrators. He wrote to the Home Secretary from the Common: 'There are I think not more than 14 or 15,000 persons'; but qualified this with the belief of his son-in-law, Mallalieu, from the Greenwich Division, that 'there are nearly 20,000'.[181] There are three further reasons why this judgment of both Mayne and Mallalieu is to be discounted.

First, Mayne sent three notes to Grey from the Common. One is timed 11.45 (and is quoted in full above, pp. 76-7) and another is 12.45. His figure is contained in the third on which, most unfortunately, he did not write the time. There is little doubt that it is the last of the sequence for he informed Grey: 'I shall go to Blackfriars Bridge presently to *act* as arranged there.' At 12.45, however, he had commented: 'more persons leaving the meeting than joining it ... Meeting seems broken up.'[182] His estimation therefore appears to relate to a period well after the climax of the demonstration – the *Sun* (and other papers) reported a dispersal so rapid and complete that by 2.00 p.m. 'there were scarcely a hundred persons on the common'.[183]

Second, there survive police reports from three of the points of assembly which estimate the numbers that collected at each. Mayne himself was on Clerkenwell Green at 9.45 a.m. and said 1,500 were there. A column from Stepney Green moved off after 9.00, 2,000 to 3,000 strong. And the report from Russell Square at 9.50 a.m. gave the size of its procession as 10,000. The demonstrators from north of the river began to arrive on Kennington Common at 11.15, at which time Mallalieu judged that 5,000 were already assembled and it is unlikely that this figure includes the contingent from a fourth assembly point that morning which had been Peckham Fields.[184] Hence four constituents of the demonstration were enumerated by policemen, of whom two were Mayne and Mallalieu, and these total 19,000, a figure exceeding Mayne's final estimate by several thousand. These

9. View of the Kennington Common meeting in the *Illustrated London News*

initial nuclei were vastly swollen *en route* as people joined the processions converging on the Common. The Rev. Henderson recollected: 'On reaching the Mile End and Whitechapel Road, the column was joined by huge crowds pouring up the Dog Row and other thoroughfares from every part of Bethnal Green';[185] a magistrate observed 'an immense body of Chartists' who 'passed thro' Spitalfields calling on the Weavers to turn out';[186] and in the Blackfriars Road a body of Confederates coalesced with the East Londoners.[187]

Third, there is the general consideration of the occupational tendency of the police to underestimate the size of popular gatherings. This is a bias shared by all in authority, just as radicals will exaggerate their support. What is required is a figure for comparison with the accepted attendances at other demonstrations (usually derived from the press). If 100,000 participated in the Copenhagen Fields meeting of 1834, how many collected on Kennington Common in 1848? Thus the numbers reported in the evening papers and the obdurate *Morning Post* are of greatest relevance. (This is the substantive point which must be pressed against the opinions of the 'military persons' of 1848 or later attempts to estimate objectively the possible turn-out. Specif-

10. Daguerreotype of the Kennington Common meeting

ically, though, attention has to be drawn to the error made by David Large.[188] He estimates the expanse of Kennington Common to have been no greater than 13,640 sq. yds – i.e., less than three acres! *The Times* on 11 April 1848, more realistically, put the maximum area at twenty acres.)

An additional essential consideration is that many of the low estimates explicitly excluded from the count – as Mallalieu had done in his 11.15 a.m. report – those standing beyond the rails surrounding the Common and classified this section of the crowd as spectators and non-demonstrators. For this there is some justification since, for example, Holman Hunt and Millais were careful not to mingle with the 'agitators' on the green itself, despite having marched with the procession from Russell Square to Kennington.[189] In addition, torrential rain had fallen overnight and the grass was 'exceedingly soft and damp' so that many had collected before the meeting outside the palings.[190]

Still, given the extreme polarization of sentiment on 10 April, any onlookers must have been overwhelmingly Chartist sympathizers;

11. Daguerreotype of the Kennington Common meeting

and confirmation of this can be inferred with reasonable certainty from the remarkable visual record existing of the meeting. Two daguerreotypes, the earliest known crowd photographs, survive in, improbably, the Royal Photograph Collection (Figures 10 and 11). The two scenes largely overlap and comparison indicates that the banner carriers in the road at the rear are stationary and, it seems, facing the Common. The engraving in the *Illustrated London News* (Figure 9) is derived mainly from the first daguerreotype (Figure 10), but presumably a third, destroyed photograph provided the detail for its left-hand portion.

At what time were the daguerreotypes taken? The car appearing in all three pictures – it can be seen to bear the inscription 'LABOUR THE SOURCE OF ALL WEALTH' – does not tally with the description given by the daily newspapers of the principal waggon drawn by six horses and also said to be 'of great size, containing almost all the delegates', as it 'contained eight seats, with six upon each, making forty-eight persons, delegates and gentlemen of the press'. It was the latter which provided the platform from which O'Connor, Ernest Jones and oth-

Table 14. *Police arrangements for Monday, 12 June 1848*

Division	Positions at 12.00 a.m.	Numbers
H (Whitechapel)		150
K (Stepney)	Bonner's Fields (300 to be	350
M (Southwark)	in the Workhouse at 9.00)	200
N (Islington)		400
E (Holborn)	In reserve at the stations ready	100
F (Covent Garden)	to move to Bonner's Fields or	100
G (Finsbury)	elsewhere as occasion may require	150
In reserve at the following stations:		
A (Whitehall)	Scotland Yard	60
B (Westminster)	King Street Station	165
C (St James's)	Vine Street Station	170
D (Marylebone)	Marylebone Lane Station	146
L (Lambeth)	Tower Street Station	125
P (Camberwell)	Park House Station and a reserve	
	to be kept at Croydon	230
R (Greenwich)	Blackheath Road Station	107
R (Greenwich)	Rotherhithe Station	50
S (Hampstead)	Albany Street Station	190
T (Kensington)	Triumphal Arch and Section	
	House	100
V (Wandsworth)	Rochester Row Station	200
Mounted men	Bonner's Fields (N, K, S Divs.)	28
	In reserve (P, R, T, V Divs.)	55
TOTAL		3076

Source: MEPO 7/14

ers were to address the crowd. The conclusion one is led to draw is that W. E. Kilburn, the photographer, took his lengthy exposures, not surprisingly, significantly before the meeting's zenith: which was the arrival of 'the triumphal car' from the John Street Institution accompanied by a great procession.[191]

12 JUNE 1848

Most of the special constables had been sworn to act for two calendar months only and their warrants therefore had lapsed by June or were due to expire before the 12th.[192] Mayne noted on the 3rd that the Home Secretary was 'of opinion that at present it is not desirable to have the Specl. Constables reappointed & sworn again';[193] but the new confrontation with the Chartists ensured that on 5 June Grey, pressed by the Chairman of the Middlesex Sessions, instructed the metropolitan magistrates to renew the appointment of such constables for a further six months. Some now presented themselves to be sworn in for the first time; but it would seem that, in general, the level of re-enrolment was low (although as many as 442 were appointed for the Grosvenor Place District and 447 for the Brentford Division of Middlesex – the latter including Isleworth, Twickenham and Ealing).[194] On 12 June the special constabulary was again on duty in the city's parishes – and remained so until dismissal at 5.00 p.m. – yet there is no indication of the numbers mobilized on this occasion.[195] Their leaders had been advised by the Commissioners that the police might be withdrawn from normal duty after midday and that: 'The number to be assembled must be fixed by each Leader keeping in mind the importance of not taking from their ordinary occupations more than are likely to be wanted to act against any body of Rioters suddenly appearing.' The instructions countered excessive middle-class enthusiasm and were designed to prevent a repetition of the *embarras de richesse* of 10 April.[196]

Memoranda of 11 June ordered the dispersion of the police shown in Table 14, involving a total of 3,076. The force ultimately mobilized for duty on the 12th, however, was substantially larger: 4,343 constables, sergeants, inspectors and superintendents received extra allowances for their duty that day.[197]

The military arrangements are detailed in Table 15. Only 400 pensioners were called out, all of them being stationed at the centre of the police operations: the Bethnal Green Workhouse (on the periphery of Bonner's Fields).

Table 15. *Military arrangements for Monday, 12 June 1848*

Corps		24-pound Howitzers	Light 6-pounders	Ammunition wagons	Officers	NCOs and rank and file	Horses	Station from which ordered up	Station occupied on Monday, 12 June
Artillery									
Royal Horse Artillery	1 Troop	1	1	1	5	34	35	Woolwich	Carlton Mews
	1 Troop	1	1	1	4	31	33		Carlton Mews
	1 Troop	1	1	1	3	31	35		Royal Mews, Pimlico
Cavalry									
1st Life Guards					25	231	231	Regents Park	3 squadrons: Regent's Park Barracks (?) 1 squadron: Eastern Counties Goods Station, Spitalfields: 9 a.m.
2nd Life Guards					25	306	183	Hyde Park	3 squadrons: Hyde Park Barracks 1 squadron: Leather Lane, Holborn: 11 a.m.
Royal Horse Guards					23	259	249	Windsor	3 squadrons: Hyde Park and Regent's Park Barracks 1 Squadron: Gardiner's Barn, Victoria Park: 9 a.m.

Infantry

Grenadier Guards 1st Batt.	35	673		Wellington Barracks	Wellington Barracks
2nd Batt.	30	529		Chichester	Millbank Prison
3rd Batt.	30	528		St John's Wood	St John's Wood
Coldstream Guards 1st Batt.	29	653		Tower of London	Tower of London
Scots Fusilier Guards 1st Batt.	28	527		St George's Barracks	St George's Barracks
2nd Batt.	28	509		Portman Street Barracks	Portman Street Barracks
SUB-TOTAL	265	4311	766		
Pensioners		400			Workhouse, Bethnal Green
TOTAL	265	4711	766		
In readiness					
12th Lancers	14	144	144	Hounslow	Hounslow
Coldstream Guards	25	544		Windsor	Windsor
MAXIMUM AVAILABLE	304	5399	910		

Source: WO 30/81

The great meetings: The maintenance of order

The defeats suffered by Chartism on 10 April and 12 June – the former only partial yet very considerable in psychological and long-term effect, the second unmitigated – are to be attributed, not to weakness in absolute numbers, but to pragmatic appreciation of the military might arrayed against the demonstrators. The Metropolitan Police, although respected as formidable opponents, were not feared. As for the special constabulary, whatever its size, Chartists would have welcomed the opportunity to set about their class enemies with stick and stone. It was the large-scale commitment of the army to the defence of the metropolis that caused the Chartist leadership to abandon the procession to Westminster on 10 April and the meeting of 12 June.

On both occasions the strategies adopted by the government had the greatest success.[198] Immediate resort was to be made to the police; and only if they failed to contain the populace were the troops to be engaged. Whereas the Chartists were fully aware of the scale of mobilization of the military – the newspapers carried extensive details and, in any case, such deployment within the capital could not be concealed – the soldiers' stations were kept out of sight. Provocation was thereby minimized, while knowledge of the consequences of any outbreak was disseminated.[199]

Sir Charles Rowan argued against prior occupation by the police of Bonner's Fields on 12 June on the grounds that such tactics would merely allow the Chartists to agree an alternative place of assembly. He recommended that, after the demonstrators had gathered, an ultimatum should be delivered to M'Douall and then, in the event of non-compliance, M'Douall should be arrested and the meeting dispersed, the police being supported by the troops if necessary. The advantage of this procedure, perilous in its consequences as it might seem, was that it was 'more calculated to limit the riot to the particular locality'. The outright prevention of the Bonner's Fields demonstration could, in contrast, initiate outbreaks by Chartists mingling with the turbulent holiday crowds in entirely unforeseen areas of London. Rowan's preferred strategy being adopted, it was possible to amass police at Bonner's Fields, and station the 400 pensioners in Bethnal Green Workhouse, while two squadrons of cavalry were ordered to the immediate vicinity with a third lying in Leather Lane. The Chartists would have been compelled to fight against substantial forces in Bethnal Green, with Buckingham Palace and Westminster fully defended and the bulk of the army available for calling from barracks.[200]

On 10 April the government was content to concede the right of meeting on Kennington Common, provided the demonstrators were unarmed and peaceable. It was obdurate in its decision that no processions should pass north of the Thames. This policy was virtually impregnable, given the seizure of the bridges (London, Southwark, Blackfriars, Waterloo, Hungerford, Westminster, Vauxhall and Battersea) after the mass of Chartists had concentrated in Kennington. As Blackfriars Bridge was the proposed point of crossing, the strongest forces were positioned there. 400 Metropolitan Police, including forty on horseback, together with a contingent from the City of London, occupied the bridge. At the Rose Inn, Farringdon Street, were two squadrons of the 1st Life Guards. The Bridewell, Bridge Street, was occupied by the 1st Battalion Coldstream Guards (minus two detachments). Four houses in Chatham Place from which the Bridge was 'effectually commanded and enfiladed' were (voluntarily) occupied by three companies of pensioners.[201] It was indeed at the southern approaches to Blackfriars Bridge that the bitterest collisions occurred on 10 April; but the situation was well within the capability of the police and support by the soldiery remained unrequired. On the other hand, the intention to prohibit all access to Westminster Bridge was not implemented and clashes broke out in Bridge and Parliament Streets.[202]

In 1848 Wellington was Commander-in-Chief – which rank he retained until his death – and a leading feature of the legend of 10 April is the image of the Iron Duke, aged almost eighty, conceiving and directing the defence of the capital.[203] In reality the strategic decision to confine the Chartists south of the river was agreed by the Prime Minister and the Commissioners of Police, elaborated by Mayne and Rowan and approved by a Cabinet meeting on the 8th to which Wellington had been invited. The precise military arrangements were then entrusted to Wellington, although orders for the movement of troops into London preceded his involvement in the preparations.[204]

In addition Wellington, unsolicited by the government, applied his mind to the tactical problems of maintaining civil order in the metropolis, producing memoranda not only in April but also in June.[205] On 5 April and 9 June, responding to newspaper reports and aware of troop movements, he produced general statements concerning the role of the military in the garrisoning of London. Unexceptionably he argued that: 'The Troops will be in their Barracks and Stations in readiness, and will not stir 'till ordered . . . But if not required it will be best not to show them!' The peculiarity of his thought lies in the strategic centrality he attributed to the parks: 'It is in my Opinion absolutely necessary to keep the Parks, that is Hyde Park, the Green Park, St James' Park, clear from Mobs as well as the Street from Trafalgar Square to the Houses of Parliament in Palace Yard', and all the park gates were to be guarded by small detachments of soldiers.[206] This unexpected emphasis is explained by Wellington thus:

That which must be the Military object on that day is to secure a communication among the Troops stationed in the several Barracks and Cantonments; and between each portion of them and the Horse Guards or Head Quarters! . . . The communications through the Parks being thus in security and clear, the Police will be at liberty to act as may be required.

For Wellington the importance of the parks lay in their periphery of executive, legislature, palaces and barracks. His logic was made more explicit – and elaborated – by Major-General Sir John Burgoyne, Inspector-General of Fortifications, in his memorandum of June 1848, 'On the measures to be adopted in London against Popular Tumults', printed in refined and more abstract form in 1859.[207] Burgoyne argued that of 'the leading public Establishments' only the Bank of England, British Museum and Post Office 'may be considered as insulated and without support'. Of the other government buildings east of Westminster, the Tower of London and Mint, the Custom House and Somerset House lay on the Thames and were thereby connected with the principal complex through 'a most valuable line of communication'. By 1859 Burgoyne could state his and Wellington's thought in lucid fashion:

in London, the parks form, in connection with the river, a valuable strategical line, and . . . nearly all the great public establishments could be combined into one system of mutual and concentrated support . . . The parks would be occupied by a general reserve force of infantry, cavalry, and artillery. These troops . . . could debouch from any part of the circuit occupied by them, in order to attack the rioters in front or flank . . . an internal line of communication, extending from the Tower to Kensington Palace . . . is securely established, and could be maintained without much difficulty.[208]

The special constables of March and April 1848 were enrolled under the provisions of the Act of 1831.[209] They were instructed in a leaflet to act on 10 April according to the principles developed by the police – and extended to the military – in the handling of the London crowd: those of, in general, unprovocative behaviour and, in particular, concealment:

1. To avoid coming into collision with persons in the Procession.
2. Not to regard any insults from people in procession.
3. Not to interfere in any case with such numbers of people, or when from other circumstances they are likely to be overpowered; to wait and get sufficient assistance to act as soon as possible.
4. To arrange that corner houses and others in commanding positions, might be occupied by Special Constables.
5. Not to show themselves in the immediate neighbourhood of any meeting.
6. A body might keep under cover near the meeting.
7. After the Meeting is over and Procession moved off, to patrol in sufficient numbers to prevent knots of persons assembling likely to cause disturbance.[210]

The euphoria of the specials on and after the 10th was such that the request was made for the institution of a formal structure; and on 11 April Wellington advised that, to combat a renewed threat, 'the Special Constables of each Parish should be more perfectly organized and arranged'.[211] Rowan wrote a 'Memorandum upon the further and more permanent organization of the Special Constables',[212] the recommendations of which were accepted by the Home Secretary (who stressed that any such arrangement was to be 'purely voluntary'), with the exception of the suggestion stemming from Wellington[213] that a portion of the special constabulary might be armed – Grey refused to allow the Chartists 'an excuse for arming themselves'.[214] Burgoyne, in June, while recognizing that it was 'the Civic mass . . . on whom eventually in our present situation the power of repression must depend', opposed the inauguration of a standing force of civilians: 'It would . . . be very unadvisable [sic] to give to even the best order of Citizens any permanent organization that would constitute a species of National Guard.'[215] With this conclusion Wellington now vehemently concurred.[216] Since Grey was not prepared to issue a public request for the specials to be more fully organized, it was left to the individual parishes to make their own arrangements. Thus on 12 June the special constabulary of St James's displayed subdivision, co-ordination and hierarchy almost martial in character and the Commissioners claimed comparable efficiency for St Martin in the Fields and St George Hanover Square. The representations of Edward Cardwell and others after 12 June resulted in the Home Office having printed the scheme of organization adopted by St James's; but Grey remained adamant that the leaflet was to be distributed only to 'such other Parishes as may ask him for assistance or hints in that respect' and no general, or official, structure was introduced.[217]

PART FOUR
The trades

Introduction

The ship-joiners were very exceptional during the Chartist years in maintaining their earnings and having no grievances whatsoever.[1] Almost every other trade had some serious challenge to confront: the intent to reduce wages (directly or indirectly), the displacement of men by machinery, the growth of injurious practices as their industry developed (e.g., engineering and boilermaking) and, in the case of the established crafts, persistent pressure to remove restrictions on increased output by employing 'illegal' men and additional apprentices, introducing piecework and sub-contracting, and replacing work in the shop by a domestic system, thereby promoting sweating. At one extreme, the large – or, at least, largish – employer was attempting to ride roughshod over trade customs; at the other, the home-working master, himself exploited by the immensely profitable wholesale or retail business, was exploiting in turn the men, women or children whom he drove to manufacture shop goods. In sum, employers sought to expand production and cut costs, in industries which remained virtually unmechanized, by enlarging the labour force and lowering wages, and effected a version of industrialization peculiar to nineteenth-century London.[2]

The earnings of the highly skilled, strongly unionized wet coopers fell, mysteriously, by a third or more over the twenty years down to 1850.[3] It was remarked, in connection with the type-founders' strike of 1843–4, that: 'The masters wanted to overflow the trade with human competition, so that they might get their work done at starvation wages.'[4] A major barrier preventing excessive 'human competition'[5] was the traditional limitation of the number of apprentices admitted to a craft; and one of the most severe conflicts of the period occurred in 1838–9 when the bookbinders successfully fought the large employers' disregard for the official ratios. One bookbinder considered that 'The present scale for apprentices ought to satisfy the most cormorant taste for apprentices', but another more realistically observed: 'masters who had many men, had also many apprentices, by whose labours they were unabled to reduce their prices; and in the shops of large masters apprentices were as numerous as blackber-

153

ries.'[6] In contrast, by 1850, the admission of apprentices to cabinet-making, including the honourable sector, was unrestricted.[7]

The continuance of apprenticeship regulations concerned several other important trades, especially the compositors, but the principal threat came from the varieties of indirect employment. These involved the utilization of intermediaries to employ workers and to spur them on to even greater productivity.[8] 'This indirect employment of workmen', Mayhew insisted, 'is the great bane of the industrious classes. Whether the middleman goes by the name of sweater, chamber-master, lumper, or contractor, it is this trading operative who is the great means of reducing the wages of his fellow working-men.'[9] Mayhew omitted from his list the 'piece-master' who, in engineering, undertook to complete a job for a specified price.[10] Similarly, in printing, work would be 'farmed' to a compositor who, with the aid of apprentices and other cheap labour, could undercut any 'respectable office'.[11]

It was, however, the four major London industries of building, shoemaking, tailoring and furniture-manufacture that were most grievously affected by 'co-exploitation'.[12] In the building trades separate portions of construction would be sub-contracted to working men who, for their part, often sub-let tasks to others. As for the other three industries manufacture was almost entirely removed from the masters' premises to the operatives' homes.[13] This physical shift enabled a man's family to assist him and the effects were far-reaching, as Place had recognized in 1824:

in those cases in which the woman and her children can generally find employment in her husband's business the very worst consequences must follow . . . In a trade say, that of a Mill-wright, the man alone can work at his trade, and his wages must be sufficient to enable him to keep himself his wife and a couple of children . . . By bringing women and children into the market, a much larger supply of labour is provided than there is a demand for . . . The consequence is, that if a man in the ordinary run of his trade has a wife and two children who can and by custom of the trade do work with him, they will altogether earn no more than he alone would earn, if men only were employed.[14]

Thus prices were diminished and it was but a short extension for the man to sweat individuals unrelated to him.[15]

There is ample evidence that such practices already flourished in some trades in the eighteenth century,[16] but they only became dominant during the second quarter of the nineteenth century and indeed it is possible to be relatively specific concerning the turning-points for the four principal industries concerned. Sub-contracting among carpenters and joiners became entrenched from about 1815–20 and 'scamping' or 'strapping shops' only grew numerous during the

1840s. In shoemaking the critical year was around 1820, for the tailors it was 1834, and 1830–5 marked the beginning of the rapid degeneration of cabinet-making.[17]

It was the cabinet-makers, 'so perfectly subdued by circumstances that they cannot, or do not, struggle against the system', whom Mayhew considered to be in the worst position of all, and the members of the fancy branch, at least, were 'far less political than they used to be. The working singly, and in their own rooms . . . has rendered them more unsocial than they were . . . as well as less regardful of their position and their rights as skilled labourers.'[18] At mid-century Mayhew concluded that almost all the metropolitan trades had 'two distinct kinds of employers; viz., those paying good and those paying bad wages; or, in other words, all handicrafts may be divided . . . into the "honourable" and "dishonourable" parts'. This principle extended so far that even scavenging and rubbish-carting had their 'good' and 'scurf' masters.[19]

In these conditions of deleterious change and economic conflict the desire of artisans to recover independence through self-employment, if largely unrealized, was, all the same, omnipresent. The schemes of the later thirties and the forties blended the utopian Owenite aspirations of the early thirties with increasingly pragmatic financial considerations concerning the advantage of employing men on strike or out of work on their own account.[20] Thus during the 1838 lock-out of the City Boot and Shoemakers it was asked:

What is there to prevent them from making this unemployed labour available? Why should they not employ those hands in the manufacture of the articles of their trade, and sell, them, aye even before the very doors of their oppressors? . . . In the boot and shoe-trades especially, middle-men are not wanted – there need not be any one between the maker and the wearer, to hoard up large profits . . .[21]

In 1836 the corkcutters had set twenty men to work on a £500 cargo of cork, thereby causing the masters to capitulate within a fortnight.[22] Crafts which entered the field in the forties were the brushmakers, without much fortune, and the bricklayers, disastrously.[23] The important Running Horse Society of Carpenters proposed to build houses or buy the 'carcases of houses' to provide its members with winter employment, while the Tailors' Protection Society was bent upon 'restricting the power of unprincipled capitalists on the one hand, and affording a refuge for the most depressed portion of the trade on the other'.[24] The popularity of the National Association of United Trades was ensured by its advocacy of similar experiments in raising 'the ill-paid and despised slaves of *capitalist-profitmongers*' to 'the dignity of independent capitalist-labourers'.[25]

Indeed the only really successful venture of this type during the period was sponsored by the NAUT after members of the strong trade belonging to the Cordwainers' Mutual Assistance Association were presented with the document by the owner of seven shops. Advertised as 'Labour's Emancipation from Capitalist Tyranny', the 'Workman's Own Shop' was opened in Drury Lane in May 1846 and supported by the formation of 'shoe clubs' of organ builders, tin-plate workers, masons, carpenters, bookbinders and others. By the end of the year the premises were too small to cope with the business and the 'Boot and Shoe Depot' was reopened at 11 Tottenham Court Road.[26]

It was in this climate of great, but mainly frustrated, enthusiasm among London working men for self-employment that the Christian Socialists, activated by Mayhew's revelations and with the economic advantages of respectability and capital (and with legislative pull in addition), from early 1850 established producers' co-operatives for tailors, needlewomen, shoemakers (men's and women's), printers, bakers, builders, piano-makers and smiths and apparently took over the running of the strong shoemakers' shop. The newly Amalgamated Society of Engineers, much influenced – and assisted – by the Christian Socialists, also set up 'associative workshops'.[27]

Another striking aspect of the trades' outlook was widespread sympathy for protectionism,[28] although this sentiment had little practical manifestation other than, most probably, to increase the antipathy towards the Anti-Corn Law League in general already felt for its personnel. One or two prominent Chartists did become active in the National Anti-League Association (and thereby politically ostracized), most notably Joseph Williams, the militant baker of 1839 and 1848;[29] but only the silk-weavers involved themselves with the Anti-League as a trade.[30]

In emergencies the London trades acted forcefully by establishing influential *ad hoc* organizations. Thus in the 1830s they formed three committees all achieving considerable success: the London Central Dorchester Committee, 1834–40, of which Robert Hartwell was secretary from 1835 to 1839;[31] the London Glasgow Cotton-Spinners Committee, 1837/8–1839;[32] and the London Trades' Combination Committee, 1838–9, to counter the activities of O'Connell's Select Committee on Combinations and which had Lovett as secretary.[33] Similarly, to aid each major metropolitan or provincial strike, a special body would be set up for the duration of the particular struggle and this would usually be a sub-committee of or be otherwise initiated by the Central Association of London Trades between 1837 and 1846 (when it ceased to be active). The objectives of the Central Association were 'a better understanding between trade societies, and the necessity of assisting each other in case of any infringements on the rights of labour'. The second aim would have been fulfilled anyway, but the existence of the Association probably did secure 'greater promptitude of action'. As for the first intention, the Association lamented in 1844: 'We are well aware that the bare idea of anything bordering on, or relative to, a general Union of the London trades, has been most generally met with apathy and indifference.'[34]

So, while inter-trade co-operation and solidarity were powerful at the level of strike support and resistance to adverse legal or legislative developments, efforts to draw the London crafts into more cohesive association were not favoured, certainly in the first half of the Chartist period.[35] This was exemplified by the failure of a campaign in 1839–41 to construct a Trades' Hall in the capital. It was estimated that the building would cost £15,000; Manchester, Birmingham and Liverpool 'each have reared a paternal mansion for their intelligent artisans'; and the scheme was promoted as having the double advantage of offering a capacious, lavishly fitted and economical meeting-place and removing trade societies from the public-house. Despite the original enthusiasm and indications that the project would prove successful, it was soon checked and evaporated entirely following the illness and resignation as secretary of its prime mover, William Farren, a printer.[36]

From 1845 the NAUT[37] took over the role of co-ordination, displacing the Central Association of London Trades (the two organizations had the same secretary: the corkcutter Thomas Barratt).[38] Not until 1848–9 did another purely London body emerge, the Metropolitan Trades' Delegate Meeting, even more firmly aligned to Chartism than the NAUT but, unlike it and the old Central Association, disregarding trade disputes, instead concentrating on the elaboration of a radical programme, political, economic and social, though seeking to combine the societies into a single body and potent force.[39]

The most spectacular development of the period among the London trades was the formation of national, general unions by the tailors and shoemakers. 'A pressure from without' did serve temporarily 'to curb the aristocratic feelings' of those who earned 'goodly wages'.[40] The two unions emanated from the capital and initially overcame the hostility of some of the Londoners. Eventually, however, in both cases, the bulk of the metropolitan membership seceded leaving the associations to organize the provinces. This was symptomatic of London's behaviour in all the crafts examined below – with the sole exceptions of hatting, the leather trades and, most strikingly, the pioneering engineers. Either London would possess its own organization distinct from societies or a union based in the country – and withdrawing from efforts at comprehensive recruitment – or, if London did belong to a national union, there would be a metropolitan faction constituted independently. Special conditions, particularly favourable or particularly unfavourable, did, of course, prevail in the city and it is not unnatural that Londoners were reluctant to be governed by others, yet equally there was an irrepressible metropolitan arrogance. The NAUT was forced to the judgment that 'in truth the metropolitan trades appear sadly deficient in public spirit'.[41] London's sectionalism in the context of national trade unionism was mirrored by factionalism internal to the metropolis – hence the weakness of intertrade movements and the failure to institute a trades council before 1860. It is, at first sight, astonishing that some of the gravest divisiveness and backbiting occurred in those industries, such as tailoring and shoemaking, economically most threatened and therefore in greatest need of trade unity. This feature can be explained by the intense traditions of the autonomy of highly local clubs, the demoralization spreading within important crafts during the second quarter of the century – the loss of the tailors' *élan* was extraordinarily acute – and the extreme divergence opening concomitantly between the most skilled, best paid and the least skilled, worst paid members of the same occupation.

The boot and shoemakers

Of the multifarious occupations of nineteenth-century Britain that of shoemaker was most ubiquitous, even the moderately sized village having its own.[42] The craft was especially numerous in London, which remained the principal centre of production, and was concentrated in the area from the West End through Holborn and the City to Tower Hamlets, and also south of the river, particularly in Southwark. The area designated by the Cordwainers' Association as its Tower Hamlets district – and which excluded Whitechapel and Shoreditch – was said to contain about 5,000 shoemakers.[43]

Machine-production and an extensive division of labour were only introduced into the British boot and shoe industry from the late 1850s.[44] Nevertheless, save in the shop of the small honourable master, substantial specialization had existed for a century and more in London, creating the craftsmen known as 'clickers', 'closers' and 'makers' by following the three principal processes in the manufacture of any pair of boots or shoes:

(1) Clicking: the cutting out of the pieces comprising upper, lining and sole. This was the most skilled task, for it demanded the combination of economy and avoidance of flaws in the leather.

(2) Closing: the sewing together of the sections of lining and upper.

(3) Making: the insole and upper were tacked to the last and then joined; the welt sewn to the insole; the sole stitched to the welt; the heel attached; and the shoe 'finished'.[45]

In addition there was a basic distinction between the manufacture of men's and women's footwear – by, respectively, men's men and women's men. Other varieties of boots and shoes were made by specialist sections: e.g., the strong trade, producing heavy boots as distinct from 'the lighter boots worn by gentlemen'.[46] The wholesale trade and sale shops had arisen alongside the traditional bespoke establishments. Shoemaking was becoming divorced from shoemending, the job of the cobbler.[47] Such was the physical separation between the branches of the trade and, often, between the different stages in the production of a given pair of shoes that, in order to collect subscriptions from non-society men, it was suggested that lists should be left at all grinders' shops, which cordwainers perforce visited to buy hemp, bristles, wax, gum, nails, ink, etc.[48]

159

During the first half of the century London's position of pre-eminence underwent relative decline as the industry developed in the Midlands, most markedly in Northamptonshire and Staffordshire.[49] Provincial products were ready-made and their prices very competitive
with those of London. This pressure from the new centres of the
trade was contemporaneous with – and accentuated – the major
development within metropolitan boot and shoemaking during the
same period and which, while in large measure geographically autonomous, was certainly attributable to the common stimuli of the export
trade (before 1815 – and after 1850), government contracts and, in
general, population growth. The wholesale trade mushroomed and
the greater portion of the craft degenerated into a dishonourable
trade.[50]

Outwork and sub-contracting, the insertion of middlemen
(whether shopkeepers or manufacturers)[51] between producers and
customers and of sweaters between the sweated and the middlemen,
the employment of female and unapprenticed labour, were the
means by which a vast slop trade, based on East London, relentlessly
expanded, beating down the prices, wages and working conditions
throughout the trade and ensuring that the honourable sector constituted a tiny minority (in terms of both employees and output). Incessant, yet increasing, labour resulted in intensified exploitation. The
Women's Men of West End and City declared:

> That some members of society should become poor through idleness,
> imprudence, or extravagance, is not surprising; but for whole communities
> to become poor by industry, is monstrous. To labour and want, and to labour
> in fear of still greater want even in the midst of abundance, is that which
> renders the condition of the British shoemaker worse than that of the negro
> slave . . . Remember the capitalists, as a class, have no sympathy for you; their
> chief object to obtain from you the greatest amount of labour at the very
> lowest price; whilst, by reducing wages, or decreasing the number of their
> workmen, they convert every change and circumstance into profit . . . For
> one moment reflect on the miserable pittance, viz. from pumps ld. to welts ls.
> per pair, doled out in many parts of the metropolis, out of which the jour-
> neyman has to provide grindery, candle, and keeping his tools in order; what
> can he then have left for his family on Saturday night? Is this not a lamentable
> state of things? yet this is not the worst side of the picture. About Somers
> Town and Bethnal Green, and the eastern part of the metropolis, a system of
> middlemen has crept in, who employ a large number of slaves to labour for
> them, at such wages as enables them to serve the manufacturers with women's
> shoes at 15s. per dozen! By the effects of such competition the condition of
> the labourer is becoming worse and worse.[52]

Two knowledgeable old-timers, John O'Neil and Allen Davenport,
dated 'the downfall of the power of the men, and the commencement
of despotism amongst the master shoemakers' from hot-headed and

overweening conduct following otherwise successful strikes in 1812 and 1813 by the men's men and women's men respectively. 'Refractory' action in 1812 resulted in 'reviling and recrimination between the City and West-end' and the permanent split between the two districts of previously united men's shoemakers, 'Drury Lane being the boundary line of separation'. During the confusion Northampton and other provincial speculators opened warehouses in London and were also able to seize the export trade (until then monopolized by the metropolis). A similarly 'arrogant proceeding' in 1813 by the ladies' shoemakers, who had at one time fourteen divisions, caused another crisis: the masters combined for the first time and entirely defeated their men.[53] By 1824 it was estimated that not more than one-fifth of shoemakers were in union.[54]

In 1836 Lovett described the operation of the outwork system in terms remarkably similar to Mayhew's more than a decade later:

The single men generally take a room to work in between three or four or any other number as they can agree, and pay for rent, fire, and candle light between them; or, if they are married men, they generally work in their own rooms. The masters who employ them have the work cut out for them at their own shops, and the workmen go and take it to their lodgings or workshop to be made up; of men's shoes generally obtaining a pair at a time – of women's two or three, as the master is disposed to give them. When they have completed them they take them back, and get their money. Of course, you will perceive that considerable loss of time is thus caused to the men, in fetching and taking home their work; some employers causing more than others, some often compelling the workmen to call three or four times for their work.[55]

John James Bezer became a 'Snob' within a year around this time, yet after two years 'never could rise above 10s.'. On the other hand, his cousin, with the assistance of his wife and one child, managed 'to earn a pound, or perhaps a little more, weekly'.[56]

It was but a step from simple outwork to the even more deleterious practice of sweating which, according to Lovett, 'within these few years . . . has been rapidly extending to the great deterioration of the trade':

Those persons who keep these cheap shoe shops, of which you see puffs of cheapness in every direction, enter into an agreement with persons called chamber masters, to supply their shops with boots and shoes at certain low prices, more especially women's (as the men's boots and shoes they get from Northampton and other parts of the country). As an instance of the lowness of price – for women's shoes, which in bespoke shops they give from ls.6d. to 3s. per pair for the making, these chamber masters will make, though in a very inferior manner, from 6d. to ls. per pair. In order, then, to fulfil their agreement they procure a number of boys from the workhouse to assist them, and by working them from 14 to 16 hours a day, they manage to make a living.[57]

Devlin, in 1839, also considered the manufacture of female footwear in London – 'the great mart for all kinds of women's cheap shoes and boots' – to be particularly dominated by the slop trade.[58]

Women had always assisted husbands and fathers in shoemaking. Certain categories of work – the closing of men's shoes and shoe binding (the closing and binding, with cloth and leather, of women's boots and shoes) – now became their prerogative, but for derisory remuneration. Earnings (for women) had once reached 22s. to 28s. and could still, in 1839, be as high as 20s., although the usual amount was from 3s. to 10s.[59]

Dishonourable techniques invaded even the honourable trade. So, in the boot trade, 'blind rands' were substituted for 'stitched rands', the journeyman was paid 5s. instead of 6s. per boot and, since his output did not increase, received reduced total earnings, and the customer continued to pay the same price for 'a much worse article'.[60]

Lovett discovered in 1836 that the cordwainers' wages had fallen by one-third in the preceding twenty years: 'where they now earn but 18s., they could in 1814 earn 27s.,[61] and so in proportion'. The ladies' shoemakers had fallen behind the men's men, 'the best paid portion of the trade', and then earned, on average, 12s. to 18s. per week.[62] So in 1837 the hierarchy of prestige was observed as 'the Boot-maker being . . . the highest, as those who make men's shoes are superior to *women's men*'.[63] The City Men's Men in 1838 subjected their earnings to an intense enquiry, claimed as 'the first document of the kind which has emanated from . . . any . . . trades' society as a society'. Boot-closers received 24s. 8d., if married, or 18s., if single and unassisted. The average wage of bootmakers was 18s. 9d. or 16s. 5d. and of shoemakers and repairers only 12s. 6d. or 12s.[64] Wages continued to decrease throughout the Chartist period. The above are gross figures, requiring the subtraction of 1s., 2s. or 3s. working costs, i.e., grindery, heating and lighting (for domestic work was the norm for all). By 1842 a man's man 'did not think, when all the deductions were made, that the present average wages were more than 10s. or 12s. a week'.[65] City boot and shoemakers gave their (gross) earnings as 11s. 6d. and 10s. in 1845 and 1846 respectively.[66] In 1844 a woman's man, raising the call for general unionism, had reported recent reductions of 10–25 per cent in piece-rates.[67] By 1850 a West End boot-closer and a maker working for the best shops could average merely 24–25s. (net) and 21s. respectively – and ordinary bootmen were down to 14s. Similarly, first-class ladies' men in the West End might earn up to 24s., but others could only make 12s.; while their counterparts in the City received 13s. net.[68] Hours remained throughout at around fourteen daily.[69]

Such conditions existed in the honourable island of the trade. Surrounded by the ocean of slop production most of its prices were dragged incessantly downwards and craftsmen denuded of their artisan attributes. 'Although there were many receiving high wages in the trade, there were also many receiving miserable low wages. This must have the effect, through the prevailing system of unprincipled competition, to pull down the high wages to the low standard, if not checked.'[70] The only checks were a (limited) demand by the well-to-do for quality products and the battered trade societies.

There were four principal societies in London: the ladies' shoemakers of the West End and of the City; and the boot and shoemakers of the West End and of the City. In March 1845 they numbered respectively 400, 200, 700 and 600.[71] (This, however, was the time of year when they began to gain size as men tramped in for the season. In 1849, for example, the West End Men's Men were 790 strong during the quarter ending in April and reached a peak of 890 during the July quarter.)[72] As these figures suggest, and as Lovett and Devlin explain and confirm, the men's trade was more favourably placed than the women's. The difference in the respective pressures of the dishonourable sector upon the two branches goes far to explain the initiative of the ladies' shoemakers in launching a general national union in 1844 and the reluctance of the men's men to combine with the movement.

A society consisted of divisions or meetings, each with a membership of around a hundred.[73] The West End Men's Men had been in union for fifty years; and of the West End Women's Men the *Northern Star* commented: 'This body of shoemakers is the most aristocratic in the kingdom.'[74] The men's and ladies' shoemakers of the Tower Hamlets – 'this vast slaughter-house . . . it is unquestionably a fact, that the work in this neighbourhood is worse paid for than in any other locality in the kingdom'[75] – and of Southwark were likewise separately organized: but their organizations were small and weak, the Borough Women's Men, for example, totalling in March 1845 under sixty.[76] Little societies also existed in other parts of the city: Chelsea and Greenwich, Hackney and Clapham. Of the strong trade, centred on Clerkenwell and Saffron Hill and said by themselves in 1848 to number 'upwards of a thousand men', as many as 240 had joined the Cordwainers' Association in 1845, their union having been reformed the preceding year.[77] The supreme aristocrats of cordwaining, who always worked on the masters' premises, were the clickers; but since

their society was for benefit purposes alone their wages varied from
£2 to £3 to as little as £1. They remained aloof from the closers and
makers and from all general agitation, trade or inter-trade, of 1838–
48.[78]

Mayhew was informed that an estimated 30,000 shoemakers in
1850 were composed thus:[79]

Men's men	10,000
Women's men	7,500
Strong trade	1,200
Clickers	2,000
Cleaners-up, and other shop assistants	2,500
Translators, repairers, and cobblers	2,800
Female workers	4,000
Total	30,000

The Chartist decade opened with dual movements of the shoemakers. One, originating in November 1838 and partially successful,
requested the employers of the Boot and Shoemakers' Clickers and
Assistants to close their shops at 8.00 in the winter and 9.00 in summer, save for Saturdays when the hours were from 7.00 a.m. until
midnight. Although the great majority of the 735 masters (including
those with no employees) concurred, the opposition of 'about twenty-
nine of the principal masters in the sale trade, most of them having
several shops situated in different first-rate thoroughfares', resulted
in a revision to 9.00 throughout the year (reducing average daily
hours by only one). Yet in December 1839 the central committee of
the society was still endeavouring to implement nine o'clock closing.[80]

During 1838 the City Men's Men engaged in two strikes. In the
summer they demanded an increase for the shoemakers and repairers, men whose earnings had been revealed as disproportionately low
compared with their fellows' (12s. against the 17s. and more of bootmakers and boot-closers). The victorious 'Coronation Strike' induced
fifty-two masters to combine and two months later the document was
presented with the insistence that there was a return to the original
wages. Rejection by the journeymen on 20 September threw 200 on
to the support of their fellows. At the end of November James Devlin[81] castigated the original strike as 'feeble, and rashly undertaken'
and correctly predicted the imminent defeat of the current resistance
to the Associated Masters – 'we have been mainly beaten by ourselves
– by our own fellow-journeymen, by some who once belonged to our
body, in conjunction with others who never so belonged'. Devlin, pro-
ponent of unity, was insistent that 'We must . . . renovate the consti-

tution of our society altogether, give it a fresh and broader basis'; and could, in postscript, eagerly announce that 'the Western Society of Boot and Shoemakers have thrown every shop open in their division, without consideration of class or prices paid'.[82]

Although the United Committee of the City, Borough, and Stepney Societies of Ladies' Shoemakers appealed to non-society men in 1839 to join 'a wide-extended union of our class' and this initiative may be connected with the 'blocking' of a City warehouse in 1840–1,[83] it was not until 1844 that concerted attempts, even then harassed and ultimately defeated by sectionalist sentiment, were made to integrate the entire trade into one union. The inspiriting progress of the Miners' Association and the favourable outcome of the campaign against the Masters and Servants' Bill resulted not only in the formation of the NAUT but also greatly aided the renewal of the shoemakers' and tailors' efforts to establish societies both national and comprehensive.

The ladies' shoemakers again took the lead and it was the exclusive and influential West End Women's Men, in February 1844, who addressed the country:

> The various Divisions of our Trade Society in the Metropolitan districts, deem it essential at the present crisis, to call upon you, one and all, to rally round the standard of your Trade, and protect yourselves from the absorbing influence of that Hydra-headed monster – Competition! which is tearing asunder the sacred bonds of civil society . . . and ultimately threatens the destruction of your trade.

They declared their society 'thrown open unconditionally' and proposed a national delegate meeting, to be held in Birmingham on 7 May, 'of our branch of trade . . . to bring about a new and better system of Organization of the whole Trade' – that is, of ladies' and men's shoemakers alike.[84]

The conference met in June, with the men's as well as the women's trade represented, and on its dispersal Alfred Hunnibell (West End Woman's Man and Chartist), a Sheffield delegate and Devlin, now editing the *Cordwainers' Companion*,[85] remained in Birmingham to prepare for publication the book of laws of the Cordwainers' General Mutual Assistance Association. Of the six members of the Committee of Management three came from the West End Women's Men: John Duncombe, Hunnibell (chairman) and James Smithyes (general secretary). Another member was George Shell of the Borough Ladies' Shoemakers.[86] By September over seventy societies throughout England had joined the Association and at the end of October there were 120.[87]

But the Men's Men of the City and West End were intent on launching their own Philanthropic Society of Boot and Shoemakers, for men's men alone though it too was to recruit non-society men and to create 'a general Union throughout the United Kingdom, similar to the Miners and other bodies'. Since the alteration of their rules they claimed an accession to the London societies of more than 300, an increase of around 25 per cent. At the end of October their membership was said to be 3,000.[88] A series of three meetings on 'Whether the Mutual Assistance Association or the Philanthropic Society of Boot and Shoemakers is best calculated to benefit the trade in general?' centred on the Men's Men's criticism of the undemocratic nature of the Mutuals, for the committee controlled finance and strikes and their rules were adjudged 'aristocratic'. The Philanthropics contended that 'if the Mutuals have not three kings sitting at Somerset House, they have five elsewhere' and denounced the Managing Committee's powers as 'at once dangerous, despotic, and altogether impracticable, inasmuch as they have the powers to lay on levies, to strike for advances, and to reject or accept reductions'. William Clark (man's man) spoke unhappily of the 'centralized democracy' of the Mutuals, who retorted: 'Some of their friends notions would do honour to the antiquated days of Adam and Eve . . . We propose to carry out the principle of representation – was not that democracy?' Plain-speaking proved constructive as it was resolved to interchange cards until the spring, when the two unions would amalgamate (an immediate national conference being rejected on grounds of expense).[89]

The united Conference opened in London on 1 April 1845, three days after the conclusion of the sessions at which the NAUT had been established. (The decision of a mass meeting of the London shoemakers on 30 March that the whole of the boot and shoe trade of the United Kingdom should be drawn into one body was hailed by the *Northern Star* as the 'First Fruits of the National Trades' Conference'.) Despite the representation of only twenty-three or so provincial towns, there were delegates from such key areas as Northampton, Leicester, Stafford and Norwich. Seven London societies participated and the proceedings lasted until 11 April. The laws of the Cordwainers' Association were revised and Smithyes re-elected as secretary.[90] The Philanthropic Society now disappeared, for during May and June all of 'the four great branches of the London Men's trade' – West End, City, Stepney, Borough – adhered to the Association. The *Northern Star* commented: 'The society of Shoemakers of the whole of England, with very few exceptions indeed, is now in union. The present union, which originated only about a year ago, is the first attempt of the kind which has ever been made in connection with this particular trade.'[91] The Mutual Association went further in its declaration that:

we are the first trade who solved the problem of whether the working-classes (of different countries) could be united for a common object . . . the boot and shoemakers were the first working-men in these realms that solved the problem . . . and they not only formed a general union, but united men, who, a few years since were deadly enemies to each other.[92]

For the eight months August 1844–April 1845 the Association had reported a membership of 4,924 (and 145 societies) – and at the end of the first quarter, August–November 1844, the total stood at 5,005. Over the following year its quarterly progress was:[93]

April–July 1845	5,385 members
July–October 1845	5,807 members
Oct. 1845–Jan. 1846	5,996 members
January–April 1846	6,061 members

Accord between the insatiably disputatious shoemakers became acrimony within a year. While William Clark had replaced Smithyes as general secretary, one division of his own West Men's Men had 'not yet been brought to join the Association'; and during the third quarter of 1845 the City Women's Men seceded. The Borough trade had been suspended prior to the 1846 conference because of non-payments.[94] Devlin, on the eve of the conference, urged the craft to do 'something towards the formation, at last, of a really "general" association. The two preceding attempts . . . have been but *attempts* – attempts, forced on, it is true, through a multitude of obstacles, as they were always endangered in their after working, from the evil results of a most bitter spirit of mere partizanship.' For, he especially insisted: 'let those of the "ancient regimen" do away for the time with some of their men's lurking misgivings, and come and "confer" at least, with their fellow workmen of the altered system, and thus the closer to examine what in reality it is'. In addition to the suspicious exclusiveness of the 'old trade', the Association was being weakened by conflicts with the masters. Early in 1846 ten towns in England and Ireland were 'either more or less on strike', while the London strong trade had been presented with the document and a levy of 3d. per member per week was retained for a second month as a bitter strike continued in Belfast.[95]

When the conference assembled in London strife was ensured by the rejection of the credentials of three delegates from the West End Men's Men – including, bizarrely, those of Devlin – since the committee of investigation reported only one section had 'respected the authority of the annual district delegate meeting as created by the general *law*, while the other sections refused to comply with the law as acted upon throughout the country'. The two excluded sections, joined by four others (out of a total of eight) and numbering 600 to 700, prepared

To establish a cheap, well-defined, and efficacious mode of assistance between town and town throughout England, Ireland, Scotland and Wales, in all properly sanctioned cases of strike, without the present cumbrous and expensive machinery of district meetings, annual conferences, administrative committees, and itinerant lecturers, but simply by a well-regulated system of correspondence, as based upon such equitable degrees of payment as shall suit . . . particular circumstances.

The 'old body' of the West End was exonerated for its refusal to combine with the Association since

it was not from any want of respect for, or faith in, the great principle of strength as involved in a general union of our trade, but from a conviction that the means proposed to this end were not the best that might be devised, nor the persons to whom, from the first, the administrative affairs of such attempted union were consigned, such as we could confide in for the honest and healthy carrying out of any such extensive undertaking.

Thus the dissentient bulk of the West End Men's Men projected a middle course between the Association and 'the old sectional modes'. Devlin was deputed to draft a polemic against the Association and proposals for a new organizational structure and his *Cordwainers' Companion* chosen as the medium for communication.[96]

At the conference Clark was re-elected secretary of the Cordwainers' Association; and Charles M'Carthy, also formerly a prominent Philanthropic, was to represent London on the Administrative Committee. The London Strong Trade, angered by non-recognition of their current dispute (they received an extraordinary payment of only £20), withdrew from the Association, followed by sections of the City Men's Men, both groups associating themselves with the new move among the Men's Men of the West End. By July 1846 it was 'pretty evident that the Association . . . is on its "last legs", in London at least', only the West End Women's Men continuing to adhere intact of the original six metropolitan divisions.[97] Total membership had slumped to 4,762 (April–July 1846), and then to 4,322 (July–October 1846) and 3,876 (October 1846–January 1847); while London affiliation had fallen from 1,980 in April–July 1845 to 873 in July–October 1846.[98] Although the majority of the Men's Men of West End and City, the advocates two years before of the Philanthropic Society, had seceded, their rumps remained influential in the affairs of the Association, Clark continuing as secretary and M'Carthy, in the autumn, being its missionary. When the 1847 Conference met at Bury the West End Women's Men, the prime initiators in the foundation of the

Association, had been suspended (on account, presumably, of the substantial arrears accumulated during 1846).[99]

To compensate for the failure to achieve general union in their own trade the four principal societies individually joined the NAUT;[100] and at the beginning of 1848 the ladies' shoemakers of the West End and City, through a committee under the secretaryship of Smithyes, renewed their appeal to non-unionists, on this occasion urging accession to the NAUT and promoting a series of successful meetings.[101]

The immediate existence of the Cordwainers' Association was not jeopardized by the removal of the metropolitan shoemakers (whose rival union remained no more than projected); and it may have survived in some parts of the country and formed one of the components which cohered, London resuming the principal role, in the United Society of Cordwainers in 1862, shortly to become the Amalgamated Cordwainers' Association, from which, in 1873–4, a breakaway of machine-workers founded the National Union of Boot and Shoe Operatives.[102]

All of the Londoners seem eventually to have concluded that there was 'something rotten in the constitution of the Mutual Association'. The expense of the system was abhorred and expenditure fiercely scrutinized. The levying powers of the executive committee resulted in the accumulation of debts for some societies and their suspension from the union. The secretary (Clark) was accused of both arbitrary acts and embezzlement. In short, the outside control of funds was resented: 'a national trade ought to have more security for their money, than mere confidence in their officers'. The loss of a cherished local autonomy proved insufferable: 'The district system is veritably bad. A district committee living together in one town and called upon to decide upon the wages of ten or twenty other societies, living sixty or seventy miles apart in some instances, is class legislation with a vengeance.'[103] These are indeed the complaints of the City Men's Men; but the original critique of the Philanthropics proved all too cogent in the context of prickly London individualism. It was organizational problems of the kind that Mutuals sought to tackle which were to be largely solved by the 'new model' of the Engineers a few years later – in a trade with quite different historical and industrial prospects.

The tailors

Outnumbered only by the shoemakers, the tailors constituted the second craft of early-Victorian London, the 1841 Census returning a total of 23,500, of whom Mayhew estimated not less than 21,000 were working artisans.[104] The trade was heavily concentrated in the great sweep from Marylebone and Westminster through to Bethnal Green and Stepney, with only five tailoring establishments in 1840 located in Southwark and Bermondsey.[105]

Originally, one man would have produced an entire man's suit, but by the nineteenth century a differentiation existed between the cutter (in small concerns usually the master, and the foreman in larger) and the tailor, while tailors specialized in coats, waistcoats or trousers. A coat generally involved three men: 'One makes the collar and sleeves, and the two others are engaged each upon one of the fore parts, or right or left side.' This division of labour was accepted throughout the honourable trade and not yet exceeded in the sweated sector, which was dependent upon (imminent) mechanical innovations for intensification of the process.[106] Under the most favourable conditions tailoring was an unhealthy occupation being entirely sedentary and conducted in 'a close and hot shop'; when sweated the workers were 'generally almost brutified with their incessant toil, wretched pay, miserable food, and filthy homes'.[107]

Severely undermined as were other major artisan trades by the tide of dishonourable practice, the tailors were especially afflicted. Their craft was closely related to dressmaking, millinery and shirtmaking, all traditional feminine skills,[108] and therefore open, in the conditions of the mid-nineteenth century, to invasion by an inexhaustible supply of female labour. The demand for cheap clothes stemmed not only from customers of limited means but also from institutional buyers. As with boots, the pressure of government contracts for army uniforms dated from the Wars, but were later supplemented by the need for police coats and trousers in particular. Custom House and Post Office clothing, even the Queen's liveries, fell into the hands of sweaters.[109]

As early as 1836 Lovett gave a succinct description of the new system of production:

a considerable quantity of work, consisting of slops, army, and police clothing, is executed chiefly by *women* and children, at wages varying from 5s. to 15s. per week. In addition to this, there is a principle of evil in operation which must continue to render [the tailors'] condition still worse. It is that of the proprietors of show and slop shops employing persons (called by the tailors *sweaters*) to do work for them at home at very low prices . . . But those sweaters, in order to make a living, will employ women and children, who work for them from 3s. to 8s. per week, frequently from six in the morning till ten at night; and thus, by a small profit on each, make up a sum equal to journeyman's wages. This pernicious and ruinous system is being extended; and those show and slop-sellers, always availing themselves of the slack season of the year for stocking their premises, render it the more difficult for the journeymen to keep up their prices, by the temptations those persons hold out for the men to do work *privately* for them at low prices. Such is the condition of the journeymen tailors of London, and of most large and populous towns throughout the country.[110]

The first public scandal concerning sweating broke in 1843 when a woman was taken to court by Messrs Moses and Son of the Minories for pawning several articles she was making up for them and it was her case which moved Hood to write 'The Song of the Shirt' (appearing in the Christmas number of *Punch*), although she was in reality a trousers hand.[111] From around this time complaints about Jewish sweaters become relatively common.[112] It was left to Mayhew to reveal fully the plight of the clothing workers in his *Morning Chronicle* articles of November and December 1849 and his findings, almost entirely omitted from *London Labour and the London Poor,* found a large readership through the medium of Kingsley's *Cheap Clothes and Nasty* and *Alton Locke,* both of 1850.[113]

The drastic deterioration in the condition of the trade was the more dramatic – and deleterious for the society man – as the tailors had occupied one of the proudest positions in the labour aristocracy. A recollection of 1844 was: 'Thirty years ago want was unknown in our trade.'[114] Place's opinion in 1818 was that: 'The system of combination of the journeymen tailors, is by far the most perfect of any.' Masters were obliged to apply to the houses of call in order to employ journeymen; and the men imposed strict craft discipline upon themselves. There was, however, already a distinction between Flints, working by the day and with upwards of thirty houses of call, and the Dungs, prepared to work also by the piece and for lower wages, but with only nine or ten houses.[115] By 1824, while the Flints outnumbered the Dungs by four to one, their houses of call had been slashed to over twenty;[116] and in the following year the West End tailors sought an assurance that their masters would cease to give out waistcoats to women.[117] The rise of piece- and home-work led the tailors to chance all in the great strike of 1834 and the consequences of defeat were disastrous.[118] The houses of call were reduced in number and wages plummeted. The weekly rate had been pushed up to 36s. in 1813 and this, together with daily hours of twelve, exclusive of meals, the Flints were able to conserve nominally, though the masters' institution of the 'log', a scale of prices per garment dependent on an estimate of the number of hours required, replaced payment by the hour with a variety of piecework. This was a critical transition, tailors judging it to have significantly accelerated the degeneration into a sweated trade.[119] From between 5,000 and 6,000 in 1821 the honourables dwindled to 3,697 in 1844, 3,000 in 1849, and 2,136 in 1856. Lovett stated average earnings in 1814 had been only 24s., yet his estimate of 17s. for 1836 seems rather too low – he calculated the rates, before deduction of working expenses and one-fifth loss of time, at 28s. for coatmakers, 22s. 6d. for trousers hands and 19s. 6d. for waistcoatmakers – and journeymen's claims of 20s. in 1839 and 18s. or 21s. in 1842 are probably more reliable. A reduction of 35 per cent was reported in 1846; and in 1849 Mayhew concluded that average wages stood at 18s. None of these figures takes account of the slop trade where Mayhew found earnings averaged 11s.[120]

In the early 1840s 'What was called the honourable portion of the trade was united in twelve societies.'[121] 'London once boasted an immense number of [houses of call] . . . what a falling off! they were poor and poverty-stricken, and distress obliged them to work for what they could get.'[122] The houses of call were situated overwhelmingly in the West End.[123] 'The four largest societies in London' were the Three Crowns, Richmond Street, Soho Square (500 members); Two Chairmen, Wardour Street; Blue Posts, Rupert Street; and King's Head, Bear Street, Leicester Square.[124] At the George, St Mary Axe, was 'one of the oldest houses of call, it having been in existence for upwards of two hundred years'.[125] The others were the Three Doves, Berwick Street; Bricklayers' Arms and Red Lion, both in King Street, Golden Square; Fleece, Little Windmill Street; Three Compasses, Silver Street (Golden Square presumably); and Robin Hood.[126] The twelfth was possibly in Red Lion Street.[127] A further reduction in the houses of call had occurred by 1847, when the London West End Tailors' Society comprised seven sections and upwards of 3,000 members; in 1849 (and also 1856) there were six societies, but in addition four 'outstanding houses' with 400 men, not in union but acting in concert with the others.[128]

In the course of 1843 the tailors, preceding the cordwainers, came together once more in an endeavour to effect general union in their craft. As a result of 'depression, suffering, and uncertainty, hitherto unparalleled', attributed principally to 'the influence of illegitimate

Establishments on the respectable and honest part of the Trade, and the misunderstandings which . . . prevail among ourselves', the Metropolitan Tailors' Protection Society had been formed – sometime during 1842, it is to be assumed – proposing the remedy of 'A UNION OF ALL THE MEMBERS OF OUR TRADE WITHOUT EXCEPTION'. The Society initially failed to consolidate itself in either London or the country and was re-established in July 1843.[129] By November it could convene a gathering of some 2,000 to counter the public statements of Moses and Son; and John Whitaker Parker, the secretary, advocated again, in the *Northern Star*, 'a general union of the whole trade, without exception, both in town and country, females as well as males'.[130]

The response from the provinces was now unambiguous. Twenty-five towns were represented by delegate or letter at a meeting in January 1844 and were declared to be in union with the metropolitan sections of the 'General United Tailors' Trade Protection Society of Great Britain and Ireland'.[131] The principal objective of the movement was stated by Francis Parrott, president of the Metropolitan Society: 'To remove from our trade its greatest reproach, namely, out-door labour, and thus destroy the accursed system of "sweating", and its attendant abominations, by inducing master tailors to confine their work to workshops provided by themselves, and under their own control.' The 1834 demand for a ten-hour day was also revived.[132] From 8 to 16 April a Tailors' Conference sat at the Parthenium Club, St Martin's Lane. Eighteen provincial districts had sent representatives and a further thirty-two were in correspondence. A plan of organization was approved and Parrott and Parker elected president and secretary, respectively, of the national society. The Executive Council was to consist of three Londoners. Proceedings concluded with a concert and ball presided over by Duncombe and at which William Prowting Roberts also was present.[133] Progress in reorganizing the craft was sluggish and, although by August forty-four sections were reported, a third of these were metropolitan.[134]

The advance of the society in London was, at first, considerable. When the Tailors' Conference met in April some fifteen metropolitan sections had been formed – only three in the West End, but two in Tower Hamlets, one each in Southwark and Greenwich, and at least five in the City.[135] Also, the houses of call now supported the Protection Society, a marked advance upon the majority refusal of July 1843.[136] The Three Crowns society 'expressed themselves perfectly satisfied, being of opinion that unless the trade generally adopt the principles of a General Union, there is no hope of making a successful stand against the encroachments of the principal capitalists'.[137] At the Conference the delegate from the George, St Mary Axe, announced:

'they threw open their books in 1834, and were perfectly ready to do so again, as they were thoroughly convinced that the Protective [sic] Society were taking the proper steps'. Yet the approbation of the most powerful members of the trade was hedged with reservations: 'they did not wish the houses of call broken up' and they ensured that there were two bodies in existence, 'general protective and partial protective', with separate business nights and separate funds.[138]

The fickleness of the aristocrats was transparent within four months:

London is the chief difficulty; it is the seat of corruption; a thousand and one interests are in existence, working against each other. It is also the seat of monopoly among the men. The high priced and constantly employed journeyman has no sympathy with his brother journeyman, who is ground to the dust. They place a barrier in the way of their brethren by the institution of a second book, in their houses of call; thus preventing many an enterprising man from obtaining his fair share of the trade. The second book system is a mere subterfuge, to keep a number of men in reserve, to supply the calls of the masters in the busy season, and to keep the first book men in their constant berths. The effect of this system is, that young men who have just finished their apprenticeship arrive from the country, full of expectation and hope, join a house of call, pay 2s. 6d. entrance, are placed on the second book; and often times are six or eight weeks before they get a call. The season is now advanced; and if they have six or seven weeks employment during the season, they are fortunate.[139] At length, the summer season is ended; they are thrown on their own resources, dispose of their clothing, &c., to purchase food, become destitute, and are compelled to solicit employment any where, for any price, and are thus converted into instruments of destructive competition against their fellow workmen, by working for eighteen pence per day or less, while the first book are receiving five or six shillings per day.[140]

A month later the Executive Council admitted a weakness additional to the continued exclusiveness of the houses of call. The newly formed sections 'have never flourished, for any length of time', 'although London has, in public meetings composed of thousands, agreed to the principles and objectives of the society'. The lack of 'some connecting interest to keep the men together' was diagnosed; and the remedy prescribed was the opening at 55 Old Bailey of 'a central "house of call" for benefit of the sections generally'. In September 1844 the society was securely established, with thirty-nine provincial sections, yet the metropolitan situation continued to deteriorate.[141] A 'squabble' ensued between the officers involving such 'slander' and 'vituperation' that the *Northern Star*, accustomed to printing virulent recriminations, declined to report the tailors' affairs for several weeks.[142] By the opening of 1845 Parrott had been displaced as president by Thomas Eames, another Londoner.[143]

The 1845 Conference was held in Manchester; and the union's national advance was indicated by the supplementation of the five-man Executive, resident in London, with members from Leeds, Birmingham, Warrington and Jersey.[144] A year later the tailors met in Leeds and the scheme of self-employment there agreed resulted in the removal of Parker – and hence the Protection Society's headquarters – to Manchester.[145] When the Conference of 1847 assembled in Manchester London was entirely unrepresented. Just as the ladies' shoemakers of London had initiated the Cordwainers' Association and by secession or suspension left it in provincial hands, so the metropolitan tailors launched the Protection Society and then, even more rapidly than the shoemakers, lapsed into sectionalism[146] and, with the sole exception of Parker, entirely broke with the national union. The tailors, it seems, were never as successful and the 1847 Conference recommended its component sections to adhere to the NAUT, Parker becoming one of its officials.[147]

The building trades

The third great metropolitan industry, building, was as acutely affected as either boot and shoemaking or the clothing trades by the transition from the relative autonomy of petty production to capitalist organization. In its case, of course, some form of domestic system was not possible. Instead contract work took hold and this involved two processes, separable theoretically, but, in practice, inextricably overlapping.

First, the large building contractor arose disrupting the world of small master craftsmen. Traditionally, a customer, whether he required a house built or merely renovated, would himself engage the individual services of the appropriate masters: bricklayer, carpenter, plasterer, etc. From the beginning of the nineteenth century there developed in contrast, from eighteenth-century origins, the career of 'master builder', a man who would undertake to perform all the operations necessary for a fixed price, 'contracting in gross', and who initially arranged for the specialist labour to be provided by sub-contractors but might then proceed to employ, following the Cubitt brothers, the different artisans directly.[148]

It was in sub-contracting that the two processes merged, for the second – and much more deleterious – tendency was the growth of speculative building,[149] whereby contract work would be sub-let and men on the job driven indiscriminately by overlookers or 'taskmasters'. Thus here also was created a vast dishonourable sector, consisting of the employees of jerry-builders or, most often, of their sub-contractors and those to whom they in turn sub-let, these two groups usually as much working men as the unfortunates they exploited, since they guaranteed to find only (the cheapest) labour, while materials were provided. Sub-contracting led inexorably to piecework, the stonemasons in 1845 believing 'that where one job is sub-contracted through piece-work, ten are made piece work [sic] through sub-contracting'.[150] Since the particular operation was being undertaken at a contracted price, all those engaged had to accept comparable terms, with the concomitant effect that it was completed in the fastest possible time.

In the building trades, therefore, sub-contracting and piecework became synonymous. Society men bitterly resisted the introduction of piecework; but even on the honourable side of the industry their labour, on time payment, could be speeded up by foremen, the most notorious of whom, George Allen, *bête noire* of the masons, provoked the great strike of 1841–2 against the eminent firm of Grissell and Peto, contractors to the government.[151] At this point too the disreputable world of the speculative developer, often without all knowledge of the trade save of the potential profits, coincided, in part at least, with that of the respectable 'master builders'. Pressure was, throughout the industry, being exerted on the worker to quicken his pace and scamp his craft – and the founders of the London Order of Bricklayers met in 1848 'to consider the propriety of taking some steps to check the pernicious tyranny of foremen of works, & the grasping rapacity of employers'.[152]

CARPENTERS AND JOINERS

Of the building trades the carpenters and joiners composed by far the largest section – Mayhew computed that the number of operatives had been 17,000 in 1841, although their trade societies' estimates were substantially lower: 13,820 and 15,000 in 1844 and 1847 respectively – so large indeed that of all the London craftsmen they were only outnumbered by the shoemakers and tailors.[153] They lived throughout the capital, but concentrations occurred in Pimlico, Marylebone and Lambeth, districts surrounding the premises of the leading masters established in the proximity of current suburban development.[154]

The principal, traditional division of labour was that between carpenter and joiner. The rule in the trade was that 'all which the plane passes over is joiners' work'. Most of the joiner's work, 'such as the wainscoting, doors, staircases, mouldings', was 'fine and finicking-like' and at the shop-bench, whereas the 'rough and rapid' carpenter, responsible for 'the larger woodwork of a building' – bond-timbers, rafters, flooring, etc. – was employed on the site. Former subdivisions within joinery were being fast eroded by 'the spirit of competition'.[155] Machinery also was reducing the carpenters' and joiners' crafts, to the extent in 1850, a joiner claimed, of eliminating labour by one-sixth.[156]

It was, however, not machinery that was the great threat to the carpenters and joiners but competition. The rise of the contract system had resulted by 1850 in only 1,770 honourable members out of a total of some 20,000, most of whom worked at not much more than half of the society men's rate of pay.[157] Over the first decade of the century the London carpenters had been able to increase their weekly wage from 20s. or 22s. to 30s. The 30s. rate was then maintained, with small fluctuations downwards, from 1810 until 1853, when there was an advance to 33s.[158] While the principle of 5s. a day (and hence 30s. per week) was the hallmark of the trade unionist in the Chartist period, normally any man was subjected to at least two months' unemployment in the year, reducing average earnings to 25s. 6d.[159] As for workers on the slop side, their earnings ranged all the way down to 14s.[160]

In 1810 the London carpenters had been organized in five societies, combining around 2,500.[161] In the course of the ensuing forty years their strength declined substantially,[162] though the number of their societies proliferated; and indeed the protean institutionalization of the carpenters rivals even that of the cordwainers and tailors. They had, however, combined during a strike of 1825; and a national union, known, interchangeably, as either the General Union of Carpenters and Joiners or the Friendly Society of Operative Carpenters, was established at Leicester in 1827 after a preliminary conference in London.[163]

In 1833 the General Union of Carpenters and Joiners became one of the seven sections of the OBU,[164] £20,000 was expended by the London carpenters in the resultant strike, and its 'odious document' was engrained in the minds of the society men of the late thirties and the forties. Charles Coleman, described by the *Charter* as 'recruiting sergeant for the document men' in that year, was assaulted in 1839 by a hundred workmen on a site in Hyde Park Square and consequently four *non*-unionist carpenters were gaoled. As late as 1846 William Cubitt was able to reduce all the carpenters he employed who had signed the document in 1834 by 3s. a week, this cut not being applicable to society men. Thus Forsyth, lately secretary of the General Union, could argue in 1839:

It was true they were not so numerous as in 1834, but what they wanted in quantity they made up in quality, and the result of the struggle which took place in 1834, was the separation of the good from the bad. They had fought the battle out, and they were now enjoying the advantages of a victory, which if it had not been obtained, would have been attended with the most deplorable consequences.[165]

By 1832 twelve societies of carpenters and joiners existed in London; in 1840 there were sixteen lodges of the Friendly Society of Operative Carpenters alone.[166] The 'United Societies of London Carpenters' had since 1823 held Whit Monday dinners at Highbury Barn Tavern, but organization was limited to this annual event and even this presumably lapsed after 1846 as the *Northern Star* ceased to report it.[167] In the spring of 1844 a Central Communicating Committee was set up by the societies to co-ordinate the carpenters' campaign against the Masters and Servants' Bill. By September twenty-one houses of call were represented on the Committee, yet, in 1844–5, there were at least nine other societies which had not sent delegates.[168] An octogenarian carpenter recalled in the 1890s for the Webbs that in 1842: 'The Clubs in London were very numerous – there were dozens of them . . . does not remember that there was any formal federation or agreement for joint action between them. But if one society struck a shop its members were sent round to all the other clubs to warn them not to work for it.'[169]

London was the seat of government of the General Union from 1834 to 1839, but the society later became known as the 'Nottingham Union' after its administration of 1844–62 and in 1860 the metropolitan carpenters believed it to be a local Nottingham club.[170] The Londoners' withdrawal from the Friendly Society of Operative Carpenters almost definitely occurred in 1846–7. National membership fell from 2,982 in 1846 to 2,174 in 1847 and by 1849 had reached 626, the NAUT lamenting for 'the great Carpenters and Joiners' Union of Great Britain' which had existed in 1846.[171]

Yet despite the retreat from national union, low unionization and the multitude of independent houses of call, Forsyth's comments of 1839 were not without foundation. The London society men *were* well placed: they were able to maintain their wage at 30s. (and increase it in 1853) and in 1847, in their only trade movement of the Chartist decade, followed the masons in securing the four o'clock Saturday, thereby reducing their weekly hours from 60 to 58½.[172]

STONEMASONS

Despite the great numerical superiority of the carpenters, the masons – of whom the *Builder* in 1853 said there were a mere 3,000[173] – were, as a trade, much more powerful. Indeed, the Operative Stonemasons' Society, established in 1831, and becoming a constituent of the OBU, was one of the two or three largest and most successful unions of the 1840s, at the beginning of the decade containing, nationally, 60 per cent of all masons.[174] In 1848 its committee pronounced: 'None come so near in principle to our trade as the joiners, & see how they are cut up into sections – two or three in one town. The consequence is that there is not a more degraded body of artisans in existence than they are. Those societies are useless when called on in time of need.'[175]

Technological change did not as yet challenge the masons' proud position, but they were compelled to conduct a fierce resistance against the growth of piecework, denunciations of which reached a crescendo in the early fifties:

This is one of the greatest curses that ever inflicted its degenerating consequences on our craft. The demon of hatred could not invent a more certain agency for destroying the health, intellect and comfort of its advocates; inducing the cringing slave by the hope of an extra shilling or two per week to sacrifice his strength; his fellow's right; & ultimately his very existence to the mercenary conscience of his Egyptian taskmaster.

By 1856 the Central Committee concluded that *their* 'noble trade' had 'become subject to misrepresentation'.[176]

From September 1841 to May 1842 the masons waged a spectacular strike against the firm of Grissell and Peto. First the Society called out the 222 men employed in the rebuilding of the Houses of Parliament and a month afterwards those erecting Nelson's Column and at Woolwich Dockyard, bringing the total to 375. Blacklegs were employed, but the struggle was then carried to the quarrymen of Dartmoor, Plymouth and Penryn. The immediate cause of the dispute was the more than petty tyranny of George Allen, the contractors' foreman, whose 'general conduct has been so debased as to be quite unbearable. He damns, blasts and curses at every turn; and to terrify us, has made a practice of threatening to discharge two or three dozen of us at a time, if we even complained of such conduct.'[177] Insufferable though this was, the fundamental objection to 'the monster Allen' was his encouragement of 'chasing', whereby the speed of a fast worker was laid down as the standard for the remainder. His attempts to beat down the daily wage, lengthen hours and introduce piecework had provoked a strike of the masons building the London and Birmingham Railway in 1837. Grissell and Peto, however, had continued to employ this highly unpopular – and profitable – intermediary.[178] By May 1842 the Society was forced to concede that an impasse had been reached: most of the strikers were by then employed elsewhere, yet Grissell and Peto had secured adequate replacements and Allen remained undismissed.[179]

The union was temporarily burdened by the financial sacrifices of the dispute, which had also drastically reduced membership.[180] Otherwise one of its few weaknesses in the period was the sectionalist spirit of the London masons. In 1840 some of the London lodges seceded and formed their own organization, the 'Anti-Society' – the Friendly Operative Masons of London Trade Society – which the following year they claimed as 300 strong. They were convinced that 'the rules, regulations and decisions emanating from a country seat of government, can never generally or successfully be carried out for the benefit of those Masons who are employed in or around London' – that is, they were uninterested in supporting either tramps or provincial strikes although they admitted the document men of 1834 and other delinquents.[181] The Grand Lodge moved from Birmingham to London in September 1841, unanimity was achieved during the great conflict which ensued, and when the seat of government was transferred to Liverpool in 1844 Thomas Carter of London was secretary. The Anti-Society not only survived, though, but prospered (until the end of the decade) and when in 1848 twenty-one masons were indicted for conspiracy three were members of the London Society as against ten from the Operative Stonemasons and eight non-unionists.[182] The charge arose out of the masons' determination to enforce the termination of work at 4.00 on Saturdays. They had initiated this movement in the spring of 1847 and their strength in London, despite their bifurcated organization, is indicated by the rapid capitulation of the major employers, among whom Grissell and Peto alone showed reluctance.[183]

BRICKLAYERS

The bricklayers had organized themselves nationally in 1829 as the Friendly Society of Operative Bricklayers, absorbed in 1833 as a section of the OBU and emerging from it in a weakly condition, yet with a newly constituted London division.[184] In 1840 there were five London lodges; and a metropolitan membership of 450 was claimed in 1845 – during a financial year in which the average figure for the country as a whole was a mere 1,369.[185] Unionism within the capital was therefore sufficiently extensive for it to withstand – and eventually profit by – the split of 1848 from which sprang the London Order, in contradistinction to the Manchester Order, of Bricklayers.[186] On foundation the London Order's membership was 115 but by 1853 it exceeded 1,000 and it ultimately became the formidable Operative Bricklayers' Society of which Edwin Coulson was secretary.[187]

Conditions had greatly deteriorated by 1848: 'the men were getting so used to the Flogging System, and the Taskmasters whipping them on, some bribing them with beer'. In 1862 it was also recalled that then:

our trade was a bye word for the operatives in the other branches to sneer at; for, what with the excess of drink amongst the men, and there being no union of purpose, everybody thought the working bricklayer was only just one step above the Railway Navvy. Let the young bricklayer be as decent and respectable as possible, directly he made known his craft, he lost cast immediately.[188]

The bricklayers' basic problem was that their trade was so readily acquired – in 1855, for instance, the twenty-one-year-old George

Howell, within six years to become a prominent member of the Operative Bricklayers, was engaged as an 'improver' at a guinea per week[189] – and it was impossible for their societies to insist on meaningful entry qualifications, the OBS certainly not imposing any.[190]

BRICKLAYERS' (AND OTHER BUILDING) LABOURERS

The low status of the bricklayers in the 1840s is to be largely attributed to the relatively narrow social distance between them and their labourers. In addition to the ease with which a labourer might become a bricklayer, the craft was unusual for the way in which the artisan and his labourer would work closely on the job (e.g., together digging foundations and carrying away the spoil).[191] And in the 1840s there are instances of bricklayers engaging, in most unartisanlike fashion, in assault and riot on building sites.[192] For Dickens the bricklayer's labourer, so often an Irishman, epitomized the lounging ruffian of St Giles: 'It is odd enough that one class of men in London appear to have no enjoyment beyond leaning against posts. We never saw a regular bricklayer's labourer take any other recreation, fighting excepted.'[193]

Yet if the position of the bricklayer was depressed so as to be, perhaps, near that of the labourer, conversely the bricklayers' labourers were remarkable in the 1830s for being organized and taking their place alongside the most skilled of craftsmen. Little is known of the detail but there is agreement that the builders' labourers were unionized in the upsurge of 1833–4.[194] In 1839–40 an Operative Labourers' Society – synonymous, it seems, with the Bricklayers' Labourers of London – still survived. T. Hurly, a bricklayer's labourer, was a member of the provisional committee of the *Charter* and a representative attended the trades' meeting at which the locked-out bookbinders requested a weekly levy of a penny – six weeks later the labourers had subscribed £2.[195]

The wage of a building labourer was 10s. to 12s. less than that of the artisan, which stood at around 30s. for all the crafts.[196]

PLASTERERS

In the early forties there were at least six societies combining 200 men. Although in 1854 there were in London an estimated 5,000 to 6,000 plasterers (working on facades as well as interiors), the union organization was then described by the *Builder* as 'flourishing'.[197] The principal objective was to exclude from the trade bricklayers' labourers as also 'hawk-boys', the unapprenticed boy assistants who were able, in their attendance upon the craftsmen, to acquire a fair knowledge of plastering – for it was from these sources that the subcontractor recruited.[198]

The plumbers (with the glaziers) and the painters formed constituent sections of the OBU, but in these crafts national union did not survive 1834 and throughout the Chartist period they were organized in London in autonomous societies.[199] Because of the original leading of windows, plumbing, painting and glazing were three intimately associated crafts. Plumbers might be admitted to a society of painters or, as in the OBU, combined with glaziers. In general, however, the London plumbers were in separate clubs while the painters absorbed the glaziers and this division reflected the current demarcation of tasks between the artisans.[200]

In 1841 the plumbers had five or so societies, with a membership of 600 by 1848 when one of their number described them as a 'very aristocratic' trade.[201] The *Labour League* declared in 1849: 'The Masons and Plumbers are the only branches of the building trades in London that have any thing which can be called an organization.'[202] Plumbing by its very nature was a craft less subject to encroachment by the untrained, but, like all the building trades, it was adversely affected by the rise of the large firm.[203]

The impact of economic change upon the painters was extremely grave. It is from around this time that casualization of the trade – and prolonged unemployment in the winter – dates. It was becoming accepted that house painting could only be undertaken during the summer (or 'about seven months in the year'); and the 30s. wage of the building craftsman might be reduced for the painter to as little as 21s. *while in work*. Save for the fortunate handful of highly skilled employees who were more or less permanent, the status and earnings of painters were both sinking to the labourers' level.[204]

In addition a traditional occupational hazard for the painter remained: poisoning by the white lead (causing 'painter's colic'), arsenic, turpentine and other ingredients of paints, although this had diminished with increasing cleanliness (plumbers and glaziers, working with molten lead, suffered from paralysis). 'One consequence of this is, that, generally speaking, a Benefit Society will not admit a painter as one of its members, from a conviction that he would be likely to draw upon the funds of the Society more frequently than other members.' As a result the ten or more painters' and glaziers' societies that existed in 1841 appear to have placed emphasis upon the provision of friendly benefits at the expense of trade protection.[205]

The silk-weavers

The immiseration of the Spitalfields weavers during the second quarter of the nineteenth century was egregious knowledge. Silk-weaving had become a major London industry with the Huguenot immigration caused by the Revocation of the Edict of Nantes in 1685. A prosperous manufacture was established, albeit one acutely prone to trade fluctuations, since it was subject to intermittent interruptions in the supply of its raw materials from overseas; to competition from French products; and, particularly, to the seasonal[206] and fashionable variations in the demand for silken goods. For much of the eighteenth century, therefore, the Spitalfields weavers were a byword for turbulence; and it was riotous pressure that produced the complete prohibition, in 1765, of foreign fabrics and then the Act of 1773 which authorized the magistrates to 'settle, regulate, and declare' wages in the industry.[207]

It is from the fifty years during which the Spitalfields Act operated that are drawn accounts of the cultured, almost arcadian, life of the silk-weaver. He would have a garden and summer-house, grow tulips and, later, dahlias, breed spaniels, canaries and pigeons, 'the best "fliers" in England'. A well-known testimony of 1840 lists the societies which had formerly existed: Floricultural, Entomological, Recitation, Musical and Columbarian, only the Mathematical (with which had merged the Historical) Society then surviving.[208]

Although the weavers continued to be affected by all the same adverse factors as before – French silks were smuggled into the country – wage regulation did ensure the maintenance of prices at an acceptable level. There can be little doubt, however, that it was in this period that the industry began its decline and that permanent poverty first appeared. Fancy lines were lost to new or growing centres of production; cottons and muslins were substituted for silk fabrics; and the recurrent depressions of the industrializing economy caused disproportionate decreases in demand for expensive luxuries such as silks and hence wholesale unemployment. Immense distress was experienced in 1816. Average earnings in 1818 were only 12s. 6d.,[209] yet provincial rates might be half as much, and the best Spitalfields craftsmen could expect 20s. to 24s. Silk-weavers elsewhere sought, therefore, the application of the Spitalfields Act beyond the capital. That such a measure remained on the Statute Book constituted a gross anomaly at the high point of classical economics and in 1824 Spitalfields was doubly struck and its downfall assured. Not only was the Act of 1773 (and its extensions) repealed but the prohibition of foreign manufactures substituted, with effect from 1826, by an import duty of 25 or 30 per cent.[210]

By the 1830s the weavers had sunk into incredible destitution, the Broad Silk Weavers Committee arguing 'that since Foreign Wrought Silks have been allow'd, to be imported into this Country, the Silk Trade has been involved in difficulties before unknown, and the Operatives have suffered privations and Distress unparelled [sic] in the Annals of the Trade'.[211] Bronterre wrote of 'these poor fellows being obliged to burn their looms for fuel, and not daring to show their half-naked squalid persons out of doors lest they might be taken up and committed as nuisances!'[212] Lovett recounts a visit to Spitalfields in 1831 with Wakley and Cleave: 'In whole streets . . . we found nothing worthy of the name of bed, bedding, or furniture; a little straw, a few shavings, a few rags in a corner formed their beds – a broken chair, stool, or old butter-barrel their seats – and a saucepan or cup or two, their only cooking and drinking utensils.'[213] In 1838 a weaver testified: 'he had six children. They lived for the last six weeks on water gruel, and the preceding morning his wife was obliged to take the shoes off her baby's feet to pledge them to get a bit of breakfast.' Another operative stated: 'he was half famished, and his wife, who was in the family way, was scarcely able to speak to him, she was so faint from hunger – they were almost naked, and slept on a bed without bed clothes'.[214] The following year it was said that: 'many a family do not taste a bit of animal food more than once a month, and that only the meanest offal . . . The chief food of the Weavers is . . . Oatmeal, Potatoes, Herrings, &c., and not enough even of these articles. Clothes they cannot get, and rent they cannot pay.'[215] The weavers had undergone physical deterioration in the nineteenth century and were especially prone to fever and cholera: 'They are decayed in their bodies; the whole race of them is rapidly descending to the size of Lilliputians . . . As they grow bigger, the children look squalid, wretched, and starved. You could not raise a grenadier company amongst them all.'[216] It was estimated in 1840 that not one-third were in employment and twelve months later that half of the looms were not in work and the remainder working half-time.[217] 'A hand of the utmost dexterity and taste' averaged not more than 12s., out of which he had to pay a boy, and another of the most skilled men worked fifteen hours daily for 9s.[218] Although the most highly paid could expect 10s. to 17s., the earnings of the majority ranged from 4s. to 8s. and both categories received wages two-thirds of those obtaining before 1824.[219] Despite the low level of wages the craft was over-stocked with hands, for whenever trade was good it was invaded by outsiders, often Irish, with or without prior knowledge of weav-ing.[220]

Silk-weaving was a domestic industry. The weaver obtained a quan-tity of thrown silk from his employer and returned home to work, assisted by his family, at his own looms – or sometimes looms pro-vided by the master – customarily receiving money on account.[221] Large manufacturers were dominant (in 1818 the fifteen principal masters employed an average of fifty-eight looms) and were growing even larger. By the 1830s there were also thriving 'great mercers or "slaughter-houses" as the trade termed them' – wholesalers or sub-stantial retailers who bought in bulk from the small masters at very low prices. This was a situation that inevitably led to price reductions all round and a new exploitation of the artisan through sweating by the introduction of a working middleman comparable to the 'under-taker' of Macclesfield and Coventry or *chef d'atelier* of Lyons.[222]

The major technical innovation in Spitalfields silk was the introduc-tion by the earlier eighteenth century of the engine loom, an inven-tion which enabled as many as twenty-four, or even thirty-six, pieces to be woven at the same time. Only narrow fabrics such as ribbons, bindings and trimmings could be so produced and when the engine loom became power operated this side of the trade migrated to Cov-entry and other towns. The number of engine looms in Spitalfields fell from about 600 in 1824 to some 100 in 1839, none of them power looms, and wages were reduced by 60 to 70 per cent.[223] Spitalfields silk was virtually synonymous with broad weaving, single pieces con-tinuing to be produced on hand-looms. Two-thirds of the weavers wove plain silks, just over a quarter velvets (the best paid branch) and the remainder, some 500 craftsmen, Jacquard (or figured) goods.[224]

Where silk is concerned 'Spitalfields' refers to a very much larger area than that of the parish of Christ Church, Spitalfields, and includes the entire weaving district which, by the Chartist period, encompassed Bethnal Green, Mile End New Town and parts of Shore-ditch and Whitechapel. In July 1838 there were 5,098 adult male weavers of whom only 415 lived in Spitalfields parish,[225] while 4,232 were in Bethnal Green. In addition the number of women, girls and boys in the industry totalled 4,204 and 894 persons were unem-ployed.[226]

The unique economic history of the silk-weavers was responsible for an inclination to accept the existing order of society and to rely upon the rich or to appeal to the monarch for succour. The Spital-fields Acts were such that they had virtually authorized the existence of weavers' organizations and the Engine-Loom Weavers rebuffed Place when he solicited their support for repeal of the Combination Acts: 'The law, cling to the law, it will protect us!'[227] Public donations were contributed 'for the benefit of the Spitalfields weavers', after their fall, in an unprecedented manner. In 1837 £5,780 was raised by 'Royal and Noble Charity', through a ball at the Opera House for the Queen Adelaide Fund (the Royal Adelaide Provident Institution being established); and in 1842 over 2,000 families were assisted with further monies, £800 of which remained in 1847, received by the Lord Mayor.[228] As late as 1838 some individuals continued to receive pensions from 'La Munificence Royale', the fund established for the support of the Huguenot refugees.[229] In 1847–8 the weavers, by then in a still worse condition, memorialized the Queen on at least three occasions within fifteen months.[230]

In contrast, they had sought to join the 'Philanthropic Society' of 1818 and provided major support for the NUWC and vendors of the unstamped. W. H. Oliver estimates that more than 1,000 silk-weavers were members of the GNCTU, the third largest contingent from the London crafts.[231] The old turbulence, also, reappeared briefly follow-ing the termination of the Spitalfields Acts – in 1828 rioting and clashes with the police caused the City to withhold £1,000 intended for the relief of distress.[232] Around 1777 the broad silk weavers had formed 'the Union', but from the 1780s rival societies existed (although there does not appear to have been any division between plain and velvet weavers) and it was not until the crisis of 1823–6 that unity was again attained.[233] At the end of the 1830s this general soci-ety was entitled the United Operative Weavers of London, publishing in 1837 five numbers of the *Spitalfields Weavers' Journal* and 'consisting of four or five Lodges ... but thinley [sic] attended, owing to the *apathy* of a *few* and the want of funds of the money [sic]'.[234] Through-out the 1840s the union, then known as the Broad Silk Hand-Loom Weavers of Spitalfields, was stable and, considering its constituency's destitution, well-supported. Membership was claimed as 1,000 in 1845.[235] The society was strongly Chartist, save that natural commit-ment to protectionism led to collaboration with the Anti-League, an alignment which was unsympathetically condemned by the Chartist mainstream.[236]

The restitution of procedures to regulate wages had been sought in 1827, 1828, 1831, 1834 and 1838–9;[237] and during the forties the Broad Silk Weavers continued to press for state intervention. In 1843 they urged the President of the Board of Trade to allow the Framework-Knitters' Commission to consider the state of the silk industry. Gladstone acceded to a separate Commission provided it could be shown to be the wish of the trade, but although a memorial signed by 8,949 weavers was presented, no enquiry was forthcoming (the flirtation with the Anti-League ensued).[238] No less than forty-one of the sixty-two broad silk manufacturers of Spitalfields supported the operatives' request in 1844 for the regulation of wages by district boards.[239] Even when demand was high, without a minimum wage, it was the employers who held 'the lion's share of the benefit':[240]

they impressed upon [Mr Gladstone] the difference between Free Trade in theory and in practice. In the former it was beautiful; but in the latter, it was horrid and demoralizing. They showed him that it set master against master, and made victims of the men . . . [Mr Gladstone] inquired whether the alteration in the Tariff had not ameliorated their condition; when the deputation informed him that *their wages had been lowered in proportion*;[241] and that if immediate steps were not taken, the best paid portion of the trade would speedily be reduced to the level of the worst.[242]

Rather than the weavers receiving greater protection, Peel's progress towards free trade resulted in the halving of the duties on manufactured silks to 15 per cent in 1846.[243] By the winter Spitalfields was 'in a more depressed condition . . . than it has been for a number of years . . . more than one-third of the hands . . . are at present unemployed; the consequence has been an immense increase of pauperism in the district'. The union now unreservedly adopted as its motto: 'Protection to British Industry, Agriculture, and Manufactures'.[244] In the first four months of 1848 two-thirds of the weavers were out of work.[245] A renewed movement was launched, in 1848–9, to protect wages directly: the establishment of local boards of trade was again advocated and a Parliamentary Bill drafted.[246]

By the end of the decade, then, the weavers had sunk to a new level of wretchedness, one of their number describing them as 'one living mass of starvation'. Average weekly earnings were down to 4s. 9d., representing a decrease, according to Mayhew, between 1839 and 1849 of 15 to 20 per cent. Weavers of 'the richest and best fabrics manufactured in the trade . . . the very finest damasks and vestings . . . altogether without rivalry in the metropolis' earned on average as little as 13s. 6d. to 14s. in 1849 – and they were currently resisting a reduction of 25 per cent by a 'large house'. John Isaac Ferdinando lamented: 'This system of unrestricted competition had not always existed in this country. In the old times – the good old times they had been not untruly called – under a protective policy the working classes could enjoy such substantive things as beef, bread, and beer, instead of the unsubstantive slops they had now to exist upon.'[247]

The metal trades

During the first fifty years of the nineteenth century the metal-working trades underwent almost total transformation and engineering progressed from subsidiary status to the verge of becoming the pre-eminent British industry. A handful of traditional crafts were multiplied – albeit gradually superseding the versatile millwrights – into a host of old and new specialisms: tin-plate workers, coppersmiths, braziers, smiths (i.e., the workers of iron), whitesmiths, brassfounders, brass cock founders, brass cock finishers, ironfounders (or moulders), pattern-makers, boilermakers, engine-makers, fitters, turners, vice-men, etc. Early in the century the artisans had the whip-hand over their employers, the case of the 'Old Society' of Millwrights being notorious,[248] but in the second quarter such was the state of flux due to expansion and technological development that they had to struggle hard to regain their position. From the 1850s most of these trades were to be numbered among the most secure, privileged sections of the proletariat. Yet down to that decade, after the abrogation of the apprenticeship clauses of the Statute of Artificers in 1814, and with the (temporary) decline in the demand for skilled labour in engineering as machine tools became widely diffused, they were subjected to piecework, 'systematic overtime' and the erosion of apprenticeship restrictions and customs.[249]

Henry Maudslay had a marked dislike for apprentices, preferring to train labourers or semi-skilled workers. Other masters employed men with related skills, such as watchmakers and mathematical-instrument-makers. It was reported in 1839 that Seawards, 'the extensive and respectable engineers at Mill-wall, Poplar', had articled an 'adult apprentice', a 'mechanic', for three years as vice-man and turner at 36s. a week – engineering wages on average ranging from 24s. to 34s. Several years later a smith earning 32s. was displaced by a workman who was to receive only a guinea.[250] Even the metal trades were afflicted with sub-contracting and the tyranny of piece-masters or, probably much more prevalent in London, of foremen. The basic issues behind the lock-out of the ASE in 1851–2 were piecework, particularly in its taskmaster form, and 'systematic overtime'.[251] While some practices could be eliminated through organized strength, others had to be pragmatically assimilated – as, for instance, in the Engineers' acceptance of any who had worked five years at the trade.[252]

In London some very large establishments were built up – the huge concerns, Maudslay's and Rennies', both of Lambeth, employing in 1840–51 1,000 and 3,500 men respectively[253] – and these employed a wide range of crafts. For example, the 'copper and lead factory' of Pontifex and Wood had on its payroll millwrights, engine-makers, brassfounders and brass-turners, in addition to coppersmiths, braziers and lead-manufacturers, and in 1851 was to be numbered with the Master Engineers. So too was the firm of Messrs Shears and Son, employers in 1848 of tin-plate workers and described then as coppersmiths.[254] On the other hand, the drawing power of the cotton industry meant that metropolitan engineering took second place, by the 1840s, to that of Lancashire; and, in general: 'The manufactures in metal are . . . carried on in London on a smaller and more divided scale than in the north, especially those which relate to iron and steel.'[255]

COPPERSMITHS AND BRAZIERS

'Copper is worked largely in London', being 'one of the metals which, for engineering purposes, are most invaluable; arising from its fitness for making vessels and boilers of various kinds' – copper was the most durable, but more expensive than iron.[256] While the coppersmiths and the braziers both worked copper (and braziers also brass) and were organized in one society, the brazier's trade was confined to 'soldering, or as it is more generally termed "brazing", such articles of copper as cannot be joined by rivets'.[257] As with the other workers in metal they were 'so peculiarly liable to attacks of ill health and premature old age' through, particularly, the inhalation of metallic vapours and particles.[258]

In April 1841 the London coppersmiths and braziers engaged in a fierce dispute with their employers over the number of apprentices. By August the society had expended £700 but its demands had been conceded by all the masters save Messrs E. and W. Pontifex and Wood of Shoe Lane. This street was the centre of the trade: 'The labours of the "Copper-smith" are in no part of London exhibited on a more extensive scale than in Shoe Lane . . . in which are many factories for articles of copper, and also of brass, lead, tin, and other metals.' Pontifex and Wood seems to have been the largest and most impressive of these concerns, with hundreds of employees of many kinds, undertaking 'the entire arrangements connected with the "fitting-up" of sugar-refineries, distilleries, and breweries, in all of which copper utensils are used on an extensive scale'. In 1842 the firm was engaged in the construction of a sugar-refinery at St Petersburg, shipping the equipment from Shoe Lane to Russia.

The previous summer the striking coppersmiths and braziers fulminated eloquently against the 'Monopolism, Combination, and Oppression' of Pontifex and Wood in their employment of twenty-three apprentices to thirty journeymen and sought instead one apprentice to every four men in the coppersmiths' department with a maximum of six apprentices and twenty-four men, and no more than two apprentices altogether in the braziers' shop. 'We . . . complain of our employment daily decreasing and becoming poorer, while our employers are daily becoming richer, through their taking and over-running the trade with a multiplicity of apprentices. We look round in the midst of increasing luxury, and we, who produce it all, are the first persons that are neglected.' The company had also introduced a greatly attenuated form of apprenticeship agreement, besides 'employing labouring men who have not secured a legal apprenticeship'. In September 1841 the coppersmiths' secretary absconded with £35 and the strike, therefore, almost certainly concluded in defeat.[259]

TIN-PLATE WORKERS

Tin-plate – sheet-iron coated with tin to prevent rusting and tarnishing – had been used for centuries to fashion a great variety of lamps, candlesticks, kettles, saucepans and other utensils. Until the early eighteenth century London had been the principal centre of tinware manufacture as Britain was dependent upon the importation of tin-plate from Northern Europe. As indigenous production was established in South Wales and the Black Country, London lost its pre-eminent position in tin-plate working (consisting of cutting, hammering and soldering), although the increasing range of articles made from tin-plate (including, for example, gas meters) ensured that its trade remained extensive. It was said in 1837 that 'the great manufacturers in London employ some 200 men each, or more, on very large premises, besides certain works requiring to be *brought up* by the hammer, which they give out to sub-masters in separate shops'. In addition, 'tin culinary vessels' were 'produced in considerable number in minor establishments'.[260]

The London Operative Tin-Plate Workers' Society was declared as 300 strong in both 1839 and 1845, its members' wages averaging 30s. to 40s. weekly.[261] The union's determination to maintain agreed piecework prices led to continual skirmishing with employers who were attempting to undercut the full book price. The society was an avid supporter of the NAUT, represented at preliminary and foundation conferences and adhering in October 1845.[262] The following year, disclosure of financial irregularities by the secretary of the Operative Society resulted in the formation of the rival Co-operative Tin-Plate Workers' Society (with headquarters at the Craven Head, Drury Lane), a schism that remained until amalgamation in 1875.[263] When in 1847 a master near Leicester Square lowered the price considerably for railway lamps, the NAUT itself employed members of the Co-operative Tin-Plate Workers' Society, the marked attraction for the tin-plate workers of self-employment dating from 1835.[264]

BOILERMAKERS

It was only towards the end of the Chartist decade that the London boilermakers emerged as a craft both strong and radical. The Boiler Makers' Society was formed in Manchester in 1834 and the first metropolitan branch, the Rose and Albion lodge, East London, was opened in 1840.[265] By 1847 there was a second East End lodge, the St James, as well as lodges in Lambeth and Greenwich (or Woolwich and Deptford district), and the London membership of the union was declared as 800 (out of a national total of 3,000) compared with 600 to 700 only three months earlier. The Londoners favoured affiliation to the NAUT – as indeed did forty of all the forty-three districts – and Harney presided at the seventh anniversary celebration of the Rose and Albion lodge.[266] The following year Alexander Fletcher, a prominent member of the London society, drew attention to the engineers' lack of inter-trade solidarity and attacked their 'aristocratic notions'.[267]

The boilers, of course, were constructed for steam engines, some destined for steam-boats. Also, as the boilermaker worked in iron or copper plates, cutting, shaping, joining and making them watertight, the craft was naturally extended somewhat to include the building of iron ships. Although in the 1840s iron-ship construction was still extremely limited, the Thames played a leading part in its development – Fairbairn, for example, built more than 100 at Millwall between 1835 and 1850. The importance of iron-ship building to the London boilermakers is possibly indicated by the formation in 1849 by some of their number of the Amicable and Provident Society of Journeymen Boiler Makers, for when it and the Scottish society were absorbed in the main union in 1852,[268] the latter took the title of the United Society of Boiler Makers and Iron Shipbuilders.[269]

The principal bane of the boilermakers, beside high unemployment,[270] was piecework. Given the formative state of both sides of their industry in the forties they adopted a conciliatory approach, while acknowledging that 'piece-work in general is very injurious to the trade'. It was not until 1848 that determined efforts were made to eradicate the practice and it proved, by then, too late to reinstate time payment.[271]

ENGINEERS

The specialist engineering works – and their employees – were situated principally in Lambeth, Southwark, Greenwich and, similarly, on the riverside of East London. The fragmentation of trade union organization (in the case of the engineers alone) was a product of the embryonic character of the industry; and in the 1840s the five principal societies in London were: the Steam Engine Makers' Society (formed in 1824 at Liverpool); Journeymen Steam Engine, Machine Makers and Millwrights' Friendly Society (1826, reconstituted 1838: the 'Manchester Society'); London Friendly Society of Engineers and Machinists (1833: the 'Old Society'); the 'New Society' of Millwrights; and the Associated London Benevolent Society of Smiths (1830). Their combined membership in 1845 appears to have been little more than 1,000.[272]

The decade saw the rise of the 'Manchester Society' (four lodges in 1840)[273] and the drive towards amalgamation. Whereas it was recalled that seeking a reduction of hours in the early thirties[274] had the effect that 'the masters treated their request as a drunken frolic, and told the men they had better have it out', by 1846 industrial relations were such that a prominent unionist (Heppell) considered that the current prosecution resulting from the Newton-le-Willows strike was inconceivable in London. Another engineer judged the source of their present strength as 'the "Great Strike" of London; from that period we had gone on progressing, and had now become a constant flowing stream, a mighty river with many tributaries'.[275]

He was referring to the eight months' strike in 1836 when several societies formed 'The Committee of Operative Engineers' and compelled 'the "long time" masters' to institute a ten-hour day and to pay at time and a quarter for the first two hours of overtime and time and a half after that.[276] In 1844 joint organization was revived, winning a further concession on hours. This was a significant event since the committee did not dissolve and marks the beginning of the unity movement.[277] The second and third anniversaries of 'the Engineers and Machinists Union' (as it was called in the *Northern Star*) were celebrated in the customary style at Highbury Barn Tavern and White Conduit House respectively; and in 1846, with William Newton as 'the talented secretary to the London Engineers', a toast was drunk to 'a speedy Union of the Societies of our Trade in Great Britain and Ireland', but London's appeal for amalgamation was rejected by the national societies.[278] Earlier that year the engineers and smiths, together with the pattern-makers and boilermakers, gained the short Saturday and thereby a general 58½-hour week, the ironfounders having led the way several months previously with a two-day strike.[279] The Londoners were therefore well positioned to throw their weight in support of the indicted Newton engineers during the winter and spring of 1846–7 and thereafter take a lead – late in 1848 their 'Central Committee' launched a campaign for the abolition of systematic overtime – in the proceedings resulting in the creation of the ASE in 1851.[280]

The furniture trades

The furniture trade was the fourth major London industry to be racked by the onslaught of a dishonourable sector. Whereas in a country town not only would a cabinet-maker produce all kinds of furniture, but cabinet-making might be combined with joinery, in the capital furniture was made by a series of distinct specialists: cabinet-makers, chair-makers, bedstead-makers, French-polishers, upholsterers, and carvers and gilders.[281]

General cabinet-makers were 'employed upon all the large work ... tables, chiffoniers, bookcases, wardrobes, sideboards, chairs, sofas, couches and bedsteads', while fancy cabinet-makers were 'the "small workers" of the trade, manufacturing the lighter articles, such as desks, dressing-cases, work-tables, and boxes, cribbage and chess boards, tea-caddies and tea-chests, &c.'.[282] Adding the chair-makers (a total of 1,325) and bedstead-makers (296) and deducting independent masters Mayhew calculated that in 1841 there were approximately 7,500 cabinet-makers. In 1850 they were organized, without correspondence with the provincial trade, in five societies: the West End General Cabinet-Makers (300); East End General Cabinet-Makers (140); Fancy Cabinet-Makers (47), of the 'Middle' district, or Clerkenwell; and Chair-Makers (130) and Bedstead-Makers (25), both situated in East London – a drastic decline from the twenty societies of 1833.[283]

Society men earned for a sixty-hour week a *minimum* of 30s. or 32s., based on the 600-page price-book of 1811,[284] since when wages had been unchanged. The book was maintained with 'very little alteration' until 1866 for the West End men; it was their exclusive society to which Lovett had the good fortune to gain admittance in the 1820s (and even more so to become their president). In 1850 their wage was 32s. with additional, elaborately specified, 'extras' for particular ornamentations. In contrast the East End General Cabinet-Makers – and the centre of the furniture trades was fast beginning to shift from Soho to Shoreditch, in and around Curtain Road[285] – received 30s. and when on piecework were paid by the job, thereby losing 'extras'. The Chair-Makers (who received 'extras') and Bedstead-Makers each earned standard wages of 32s. As their numbers indicate the Fancy

Cabinet-Makers were in the weakest position: they 'very rarely' obtained their 'legitimate' wages of 30s. – 20s. was a good sum – worked mainly at home and were most prone to the incursions of the slop trade. But as Lovett's experiences testify general cabinet-making was far from immune.[286] Good West-End shops in 1836 would pay 65s. for a loo table and 'linendrapers' or 'carpet-sellers' only 21s. By 1850 the price might be as low as 5s.; and the unresting slaves of the slaughter-houses were earning between 10s. and 25s. per week.[287]

East London cabinet- and chair-makers had joined the GNCTU;[288] but afterwards the societies of the cabinet-makers proper evinced no support for Chartism or radical trade union developments until 1848.[289] Mayhew was told that the general cabinet-makers 'care little' about politics and that the fancy cabinet-makers were 'far less political than they used to be'.[290] Only the London Chairmakers and Carvers affiliated to the NAUT, which successfully mediated when the employees of a Tabernacle Row chair and sofa manufacturer struck.[291]

French-polishing was still of recent introduction and not until the early 1850s is there evidence that a society – in fact, several – existed.[292] In the mid-twenties the upholsterers were regarded as superior to most other artisans and charged 'enormous premiums' for admission to apprenticeship. 'The most important part' of their work was 'arranging draperies for window curtains' and they were 'often required to cut out carpets'; but they also worked in conjunction with cabinet- and bedstead-makers and, in 1837, Whittock and his collaborators treated the 'Cabinet-maker and Upholsterer' as a combined trade. The competition of 'large houses' of linen drapers (coinciding with a great increase in demand on account of the developing taste for elaborate upholstery) led to a dramatic deterioration in the workmen's position. In 1846 London upholsterers were 'working for themselves'; and it was the unemployed members of the Upholsterers' Institute who in 1848 convened the Metropolitan Trades Delegates' meetings.[293]

Of the several furniture trades only the carvers and gilders were consistently radical.[294] They had constituted a (small) lodge of the GNCTU; one society 'approved' of the Charter as early as August 1838; although the attempt to introduce the Charter as a trade measure failed, a carvers and gilders' locality was formed in 1842; two societies were represented at the foundation conference of the NAUT; and their voices were prominent at a Trades' Delegate meeting in 1848.[295] During 1833–40 three societies existed. By 1844–5 there were six: Phoenix, Stacey Street; King's Arms, Poland Street; Golden Lion, Wardour Street; George and Dragon; Green Man, Berwick Street (fifty); and Three Tuns (thirty-one).[296] The carvers who worked in conjunction with cabinet- and chair-makers[297] were seldom connected with the separate craft of carving and gilding, as much allied to house-painting, and which proved the *gilt* frames (carved or moulded) for mirrors, fixed permanently on walls, and for pictures and the gilding in interior decoration. The society men insisted, in 1840, on a minimum wage of 30s., but others had to accept 20s. 'A great number of workmen' were 'chamber masters': 'This mode of doing business has largely increased within a few years.'[298]

The hatters

Hats were manufactured 'to a greater extent in London than any-where else';[299] and the 3,500 hatters were one of the most localized of metropolitan trades.

At about the end of the last century and the beginning of the present, the 'Maze' . . . Tooley Street, the northern end of Bermondsey Street, and other streets in the immediate vicinity, formed the grand centre of the hat-manu-facture in London; but since then some commercial motive-power has exerted a leverage which has transferred nearly the whole assemblage farther westward.

Thus, by the 1840s, hatting was largely contained within the area between Borough High Street and Blackfriars Road, though some establishments remained in Bermondsey, including 'the largest in the world'.[300]

The hatters' was a fashion trade and therefore subject to seasonal employment.[301] Additionally, a change in hat-style could entail radical adjustment in labour or skills.[302] The supersession during the forties of 'stuff' by silk hats involved so complete an alteration of manufacturing techniques 'that old hands, when they could not get employment in "stuff", had almost to re-learn their craft on "silk." ' In stuff (or beaver) hats, fur from beaver, musquash or coypu adhered to a body of 'fine wool and coarse fur' in the process of 'felting', whereas silk or velvet hats had a body of 'coarse felted wool, or of some light material such as willow or stiffened cambric' to which a hood of silk plush was joined with a heated iron. By 1850 the use of beaver skins had declined to one-twentieth of what it had been twelve years earlier; and, for example, a stuff body maker earned, on average, 36s. in contrast to the 55s. to 60s. of twenty years before. Yet in 1841 stuff hatters still held their own despite the cheapness of the alternative headgear (which demanded considerably less craft) and not less than 500 remained in union as late as 1853.[303]

The trade was also weakened by its division into the 'fair' (honour-able) and 'foul' (slop). This nomenclature dated from at least the 1820s, when it simply referred to the observation of apprenticeship regulations. By the forties, however, the gravamen was of primary

199

import to silk hatters, for the thousand or so 'foul' 'little masters' of 1850 manufactured silk hat bodies alone. They averaged but 10s. to 12s. per week, while earnings in the 'fair' trade ranged from 30s. to 40s. according to the particular skill – and the principal sweated occupations could be named as shoemaking, tailoring, shirtmaking and hatting.[304]

On the other hand, the Hatters' Society was a well-organized national union (possibly the oldest in England), limiting every master, however many men he employed, to only two apprentices.[305] Although there is no record of trade disputes in London in the Chartist period, the union pursued a militant policy throughout the country and in Southwark (and Bermondsey) the hatters were active not only in politics but in inter-trade movements. Hence £17,000 was expended on the (unsuccessful) Lancashire strike of 1840; and it was at a meeting convened by the journeymen hatters' committee that the Duncombe Testimonial Committee was initiated.[306] Separate societies of stuff hatters and silk hatters existed;[307] and, despite the strain induced by the commercial rivalry of their respective products, cohered through a joint committee, the Hatters' Society. This body, inaugurated perhaps in 1759, continued in the latter decades of the century as the union of silk hatters and exercised, according to the Booth Survey, 'almost despotic power' in that branch of the industry.[308]

The leather trades

The leather trades were principally conducted south of the Thames; and there were agglomerated in Bermondsey, 'that land of leather, that region of skins and pelts', which 'has been for many years the principal seat of the leather-manufacture in England,[309] and derives from this circumstance a character and appearance different from those presented by any other district in London.' The special architectural features were the tanyards with towering chimneys and low sheds surrounding the pits, 'filled to the brink with a dark, chocolate-coloured, thick liquid'; the 'long, and somewhat high, and always black' drying-lofts of tanneries, curriers' and leather dressers'; and the lofty stone wool-warehouses.[310]

The broad, but fundamental, distinction, from which the differentiation of the leather crafts largely derived, was between *hides* – the skins of oxen, bulls, cows, horses, etc. – and *skins,* those of calves, sheep, goats, pigs, etc.[311]

All the London tanneries but one were in Bermondsey where tanning 'is carried on to a greater extent . . . than in any other part of the kingdom'.[312] Tanners converted hides into leather in three stages, none requiring especial skill. The hides were stripped of hair and flesh by beam-men and prepared for the yard-men, who placed them in the tan-pits. This process of steeping was lengthy, lasting for months and sometimes for as long as two years. Finally the hides were passed to shed-men, who hung them to dry and beat and/or rolled them. Mayhew found average wages ranging from 18s. for yard-men to between 21s. to 25s. for shed work. There was a national union (formed in 1822) whose three London branches had 272 members in 1850.[313] Although the tanners had formed a lodge of the GNCTU and seventeen had been sentenced to imprisonment after striking in 1834, for the next fifteen years at least they resorted to neither major trade nor other action.[314]

Hides which had been merely tanned were primarily used for the soles of boots and shoes. If the leather was for shoe uppers or to be used by saddlers or coachbuilders, it had also to be curried. Curriers softened, shaved, smoothed, coloured, etc., leather through a variety of means. Of the leather manufacturers it was only the curriers who, although Bermondsey was their 'headquarters', worked in considerable numbers elsewhere. Their wages, agreed in 1812, remained unchanged in 1850 – the very best earnings being from 30s. to 42s. – except that 'black' masters employed 'slushers' (non-society men) at lower prices. This was 'the great grievance' of the honourable or 'fair' trade, but the curriers were as little disposed to radical action as the tanners; although there were many small disputes, no general turn-out occurred between 1812 and 1877.[315] The London society, part of a federal union established in the later eighteenth century (and reorganized in 1843 – or 1845), was 'the largest & richest' in the country, numbering 1,200 in 1850.[316]

From 1603 to 1830 combination of tanning and currying on the same premises was forbidden by law. On repeal of the act, however, vertical integration in the industry developed only gradually.[317]

Skins, being thinner than hides and some arriving in Bermondsey already cured, were the province of the leather dressers, who employed sumach, alum and oil, but not the oak-bark of the tanners, in the preparation of their leathers. The leather dresser *tout court* dealt with the goat and kid skins, grounders scraped them clean, while finishers coloured and otherwise fitted them for use. In 1850 a finisher could earn £2 a week regularly, whereas twelve years previously he had made 50s. or £3; and about 100 of the leather dressers were society men, with twice as many 'blacks'.[318]

An important branch of leather dressing was the Morocco trade, many of the goat-skins prepared for ladies' shoemakers, upholsterers and bookbinders still being imported from North Africa. There was a fivefold division in the trade: skinners removed the hair, puremen treated the skins with pure (dogs' or bird dung) and sumach, shavers equalized their thickness, dyers coloured them (this work was the finishers' until the strike of 1843) and finishers, whose craft was the most skilled and laborious, gave the leather its grained appearance. Roans (imitation Morocco) – for 'common bookbinding, hat-linings, pocket-books, work-box covers, and other cheap purposes' – were prepared by a similar, though less exacting, process after a sheepskin had been split into two thinner skins. There were fifty society and one hundred non-society men in 1850, when unionists' wages were about the same as curriers', a Morocco leather finisher, in good employment, receiving an average of 30s.

Finishers traditionally employed a grooved wooden roller. But the Webbs were informed of the demise of 'an old tramping society which had its Head Quarters in London . . . & which was very powerful in the Trade'; for:

In 1843 the first machinery was invented & brought into the Trade. The old London Society determined to oppose its introduction by every possible means & struck against it all over the country spending very large sums of money in the attempt. But they were defeated. Outsiders & unskilled men were brought in & supplanted the old ones & the old Society was completely smashed.

From 1844 to 1846 there was no national organization (and a reduction was enforced in 1845) and when in 1846 the Londoners attempted to reconstitute the union many country towns, disgusted with the recent failure, supported a rival society based in Leeds. Mayhew reported in 1850:

In this department of the leather trade, the system of little masters and of hawking prevails rather extensively. In some establishments when the slack time comes, hands are discharged, and being unable to get work elsewhere, or preferring as some do to work on their own account, wretched as is their remuneration, they start to 'make for hawking'.[319]

It is difficult to distinguish always between the leather finishers *tout court* and the Morocco leather finishers. The reports are that it was a majority of 'the leather finishers' trade' who resolved to found a Chartist locality.[320] Otherwise it was the Morocco leather finishers who were exemplary radicals. In 1839, when there were two metropolitan societies, 'the London Trade' donated £7 to the Chartist Convention. They were represented at the preliminary meeting and inaugural conference of the NAUT (when they numbered 156); and a member, Frederick Green, was soon elected to the Central Committee.[321]

The printing and book trades

Whether we regard the arrangements connected with the printing of a book, of a newspaper, or of parliamentary proceedings, London undoubtedly takes the lead among the cities of the empire. In no other British town or city are there printing-offices on so large a scale, or so many printing-machines congregated in one spot, or so many workmen contributing to this object by their combined exertions . . . The binding of books is, like the printing, a department of labour essentially metropolitan.[322]

The printing trade was concentrated in the centre: the western part of the City – Fleet Street was already very important – Holborn, the Strand and St Martin's Lane; and bookbinding was situated in the same area or, on its periphery, in Soho and Clerkenwell.[323] Despite the large number of operatives, their economic vicissitudes in the period and general intellectualism (or maybe on account of this factor), the trades remained comparatively remote from radical political or industrial action.

In 1834 two rival clubs had coalesced to form the London Union of Compositors, whose membership peaked at around 2,000 in 1836 but had fallen to 600 by 1844 when it joined, at the outset, the first countrywide union, the National Typographical Association. It now became the London Society of Compositors and within the first month more than 1,400 joined, a maximum of 2,200 being reached in 1846. During 1847–8 the Association fell apart; the London Society of Compositors withdrew in 1848, reconstituted itself under this name and proceeded to organize London in isolation from the rest of the country. Initial membership was 1,100, though it reached 2,600 in 1853. This secession, for once, was not an instance of metropolitan separatism, nor – in the early years, at least – was the refusal of the Londoners to adhere to the reorganized Typographical Association of 1849.[324]

The principal disputes of the Chartist years were minor but frequent and 'crippled' the society's means.[325] Compositors were usually paid by the piece (per 1,000 letters). In 1838–9, there was a flare-up of the standing problem of periodical wrappers, in which there was 'fat', for the men charged full prices even though only minor alterations for each issue might be made to existing formes. They now con-

ceded three out of the four pages of a cover.[326] Another brief, partial strike occurred in 1845 over the issue of 'Appeal Cases' (the printing of appeals to the House of Lords).[327] The implementation of stern new apprenticeship regulations produced a strike in 1846–7 and an experiment in self-employment, since about twenty strikers with fifteen unemployed members launched the weekly *People's Newspaper*, which ran from May to August 1847.[328] During the strike of 1838–9 average earnings of 20s. (for 'by far the greater number') and 27s. were claimed; but: 'Almost any compositor can earn about thirty shillings per week, if in full work. A clean and quick compositor may on some works earn from two to three pounds.' Men on 'the establishment' were paid the weekly wage of 26s. – which a piece-hand would expect to exceed.[329]

Compositors confronted two major problems: overmanning and hence unemployment. Inability to limit apprentices, as the industry expanded tremendously in the course of the century (gross output in letterpress printing doubled between 1831 and 1851),[330] led to an escalating labour supply.[331] The number of all printing workers aged over twenty rose from 3,628 in 1831 to 5,533 (and 1,020 under twenty) in 1841 to 8,077 (and 2,228 under twenty) in 1851.[332] October to March was the brisk period for the book trade, but the lengthy parliamentary recess curtailed government work in the last quarter of the year. The problems caused by such seasonality of employment were aggravated by instability within, as well as outside, the industry. In the Chartist decade there are repeated laments of extensive unemployment, markedly in the traditionally good autumn season (in October 1841 there were 1,200 compositors out of work).[333] The authority on the history of metropolitan printing believes that conditions were never worse than during the decade from 1826 and that only a gradual improvement followed.[334]

The compositors had not been unsympathetic to the developments of 1833–4.[335] The Londoners represented the National Typographical Association at the inaugural conference of the NAUT and Robert Thompson became a member of the provisional Central Committee, although the Association declined to affiliate by an overwhelming majority.[336] William Edwards and Thompson, Secretary and Registrar respectively of the LUC, were members of the *Operative*'s Committee of Management; and Edward Edwards, then secretary of the LSC, was chairman of the Metropolitan Trade Delegates of 1848.[337]

Compositors set and distributed the type; it was pressmen (the printers proper – and letterpress printers as distinct from those in the copper plate branch) who worked the presses by hand and produced the printed page. There were said in 1838 to be 1,000 (and 850 men with 450 boys in 1850) who could earn 30s. to 25s. in full work, but the introduction of printing-machines (from 1814 by *The Times*) was savagely reducing their proportion in the trade. 'It is only for short numbers, for very fine work, and in offices too small to keep a machine, that they can now find employment.' A Grand Lodge of Operative Letterpress Printers was formed in 1834, with Hartwell as secretary, and ran a Union Printing Office. While their difficulties were probably the greatest of any afflicting the printing and book trades, they were inactive throughout the 1840s, although the London Union of Pressmen dated from 1834 (and by 1849 had split in two).[338]

The very first stage in the printing process was, of course, the casting of the type, although by the nineteenth century the craft of type-founding was 'now almost invariably separated' from that of the printer (and could have been considered, with justification, with the metal trades above). The work was unhealthy for type was cast from lead and antimony, rubbing and dressing resulted in the inhalation of metallic dust and an extreme temperature was necessitated by the molten metal – no benefit society would accept a type-founder as member.[339] The principal London masters were in intermittent combination between 1793 and 1820, primarily to combat Scottish price-cutting, and crushed a strike and formation of a society by the journeymen in 1818, when the existence of garret-masters was noted – but the real threat to the workmen continued to come from the large capitalists. A renewed society fought a reduction for at least four months in 1837 and an even longer contest ensued in 1843–4. By 1853 the trade appears to have been highly unionized – 680 men were organized in two societies.[340]

After several leading employers had come together again (to drive their competitors from the market), on 1 July 1843 they demanded reductions of 10–20 per cent to which the journeymen acquiesced. Before this 'a crack workman' could average no more than 25s., wages always having been below 'the general standard', and now 18s. became the norm. When the masters proceeded, immediately, to submit a further list of price reductions of 23–75 per cent, up to one hundred type-founders of the three London firms resisted, together with eighty in Sheffield. The Sheffield men were victorious after twelve weeks, but the London strike dragged on into 1844 and after six months an exercise in self-employment, the Operatives' Type-Foundry Association, under the patronage of W. B. Ferrand, was launched.[341] It is scarcely surprising that the London society decided to join the NAUT – though only as late as 1847[342] – or that they had made a donation to the Second Chartist Convention.[343]

With the exception of the masons' strike of 1841–2, the longest, fiercest and most extensive trade dispute of the Chartist decade occurred at the very outset. This was the lock-out in 1838–9 of 250 bookbinders by members of the Masters' Association, which had been formed in February 1837. The principle at stake concerned the proportion of apprentices to journeymen. The scale recognized by the union was one to one; two to six; three and one son to ten; four to fifteen; five to twenty; six to twenty; seven to forty; and eight and two sons to fifty. Here the scale ended, although the two largest houses, those of Westley, Son & Jarvis[344] and Remnant & Edmonds, each employed from ninety to one hundred men. There had been pressure on the apprentice–journeyman ratio from early in the century; and 1838 had seen several skirmishes on the issue, which was becoming increasingly important for the masters given the financial incentives to develop the mass-production of books.[345] The lock-out was therefore the culmination of minor but continuous altercations between employers and journeymen and was equally a struggle between the large and small masters – the 'unassociated masters' proceeded to form a Friendly Society which gave vehement support to the men.

The dispute originated on 15 December 1838 in a Blackfriars shop and eleven men quit their employment. As a result Westley's, Remnant's and a third substantial employer, Leighton & Eales, told their bookbinders that they would be dismissed if they did not leave the trade society; and sixteen men appeared at the Guildhall on 7 and 9 January on charges of conspiracy. First with the support, and even pressure, of their customers (the publishers and booksellers) and then by using blackleg labour to keep them content, the four employers, with the backing of the Masters' Association, were enabled to prolong their offensive. The ability of the journeymen to resist was grounded upon inter-trade solidarity, for initially their funds were 'exceedingly low', 'not more than £150', and the final cost to the bookbinders was almost £6,000. A compromise, very much to the workmen's favour, was eventually reached on 28 August, with the approach of the 'busy season' when the annuals were printed and bound for both London and American markets. The indictments for conspiracy were dropped and with respect to apprentices the employers agreed 'that they will . . . do that which the journeymen – who have conceded some things in these matters – have wished to be the rule of their trade'. The large masters had been checked, a clear indication of this being the decline in membership of the Masters' Association from fifty-seven to thirty-three.[346]

The Trade Society of Journeymen Bookbinders of London and

Westminster, dating from the 1780s, had 743 members by 1838 in three branches (Plough, Museum Street; Crown and Anchor, King's Head Court, Shoe Lane; Sekforde Arms, Clerkenwell). The conflict of 1838–9 caused the Londoners to concentrate their lodges into one and, also in 1840, to initiate the countrywide Bookbinders' Consolidated Union; but, weighted with financial liabilities and producing some ill-feeling, they defected as the London Consolidated Society of Journeymen Bookbinders from the national union before the end of the year.[347] The capital's isolation was shortly to descend into factionalism. The craft consisted of three principal stages: 'making-up' – folding and sewing the sheets ('almost invariably' performed by women); 'forwarding' – covering the book in either leather or cloth; and 'finishing' – lettering and decorating the volume.[348] In 1844 both finishers and forwarders formed separate Friendly Associations to protect their interests, though within the framework of the Consolidated Society. In 1850 they coalesced as a breakaway union, the Dayworking Bookbinders' Society, contending that the parent society subordinated their needs to those of the pieceworkers. Piecework was general in the City binderies, specializing in the semi-mass-production of bibles and the like, while the best class of work was conducted in the West End. The Forwarders' Association was designed, in fact, to safeguard the 'extra forwarders', those engaged in extra special binding. In 1860 the Dayworkers' Society numbered 357 to the Consolidated Society's 634.[349]

The average wage ranged from 30s. to 2 guineas and, while some bookbinders had formed a lodge of the GNCTU, such was their privileged position that it was admitted in February 1839 that 'there was a time when the trade had considered it expedient to keep aloof from other bodies' (i.e., trade organizations) – in practice until eighteen months previously. The shock of the lock-out of 1838–9 resulted in the bookbinders' radicalization. There were three on the Committee of the *Charter,* including John Jaffray and T. J. Dunning, the two leading figures in the London society (of which Dunning became secretary in 1840). They even adhered to the NAUT – and the Webbs suggest that Dunning's moderating influence may be detected in the document prepared by the preliminary meeting.[350]

The jewellery trades and watchmaking

George Dodd commented in 1843:

Those decorative appendages which remind us that 'all is not gold that glitters', such as chains, guards, rings, &c., are largely manufactured at Birmingham, as well as a portion of the really valuable jewellery: but it is probable that the larger portion of the gold, silver, and jewel manufacture, in its highest and most costly form, is carried on in London.[351]

Goldbeaters hammered rolled gold into the very fine leaf used for all kinds of gilding; and had organized themselves as early as 1777. In 1836 they engaged in a 'severe strike' against a reduction, but had, three years later, increased their numbers from 50 to 150, thereby 'embracing nearly the whole of the journeymen in the trade'. It was observed in 1837: 'The trade of a Gold-beater has been a very brisk one of late years, owing to the increased taste for [gilding].' Wages had been lowered since 1830 by nearly 33 per cent, but in 1843–4 the goldbeaters confronted a further reduction of 30 per cent, which would entail a maximum of 17s., whereas in 1812 they had received not less than 30s. a week. It was therefore agreed to consolidate their two societies into the General Goldbeaters' Protection Society. Not surprisingly, they were represented at the second conference of the NAUT, and had formed a lodge of the GNCTU, as had the goldsmiths, silversmiths and jewellers.[352]

Goldsmiths produced brooches, bracelets, etc., while jewellers both made the mounts and set the gems in those items with precious stones. The other indication of the trade's radicalism was that the secretary of the Goldsmiths' and Jewellers' Society (for the Prevention of the Increase of the Hours of Labour) was on the *Operative*'s Committee of Management.[353] Silversmiths were responsible for plate (but as most of it was gilded they then became, in effect, goldsmiths), small objects of different kinds and cutlery. A notable example of inter-trade generosity was the loan in 1839 by the 160 silver spoon makers of £150 to the locked-out bookbinders.[354]

The jewellery trades were located in Clerkenwell and its environs; but it was for another, related, manufacture that Clerkenwell was renowned: 'it is scarcely an exaggeration to say that nearly the whole prosperity and industry of the district are dependent on the making of clocks and watches'.[355] Of all the sizeable metropolitan crafts this is exceptional in that not a single reference to it has been found in the Chartist press.[356] Although chamber-masters in watchmaking dated from the eighteenth century this did not prove injurious. An equally long-established, minute division of labour entailed that 'there are thirty or forty distinct classes of tradesmen, comprising, perhaps, three times that number of minor subdivisions, all living and working at their own homes'. In this trade alone, therefore – while a 'watch-manufacturer' bought Birmingham or Lancashire movements and hired 'the services' of others to complete a watch – independent specialist artisans continued to flourish (and even as late as the Booth Survey no trade union had been formed), despite the employment by some of journeymen. There were not, in 1842, 'two or three hundred men employed in a large factory, to make a watch throughout'.[357]

The riverside trades

Shipbuilding, situated principally between Limehouse and Blackwall and, on a smaller scale, in Rotherhithe,[358] consisted of a variety of separately organized crafts. Shipwrights were distinguished from ship-joiners in much the same way as house carpenters from joiners – that is, the joiners made and fitted the cabins while the wrights were responsible for the main structure from keel to decks. In addition there were the trades of the caulkers, mast-makers, etc., as well as boat- and barge-builders. The 2,000 shipwrights easily outnumbered the other trades in what was, as regards numbers employed, a sur-prisingly small industry, although London retained its predominance over the other ports: 'The fine vessels for the East India trade have been all along made principally in the Thames.' (It was not until the 1860s that the workforce reached a maximum and metropolitan ship-building underwent a crisis resulting in acute contraction.) Their society was the Thames Shipwrights' Provident Union, founded in 1824 with John Gast as secretary. Day-rates were 6s. or 7s., but as the price of a job was bargained for by a gang working to contract, May-hew found the top earnings in 1850 were 40s. to 50s. a week during nine months of the year (joiners' and caulkers' wages being 10–15 per cent less). He judged them 'great politicians', yet they had evinced little interest in Chartism – their twenty years of difficulty had ended in 1834–5 – and their trade unionism was as placid as it was power-ful.[359] While it is the construction of wooden ships alone which has been considered here the transition on the Thames to iron ships was effected smoothly.[360]

The rope-makers were strangely quiescent throughout the forties considering the disturbed state of their craft in the two previous decades. Lovett, driven from the Cornish trade which was depressed by the substitution of chains (and soon wire ropes were to be intro-duced), was unable to obtain work in London and had to turn to cab-inet-making. The introduction of machinery also caused hardship in the twenties; Oliver has computed 303 rope-makers to have been members of the GNCTU (only 867 being returned in the 1831 Cen-sus); and in 1836 they organized a co-operative venture in the Port of London to provide employment. In 1839 the Society of Operative

Rope Makers were denouncing a further attempt by some employers to reduce wages. From the 1820s through to the 1850s high union-ization was maintained.[361]

After frequent strikes in the thirty years down to 1834 coopering remained tranquil until, at least, 1850. A fourfold division of the craft existed. Dry coopers constructed casks for solid goods; but wet coo-pers were the most skilled as they made barrels for liquids (primarily beer, wines, spirits and molasses) and it was they who chiefly (proba-bly exclusively) constituted the four trade societies, apparently based on the different varieties of wet work. White work produced tubs, pails, churns, was non-unionized and the worst paid. 'Coopers in gen-eral' could turn their hands to all the three other branches and found ready employment in the docks, although dock work, consisting pri-marily of repairs, was almost a specialism in its own right. In 1850 Mayhew observed that only dry and white work had been invaded by a slop trade, white coopers' earnings having been reduced by two-thirds within twelve years – although even the wages of wet coopers on the best work had fallen by a third over two decades.[362]

There were also four types of sawyer, not all working by the river: cooper's stave, shipwright, hardwood (sawing for the furniture trade) and timber (cutting wood for builders). With the exception of the cooper's stave sawyers (who accounted for merely one-sixteenth of the workmen in 1850), they were being 'extensively superseded by machinery'. The fifteen steam saw-mills of 1841 had increased to sixty-eight by 1850 and the number of sawyers almost halved to 1,595. Wages had been similarly slashed over twenty-five years: to an annual average of around £1 per week from 'full double that' in the mid-1820s. The sawyers were attracted to the movement of 1833–4, when their society had 1,500 members. Strikes in 1833 and 1834 had been their last; they thereafter employed 'more conciliatory measures'. The metropolitan society was reduced to 290 by mid-century and the national union, originating in 1824, and of which London provided the seat of government in 1840, was collapsing correspondingly. The Surrey sawyers (timber and hardwood – or 'general') were repre-sented at the inaugural conference of the NAUT and at least one district (not Surrey) became affiliated. It was Mayhew's assessment that: 'As a body of men they are essentially unpolitical. I could not hear of one Chartist among them.'[363]

The bakers

The *Northern Star* assessed baking as 'one of the hardest-worked, worst-used, and badly-paid trades in London'. Ten years before the *Charter* had denounced it as 'this incessant health-destroying trade'; and bakers were known for their pale complexions and greatly reduced expectation of life, 'scarcely ever exceeding the age of forty years'.[364] The journeymen's day started at 11.00 p.m. when they made the dough and fired the oven. This might be followed by one or two hours' relaxation, but at 2.30 a.m. the dough had to be worked, 'scaled off' into the portions for individual loaves and placed in the oven. By the time this was completed it would be 5.00 a.m. At 6.00 or 7.00 the bread was drawn and taken to the shop, a second batch set in the oven and the ferment fixed for the following day. Breakfast was eaten at 8.00 and from then until dinner at 1.00 p.m. the bakehouse and its tubs and troughs were cleaned and the second baking began to be drawn. After dinner there was more bread to carry out, the 'sponge' to be set (for the new day) and various other jobs, all of which kept the bakers busy until 5.00 or 6.00 p.m. Their 'leisure time' was therefore from around 5.00 up to 11.00 p.m., when they would sleep – or drink. There were the two opportunities for naps during the early hours, with the baker lying 'on the top of the trough with a tin baking-pan for his pillow': 'This is called "having a pitch", the word *sleep* never being used by journeymen bakers talking to each other.' The baker worked in an unwholesome cellar and was frequently exposed to the fierce heat of the oven. His single advantage was the regularity of employment, though the average wage was only 20s.[365]

The London bakers had demonstrated interest in the GNCTU in 1835, when they had campaigned against nightwork; but in 1842 they had no local union, only clubs, and missionaries from Dublin and Liverpool failed, despite a warm reception and the formation of a metropolitan central committee, to incorporate them into 'a union of the trade throughout Great Britain and Ireland', for 'the abolition of night and Sabbath working, and other grievances'.[366] An extensive agitation was not initiated until late in 1846 with the visit of a deputation which included George Read, secretary of the Operative Bakers' Society. The new movement had originated in Scotland and its

213

twin aims were a twelve-hour day and the abolition of nightwork, the first of which the Scots had attained.[367] Considerable support was forthcoming from the journeymen and shortly from such figures as Wakley, Oastler, Charles Cochrane, Lord John Manners (who became a vice-president of the society) and, particularly, from the zealous Sabbatarian, Lord Robert Grosvenor. The committee therefore declined to join the NAUT, preferring to work with the latter 'able auxiliary'. The disappointing result was that, when the bakers' petitions were presented to the Commons on 30 May 1848, Grosvenor's motion for a select committee to consider them was defeated. The Bakehouses' Bill for the abolition of nightwork (between 6.00 p.m. and 4.00 a.m.), which he proceeded to introduce on 17 July, was abandoned on 2 August, but Grosvenor retained the extra-parliamentary support of the Bakers' Society and a year later was preparing to reintroduce his bill.[368] By the end of the century, however, conditions had improved only slightly and the legislative prohibition of night and Sunday work was still being sought.[369]

The linen drapers' assistants – and other non-manual workers

The young men employed as linen drapers' assistants put in hours almost as long as the bakers and for the same remuneration, although, of course, their work was nothing like as laborious.[370]

At a meeting in 1825 'the Principals engaged in the linen drapery, silk mercery, haberdashery, and hosiery trade of the Metropolis' had recommended that shops should be closed at 7.00 p.m. in November, December, January and February, at 8.00 p.m. in March, April, September and October, at 9.00 p.m. in May, June, July and August, and on Saturday nights, 'for the convenience of the public', one hour later whatever the season. This merely remained a declaration of good intent for, some fifteen years later, the assistants still worked 'from six and seven o'clock in the morning to eleven, twelve, and often one o'clock at night, with the brief intermissions allowed for taking their meals'; and were paid £50 a year. In 1838 the drapers' assistants began a campaign to *persuade* the employers to adhere to their 1825 resolution and formed a permanent organization, the Assistant Drapers' Association, which was to be not a union nor combination but a society – that is, an 'anti-coercion society' – for they did not have the temerity to intimidate the retailers or provide financial support for any member dismissed for advocating their cause. The city was divided into eighteen districts, each holding a meeting with a committee member as chairman, and delegates proceeded to solicit the shopkeepers for signed assent to the new hours.

Many employers were unyielding, and even friendly ones proved backsliding; and in the following year the assistants dropped the request for winter closing at 7.00 p.m. and contended for 8.00 p.m. and 9.00 p.m. closures (still with the exception of Saturday), continuing to operate the same system of agitation. This steadfast adherence to district meetings, 'addressing respectful expostulatory letters to their employers' and 'putting forth public circulars, stating the hardship of their case' was, three years afterwards, showing definite indications of success. By 1846 the immediate objectives had been attained (and deferential restraint was abandoned in 1847 with the smashing of a window of a recalcitrant Lambeth retailer). The Assistant Drapers' Association had already widened its activities by becoming in 1842 the Metropolitan Early Closing Association with extensive aristocratic and clerical patronage.[371]

Other shopmen – the chemists and druggists, grocers and hosiers – had certainly been stimulated by the example of the linen drapers to seek limitations of their hours in 1838–9, yet their efforts were transitory and none rallied to the Early Closing Association in the forties.[372] Nor did the tens of thousands of clerks stir, even though, as a Chartist correctly wrote, 'A Lawyer's copying-clerk is an ill-paid drudge, verily a hard working-man; he slaves from nine o'clock in the morning till eight in the evening, for the paltry wages of about 15s. per week.'[373]

Labourers

While labourers constituted an important component of the Chartist crowd, they otherwise behaved similarly to the 'white-collar workers' in shunning the Chartist localities and accepting their economic lot passively, although the unskilled too threw up one movement for better conditions.

This exception was provided by the coal-whippers, who, it is well known, received protective legislation in 1843, though it has been overlooked that this was attained through a strike the previous year (their petitioning of both the City and Parliament from at least as early as January 1841 having proved ineffective). Whippers unloaded colliers by means of basket and pulley: baskets of coal were jerked or 'whipped' by gangs of nine out of the holds and emptied into barges alongside. (This method had, by the early-nineteenth century, superseded coal-heaving, whereby the coal was shovelled up from platform to platform.) Despite a series of acts passed on their behalf (in 1758, 1770, 1803 and 1807) the whippers continued to be afflicted by truck, since they were hired by 'undertakers' who were publicans (or grocers and other shopkeepers) and 'only employed those who run up long scores'. The Act of 1807 proved ineffective with respect to truck, but did fix wages (at 3s. per man per score of chaldrons). In 1831, however, both provisions were repealed and the whippers' condition grew desperate.[374]

By 1834 average daily earnings had fallen from 6s. 3d. to 4s. 1d., the whippers rioted and formed a lodge of the GNCTU – it is this union which appears to have been 'broken up' about four years later.[375] In the summer of 1842 the whippers, whose number they themselves always put at 2,000, were in 'awful distress', on 24 August 'a general strike among the coalwhippers on the river' began and at the end of October the men were still out. The whippers proposed the establishment of an office for registration, free 'from the clutches of the publicans', and a fixed scale of prices – they initially contended for 1¼d. per man on every ton, the pre-1831 payment,[376] but later settled for 1d.[377] In consequence the Act of 1843 instituted the Coal-Whippers' Office, jointly administered by the Board of Trade and Corporation of London, and compulsory registration and, while a standard rate of pay was not forthcoming, a pension fund was introduced and the measure gave such satisfaction that the whippers volunteered to act as special constables in 1848. One man told Mayhew: 'When the new system first came into operation, I felt almost in a new world. I felt myself a free man.' In 1851, as in 1830, average earnings were around 16s. weekly.[378]

The ballast-heavers were released from 'the terrible thraldom' of the publican by the intervention of a group of aristocratic and upper-middle-class heavyweights in the early fifties, but the lumpers (who unloaded timber) remained in 'bondage to the beer-house'.[379]

Before 1800 nearly all cargoes had to be discharged into lighters and then landed at the wharves lining the Thames, mostly upstream of the Tower. There were no commercial wet docks until the opening of the West India Docks in 1802 and between then and 1828 the London, East India, Surrey, Commercial and St Katherine Docks were constructed (and not until 1855 did a new company complete the (Royal) Victoria Dock).[380] One result was the protracted demise of the privileged City Porters;[381] another was the growth of a huge dock (and wharf) labour force, largely in casual employment, which was estimated in 1839 to amount to between 8,500 and 10,000, while Mayhew, at mid-century, considered a rough aggregate to be at least 20,000.[382] This 'numerous, but oppressed body of men'[383] remained quiescent until July and August 1853 when labourers struck on both sides of the river for an increase in pay.[384]

There were 50,000 labourers in Chartist London. This total excludes such 'specialist' unskilled workers as the coal-whippers, ballast-heavers, porters, etc., who were returned separately in the Occupation Abstracts of the Census. Of general labourers there is minimal information relating to their lives and work. Average earnings seem to have ranged from 10s. to 20s. weekly.[385]

In 1841 there were recorded as living in the metropolis 2,504 agricultural labourers and 4,785 gardeners. The latter constituted an important occupation of mid-Victorian London (their numbers had increased to 8,650 by 1851) working not only for householders but in the market gardens – of Brompton, Chelsea, Fulham, Hammersmith, Battersea, Camberwell, Bermondsey, Rotherhithe, Deptford and elsewhere.[386] Some were attracted to Chartism; and a Grand Lodge of Operative Gardeners had been established in 1834.[387] They worked from 6.00 a.m. to 6.00 p.m., or even 5.00 a.m. to 7.00 p.m., in summer, and 'from light to night' in winter for pay of 12s. to 15s. In August 1853 'a general strike' to advance wages occurred in the gardens of Fulham.[388]

Conclusion

Conclusion

The traditional conception of London Chartism – as minimal, ineffective, disorganized, passive – does not then accord with the reality.[1] During the 1840s London was a major Chartist centre, with a mass movement from 1841 and in 1843–4 becoming the headquarters of both the Executive and the *Northern Star*. Londoners contributed significantly to the national leadership not only with men of the stature of Harney and Ernest Jones but also with such neglected, yet influential, figures as two of the NCA's full-time officials: Philip M'Grath and Thomas Martin Wheeler. Nor is the familiar account of 1848, as a year of 'fiasco', to be accepted; rather the *Labour League*'s sober assessment:

It was not to be expected that, in the midst of the universal excitement which pervaded all the nations of the Continent, the people of the 'sea girt isle' should escape the prevalent influence. The memorable 10th of April, and the Chartist trials and convictions which have succeeded, are momentoes of the force with which public opinion set in the direction of political changes, and of the fears of the ruling classes lest these changes should be effected.[2]

It was not in 1848, nor 1842, that the capital failed Chartism but, probably fatally, in 1838–9. The course the movement ran in London would seem the reverse of the experience of the country as a whole. So it was in 1848 that metropolitan Chartism was most dangerous, most insurrectionary, whereas nationally the spontaneity or strength of the first phase was perhaps never repeated. Certainly once the alarms of 1838–9 had been weathered Chartism was not again viewed, particularly by the local authorities, as a serious challenge to the state until March to June 1848 – when London was disturbed.

This initial weathering was incomparably aided by the virtual absence of an agitation in the metropolis during 1838–9. 'Why did the Chartists fail?' asked H. M. Hyndman in 1885. 'Largely . . . because they had never touched London. When they came to London from the country the great mass of the people in this vast metropolis knew them not at all.'[3] Although London is indeed not England – 'in all onward movements of the people Paris is France, for the rest of France moves at her bidding'[4] – Chartism stood no chance of success without a substantial metropolitan contribution. Despite their proud independence and initiation of so many agitations, including in effect Chartism, the provinces ultimately looked to London, especially if matters took a revolutionary turn. (As Liverpool remarked to Chateaubriand: 'one insurrection in London and all is lost'.)[5] There was a tacit, pragmatic realization that no fundamental challenge to the existing order could succeed unless the capital adhered to the cause. The psychological importance of London's wholehearted participation in any movement was twofold, for in addition it was both the seat of government and the social centre of the ruling class. The strategic centrality of the city therefore also lay in the physical proximity of any London movement to the nation's moulders of opinion and decision-makers. As the *Chartist* put it:

unless the metropolis be set working, all agitation elsewhere is useless. It is here that the seat of Government is. A demonstration in the streets of London comes before the very eyes of those who make the laws. An atmosphere of agitation here does not dissipate without first involving the two houses of legislation in its influence. A hundred demonstrations in the country are only heard of through the newspapers of the factions, which invariably describe them as contemptible, diminish the numbers, and caricature the speeches.[6]

Early-nineteenth-century London had been seized by three outbreaks of major civil disorder within seven years: the protests against the Corn Bill in 1815, the Spa Fields Riot of 1816 and the Queen Caroline disturbances in 1821.[7] Although Peel made no mention of riot control in 1829, various writers emphasize that the essential background to the establishment of the Metropolitan Police that year lay in the inadequacies of the troops in the handling of the events of 1815–21.[8] It has been argued in Part Three that it was to a great extent the achievement of the new police that London Chartism was contained when it developed riotous features in 1842 and 1848. And it is a commonplace that the Revolutions of 1848 occurred in cities which lacked police forces trained to quell riots and where the governments were reliant on the military to suppress the uprisings.[9]

Besides possessing an effective, modern police, London differed from the cities of France, Italy, Germany and the Habsburg Empire (as well as those of Britain) in at least one other outstanding respect: its vast size. London's population was double that of Paris, which had between a million and one million and a quarter inhabitants in 1846. The next largest cities were Vienna, Berlin and Naples with only over 400,000 inhabitants.[10] E. J. Hobsbawm considers that sheer size drastically reduces a city's 'riot potential', pointing out that, approximately, London ceased to be riotous as its population grew from one to two million during the first half of the nineteenth century.[11] As a commentator observed in 1856:

Those who shudder at the idea of an outbreak in the metropolis containing two millions and a half of people and at least fifty thousand of the 'dangerous classes' forget that the capital is so wide that its different sections are totally unknown to each other. A mob in London is wholly without cohesion, and the individuals composing it have but few feelings, thoughts or pursuits in common.[12]

London's diminishing propensity for riot was accompanied by the increasing difficulty of organizing any kind of metropolitan agitation, however legal and respectable. For example, both Owenism and temperance reform were hampered by the inertia of London.[13] In 1839 Thomas Attwood claimed in the Commons that London had not led national opinion since Burdett's imprisonment of 1810, since which it had been 'remarkable for its soporific character'.[14] So while a strong Chartist movement did take root in the 1840s it was undoubtedly not commensurate with the total population of the capital.

The basic problem confronting radicals, and its origins in London's heterogeneity and fragmentation, enormous population and fast expanding area, was most comprehensively expounded by Place to Cobden in a letter of March 1840 concerning the metropolitan prospects of the Anti-Corn Law League:

London differs very widely from Manchester, and, indeed, from every other place on the face of the earth. It has no local or particular interest as a town, not even as to politics. Its several boroughs in this respect are like so many very populous places at a distance from one another, and the inhabitants of any one of them know nothing, or next to nothing, of the proceedings in any other, and not much indeed of those of their own. London in my time, and that is half a century, has never moved. A few of the people in different parts have moved, and these, whenever they come together, make a considerable number – still, a very small number indeed when compared with the whole number – and when these . . . are brought to act together, not only make a great noise, which is heard far and wide, but which has also considerable influence in many places.

Place continued to observe that in London men were isolated, 'living as they do at considerable distances, many seven miles apart'.[15] Similarly the *Northern Star* ten years later was convinced that agitation 'must be rolled up to London from the country':

London is always the last to stir, or when it takes the initiative, such is its overwhelming bulk, and the consequent segregation of its parts, that no powerful and well compacted concentration of popular energy is produced . . . When you do get a large meeting it is not London, but the friendly parties who reside in different parts of it that are brought together by a common feeling. The outer public is scarcely stirred. How different all this is in a provincial town! There the movement, if popular at all, is a real one, and carries all classes with it. The workshops, factories, warehouses, counting-houses, shops and street-corners, all reflect its influence.[16]

The analyses of Place and the *Northern Star* were enunciated piece-meal by trade unionists and Chartists alike, disconcerted by the problem of arousing the capital. A baker 'expressed his doubts of their ever being successful, London being such an huge overgrown place, that he is hopeless of their energies being concentrated'. The tailors announced 'London is an unwieldy place' and 'London is the chief difficulty . . . a thousand and one interests are in existence, working against each other.'[17] Coombe, secretary of the LDA, considered: 'London is too huge a place to carry out the details of organization, in a business-like or satisfactory manner; and besides, the people are not sufficiently known to, or have they the necessary confidence in each other.'[18] Hartwell, addressing the First Convention, explained that

there was not sufficient consideration for the position of London, which possessed many conflicting interests, where the people were strangers to each other, engaged day and night at their various trades; whereas the people of the manufacturing towns knew each other individually. There are other causes . . . the enormous extent of the city prevents the people assembling and acting . . . The working men could not be concentrated so easily as the people of the country.[19]

If on the level of total, ultimate, numbers in the 1840s metropolitan Chartism was a failure relative to the strongholds with many less inhabitants elsewhere in Britain, in terms of Chartist unity it was, with few reservations, a remarkable success. London's labourers and street-folk were, essentially, uneducated, ill-informed and apolitical – except, as Mayhew makes clear, for their overwhelming inclination to Chartism. As with the dustmen:

I cannot say that they are Chartists, for they have no very clear knowledge of what 'the charter' requires. They certainly have a confused notion that it is something against the Government, and that the enactment of it would make them all right . . . They have a deep-rooted antipathy to the police, the magistrates, and all connected with the administration of justice, looking upon them as their natural enemies.[20]

In contrast, Mayhew reported 'The artisans are almost to a man red-hot politicians' – that is, Chartists, 'entertaining violent democratic opinions'.[21] Inherently there was profound divisiveness between the most skilled and the dishonourable sector of the same craft and between prospering and declining trades.[22] But the stresses of economic change, examined in Part Four, were so great – as the proletarianization of the London artisans was completed – that otherwise disparate groups of workers rallied behind the Charter. Iorwerth Prothero's distinction between 'lower', Chartist trades and 'upper' or 'aristocratic', non-Chartist trades does not give a true reflection of the facts.[23] Without doubt trades, like the shoemakers, weavers, carpenters and tailors, whose members were most threatened, were exceptionally prominent among Chartist militants. On the other hand, crafts which were 'aristocratic' *and* Chartist included the stonemasons, hatters, leather finishers, and carvers and gilders. The bookbinders cannot be realistically designated as 'aloof' from Chartism[24] nor were the engineers unaware of the necessity for radical industrial or political action[25] and, as has been shown, were 'markedly Chartist'. The coopers were scarcely 'aristocratic' but not Chartist; and of trades relegated to the ranks of the 'lower', the painters evinced no appreciable, and the sawyers an imperceptible, interest in politics. Overall, however, the 1840s saw a closing in the ranks of the metropolitan crafts and impressive solidarity in the demand for political and social emancipation. It was only in the third quarter of the century that the labour aristocracy was to develop an exclusive, reformist programme.

Appendix I. Economic fluctuations in London

	Real wages[a] (1900 = 100)	Excise duty paid on bricks[b] (£000)	Ratio of days cabinet-makers were unemployed to those employed[c] %
1834	57.3	15.7	2.1
1835	57.2	17.7	2.2
1836	53.5	19.9	1.4
1837	50.4	20.9	4.0
1838	50.3	20.3	5.0
1839	46.7	23.9	3.2
1840	49.2	26.7	4.7
1841	47.9	25.9	7.1
1842	54.7	26.4	9.4
1843	55.3	19.8	6.4
1844	55.8	25.8	2.8
1845	53.2	31.3	1.0
1846	48.7	33.7	2.0
1847	46.7	34.9	7.3
1848	52.0	19.4	13.4
1849	55.1	26.0	8.3

Sources:
[a]Rufus S. Tucker, 'Real Wages of Artisans in London, 1729–1935', *Journal of the American Statistical Association,* XXI (1936).
[b]A. K. Cairncross and B. Weber, 'Fluctuations in Building in Great Britain, 1785–1849', reprinted in E. M. Carus-Wilson (ed.), *Essays in Economic History,* III (1962), p. 328.
[c]Mayhew, *UM,* pp. 360–2.

It has been maintained in Part Two that while the depression of 1837(–9) was scarcely felt in London, that of 1841–2 was intense and in 1847–8 the capital was struck with extreme severity. This argument is largely dependent on qualitative observations and isolated quantitative claims. Neither of the recognized economic indices for London – compiled by Tucker[1] and Cairncross and Weber[2] – entirely provide support; but figures calculated by Mayhew, for 1834–49, utilizing the records of the Cabinet-Makers' Society, confirm the claimed pattern of fluctuation with extraordinary consistency.

Appendix II. Dates and locations of the delegate meetings of the 1848 conspiracies, with attendance as known

Tuesday, 6 June. Windsor Castle, Holborn. H. Mander May (?), Plume (?).

Monday afternoon, 12 June. Albion, Bethnal Green Road. 25 present. M'Douall (chair), Henshaw, Honeybold, Percy, Pitt. George Davis.

Tuesday, 13 June. Windsor Castle, Holborn. James Bassett (chair), Henshaw, Honeybold, William Lacey, Percy, Pitt, George Shell. George Davis.

Wednesday morning, 14 June. Literary Institution, John Street. 14 present. M'Douall (chair), James Bassett (vice-chair), Child, William Lacey, George Bridge Mullins, Pitt, George Shell. George Davis.

Wednesday evening, 14 June. Lord Denman, Great Suffolk Street, Blackfriars Road. 8 present. James Bligh. George Davis.

Monday, 10 July. George, Old Bailey. 13 or 20 present. Brewster, Lacey, Mullins, Payne, John Rose, Smith. George Davis.

Thursday, 13 July. Lord Denman, Great Suffolk Street. Brewerton, Morgan.

Thursday, 20 July. Black Jack, Portsmouth Street, Lincoln's Inn Fields. 14 present. William Allnutt, Bassett, Battice, Brewster, William Dowling, Mullins, Payne, John Rose. Davis, Thomas Powell (alias Johnson) (1st time).

Sunday morning, 23 July. Denny's Coffee House, Great St. Andrew's Street, Seven Dials. 10 present. Allnutt, Brewster, Dowling, Gurney, Mullins, Payne, Rose. Davis, Powell.

Sunday evening, 23 July. Cartwright's Coffee House, Redcross Street, Cripplegate. Brewster, Mullins, Payne, Rose. Powell.

Wednesday, 26 July. Hopkinson's Coffee House, Saffron Hill. 18 present. Allnutt, Brewster, Dowling, Ferdinando, Flanagan, Mullins, Payne, Pedley, Rose, Smith, Stephens (?), Thompson. Davis, Powell.

Friday, 28 July. Hopkinson's Coffee House, Saffron Hill. 14 present. Brewster, Fay, Ferdinando, Flanagan, Hopkinson, Horn, Mullins, Page, Payne. Powell.

Sunday afternoon, 30 July. Cartwright's Coffee House, Redcross Street. 28 present. Bassett, Brewster, Donovan, Dowling, Fay, Ferdinando, Hayman, Kirby, Lindsay, Mullins, Nash, Nowlan, Payne, Rose, Stephenson (or Stevenson). Davis, Powell.

Tuesday, 1 August. Dispatch Coffee House, Bride Lane, Fleet Street. 34 or 29 present. Allnutt, Bezer, Brewster, Collins, Donovan, Dowling, Fay, Ferdinando, Fuzzen, Hayman, Lynch, Mullins, Payne, Raymond, Rose, Thompson, Warry. Davis, Powell.

Friday, 4 August. Cartwright's Coffee House, Redcross Street. 32 present.

Bassett, Bligh, Brewster, Cuffay, Donovan, Dowling, Gurney, Lynch, Mullins, Payne, Rose, Thompson. Davis, Powell.

Sunday morning, 6 August. Denny's Coffee House, Great St. Andrew's Street. Brewster, Fay (?), Lynch (?), Mullins, Payne, Rose, Thompson. Davis.

Sunday afternoon, 6 August. Dispatch Coffee House, Bride Lane. 24 to 30 present. Allnutt, Bligh, Brewster, Cuffay, Fay, the two brothers Granshaw, Hammond (=Hayman?), Mullins, Page, Payne, Rose, Warry. Davis, Powell.

Monday, 7 August. Denny's Coffee House, Great St. Andrew's Street. About 30 present. Allnutt, Bassett, Brewster, Cuffay, Donovan, Dowling, Fay, Lynch, Mullins, Payne, Ritchie, Rose, Thompson, Warry. Davis, Powell.

Wednesday, 9 August. Lord Denman, Great Suffolk Street, Blackfriars Road. 28 present. Allnutt, Bassett, Bligh, Brewster, Cuffay, Donovan, Dowling, Fay, Flanagan, Fuzzen, the 2 Granshaws, Gurney, Horn, Lynch, Mullins, Nash, Payne, Pedley, Ritchie, Rose. Davis, Powell.

Friday, 11 August. Perry's Coffee House, Church Street, Shoreditch. Cancelled.

Sunday morning, 13 August. Hopkinson's Coffee House, Saffron Hill. Allnutt, Bligh, Brewster, Fuzzen, Mullins, Payne, Ritchie, Salmon. Davis.

Sunday afternoon, 13 August. Breedon's Beershop, Shouldham Street, Crawford Street, Marylebone. 26 or 30 present. Bligh, Cuffay, the 2 Granshaws, Hayman, Mullins, Nash, Payne, Ritchie, Warry. Davis.

Monday, 14 August. Orange Tree, Orange Street, Red Lion Square. 25 or 30 present. Allnutt, Bligh, Brewster, Cruikshank, Cuffay, Fay, Fleming, Ford, the 2 Granshaws, Gurney, Hayman, Mullins, Nash, Payne, Pearce, Ritchie, Scurrey (or Scurry), Simmonds, Warry. Davis, Powell.

Tuesday, 15 August. Lord Denman, Great Suffolk Street. 30 or 40 present. Allnutt, Brewster, Cruikshank, Cuffay, Donaldson, Dowling, Fay, Ferdinando, Fleming, the 2 Granshaws, Gurney, Lacey, Mullins, Page, Payne, Pedley, Ritchie, Simmonds. Davis, Powell.

Sources: HO 45/2410/Part 1; TS 11/138/380; TS 11/139/381; TS 11/142/389; CCC, XXVIII, pp. 733–5, 824, 926, 928, 934–9

Appendix III. Memorandum of Sir George Grey, 9 April 1848

In case, notwithstanding the notice issued by the Directions of the Government, with regard to the proposed Chartist assemblage and procession tomorrow, an attempt should be made to accompany the Chartist Petition to the House of Commons by an excessive number of people, it has been determined that the following measures shall be taken.

In order to avoid as far as possible the probability of collision between the authorities and the people taking part in the proposed meeting and procession, and to enable the Police to act with the greatest advantage and efficiency, it is intended that while a body of Police will attend in the neighbourhood of Kennington Common being the place announced for the formation of the Procession, no opposition shall be offered to the assembling of persons on the Common, provided they do not appear armed and their conduct and demeanour is peaceable and orderly. If however, they should form a Procession according to the announced intention, the Police authorities will give them notice the Petition will be allowed to proceed, but that orders have been given not to permit such Procession to pass over any of the Bridges and that a sufficient force will be stationed at each Bridge effectually to prevent any attempt to force a passage across it.

Assuming that the line announced for the Procession will be adhered to, a strong body both of the Metropolitan and City of London Police will be posted upon Blackfriars Bridge with orders to offer no obstruction to the Petition being carried over it, accompanied by only a small number of persons, but to prevent the passage of any Procession or of any large number of persons accompanying such Petition. If an attempt shall be made to force a passage, it is confidently anticipated that the Police will be able successfully to resist such an attempt.

In order however to be prepared against the contrary contingency, a Military Force composed of both Cavalry and Infantry will be posted in the immediate neighbourhood of the Bridge and on the requisition of a Magistrate or one of the Commissioners of the Police they will give the necessary support to the Police.

Each of the other Bridges will be occupied by a Body of Police accompanied by a Magistrate, and a Military Force will be stationed in the immediate neighbourhood of each.

After the Petition has passed over the Bridge the persons bearing and accompanying it must not be allowed to remain stationary but must be compelled to proceed towards their destination.

If the conduct of the persons whose progress shall have been stopped shall be peaceable and orderly, they may be allowed, on the expiration of an hour after the Petition has gone forward, to pass over any of the Bridges except Westminster Bridge in small numbers at a time in order to disperse or to repair to their respective homes, and parties of Police and of Special Constables will patrol the streets and prevent the assemblage of any number of persons and any obstruction to the thoroughfares.

In order to avoid an unnecessary interruption of ordinary traffic carriages and passengers pursuing their usual avocations may, at the discretion of the Police authorities on the spot, be allowed to pass over the Bridges, but if circumstances should render it expedient, the passage across any Bridge may be altogether prevented.

In case it shall be ascertained that any change of intention takes place as to the proposed route of the Procession, arrangements will of course be made to meet the altered circumstances.

Source: draft copy in HO 45/2410/Part 5; completed copies in HO 41/26, MEPO 2/65 and WO 30/111

Appendix IV. Memorandum of Sir Charles Rowan, 10 June 1848

If it be determined to prohibit the Chartist Meeting on Monday there appears to be two methods of proceeding:

The first plan is to prevent the assemblage altogether on the spot where the meeting is called, by the Police occupying it in force previous to the hour of the meeting, and having strong detachments of Police in all the neighbouring Streets, thoroughfares and open spaces to a considerable distance. This would probably render abortive any attempt at a meeting in that particular place.

The above plan is liable to the following objections the Leaders will be upon their guard, having seen the notice, and with their present organization they may arrange either beforehand or at the moment, to give out another place for the meeting to assemble, say Copenhagen Fields, there will be tens of thousands of holiday people on foot all over the Metropolis, with whom they would of necessity be mixed up in going to such place, and it would be difficult for many reasons to prevent them, or they might arrange some scheme for an outbreak or mischief after dark, or at such a place as the British Museum where perhaps there will be thirty or forty thousand people on that day.

The second plan is, for the Police to give notice to Mr. McDouall that if they persisted in holding a meeting after the public notice they had received it would be at their peril and they would be dispersed. – To have the Police very strong in the neighbourhood, and to disperse them at whatever moment appeared most desirable taking the Chairman into Custody. – In this case it would be necessary to be very decided, it would otherwise lead to the thronging and blocking up all the neighbouring Streets and thoroughfares throwing stones &c, it might happen if they are determined that to protect these and to cause riot and commotion that they would occupy the Houses with such firearms as they may be provided with, and if so it might be necessary to call in Troops in order to disperse them and make prisoners of those in the Houses. This plan would appear to be more likely to succeed than the other to bring matters to a final settlement, and to be more calculated to limit the riot to the particular locality. This is taking it for granted that the law is clear as to the dispersion. –

Source: MEPO 2/59

Notes

The following abbreviations are used in the notes.

Add. MSS.	Additional Manuscripts, British Library
BL	British Library
HO	Home Office Papers
MEPO	Records of the Metropolitan Police Offices
PC	Place Collection
PRO	Public Record Office
RA	Royal Archives
TS	Treasury Solicitor's Records
WO	War Office Records
Webb TU MSS.	Webb Trade Union Collection, Section A

BSSLH	*Bulletin of the Society for the Study of Labour History*
CCC	Central Criminal Court, *Sessions Papers*
Clapham I	J. H. Clapham, *An Economic History of Modern Britain: The Early Railway Age, 1820–1850*
Clapham II	J. H. Clapham, *An Economic History of Modern Britain: Free Trade and Steel, 1850–1886*
ECC	*English Chartist Circular*
Econ HR	*Economic History Review*
1841 Census	*Occupation Abstract, Part I, England and Wales*, 1844, XXVII [587]
1851 Census	*Population Tables, II, Ages, Civil Condition, Occupations, and Birth-Place of the People*, 1852–3, LXXXVIII Part 1, I [1691–I]
ELP	*East London Papers*
HJ	*Historical Journal*
IRSH	*International Review of Social History*
L&S	William Lovett. *Life and Struggles of William Lovett*
LL&LP	Henry Mayhew, *London Labour and the London Poor*
NS	*Northern Star*
P&P	*Past and Present*
UM	Henry Mayhew. *The Unknown Mayhew*, ed. E. P. Thompson and Eileen Yeo

GNCTU	Grand National Consolidated Trades Union
LDA	London Democratic Association
LWMA	London Working Men's Association
NAUT	National Association of United Trades
NCA	National Charter Association
NPU	National Political Union
NUWC	National Union of the Working Classes
OBU	Operative Builders' Union

All books are published in London unless otherwise stated (with the exception of Penguin editions which are published in Harmondsworth).

Preface

1 In Asa Briggs (ed.), *Chartist Studies* (1959).
2 Asa Briggs, 'Open Questions of Labour History', *Bulletin of the Society for the Study of Labour History* [hereafter *BSSLH*], no. 1 (Autumn 1960), p. 2.
3 D. J. Rowe, 'Chartism and the Spitalfields Silk-weavers', *Economic History Review* [hereafter *Econ HR*], 2nd Ser., XX (1967); and D. J. Rowe, 'The Failure of London Chartism', *Historical Journal* [hereafter *HJ*], XI (1968). His article on the pre-Chartist period, 'The London Working Men's Association and the "People's Charter" ', *Past and Present* [hereafter *P&P*], no. 36 (April 1967), is appraised below, p. 241 n6.
4 Iorwerth Prothero, 'Chartism in London', *P&P*, no. 44 (Aug. 1969); and Iorwerth Prothero, 'London Chartism and the Trades', *Econ HR*, 2nd Ser., XXIV (1971).
5 Prothero, 'Movements', p. ii.
6 See Prothero's candid admission that 'this short chapter ... deals with only a few points, and relies less completely on original research than preceding ones', since, he asserts, the events of 1848 are 'so well known' (*ibid.*, p. 259). Prothero's impressive book, *Artisans and Politics in Early Nineteenth-Century London: John Gast and his Times* (Folkestone, 1979), is by no means a published version of his doctoral research, though manifestly inspired by it – for one thing, it ends where the present book begins. The thesis remains essential reading for all students of the subject.
7 In John Stevenson (ed.), *London in the Age of Reform* (Oxford, 1977).
8 This conclusion, originally stated in my 'Chartism in London', *BSSLH*, no. 20 (Spring 1970), p. 14, is not accepted (but, it should be insisted, partly misinterpreted) by Large, in Stevenson, *London*, p. 193.
9 The term is Prothero's ('Movements', p. 259).
10 They are necessarily treated with brevity by Mather in *Public Order in the Age of the Chartists* (Manchester, 1966 edn), pp. 97–105, but their handling by Keller, who takes Chartism as one of her four 'case studies', is plainly inadequate ('Public Order in Victorian London: The Interaction Between the Metropolitan Police, the Government, the Urban Crowd, and the Law' (Cambridge PhD thesis, 1977), pp. 81–93, 105, 110). Large, in Stevenson, *London*, is only impressed by – and therefore devotes any especial attention to – the disturbances of 4 June 1848.

Part One. The character of London and its Chartism

1 See François Bédarida, 'Londres au Milieu du XIXe Siècle: une Analyse de Structure Sociale', *Annales: Économies-Sociétés-Civilisations*, XXIII (1968), p. 271; François Bédarida, *A Social History of England, 1851–1975* (1979), p. 20.
2 See *Smith's New Map of London and Environs* (1848), Guildhall Library, and – for 1833 – Francis Sheppard, *London, 1808–1870: The Infernal Wen* (1971), Plate 8, between pp. 84–5. Cf. Donald J. Olsen, *The Growth of Victorian London* (1976), pp. 187–96. The most useful studies of London's nineteenth-century growth are: Janet Roebuck, *Urban Development in 19th-Century London: Lambeth, Battersea & Wandsworth, 1838–1888* (Chichester,

1979), chaps. 1, 7; H. J. Dyos, 'The Suburban Development of Greater London South of the Thames, 1836–1914' (London PhD thesis, 1952); A. D. Grady, 'The Lower Lea Valley: A Barrier in East London', *East London Papers* [hereafter *ELP*], II, no. 1 (April 1959); W. Ashworth, 'Types of Social and Economic Development in Suburban Essex', in Centre for Urban Studies, *London: Aspects of Change* (1964); Hugh C. Prince, 'North-west London 1814–1863' and 'North-west London 1814–1914', in J. T. Coppock and Hugh C. Prince (eds.), *Greater London* (1964); D. A. Reeder, 'A Theatre of Suburbs: Some Patterns of Development in West London, 1801–1911', in H. J. Dyos (ed.), *The Study of Urban History* (1968).

3 John Hogg, *London as it is: Being a Series of Observations on the Health, Habits, and Amusements of the People* (1837), pp. 224–6; *Charter*, 29 Sept. 1839; George Godwin, *Town Swamps and Social Bridges* (1859; Leicester, 1972 edn), pp. 12–15; Dyos, 'Suburban Development', p. 63.

4 Hogg, pp. 218–20; Charles Knight (ed.), *London* (6 vols., 1841–4), II, pp. 319–22.

5 Knight, I, p. 111. See too M. E. Falkus, 'The British Gas Industry before 1850', *Econ HR*, 2nd Ser., XX (1967); Sheppard, *London*, pp. 183–5; J. J. Tobias, *Crime and Industrial Society in the Nineteenth Century* (Penguin edn, 1972), pp. 221–2.

6 E.g., see Charles Reith, *British Police and the Democratic Ideal* (1943), pp. 250–1.

7 It can, of course, be immensely difficult to distinguish between the influence of, for instance, the new police and that of other, concurrent social changes (cf. Wilbur R. Miller, *Cops and Bobbies: Police Authority in New York and London, 1830–1870* (Chicago, 1977), pp. 109–11; Reith, *British Police and Democratic Ideal*, pp. 218–19; John Stevenson, *Popular Disturbances in England, 1700–1870* (1979), pp. 321–3).

8 M. Dorothy George, *London Life in the Eighteenth Century* (Penguin edn, 1966), Introduction and pp. 158–9, 207–8; Elizabeth W. Gilboy, *Wages in Eighteenth Century England* (Cambridge, Mass., 1934), pp. 5–6, 21–2, 33–5. But, regarding the opinions of foreign visitors, cf. Leon Radzinowicz, *A History of English Criminal Law and its Administration from 1750* (4 vols., 1948–68), I, Appendix 3. An 1840s review of the 'alien' world of eighteenth-century London is provided by Knight, II, chap. 47. In contrast, George Rudé, *Hanoverian London, 1714–1808* (1971), pp. 90–9, sketches a far mellower scene.

9 Collections relating to manners and morals, Place Papers, British Library [hereafter BL] Add. MSS. 27,825–30; also Francis Place, *The Autobiography of Francis Place (1771–1854)*, ed. Mary Thale (Cambridge, 1972).

10 W. E. S. Thomas, 'Francis Place and Working Class History', *HJ*, V (1962); E. P. Thompson, *The Making of the English Working Class* (1963), esp. pp. 486–7. Caution is counselled even by D. J. Rowe, 'Francis Place and the Historian', *HJ*, XVI (1973).

11 Add. MS. 27,828, ff. 118–25, 129–30. Cf. the speculation of Thompson, *Making*, p. 814n.

12 Add. MS. 27,834, ff. 86–7. (Punctuation as in the original.)

13 Add. MS. 27,827, f. 30; Theo Barker, 'The Early Railway Age', in Theo Barker (ed.), *The Long March of Everyman, 1750–1960* (Penguin edn, 1978), pp. 120–1; William Lovett, *Life & Struggles of William Lovett in His Pursuit of Bread, Knowledge, and Freedom: With some Short Account of the Dif-*

ferent Associations He Belonged To and of the Opinions He Entertained (1876; 2 vols., 1920 edn) [hereafter Lovett, *L&S*], I, pp. 24, 32–3. Similar statements are cited by H. A. Shearring, 'The Social Structure and Development of London, circa 1800–1830', (Oxford DPhil thesis, 1955), pp. 358–60.

14 Charles Manby Smith, *The Working Man's Way in the World* (1853; 1967 edn), pp. 261–70, describes (and reflects on) the spectacle in 1836. In general see Radzinowicz, I, chaps. 6, 7, and IV, chap. 8, sect. 5.

15 *St Crispin*, 5 June 1869, 19 Feb., 10 Sept. 1870. See also Rev. J. Richardson, *Recollections, Political, Literary, Dramatic, and Miscellaneous, of the Last Half-Century* (2 vols., 1856), esp. I, chap. 1, and II, pp. 225–6; Henry Mayhew, *London Labour and the London Poor* (4 vols., 1861–2) [hereafter Mayhew, *LL&LP*], II, pp. 47, 54–7; Gareth Stedman Jones, 'Working-Class Culture and Working-Class Politics in London, 1870–1900; Notes on the Remaking of a Working Class', *Journal of Social History*, VII (1973–4), pp. 476, 503 n57.

16 Knight, III, pp. 65–6. (Lynn Lees, 'Metropolitan Types: London and Paris compared', in H. J. Dyos and Michael Wolff (eds.), *The Victorian City: Images and Realities* (2 vols., 1973), I, provides an interesting modern comparison of the nineteenth-century cities.)

17 See pp. 27–31, 221–2.

18 *Knight's Cyclopædia of London* (1851), pp. 484–5. See, too, J. H. Clapham, *An Economic History of Modern Britain: The Early Railway Age, 1820–1850* (Cambridge, 2nd edn, 1930) [hereafter Clapham I], pp. 3–4; and J. H. Clapham, *An Economic History of Modern Britain: Free Trade and Steel, 1850–1886* (Cambridge, 1932) [hereafter Clapham II], pp. 519–20; and, for London's relative decline as a port from 1700 onwards, Rudé, *Hanoverian London*, pp. 28–30, 230.

19 Of which, undoubtedly, a significant proportion were re-exports (cf. Clapham II, pp. 230–1).

20 P. G. Hall, *The Industries of London: Since 1861* (1962), pp. 9–10, 21–3, 114.

21 John Weale (ed.), *London Exhibited in 1851* (1851), cited by Hall, *Industries*, p. 9.

22 George Dodd, *Days at the Factories; Or, The Manufacturing Industry of Great Britain Described, and Illustrated by Numerous Engravings of Machines and Processes. Series 1. – London* (1843), pp. 1–2.

23 For views of London's industries through technological blinkers of varying obscurity, see Clapham I, pp. 67–70; Paul Thompson, *Socialists, Liberals and Labour: The Struggle for London, 1885–1914* (1967), pp. 13–6; and Lees, in Dyos and Wolff, pp. 419–22. In contrast, Bédarida, 'Londres', pp. 272–3, offers a refreshingly realistic and balanced assessment. See too Sheppard, *London*, pp. 158–9.

24 Cf. Gareth Stedman Jones, *Outcast London: A Study in the Relationship Between Classes in Victorian Society* (Oxford, 1971), esp. chap. 1.

25 But see 'A Day at a Hat-Factory', *Penny Magazine*, Jan. Supp., 1841, for the practice of Christys', the leading firm.

26 R. J. Hartridge, 'The Development of Industries in London South of the Thames, 1750 to 1850' (London MSc (Econ.) thesis, 1955), pp. 5–6, 81; Dodd, *Days*, chap. 1 (which provides a fascinating analytical overview of London industry).

27 Henry Mayhew, *The Unknown Mayhew: Selections from the 'Morning Chronicle', 1849–1850*, ed. E. P. Thompson and Eileen Yeo (1971) [hereafter

Mayhew, *UM*], p. 104; 'A Day at a Sugar-Refinery', *Penny Magazine*, April Supp., 1841; Hall, *Industries*, pp. 25, 39.

28 Bédarida, 'Londres', pp. 276–7, provides a useful analysis of these Census data. See also Jones, *Outcast London*, p. 374.

29 *Smith's New Map.*

30 'Day at Hat-Factory', *Penny Magazine*, Jan. Supp., 1841. Dodd's *Penny Magazine* articles, invaluable for their technical detail, were, with one exception, collected and published with an introductory chapter as *Days at the Factories.*

31 So, although of the fifty-three 'legal' brushshops in 1835 only twenty-seven employed five or more journeymen and apprentices and the largest but twenty-seven, it was around this time that 'employers' began to replace small, working masters and middlemen appeared (William Kiddier, *The Old Trade Unions: From Unprinted Records of the Brushmakers* (2nd edn, 1931), pp. 54–8, 66–9, 99–101).

32 *Charter*, 20 Oct. 1839.

33 *Ibid.*, 14 April 1839.

34 *English Chartist Circular* [hereafter *ECC*], no. 32.

35 *Northern Star* [hereafter *NS*], 26 Oct. 1839.

36 Mayhew, *UM*, p. 203.

37 *NS*, 18 March 1848. See also, *Morning Chronicle*, 18 Dec. 1849, and *Reynolds's Political Instructor*, 2 Feb. 1850. These claims are confirmed by N. Whittock, J. Bennett, J. Badcock, C. Newton, and Others, *The Complete Book of Trades* (1837), p. 432. For the 'country houses' and 'thousands' of speculators in shoemaking: Mayhew, *UM*, p. 273. (Mayhew's original articles in the *Morning Chronicle* are only cited when the relevant passages are not reprinted in Mayhew, *UM*.)

38 *Operative*, 16 June 1839.

39 'Poetical Broadsides, Etc.', II, f. 309, BL press mark 11621. k. 5. An expurgated version is printed in John Ashton, *Modern Street Ballads* (1888), pp. 17–20.

40 Cf. George, *London Life*, pp. 164–5.

41 Clapham I, p. 70; Census, 1841, *Occupation Abstract, Part I, England and Wales*, 1844, XXVII [587] [hereafter 1841 Census], pp. 46–7 (reprint of 1831 Abstract); Dodd, *Days*, p. 15.

42 Lees favours the first proposition, but apparently sees no inconsistency in identifying a 'working class' (in Dyos and Wolff, pp. 420–1, 423–4).

43 Bédarida, 'Londres', pp. 285–92. His calculation is supported by Lees's proportion of 79.1 per cent (in Dyos and Wolff, pp. 423–4). Cf. the very interesting conclusions of L. D. Schwartz, 'Income Distribution and Social Structure in London in the Late Eighteenth Century', *Econ HR*, 2nd Ser., XXXII (1979).

44 Hall, *Industries*, pp. 115–17, discusses the London market. See also George, *London Life*, p. 162.

45 Cf. the important comments of Thompson, *Making*, pp. 260–2. Comparable reasoning that industrialization is not synonymous with mechanization and artisan producers can form a proletariat has been adduced in the case of France – and, in particular, of Paris – where sweating and its associated practices also proved a decisive solvent of the traditional industrial structure, by Christopher H. Johnson, *Utopian Communism in France: Cabet and the Icarians, 1839–1851* (Ithaca, N.Y., 1974), pp. 158–65, 175–84; and Christopher H. Johnson, 'Economic Change and Artisan Discontent: The

Tailors' History, 1800–48' (in Roger Price (ed.), *Revolution and Reaction: 1848 and the Second French Republic* (1975)); and Bernard H. Moss, 'Parisian Producers' Associations (1830–51): The Socialism of Skilled Workers' (in Price, *Revolution and Reaction*); and Bernard H. Moss, *The Origins of the French Labor Movement, 1830–1914: The Socialism of Skilled Workers* (Berkeley and Los Angeles, 1976), pp. 9–19. Recently, also, Raphael Samuel has stressed, with impressive detail, not only the sheer size of the non-mechanized sector but the importance of its contribution to the economy of the 1850s and 1860s ('Workshop of the World: Steam Power and Hand Technology in mid-Victorian Britain', *History Workshop Journal*, no. 3 (Spring 1977)).

46 The views of D. J. Rowe – expressed most fully in 'Class and Political Radicalism in London, 1831–2', *HJ*, XIII, (1970) – as well as of Patricia Hollis (*The Pauper Press: A Study in Working-Class Radicalism of the 1830s* (1970), pp. 303–5, and 'Introduction', *The Poor Man's Guardian, 1831–1835*, I (1969), p. xxxix) are therefore rejected. But see Prothero, *Artisans and Politics*, pp. 303, 333–4; also Asa Briggs, 'Introduction' to William Lovett and John Collins, *Chartism: A New Organization of the People* (1840; Leicester, 1969 edn), pp. 9–11.

The case of the NPU of 1831–3, which existed alongside the NUWC, is complex. It too enjoyed mainly working-class support – the overlapping membership of ultra-radicals scared off middle-class reformers – and the extremist small-shopkeeper parish agitators not unsuccessfully struggled to gain control of the NPU, which Place had intended as his creature and which he continued to project as supported equally by both classes (see, for example, Prothero, *Artisans and Politics*, pp. 287–9, 291–3; and, also, *idem*, 'Movements', pp. 122, 126–8; Michael Brock, *The Great Reform Act* (1973), pp. 255–6; Joseph Hamburger, *James Mill and the Art of Revolution* (New Haven, Conn., 1963), pp. 87, 131 n20). The Metropolitan Political Union, in 1830, had disintegrated because of divergent class interests (David Large, 'William Lovett', in Patricia Hollis (ed.), *Pressure from Without: in Early Victorian England* (1974), p. 118).

For Birmingham see Conrad Gill, *History of Birmingham, I: Manor and Borough to 1865* (1952), pp. 91–112, 292–309; the three articles of Asa Briggs ('Thomas Attwood and the Economic Background of the Birmingham Political Union', *Cambridge Historical Journal*, IX, no. 2 (1948), esp. pp. 199–200; 'Social Structure and Politics in Birmingham and Lyons (1825–1848)', *British Journal of Sociology*, I (1950); 'The Background of the Parliamentary Reform Movement in Three English Cities (1830–2)', *Cambridge Historical Journal*, X, no. 3 (1952), esp. pp. 297–8) and also his *Victorian Cities* (Penguin edn, 1968), pp. 186–9; and the three articles by Trygve R. Tholfsen ('The Artisan and the Culture of Early Victorian Birmingham', *University of Birmingham Historical Journal*, IV, no. 2 (1954), esp. pp. 151–2; 'The Chartist Crisis in Birmingham', *International Review of Social History* [hereafter *IRSH*], III (1958); 'The Origins of the Birmingham Caucus', *HJ*, II (1959)). (This orthodoxy is challenged by Clive Behagg, 'Custom, Class and Change: the Trade Societies of Birmingham', *Social History*, IV (1979).)

Widespread use of steam-power by small producers in Birmingham distinguished them additionally from their London equivalents (Douglas A. Reid, 'The Decline of Saint Monday, 1766–1876', *P&P*, no. 71 (May 1976), pp. 94–6). For Sheffield there is only (the admirable) Sidney Pollard, *A History of Labour in Sheffield* (Liverpool, 1959), pp. 40–59. In contrast, G. D. H. Cole, *Studies in Class Structure* (1955), pp. 33–4, makes the interesting suggestion of a connection, by no means irrelevant to London history, between sweating and Parisian *émeutisme*.

47 For which see Lovett, *L&S*, I, pp. 41–54; Prothero, *Artisans and Politics*, chap. 13; W. H. Oliver, 'The Labour Exchange Phase of the Co-operative Movement', *Oxford Economic Papers*, New Ser., X (1958), pp. 355–61; W. H. Oliver, 'Organizations and Ideas behind the Efforts to Achieve a General Union of the Working Classes in the Early 1830s' (Oxford DPhil thesis, 1954), pp. 43–6, 111–23. (Working-class Owenism, in general, is considered by J. F. C. Harrison, *Robert Owen and the Owenites in Britain and America: The Quest for the New Moral World* (1969), pp. 195–216.)

48 R. W. Postgate, *The Builders' History* (n.d.), pp. 56–111; W. S. Hilton, *Foes to Tyranny: A History of the Amalgamated Union of Building Trade Workers* (1963), pp. 34–53; Sidney and Beatrice Webb, *The History of Trade Unionism* (1894), pp. 110–17, 135–6; G. D. H. Cole, *Attempts at General Union: A Study in British Trade Union History, 1818–1834* (1953), pp. 101–6; Prothero, *Artisans and Politics*, pp. 301, 304; *idem*, 'Movements', pp. 164, 171–2; David Brian Viles, 'The Building Trade Workers of London, 1835–1860' (London MPhil thesis, 1975), pp. 45–9.

49 Webb, *History*, p. 120.

50 W. H. Oliver, 'The Consolidated Trades' Union of 1834', *Econ HR*, 2nd Ser., XVII (1964–5), pp. 84–6, but he provides the detailed analysis in his thesis, 'Organizations', pp. 208, 210–13. Prothero, 'Movements', pp. 414–15, gives a definitive list of the London lodges.

51 Prothero, 'Movements', p. 173 (but cf. *idem*, *Artisans and Politics*, p. 304).

52 A 'great strike' in August 1830 had failed to prevent the masters reducing wages (Mayhew, *UM*, pp. 234–5; *Morning Chronicle*, 7 Feb. 1850).

53 T. M. Parssinen and I. J. Prothero, 'The London Tailors' Strike of 1834 and the Collapse of the Grand National Consolidated Trades' Union: A Police Spy's Report', *IRSH*, XXII (1977); F. W. Galton (ed.), *Select Documents Illustrating the History of Trade Unionism: I. The Tailoring Trade* (1896), pp. lxxx–xciii, 179–210; Cole, *Attempts*, pp. 131, 144–5; Oliver, 'Consolidated Trades' Union', pp. 79–80, 95; *idem*, 'Organizations', pp. 166–72, 320–6; Prothero, 'Movements', pp. 160–2, 164–5, 173; *idem*, *Artisans and Politics*, pp. 300–4.

54 Lovett, *L&S*, I, pp. 38–9; Webb, *History*, p. 132; Trades Union Congress, *The Book of The Martyrs of Tolpuddle, 1834–1934: The Story of the Dorsetshire Labourers Who Were Convicted and Sentenced to Seven Years' Transportation for Forming a Trade Union* (1934), pp. 63–6; Cole, *Attempts*, p. 129; Oliver, 'Consolidated Trades' Union', p. 85; Prothero, 'Movements', p. 175; Joyce Marlow, *The Tolpuddle Martyrs* (1971), pp. 125–30. See too J. F. C. Harrison, Plate 27, facing p. 196.

55 *NS*, 23 Oct. 1847. For the carpenters' favourable recollections see below, p. 178, and *Charter*, 26 May 1839 (but cf. *Charter*, 21 April 1839).

56 Not surprisingly, the sceptics included the shoemakers (*NS*, 26 Oct. 1844; *The Last*, 1 Nov. 1844). (John O'Neil had been a critic at the time of 'the great bubble' of 'the consolidated humbug' (*St Crispin*, 11 Dec. 1869).) Tailors' attitudes were uneasily ambivalent (see *NS*, 13 April 1844).

57 Cf. Robert F. Wearmouth, *Some Working-Class Movements of the Nineteenth Century* (1948), p. 197.

58 E. J. Hobsbawm, *Primitive Rebels: Studies in Archaic Forms of Social Movement*

in the 19th and 20th Centuries (Manchester, 1959), p. 128; Jones, *Outcast London*, pp. 337–41; Paul Thompson, chap. 2. Edward Royle, *Victorian Infidels: The Origins of the British Secularist Movement, 1791–1866* (Manchester, 1974), is the first scholarly history of (early) freethought –see esp. chaps. 2 and 3 for some of the interconnections between secularism and Chartism in London and, also, App. 2.

59 See, for example, *Charter*, 10 Feb. 1839; *NS*, 14 Nov. 1840, 6 Feb. 1847, 5 Feb. 1848, 3 Feb. 1849. Cf. David Jones, *Chartism and the Chartists* (1975), p. 61.

60 For Alfred's reputation and the theory of the Norman Yoke, see Christopher Hill, 'The Norman Yoke', in *Puritanism and Revolution: Studies in Interpretation of the English Revolution of the 17th Century* (Panther edn, 1968); but Hill underestimates the extent to which Chartists continued to cling to the belief in its entirety (pp. 113–14, 119–21).

61 See Louis James, *Fiction for the Working Man, 1830–50: A Study of the Literature produced for the Working Classes in Early Victorian Urban England* (Penguin edn, 1974), p. 86, for the popularity of Tell.

62 Cf. the 'Chartist Calendar', *Evening Star*, 30 Nov. 1842. Hollis in her impressive, detailed examination of ideology reaches broadly similar conclusions (*Pauper Press*, chaps. 6, 7, pp. 285–90, 299–300). See also Trygve R. Tholfsen, *Working Class Radicalism in Mid-Victorian England* (1976), pp. 83–97, who rightly stresses the Chartist insistence on a fundamental change in class relations.

63 Cf. John Saville, 'Introduction: R. G. Gammage and the Chartist Movement' to R. G. Gammage, *History of the Chartist Movement, 1837–1854* (New York, 1969 edn), pp. 39–45; and John Saville, 'Some Aspects of Chartism in Decline', *BSSLH*, no. 20 (Spring 1970).

64 Stan Shipley, *Club Life and Socialism in Mid-Victorian London* (Oxford, 1971), esp. pp. 24–6, provides such a pointer.

65 Alfred Plummer, *Bronterre: A Political Biography of Bronterre O'Brien 1804–1864* (1971), chaps. 10–12, App. C; Shipley. However, in his very important article, 'Working-Class Culture and Working-Class Politics', esp. pp. 480–1 (but cf. pp. 484–5, 499), Jones argues that it was not until as late as the 1890s that the tradition of artisan radicalism had been extinguished in London.

66 Prothero, 'Chartism in London'; and *idem*, 'London Chartism and the Trades'.

67 Cf. F. C. Mather, *Chartism* (1972 edn), p. 11.

Part Two. The course of events

1 Narrative accounts by Lovett in Add. MS. 27,822, ff. 15–27 (rather than Place's highly inaccurate transcription in Add. MS. 27,791, ff. 243–57), and Lovett, *L&S*, I, pp. 43–88. The NUWC has still to find its historian, although we now have Prothero's learned, illuminating, yet immensely compressed, treatment in *Artisans and Politics*, chap. 14 (see, additionally, Prothero, 'Movements', esp. pp. 421–2 for a list of branches and some of the eighty-six classes; Graham Wallas, *The Life of Francis Place, 1771–1854* (4th edn, 1925), chap. 10; Rowe, 'Radicalism in London', pp. 47–116; *idem*, 'London Radicalism in the Era of the Great Reform Bill', in Stevenson, *London;* Hollis, *Pauper Press*, esp. pp. 40–6, 263–72, 276–7). The police action at Coldbath Fields is considered below, pp. 123–4. T. M. Parssi-

nen, 'Association, Convention and Anti-parliament in British Radical Politics, 1771–1848', *English Historical Review*, LXXXVIII (1973), is a penetrating exploration of the entire convention tradition (see too Iorwerth Prothero, 'William Benbow and the Concept of the "General Strike" ', *P&P*, no. 63 (May 1974), pp. 135–41).

2 There are two excellent histories of the unstamped. Joel H. Wiener, *The War of the Unstamped: The Movement to Repeal the British Newspaper Tax, 1830–1836* (Ithaca, N.Y., 1969), provides a national survey and Hollis, *Pauper Press*, is an admirable study of London.

3 Lovett, *L&S*, I, pp. 93–4; Birmingham Reference Library, Lovett Collection, I, ff. 1, 175; BL Add. MSS. 27,819, ff. 20–35; 27,821, f.320; 27,827, f. 32; D. J. Rowe (ed.), *London Radicalism, 1830–1843: A Selection from the Papers of Francis Place* (1970), pp. 151–2; BL, Place Collection [hereafter PC] set 56, vol. I, f. 1 of preface to volume, and f. 1; Wiener, p. 98 *et seq.*, 252–3, 275–6; Hollis, *Pauper Press*, pp. 77, 303–5.

4 Minutes of the Working Men's Association, BL Add. MS. 37,773, f. 1 *et seq.;* Lovett, *L&S*, I, p. 99.

5 PC set 56, vol. I, ff. 1–2 of preface; Add. MSS. 27,819, ff. 46, 205–6; and 27,835, ff. 131–2; Wallas, pp. 359–61.

6. Lovett, *L&S*, I, pp. 104–5, 113–14, 168–9; Add. MS. 37,773, ff. 50–5, 82, 100–6; Lovett Collection, I, f. 170. Place's accounts are in PC set 56, vol. I, ff. 8–9 of preface; Add. MSS. 27,820, ff. 96, 98–9; 27,882, ff. 79–80; 27,835, ff. 135, 160; Wallas, p. 367. In the brief summary, above, of the origins of the LWMA it will be seen that the account by D. J. Rowe, 'The London Working Men's Association and the "People's Charter" ', *P&P*, no. 36 (April 1967), pp. 74–81, is largely accepted. On the other hand, his contention that 'working-class political consciousness was not strong enough in the mid-1830s to formulate its own ideas and programme . . . it still needed the initiative to come from a middle-class radical source' is clearly misplaced – it is only necessary to consider the multifarious working-class activities of the early thirties. As for the production of the Charter, despite Rowe's initial denial that Lovett was 'the principal author', his final position does not radically challenge this attribution (*ibid.*, pp. 81–5, but cf. his extraordinary assertion in 'The London Working Men's Association and the "People's Charter": Rejoinder', *P&P*, no. 38 (Dec. 1967), p. 176). For various criticisms of Rowe's claims see Iorwerth Prothero, 'The London Working Men's Association and the "People's Charter" ', *P&P*, no. 38 (Dec. 1967); Dorothy Thompson, 'Notes on Aspects of Chartist Leadership', *BSSLH*, no. 15 (Autumn 1967), pp. 31–2; Wiener, p. 276n; R. S. Neale, *Class and Ideology in the Nineteenth Century* (1972), pp. 35–6. The *Operative*, 3 Feb. 1839, contains an interesting item on the authorship of the Charter. George Howell, *A History of the Working Men's Association from 1836 to 1850* (Newcastle upon Tyne, n.d.), is little more than an incomplete précis of the LWMA's minutes.

7 Add. MS. 37,773.

8 Wiener, pp. 254–7; Add. MS. 27,835, f. 67; Wearmouth, pp. 59–60, 65; Hollis, *Pauper Press*, pp. 266–7; Prothero, 'Movements', pp. 185 *et seq.*, 424–5; *idem, Artisans and Politics*, pp. 307–8, 312–13, 315; Rowe, 'Radicalism in London', pp. 203–5; PC set 56, vol. I, ff. 2–3 of preface, and ff. 6–7, 11, 16; Add. MS. 27,819, ff. 32–5, 194. James A. Epstein, 'Feargus O'Connor and the English Working-Class Radical Movement, 1832–1841; A Study in National Chartist Leadership' (Birmingham PhD thesis,

1977), pp. 30–42, provides the fullest and most sympathetic discussion of the Radical Associations; but his assessment of the Universal Suffrage Club (pp. 51–6) appears unduly generous.

9 See Donald Read and Eric Glasgow, *Feargus O'Connor: Irishman and Chartist* (1961), pp. 44–7, and Epstein, 'O'Connor and Radical Movement', pp. 30, 42–3.

10 Cf. Add. MS. 37,773, f. 80, and *NS*, 27 Jan. 1838; although see also *NS*, 22 Dec. 1838. In any case Prothero, 'Movements', p. 193, is incorrect to maintain that in December 1837 the Surrey Radical Association was the last survivor, as Lambeth's remained active in February 1838 (PC set 56, vol. I, ff. 186–7).

11 F. H. W. Sheppard, *Local Government in St Marylebone 1688–1835: A Study of the Vestry and the Turnpike Trust* (1958), chaps. 16, 17; and Rowe, 'Radicalism in London', chaps. 2, 5, treat their agitation. James Williamson Brooke, *The Democrats of Marylebone* (1839), is a virulent, but highly informed, attack. See too Prothero, 'Chartism in London', pp. 91–4 (who, though, underestimates the Chartist commitment of Webb in the forties – for example, he chaired an angry mass meeting in August 1842 (*The Times*, 19 Aug. 1842) – and John Savage, who returned to full activity in 1848). Rowe, in Stevenson, *London*, p. 173 n31, usefully draws attention to the ease with which John Savage can be confused with James Savage, another radical of the 1830s.

12 Good accounts are given by: Schoyen, pp. 17–21; Plummer, *Bronterre*, pp. 80–4; and, especially, Epstein, 'O'Connor and Radical Movement', pp. 69–79.

13 'Prospectus of the East London Democratic Association', Lovett Collection, I, f. 35 (reprinted in Dorothy Thompson, *The Early Chartists* (1971), pp. 55–6); PC set 56, vol. I, f. 56; Add. MS. 37,773, f. 44; J. A. Bennett, 'A Study in London Radicalism: The Democratic Association, 1837–1841' (Sussex MA thesis, 1968), pp. 3–6.

14 The case is examined by W. H. Fraser, 'The Glasgow Cotton Spinners, 1837', in John Butt & J. T. Ward (eds.), *Scottish Themes: Essays in Honour of Professor S. G. E. Lythe* (Edinburgh, 1976).

15 Add. MS. 37,773, ff. 85, 87, 90–1, 93–8; Lovett Collection, I, ff. 154, 172, 276; Lovett, *L&S*, I, pp. 162–7; Schoyen, pp. 23–6.

16 Public Record Office [hereafter PRO], Home Office Papers [hereafter HO] 44/52, 'The Constitution . . .' and membership card of LDA. But see *NS*, 23 June, 7, 21 July 1838, 16 Aug. 1845; Schoyen, p. 28.

17 Add. MS. 27,820, esp. ff. 91, 109–23, 130–1, 136–40, 170–83; Briggs, 'The Local Background to Chartism', in Briggs, *Chartist Studies*, pp. 22–6; Kenneth Judge, 'Early Chartist Organization and the Convention of 1839', *IRSH*, XX (1975), pp. 371–2; Hovell, pp. 105–7.

18 R. G. Gammage, *History of the Chartist Movement, 1837–1854* (Newcastle-on-Tyne and London, 2nd edn, 1894), chaps. 3, 4.

19 *NS*, 22 Sept. 1838. Gammage, p. 46, puts the figure at 30,000, but appreciates that the demonstration was 'comparatively insignificant' and 'a decided failure'. The Commissioners of Police produced the characteristically modest estimate of 4,000 (PRO, Records of the Metropolitan Police Offices [hereafter MEPO] 1/45; HO 61/21), but cf. the equally astringent assessments of Place (Add. MS. 27,820, f. 202) and the *Globe*, 11 April 1848. At the other extreme – of up to 50,000 – see PC set 56, vol. II, ff. 103–5, 114–17.

20 Add. MS. 37,773, ff. 109–10, 115, 117; Lovett Collection, I, ff. 170, 174, 180; HO 61/21.
21 Add. MS. 27,820, ff. 200–1; Lovett, *L&S,* I, p. 185.
22 Add. MS. 37,773, ff. 119–20; PC set 56, vol. II, ff. 3, 34.
23 *Operative,* 28 April, 5 May 1839.
24 PC set 56, vol. II, ff. 327–8; *NS,* 5 Jan. 1839. Cardo had been active in the GNCTU; and in 1840, with other renegade Chartists, became a lecturer on foreign affairs for Urquhart's committee, in his case as early as January – indeed he was arrested in Newport shortly after the Rising of 1839, which he stated to be 'the result of a Russian agency' (Prothero, 'Movements', p. 203n; Robert Lowery, *Robert Lowery: Radical and Chartist,* ed. Brian Harrison and Patricia Hollis (1979), p. 162n.; Hovell, pp. 181–5; Epstein, 'O'Connor and Radical Movement', p. 503 n4; *Charter,* 24 Nov. 1839).
25 HO 61/21.
26 The protest meeting on behalf of the Dorchester labourers in 1834, the crowd which presented the Second Chartist Petition to Parliament in 1842 and the demonstration on Kennington Common on 10 April 1848 all appear to have exceeded 100,000.
27 PC set 56, vol. II, ff. 275, 310; *NS,* 29 Dec. 1838.
28 Cf. Hovell, pp. 74–6, and Schoyen, p. 41.
29 PC set 56, vol. II, ff. 308–9; *NS,* 29 Dec. 1838; *Operative,* 23 Dec. 1838. For Place's caustic comments: Add. MS. 27,820, ff. 354–6.
30 *Operative,* 10 March 1839.
31 *Charter,* 21, 28 Apr. 1839. For the LDA's version of events, see letter from Thomas Ireland, *Operative,* 28 Apr. 1839; and for the acrimonious controversy surrounding the affair, which had its roots in the manipulation of the Palace Yard elections, *ibid.,* 31 March, 14, 21, 28 April, 5 May 1839.
32 *Charter* and *Operative,* 28 April 1839; Correspondence and Papers of the General Convention of the Industrious Classes, 1839, BL Add. MS. 34,245A, ff. 214, 283, 309, 331, 362; HO 40/44.
33 *Charter,* 5, 12 May 1839; *Operative,* 12 May 1839; Add. MS. 34,245A, ff. 285, 364, 384–7. For the opposition in East London when the LDA's intentions became known, see *Charter,* 21, 28 April, 5 May 1839, and *Operative,* 28 April 1839.
34 Schoyen, pp. 64–6, views the activities of the LDA described above very differently, maintaining that they demonstrate its strength and that it was 'the dominant London working-class organization'. (See also, *ibid.,* pp. 31–2, 56–7.) He is able to pursue his unacceptable argument by, in part, regarding the notoriously small LWMA as the LDA's principal adversary, in 1839 as in 1838. The LWMA, however, rapidly shrank into a more-or-less localized organization, most metropolitan Chartists became members of associations in their own localities and it was these new societies which mobilized themselves against the LDA's manoeuvres. In this context (alone) the remarks of Rowe, 'Chartism and the Spitalfields Silk-Weavers', esp. pp. 486–7, are salutary. See too Prothero, 'Chartism in London', pp. 78–80.
35 For the figures: *Charter* and *Operative,* 10 Feb. 1839; Add. MS. 34,245B, ff. 219–22.
36 *NS,* 9 Nov. 1839.
37 But for the initial discussions of 'the apathy of the London radicals', see *Operative* and *Charter,* 10 Feb. 1839.

38 Even a police superintendent estimated a crowd of 5,000 to 6,000 (whereas an inspector put it at 1,000) (HO 44/52, reports of 15 Feb. 1839).
39 *Charter* and *Operative*, 17 Feb. 1839; *Chartist*, 16 Feb. 1839. The *London Democrat*, 20 April 1839, regarded that at White Conduit House as one of the most encouraging meetings to have been held in London, since the 'brown jackets' for once were in the majority.
40 *Charter* and *Operative*, 24 Feb. 1839; *NS*, 2 March 1839.
41 *Charter*, 3 March 1839. On the other hand there are contemptuous reports of four of these meetings by policemen and a shorthand reporter (HO 44/52).
42 *NS*, 2 March 1839.
43 *Operative*, 5, 12 May 1839; *Charter*, 12 May 1839. Place's interesting observations on the removal are in Add. MS. 27,821, ff. 93–4, 113–15. Parssinen, 'Association, Convention and Anti-parliament', p. 524, rewardingly views it as indicating that the Convention had opted to act as an 'anti-parliament', not as an 'association'.
44 *Charter* and *Operative*, 12 May 1839. (D. J. Moss, 'A Study in Failure: Thomas Attwood, MP for Birmingham, 1832–1839', *HJ*, XXI (1978), pp. 566–7, describes Attwood's extremely ambivalent attitude by this time towards both the Chartists and the Petition.) For the actual delivery of the Petition to the Commons: *Operative*, 16 June 1839. See the remarks of the *Chartist*, 30 June 1839.
45 HO 40/44, report of 26 March 1839. Cf. Vincent's sentiments, HO 44/52, report of 8 May 1839.
46 HO 40/44, report of 29 March 1839.
47 *NS*, 9 March 1839.
48 *Charter*, 31 March 1839.
49 PC set 56, vol. II, ff. 308–9; *NS*, 29 Dec. 1838.
50 *Operative*, 31 March 1839; HO 40/44, report of 26 March 1839.
51 *NS*, 16 Feb. 1839.
52 *Ibid.*, 5 Sept. 1840.
53 *London Democrat*, 20 April, 18 May 1839.
54 *Charter* and *Operative*, 31 March 1839.
55 *Charter*, 28 April 1839.
56 *Ibid.*, 27 Oct. 1839.
57 *Ibid.*, 15, 29 Dec. 1839.
58 *Operative*, 9 Dec. 1838.
59 Add. MS. 34,245A, ff. 76–7; *Charter* and *Operative*, 10 March 1839. See also *Operative*, 17 March 1839.
60 *Charter* and *Operative*, 24 March 1839. See also, *Operative*, 17 March 1839.
61 *London Democrat*, 20 April, 18 May 1839.
62 HO 40/44, report of 19/20 April 1839.
63 *London Democrat*, 20 April 1839.
64 *Charter*, 28 April, 5, 12 May 1839; *Chartist*, 5 May 1839; *Operative*, 12 May 1839; HO 40/44.
65 *Chartist* and *Operative*, 12 May 1839; HO 40/44.
66 This explicit reason for the ensuing police action is not appreciated by Schoyen, pp. 67–8.
67 *Operative* and *Charter*, 12, 19 May 1839; *NS*, 18 May 1839, 26 Dec. 1846; HO 40/44; HO 61/22; MEPO 1/32.
68 Frank F. Rosenblatt, *The Chartist Movement: In Its Social and Economic*

Aspects (New York, 1916), pp. 172–3; *Chartist, Operative* and *Charter,* 26 May 1839; HO 40/44.

69 *Charter,* 28 July, 4, 11, 18 Aug. 1839; *NS,* 10, 17 Aug. 1839; HO 40/44.

70 *Charter,* 10, 17 Nov. 1839.

71 *Ibid.,* 2, 9, 16 Feb. 1840; *Southern Star,* 16 Feb. 1840; *NS,* 15 Feb. 1840.

72 *Charter* and *Southern Star,* 19, 26 Jan. 1840; HO 61/25; HO 40/57, letter from Dr Wade, 17 Jan. 1840; MEPO 7/6, 14 Jan. 1840; HO 41/15; HO 65/13.

73 Apparently from W. P. Stuart (see HO 61/24, letters of 24 Dec. 1839).

74 HO 40/44, letters of Nov. 1839; HO 40/52, letters from T. R. Reading, 11 Nov., and John Dale, 18 Nov. 1839; HO 61/24, letters of 24 Dec. 1839. A. J. Peacock, *Bradford Chartism, 1838–1840* (York, 1969), esp. pp. 34–9, has gone furthest in unravelling the conspiratorial activity of November 1839 to January 1840. However, Lowery, who left the only inside account of the Convention of 19 December–8 January (now reprinted in *Robert Lowery: Radical and Chartist,* pp. 157–60), explains that the delegates failed to provide central direction for 12 January – and comments at some length on Beniowski's conduct. (See, too, John L. Baxter, 'Early Chartism and Labour Class Struggle: South Yorkshire 1837–1840', in Sidney Pollard and Colin Holmes (eds.), *Essays in the Economic and Social History of South Yorkshire* (Sheffield, 1976), pp. 146–50, and Thompson, *Early Chartists,* Part 5.)

75 HO 45/102, police report of 16 July 1839. On the evening of 23 January rockets *were* seen in the air by two constables in the Whitechapel Road, while that morning three rockets had been discovered behind a Bethnal Green pub (*ibid.,* report of 24 Jan. 1840).

76 Quoted by *Southern Star,* 19 Jan. 1840. The argument by Bennett, pp. 28–32, that London was playing a diversionary role is ingenious, but not convincing.

77 Although the importance of the provocative acts of Joseph Goulding seems to have been overestimated by Mather, *Public Order,* p. 210; and Schoyen, p. 63 (cf. *Southern Star,* 15 March 1840, and *NS,* 7 March, 25 April 1840, with the letter from Goulding (HO 61/25) which is printed in Reith, *British Police and Democratic Ideal,* pp. 241–4).

78 *NS,* 21 March 1840; *Southern Star,* 5 April 1840; HO 44/35, letters from and to Joseph Hume, July 1840; HO 41/16, letter to Hume, 4 Aug. 1840; *ECC,* no. 1.

79 *Operative,* 4 Nov. 1838, 24 Feb. 1839. See, however, *ibid.,* 2 Dec. 1838; also, Plummer, *Bronterre,* pp. 87–8.

80 PC set 56, vol. II, ff. 125, 128–9; Add. MS. 27,820, ff. 221, 381–3, and 27,821, ff. 22–3; *Charter,* 31 March 1839; Lovett, *L&S,* II, p. 248. For the curious demise of the *Charter*: Rowe, *London Radicalism,* pp. 201–3, 217; PC set 66, ff. 1–9; Lovett, *L&S,* II, pp. 248–9; *Charter,* 9 Feb., 1, 15 March 1840; *Southern Star,* 8 March 1840.

81 *Operative,* 14 April 1839; *Charter,* 14 April, 5 May, 22 Sept. 1839; Add. MS. 34,245A, f. 378.

82 *Charter,* 21 April 1839.

83 *Ibid.,* 6, 13 Oct., 1 Dec. 1839.

84 *Operative* and *Charter,* 5, 12 May 1839.

85 Add. MS. 37,773, f. 116.

86 *Charter,* 17 March 1839.

87 Add. MS. 34,245A, f. 246.
88 *Operative* and *Charter,* 12 May 1839.
89 *Operative* and *Charter,* 26 May 1839.
90 *Charter,* 25 Aug. 1839, 2 Feb. 1840.
91 *Ibid.,* 8 Sept. 1839.
92 *Ibid.,* 13 Oct. 1839.
93 *Charter* and *Operative,* 7, 28 April 1839; *NS,* 2 March 1839.
94 *Operative* and *Charter,* 27 Jan. 1839. For the highly industrial character of the Wandle valley, from Mitcham to Wandsworth, see Sheppard, *London,* pp. 161–2, and Roebuck, pp. 133–4.
95 *Charter,* 28 April 1839.
96 *Charter* and *Operative,* 14 April, 12 May 1839.
97 24 March 1839.
98 Add. MS. 37,773; Minutes of the National Association, BL Add. MS. 37,774; Lovett, *L&S,* II, pp. 264–5. In June 1840 he loyally offered, as an eye-witness, information on the unsuccessful attempt by Edward Oxford on the life of the Queen (HO 44/36).
99 See below, pp. 42–4.
100 He died in 1842, aged seventy-five (*NS,* 16 July, 13 Aug. 1842).
101 HO 40/44, report of 21 May 1839. Ackerley is mentioned by Thomas Frost as having 'claimed to have invented a wonderful lamp, which possessed the property of curing all diseases, and was named by him the "Lamp of Life". He sometimes made an appearance on the platform at political meetings, whence he spoke for a few minutes on the question of the occasion, but invariably strayed from it to the "Lamp of Life". Mysterious advertisements in cipher were occasionally inserted by him in the evening journals, these also referring, as far as they were intelligible, to his alleged discovery' (*Forty Years' Recollections: Literary and Political* (1880), p. 314n). Ackerley attended radical meetings regularly throughout the forties, speaking – and often interrupting – to either the amusement or the indignation of his auditory. For his antics in the Forest of Dean in 1838, see HO 40/36; also PC set 56, vol. II, ff. 103–16, and Add. MS. 34,245A, ff. 24–5.
102 For example, see the record of their impressive attendance at meetings during the three weeks ending 23 March in the *Charter,* 10, 17, 24 March 1839.
103 Cf. the similar remarks of Prothero, 'Chartism in London', pp. 77–8. Lovett from February 1839 (as Judge, p. 377, points out) was completely occupied as secretary to the Convention, but he was an extremely infrequent speaker both before and after 1839 (Prothero, 'Chartism in London', p. 97).
104 E. J. Hobsbawm, 'The Nineteenth Century London Labour Market', in Centre for Urban Studies, p. 3; Gilboy, esp. chap. 8.
105 *Operative,* 10 Feb. 1839; *Chartist,* 30 June 1839. Cf. R. C. O. Matthews, *A Study in Trade-Cycle History: Economic Fluctuations in Great Britain, 1833–1842* (Cambridge, 1954), p. 156; and see Appendix I.
106 For the relationship between the Anti-Poor Law Movement and Chartism, see Hovell, esp. chap. 5; M. E. Rose, 'The Anti-Poor Law Agitation', in J. T. Ward (ed.), *Popular Movements, c. 1830–1850* (1970); Nicholas C. Edsall, *The Anti-Poor Law Movement, 1834–44* (Manchester, 1971), esp. chap. 8; and for the insignificance of the former in London, Edsall, pp. 134–7, and, also, David Ashforth, 'The Urban Poor Law', in

Derek Fraser (ed.), *The New Poor Law in the Nineteenth Century* (1976), p. 128.

107 *Southern Star*, 22 March, 3 May 1840; *NS*, 25 April 1840.

108 *NS*, 29 Aug. 1840.

109 *Southern Star*, 21 June 1840; *NS*, 20 June 1840.

110 HO 45/102, report of 14 July 1840; *NS*, 11, 25 July, 29 Aug., 19 Sept. 1840.

111 *NS*, 12 June, 17, 31 July 1841.

112 *Ibid.*, 29 Jan., 5, 12 Feb., 9–30 July 1842.

113 Indeed, Epstein, 'O'Connor and Radical Movement', pp. 407–8, names London as one of the four districts of considerable early support for the NCA.

114 Add. MS. 37,773. See also Lovett, *L&S*, I, p. 96.

115 *Operative*, 28 April 1839.

116 Lovett's essential liberalism is astutely analysed by Large, 'William Lovett', pp. 108–11.

117 Lovett, *L&S*, esp. II, pp. 250–7; *NS*, 10 April 1841 *et seq.*

118 Add. MS. 37,774; Lovett, *L&S*, II, pp. 250, 264n; Lovett Collection, II, f. 200. Cf. West, p. 168, and Epstein, 'O'Connor and Radical Movement', p. 475. Not until 1847 was Cleave arraigned as one of O'Connor's enemies (*NS*, 6 Nov. 1847).

119 *NS*, 25 Aug. 1849; George Jacob Holyoake (ed.), *The Life and Character of Henry Hetherington* (1849); Ambrose G. Barker, *Henry Hetherington, 1792–1849: Pioneer in the Freethought and Working Class Struggles of a Hundred Years Ago for the Freedom of the Press* (n.d.), p. 29 *et seq.*

120 It is striking how fleetingly Watson passed over his participation in the LWMA and Chartism in the autobiographical speech he delivered on his retirement in 1854 ('Reminiscences of James Watson', in David Vincent (ed.), *Testaments of Radicalism: Memoirs of Working Class Politicians, 1790–1885* (1977)).

121 Lovett, *L&S*, II, pp. 264–5; *NS*, 18 Sept. 1841; Add. MS. 37,774.

122 Notably, and seminally, by Hovell, and West. Prothero, 'Chartism in London', esp. pp. 76–8, presents an identical verdict.

123 *NS*, 23 April 1842 (also, 11 Sept. 1841); West, pp. 159–61; Large, 'William Lovett', p. 119; Lovett, *L&S*, II, esp. pp. 292–4. In fact, the bourgeois advocates of universal suffrage (e.g. Dr J. R. Black, Joseph Hume, Dr Bowring, Henry Warburton, W. H. Ashurst, Dr Epps, Place) had their own Metropolitan Parliamentary Reform Association from March 1842 to March 1843 (Add. MS. 27,810 – from which a generous selection is printed in Rowe, *London Radicalism*, pp. 220–49).

124 *NS*, 17, 24 April, 1, 8 May 1841.

125 W. J. Linton, *James Watson: A Memoir of the Days of the Fight for a Free Press in England and of the Agitation for the People's Charter* (Manchester, 1880), p. 50. Cf. Large, 'William Lovett', p. 121.

126 Cleave disapproved and was not a member of the organizing committee (Prothero, *Artisans and Politics*, p. 295; but cf. Parssinen, 'Association, Convention and Anti-parliament', p. 520).

127 Lovett, *L&S*, I, pp. 83–5, 88–9.

128 For a rare sympathetic assessment of O'Connor's appeal: Saville, 'Introduction: R. G. Gammage', pp. 62–5.

129 Lovett, *L&S*, II, p. 256; *NS*, esp. 11 Sept. 1841.

130 *NS*, 18 Sept. 1841.

131 *NS*, 18 Nov. 1843, 12 Feb., 16 Dec. 1848. There is a biographical sketch in *Reynolds's Political Instructor*, 27 April 1850. See also Prothero, 'Movements', p. 140; and *idem, Artisans and Politics*, pp. 272–3, 299.

132 *NS*, 12 March 1842.

133 Prothero, 'London Chartism and the Trades', p. 202n; *NS*, 9 Dec. 1843, 2 Oct. 1847; William Stevens, *A Memoir of Thomas Martin Wheeler, Founder of the Friend-in-Need Life and Sick Assurance Society . . .* (1862), p. 25. His full name appears to have been Daniel William Ruffy Ridley (HO 45/248, letter from W. H. Lander, 3 Sept. 1842).

134 *NS*, 9 Oct. 1841, 16 Sept. 1843, 6 Nov. 1847; Stevens; J. A. Epstein, 'Feargus O'Connor and the *Northern Star*', *IRSH*, XXI (1976), p. 92n.

135 *NS*, 14 Aug., 18 Dec. 1841, 16 Sept., 14 Oct. 1843; Georg Weerth, *A Young Revolutionary in Nineteenth-Century England: Selected Writings of Georg Weerth*, ed. Ingrid and Peter Kuczynski (Berlin, 1971), p. 167. The biographical outline in *Reynolds's Political Instructor*, 20 April 1850, is disappointingly unrevealing. Prothero, 'Chartism in London', p. 97, is incorrect in identifying another member of O'Connor's entourage, William Dixon, as a 'Chelsea plasterer'. He was instead a Lancastrian, a weaver by trade and an organizer for the Miners' Association, who became first a trustee, then a director of the Land Company (Raymond Challinor and Brian Ripley, *The Miners' Association: A Trade Union in the Age of the Chartists* (1968), esp. pp. 219–22; *NS*, 13, 20 Dec. 1845, 28 Aug. 1847; Gammage, p. 402).

136 For M'Grath: Gammage, p. 402; Thomas Frost, *Reminiscences of a Country Journalist* (1886), esp. p. 94. The proletarian institutions of self-help in Victorian Britain demand, as a whole, intensive examination; but for Chartist links see also West, pp. 271, 282–3, and Stan Newens, 'Thomas Edward Bowkett: Nineteenth Century Pioneer of the Working-Class Movement in East London', *History Workshop Journal*, no. 9 (Spring 1980).

137 For this renewal of agitation see Wallas, p. 391 *et seq.;* Norman McCord, *The Anti-Corn Law League, 1838–1846* (2nd edn, 1968), pp. 75–7; Add. MS. 27,822, ff. 152–63.

138 *NS*, 21 March 1840.

139 Cited by Wallas, p. 376.

140 Quoted in *NS*, 6 March 1841. For Place's despairing reaction: Wallas, p. 377.

141 *NS*, 27 March 1841.

142 James B. Jefferys, *The Story of the Engineers, 1800–1945* (1945), pp. 37–42, 44–5.

143 *NS*, 3 April 1841.

144 *Ibid.*, 12 Feb. 1842. Smith's claim that eventually 'the first Great London Meetings . . . overawed the Chartists, who had formerly routed public meetings' (Add. MS. 27,822, f. 160) appears justified only to the extent that the League had achieved the successful management of its meetings and should be compared with the remarks of Charles Mackay, *Forty Years' Recollections of Life, Literature, and Public Affairs: From 1830 to 1870* (2 vols., 1877), I, pp. 107–9; II, p. 50. In 1843 the League launched an offensive to win over London. See McCord, pp. 139–42, 178–9.

145. *NS*, 6 May 1843.

146 But the Chartists did not pay men to pack meetings as the League reputedly did. See, for example, the complaint that forty or fifty Irishmen

from St Giles's were hired to attend a discussion between the Chartists and one of the League's lecturers (*ibid.*, 26 March 1842). Cf., however, McCord, pp. 99–103, and J. H. Treble, 'O'Connor, O'Connell and the Attitudes of Irish Immigrants toward Chartism in the North of England 1838–48', in J. Butt and I. F. Clarke (eds.), *The Victorians and Social Protest: A Symposium* (Newton Abbot, 1973), pp. 51–5.

147 *NS*, 5 March 1842.
148 Around this period there were only seventy or eighty towns in the NCA (*ibid.*, 30 April 1842).
149 In December 1841 there were 298 branches of the NCA throughout the country (*ibid.*, 24 Dec. 1841).
150 There were then about 350 towns in the NCA (*ibid.*, 30 April 1842).
151 *Ibid.*, 5 March 1842.
152 *Ibid.*, 3 July 1841.
153 *Ibid.*, 18 Sept. 1841.
154 See below, p. 180.
155 *NS*, 13 Nov. 1841.
156 See below, pp. 191–2.
157 *NS*, 7, 21 Aug., 25 Sept. 1841.
158 *Ibid.*, 5 March 1842.
159 *Evening Star*, 25 Aug. 1842; *NS*, 27 Aug. 1842.
160 *Evening Star*, 20 Sept. 1842; *NS*, 24 Sept. 1842.
161 *NS*, 15 Oct. 1842; *Evening Star*, 13 Oct. 1842.
162 *NS*, 5 Feb., 5, 12 March 1842.
163 *Evening Star*, 31 Aug. 1842.
164 *Ibid.*, 13 Sept. 1842; *NS*, 17, 24 Sept. 1842.
165 *Evening Star*, 26 Oct. 1842; *NS*, 29 Oct. 1842.
166 *NS*, 9 April 1842.
167 Epstein, 'O'Connor and Radical Movement', pp. 411–14 and App. C.
168 This remark referred to the 'unpleasant feeling' dividing the Middlesex and Surrey County Councils.
169 I.e., of 1841.
170 *NS*, 23 April 1842.
171 *Ibid.*, 7, 21 May 1842.
172 Delegate for North Lancashire. For the weavers in 1841–2 see below, pp. 186, 188.
173 Cf. Matthews, p. 164.
174 *NS*, 23 April 1842.
175 *Ibid.*, 18 Dec. 1841. Almost two-thirds of the tailors had been claimed unemployed in October 1841 (E. J. Hobsbawm, *Labouring Men: Studies in the History of Labour* (1964), p. 77). See also *ECC*, no. 52.
176 *NS*, 2 July 1842.
177 *Ibid.*, 20 Nov. 1841. For building workers: *ibid.*, 16 April, 11 June 1842; and, in general: *Evening Star*, 9 Aug. 1842. See Appendix I.
178 Quoted by *The Times*, 7 May 1842.
179 *NS*, May 1842. 50,000 was given as the size of the assemblage outside Parliament by *The Times*, 3 May 1842, judging only 12,000 or 15,000 to have taken part in the procession, which, according to *Punch*, II (1842), p. 206, was 17,000 strong.
180 *NS*, 30 April 1842.
181 *Ibid.*, 7 May 1842. See also *The Times*, 3 May 1842.
182 *The Times*, 15, 18, 19, 20 Aug. 1842; Graham Papers (on microfilm at the

University Library, Cambridge), Bundles 52A and B; *NS,* 20 Aug. 1842; *Evening Star,* 19 Aug. 1842. Lord Hill requested to be relieved of the command on 9 August and Wellington accepted the post on the 12th (Arthur Christopher Benson and Viscount Esher (eds.), *The Letters of Queen Victoria: A Selection from Her Majesty's Correspondence Between the Years 1837 and 1861* (3 vols., 1908), I, pp. 419–21). For a more detailed account of August 1842 see below, pp. 106–11.

183 *NS,* 20 Aug. 1842.

184 *Ibid.,* 20, 27 Aug. 1842; *The Times,* 17, 18 Aug. 1842.

185 *NS,* 20 Aug. 1842; *The Times,* 18 Aug. 1842; *Evening Star,* 18 Aug. 1842.

186 Published in Benson and Esher, I, p. 427.

187 *The Times,* 19 Aug. 1842; *NS,* 27 Aug. 1842; Royal Archives [hereafter RA], Windsor Castle, B5/59, letter from Graham to Queen, 19 Aug. 1842; Graham Papers 52A; MEPO 1/43, letters from Mayne to Sutton, 20, 31 Aug. 1842; Alfred Jenkin, 'Chartism and the Trade Unions', in Lionel M. Munby (ed.), *The Luddites and Other Essays* (Edgware, 1971), p. 86.

188 *NS,* 27 Aug. 1842; *The Times,* 20 Aug. 1842; RA B5/60 and Graham Papers 52B, letter from Graham to Queen, 20 Aug. 1842 (published in Benson and Esher, I, p. 427); HO 45/252.

189 *NS,* 27 Aug. 1842.

190 *The Times,* 23 Aug. 1842.

191 *NS,* 27 Aug. 1842; *Evening Star,* 23 Aug. 1842; *The Times,* 23 Aug. 1842; *Illustrated London News,* 27 Aug. 1842; Graham Papers 52B; MEPO 7/8.

192 *NS,* 27 Aug., 3 Sept. 1842; *Evening Star,* 24, 29, 30 Aug. 1842; *The Times,* 24 Aug. 1842; HO 45/267; Thomas H. Duncombe (ed.), *The Life and Correspondence of Thomas Slingsby Duncombe, Late MP for Finsbury* (2 vols., 1868), I, pp. 309–10.

193 *NS,* 27 Aug. 1842. Cf. *The Times,* 26 Aug. 1842.

194 For the whippers' movement see below, pp. 217–18. The account of the metropolitan disturbances in Mick Jenkins, *The General Strike of 1842* (1980), pp. 165–71, relies heavily on the Manchester press (and mistakes the events of 19 August as occurring on the 20th). The inadequacy of the traditional assessment of London Chartism is fully displayed in Julius West's comment (p. 190) that 'Even lethargic London was affected' by the Plug Riots, mentioning merely the Stepney Green meeting.

195 *NS,* 28 Aug. 1841.

196 *Ibid.,* June–Sept. 1844, *passim.*

197 *Ibid.,* 13, 20, 27 April, 4 May 1844.

198 *Ibid.,* 4, 11 May *et seq.,* 1844; 29 March, 8 Nov. 1845; 4, 25 April 1846.

199 *Ibid.,* 9, 16 Nov. 1844; 4, 11, 18 Jan., 8, 15 Feb., 29 March, 5 April 1845. Pollard, *History of Labour in Sheffield,* pp. 74–5, briefly outlines the Sheffield background to the Association.

200 Pp. 155–6.

201 Cf. *NS,* 29 May 1847.

202 For the objectives of the Association and the plans of organization see *NS,* 29 March, 9 Aug. 1845; also, *Monthly Report of the National Association of United Trades for the Protection of Industry,* 1 Dec. 1847; Webb, *History,* pp. 170–2; and G. D. H. Cole and A. W. Filson, *British Working Class Movements: Select Documents, 1789–1875* (1965 edn), pp. 469–74. The strain of the depression of 1847–8 resulted in the winding up of the

'Employment Association' and the two Associations becoming one at the conference of June 1848, but 'the reproductive principle' was not abandoned (*Cause of the People*, 8 July 1848).

203 RA A14/32, letter from Peel to Queen, 29 March [1843]. An indication of his Chartism may be gained from Duncombe, I, chaps. 14, 17.

204 *NS*, 5 April 1845.

205 British Library of Political and Economic Science, Webb Trade Union Collection, Section A [hereafter Webb TU MSS.], II, ff. 36, 51, 65; Duncombe, II, p. 102. Fleming had, in addition to working on the *Northern Star*, edited the *New Moral World* for many years (Epstein, 'O'Connor and *Northern Star*', p. 82; Read and Glasgow, p. 65).

206 George Howell, *The Conflicts of Capital and Labour* (2nd edn, 1890), p. 122. The foregoing assessment of the Association concurs largely with that of Prothero, 'London Chartism and the Trades', pp. 205, 213–19. The dismissive judgments of A. E. Musson (*British Trade Unions, 1800–1875* (1972), p. 49, and *Trade Union and Social History* (1974), pp. 18, 24 – but see also R. G. Kirby and A. E. Musson, *The Voice of the People: John Doherty, 1798–1854: Trade Unionist, Radical and Factory Reformer* (Manchester, 1975), p. 302) can be accounted for by his reluctance to appreciate that an organization may be important without achieving much practically or may be significant yet not fit neatly into a continuous progress by the technologically advanced (or otherwise favoured) sectors – much as is the situation with Chartism itself, of course. In any case, Musson ignores (and Prothero underestimates this attraction ('London Chartism and the Trades', p. 212)) the adherence to and/or very great interest in the Association by such crafts of the future as the engineers and boilermakers (*NS*, 29 March 1845, 1 Aug. 1846, 23 Jan., 13 Feb., 3 April 1847, 16 June 1849; *Monthly Report*, 1 Dec. 1847).

207 See *Monthly Report*, 1 Dec. 1847. For its demise and the reversion to the use of the *Northern Star*: *NS*, 9, 30, June 1849.

208 See, for example, National Association of United Trades, *Report of the Central Committee of United Trades on the Proceedings Connected with the 'Combination of Workmen Bill' in the Parliamentary Session, 1853* (1853); and National Association of United Trades, *Arbitration of Disputes Between Employers and Employed* (1854).

209 Webb, *History*, pp. 168–78, still provides the fullest account of the Association; and George Howell, *Conflicts*, pp. 121–2, 394–5, and *Labour Legislation, Labour Movements, and Labour Leaders* (1902), pp. 94–5, 154–5, 437–8, have some useful details. Michael A. Shepherd, 'The Origins and Incidence of the Term "Labour Aristocracy" ', *BSSLH*, no. 37 (Autumn 1978), contains helpful information and provocative ideas concerning (not only) the NAUT, but is also unusual for according it the attention that it demands. On the question of the date of its ultimate disappearance, see also Musson, *Trade Union and Social History*, p. 57 n9.

210 *NS*, 24 Jan. – 7 March 1846; Lovett, *L&S*, II, pp. 319–26; Schoyen, pp. 138–9.

211 See *NS*, 16, 23 Aug., 27 Sept. 1845, 7 March, 26 Sept. 1846; Schoyen, pp. 133–41.

212 See *NS*, 21, 28 March 1846; Frank Gees Black and Renee Métivier Black (eds.), *The Harney Papers* (Assen, 1969), pp. 244–5; Schoyen, pp. 139–40. For the Fraternal Democrats see also Th. Rothstein, *From Chartism to*

Labourism: Historical Sketches of the English Working Class Movement (New York, 1929), p. 128 *et seq;* and Henry Weisser, *British Working-class Movements and Europe, 1815–48* (Manchester, 1975), Part 4 and Appendix.

213 *NS*, 26 April, 3 May 1845.

214 W. H. G. Armytage, *Heavens Below: Utopian Experiments in England, 1560–1960* (1961), p. 227.

215 See, for example, *NS*, 22 Aug. 1846, 29 May 1847.

216 *Ibid.*, 28 June 1845.

217 *Ibid.*, 30 May 1846.

218 *Ibid.*, 17 Oct. 1846. David Jones, pp. 10, 132–3, gives the national distribution in July 1847.

219 *NS*, 16 Dec. 1848. See too, *ibid.*, 25 Dec. 1847.

220 *NS*, 20 Dec. 1845, 26 Aug., 30 Sept. 1848. For the Land Scheme generally, see Joy MacAskill, 'The Chartist Land Plan', in Briggs, *Chartist Studies*, and Alice Mary Hadfield, *The Chartist Land Company* (Newton Abbot, 1970). The latest survey is Dennis Hardy, *Alternative Communities in Nineteenth Century England* (1979), pp. 75–8, 83–105. John Saville, 'The Chartist Land Plan', *BSSLH*, no. 3 (Autumn 1961), and Mather, *Chartism*, pp. 12–13, offer brief, sensitive reappraisals, and Saville, 'Introduction: R. G. Gammage', pp. 48–62, provides a substantial basis for historical revision.

221 *NS*, 20 Feb. 1841, 2 April 1842, 18 Nov. 1843; Gammage, p. 261.

222 Thomas Cooper, *The Life of Thomas Cooper: Written by Himself* (2nd edn, 1872), p. 258; *NS*, 20 Sept. 1845.

223 *NS*, 31 Jan., 7, 14 Feb. 1846. For Cooper's *Two Orations Against the Taking Away of Human Life under any Circumstances* of Feb. and March 1846, see Robert J. Conklin, *Thomas Cooper the Chartist (1805–1892)* (Manila, 1935), pp. 277–84.

224 Cf. Black and Black, p. 240.

225 *NS*, 11 April, 9 May 1846.

226 *Ibid.*, 13, 20 June 1846.

227 For Jones's entry into Chartism, see John Saville, *Ernest Jones: Chartist. Selections from the Writings and Speeches of Ernest Jones with Introduction and Notes* (1952), p. 17 *et seq.*; *NS*, 9, 30 May 1846.

228 *NS*, 4, 25 July, 1, 8 Aug. 1846; Saville, *Ernest Jones*, pp. 22–3, 248–51. For the breach with O'Connor, see also Cole, *Chartist Portraits*, pp. 211–12, and Weisser, pp. 161–3. In his autobiography (p. 258 *et seq.*) Cooper considerably underplays the extent of his personal activity in London Chartism during 1845–6. Only in the 1850s did O'Brien's small group of London disciples emerge (Plummer, *Bronterre*, chap. 10).

229 *NS*, 25 March, 15 April, 16 Sept., 25 Nov. 1843.

230 *Ibid.*, 27 April, 18, 25 May 1844.

231 *Ibid.*, 27 July, 24 Aug., 7, 21 Sept., 5 Oct. 1844.

232 *Ibid.*, 25 Oct. 1845.

233 *Ibid.*, 15 Aug. 1846. Cf. *ibid.*, 20 Nov. 1847, 8 Jan. 1848.

234 This phenomenon helps to place in perspective the minority, though familiar, tendency of Teetotal Chartism (for which see Brian Harrison, 'Teetotal Chartism', *History*, LVIII (1973)).

235 *NS*, 16 Sept. 1843, 20, 27 April, 19 Oct. 1844. Cf. Kirby and Musson, p. 248.

236 *Evening Star*, 23, 24 Aug., 18 Nov. 1842, 21 Jan., 1 Feb. 1843. See

Epstein, 'O'Connor and *Northern Star*', pp. 91–2; but the details in Read and Glasgow, pp. 63–4, are inaccurate.

237 E. Strauss, *Irish Nationalism and British Democracy* (1951), pp. 90–102, 107–13; R. B. McDowell, 'Ireland on the Eve of the Famine', in R. Dudley Edwards and T. Desmond Williams (eds.), *The Great Famine: Studies in Irish History 1845–52* (Dublin, 1956), pp. 71–5; Angus Macintyre, *The Liberator: Daniel O'Connell and the Irish Party, 1830–1847* (1965), chap. 2 and pp. 126–46.

238 Read and Glasgow, chap. 4 and pp. 48–50; Macintyre, pp. 126, 266n; Treble, pp. 34–7. But the fullest and most satisfactory account of this phase, as others, of O'Connor's career is now Epstein, 'O'Connor and Radical Movement', pp. 7–24, 56–62. For a vituperative summary by O'Connor in 1838 of his years in Parliament, see PC set 56. vol. II, f. 310.

239 Maurice R. O'Connell (ed.), *The Correspondence of Daniel O'Connell* (Shannon and Dublin, 8 vols., 1972–), VI, p. 187.

240 For the contributions from Britain see John Denvir, *The Irish in Britain from the Earliest Times to the Fall and Death of Parnell* (1892), p. 117; and, also, Treble, pp. 45–6.

241 McDowell, in Edwards and Williams, pp. 75–8; Macintyre, pp. 262–78; Kevin B. Nowlan, *The Politics of Repeal: A Study in the Relations between Great Britain and Ireland, 1841–1850* (1965), esp. chap. 2.

242 Cf. Large, 'William Lovett', pp. 118–19.

243 Add. MS. 37,773, ff. 53–5.

244 See above, p. 23.

245 Lovett, *L&S*, I, p. 169; Add. MS. 27,820, f. 325.

246 O'Connell, VI, pp. 174–6, 183–8; Treble, pp. 38, 42–3.

247 W. J. FitzPatrick (ed.), *Correspondence of Daniel O'Connell, The Liberator* (2 vols., 1888), II, p. 215.

248 Rachel O'Higgins, 'Irish Trade Unions and Politics, 1830–50', *HJ*, IV (1961), pp. 214–15; FitzPatrick, II, pp. 222–3. Lowery's own accounts are in his reports to the Convention and autobiography (Add. MS. 34,245B, ff. 121–2 *et seq.*; Lowery, *Robert Lowery: Radical and Chartist*, pp. 144–8). The incident was not forgotten by those Irish Chartists involved (*NS*, 11, 18 Dec. 1847). As Prothero suggests, the withdrawal of Irish support probably contributed significantly to the weakness of London Chartism in 1838–9 ('Chartism in London', pp. 90–1).

249 Rachel O'Higgins, 'Ireland and Chartism: A Study of the Influence of Irishmen and the Irish Question on the Chartist Movement' (Trinity College, Dublin, PhD thesis, 1959), pp. 198–200; Treble, pp. 55–9; *NS*, 10, 17 June 1843. Lynn Hollen Lees, *Exiles of Erin: Irish Migrants in Victorian London* (Manchester, 1979), pp. 225–30, provides another, related account of the politics of the London Irish during the 1840s.

250 *NS*, 3, 24 June 1843.

251 Cf. Read and Glasgow, esp. p. 35 and chap. 13; Treble, p. 220 n16. The first issue of the *Northern Star*, 18 Nov. 1837 (partially preserved in PC set 56, vol. II, f. 155), contained a statement on Ireland by O'Connor.

252 *NS*, 22 July 1843.

253 *Ibid.*, 6 July 1844.

254 The 'Repeal in London' column lasted from 13 July 1844 to 4 Jan. 1845.

255 *NS*, 30 Nov. 1844.

256 Census, 1841, *Enumeration Abstract, Part I, England and Wales*, 1843, XXII [496], p. 469; 1851 Census, p. 31. They came chiefly from Munster, especially county Cork (Rev. Samuel Garratt, 'The Irish in London: A Lecture Delivered on Monday, Dec. 6th, 1852, at the Music Hall, Store Street', in *Motives for Missions: A Series of Six Lectures Delivered Before the Church of England's Young Men's Society in the Autumn of 1852* (1853), p. 194; Mayhew, *LL&LP*, I, p. 113; Lees, *Exiles*, p. 51).

257 *NS*, 27 July 1844. The *Catholic Directory* estimated there were 200,000 London Catholics in 1840 (John Archer Jackson, *The Irish in Britain* (1963), p. 138). In contrast, Lees puts the number of Irish Catholics for the same year as low as 110,000–125,000. Her figure of 156,000 for the metropolitan Irish community in 1851 is also exceedingly modest, but this is a minimum size calculated on the basis of households with at least one Irish-born member (*Exiles*, pp. 46–8, 180). See too Jackson, *Irish in Britain*, p. 9. Garratt, p. 188, observes that 'a most decided animosity' existed between the native and 'Cockney' Irish.

258 Lees, *Exiles*, Tables 4.1, A.2, and pp. 97–8; Lynn H. Lees, 'Patterns of Lower-Class Life: Irish Slum Communities in Nineteenth-Century London,' in Stephan Thernstrom and Richard Sennett (eds.), *Nineteenth-Century Cities: Essays in the New Urban History* (New Haven, 1969), p. 369; *idem*, in Dyos and Wolff, pp. 424–5; John A. Jackson, 'The Irish in East London', *ELP*, VI, no. 2 (Dec. 1963), pp. 107–9. In her commentaries, however, Lees underemphasizes the proportion of skilled Irish males; and, in Dyos and Wolff, p. 425, she actually misstates her calculations by claiming that 'under 10 per cent had skilled jobs of any sort'. She also, in my opinion, exaggerates both the extent to which Irishmen fell victims to sweating and their inactivity in craftsmen's organizations (*ibid.; Exiles*, pp. 93–4, 98, 101–2, 239–40). Certainly according to Mayhew, *LL&LP*, I, p. 104, 'The greater part of the Irish artizans who have arrived within the last five years are to be found among the most degraded of the tailors and shoemakers who work at the East-end for the slop-masters'; but it is not possible to ascertain whether, during the 1840s, the Irish – and particularly Irish as opposed to other migrants – were disproportionately represented in the dishonourable trades. See also *Morning Chronicle*, 18 Dec. 1849; Mayhew, *UM*, pp. 215, 223–6, 426–7.

259 This is substantially confirmed by the 'Returns of Places where Political Meetings are held . . . with Particulars relative thereto' of 22 June 1848 (MEPO 2/59), oddly the only attempt by the police in the Chartist decade to produce a comprehensive survey of the ultra-radical societies in London – though significantly covering the Confederates as well as Chartists.

260 Cf. Lees, *Exiles*, p. 225.

261 *NS*, 21 Sept. 1844, 26 June 1847.

262 PRO, Treasury Solicitor's Records [hereafter TS] 11/136/373; Robert Crowe, *The Reminiscences of Robert Crowe, The Octogenerian Tailor* [sic] ([New York], n.d.), pp. 7–8 (two of Crowe's short chapters were first published as 'The Reminiscences of a Chartist Tailor', *The Outlook* (New York), 9 Aug. 1902).

263 See, for example, *NS*, 3 June, 5 Aug., 25 Nov. 1843, 30 March, 16 Nov. 1844.

264 McDowell, in Edwards and Williams, pp. 81–4.

265 Nowlan, pp. 93–115.

266 O'Higgins, 'Ireland and Chartism', pp. 203–4. For Harney's succinct

class analysis at the Convention of the Young Irelanders' position: *NS*, 8 Aug. 1846.

267 Sir Charles Gavan Duffy, *Young Ireland: A Fragment of Irish History, 1840–1850* (1880), p. 171.

268 W. J. Linton, *Memories* (1895), pp. 107–9; Sir Charles Gavan Duffy, *Four Years of Irish History, 1845–1849: A Sequel to 'Young Ireland'* (1883), p. 450n; F. B. Smith, *Radical Artisan: William James Linton 1812–97* (Manchester, 1973), pp. 67–71.

269 Cf. Treble, pp. 64–8. Nowlan, p. 182 *et seq.*, discusses the impact in Ireland of the events in France.

270 Cf. J. H. Treble, 'The Irish Agitation', in Ward, *Popular Movements*, p. 177.

271 O'Higgins, 'Ireland and Chartism', pp. 204–7. For enthusiastic comments on O'Connor's tactics by the London Confederates see *NS*, 4–25 Dec. 1847. A disparaging assessment is given by Kevin B. Nowlan, 'The Political Background', in Edwards and Williams, pp. 182–4.

272 Nowlan, *Politics of Repeal*, chap. 8 and pp. 171–3; O'Higgins, 'Ireland and Chartism', pp. 207–9.

273 O'Higgins, 'Ireland and Chartism', pp. 213–19; Treble, pp. 65–7.

274 *NS*, 19 July 1845, 5 Sept., 24 Oct. 1846, 28 Aug. 1847; Denvir, *Irish in Britain*, p. 133. For a previous dispute, involving the permanent expulsion of Dwaine, see *NS*, 27 July 1844. For initial metropolitan support, in 1846, for the seceders and the resignation of Daly, 'a notable warden in London', see Duffy, *Four Years*, pp. 286–7, 294.

275 *NS*, 20 March, 24 April, 15 May, 17, 31 July, 4, 18 Sept. 1847.

276 O'Higgins, 'Ireland and Chartism', pp. 102–3.

277 *NS*, 28 Aug., 11 Sept., 2 Oct. 1847.

278 *Ibid.*, 18 Dec. 1847, 15 July, 30 Sept. 1848.

279 See entry in the *Dictionary of National Biography*; John Saville, 'The Background to the Revival of Socialism in England', *BSSLH*, no. 11 (Autumn 1965), p. 15. The Confederation had refused to endorse Kenealy as their candidate for Dublin University in the 1847 election and later declined to accept his nomination by the Davis Club for membership of the Council, since he was not regarded as 'sincere and reputable'. He had written ill of the dead Davis, an unforgivable act (Duffy, *Four Years*, pp. 422–4, and *Young Ireland*, p. 766n).

280 *NS*, 2, 16 Oct. 1847.

281 *Ibid.*, 28 Aug. 1847–29 April 1848.

282 *Ibid.*, 26 Feb., 25 March, 1, 8 April 1848.

283 *Ibid.*, 31 July, 2 Oct., 4 Dec. 1847; 29 Jan., 8 April 1848.

284 *Ibid.*, 8 April 1848.

285 Quoted by O'Higgins, 'Ireland and Chartism', p. 220.

286 Black and Black, p. 317.

287 *NS*, 15 April 1848.

288 J. T. Ward, *Chartism* (1973), pp. 200–2; John Prest, *Lord John Russell* (1972), pp. 283, 285; M. Creighton, *Memoir of Sir George Grey, Bart., G.C.B.* (Newcastle-upon-Tyne, 1884), p. 65; F. C. Mather, 'The Government and the Chartists', in Briggs, *Chartist Studies*, pp. 394–5; Nowlan, pp. 196–200.

289 *The Times*, 10 April 1848.

290 Indeed, it has been computed that 1848 is the year with London's highest recorded level of convictions for (indictable) offences against public

order – in the span from 1834 to 1972 (Ted Robert Gurr, Peter N. Grabosky and Richard C. Hula, *The Politics of Crime and Conflict: A Comparative History of Four Cities* (Beverly Hills, 1977), pp. 70–2, 655–8).

291 Preston William Slosson, *The Decline of the Chartist Movement* (New York, 1916), p. 94, considers that the renewed agitation can be traced as far back as early 1846.

292 *NS,* 4 March 1848.

293 *Ibid.,* 26 Feb. 1848. For Harney's recollection of his ecstatic reaction: Black and Black, p. 355.

294 *NS,* 4 March 1848.

295 *Ibid.,* 4, 11 March 1848; *Reynolds's Political Instructor,* 20 April 1850.

296 D. Morier Evans, *The Commercial Crisis, 1847–1848* (1849; Newton Abbot, 1969 edn), Epoch the Third.

297 See, in addition to the following, Appendix I.

298 *NS,* 8, 15, 29 Jan., 5, 12 Feb., 18 March 1848.

299 Webb TU MSS., XI, ff. 288–9; Postgate, *Builders' History,* pp. 8–9. Cf. Francis Sheppard, Victor Belcher and Philip Cottrell, 'The Middlesex and Yorkshire Deeds Registries and the Study of Building Fluctuations', *London Journal,* V, no. 2 (Nov. 1979), p. 196.

300 *Morning Chronicle,* 7 Feb. 1850.

301 *Spirit of the Age,* 30 Dec. 1848.

302 *Weekly Dispatch,* 16 April 1848. Cf. the windowblind-maker's and upholsterer's statements, PC set 58, vol. I, f. 256, and *Morning Chronicle,* 16 Nov. 1849. For Harney on metropolitan destitution: *NS,* 11, 25 Dec. 1847, 29 Jan. 1848.

303 James Knox Laughton, *Memoirs of the Life and Correspondence of Henry Reeve, C.B., D.C.L.* (2 vols., 1898), I, p. 190.

304 There were comparable estimates in October and November 1848 (*Spirit of the Age,* 21, 28 Oct., 11 Nov. 1848).

305 For the analysis see *NS,* 29 April 1848, and *Labour League,* 12 Aug. 1848; also *The Times,* 1 April 1848. It should be noted that when he discusses employment Mayhew gives these proportions as the *permanent* condition of British workers at mid-century (*LL&LP,* II, p. 300). The statement by 'R. E. . . . a working tailor', printed in the *Morning Chronicle,* 18 Dec. 1849, appears to provide the connection between the Trades' Delegates' findings and Mayhew's unjustified conclusion (but cf. Walton's pronouncement, *NS,* 10 March 1849). The distress caused by the interaction of this very severe downturn in the trade cycle – and the cholera of 1849 – with the deleterious economic structural changes (discussed in Part Four) resulted in Mayhew's *Morning Chronicle* commission, which in turn accounts for our considerable knowledge of the latter. (I owe this point to T. C. Barker.) This book in places draws heavily on Mayhew's reports and *London Labour and the London Poor.* I have no reservations (the preceding point is exceptional) about their reliability – in my experience Mayhew's findings have frequently been substantiated by independent sources – but the conclusions of F. B. Smith, 'Mayhew's Convict', *Victorian Studies,* XXII (1978–9), demand respect.

306 For the French connection, see the address, inaugurating the Trades' Demonstration Committee, signed by Hawson and Nicholson, *NS,* 18 March, 1 April 1848.

307 *Ibid.,* 11, 18, 25 March, 1, 29 April 1848.

308 *Spirit of the Age*, 5 Aug., 2 Sept. 1848; *NS*, 9 Sept. 1848, 10 March 1849.
309 *Spirit of the Age*, 14 Oct. 1848; *NS*, 18 Nov. 1848.
310 See, esp., *NS*, 6 Jan., 3, 10 March, 14 April, 12 May, 10, 17, 24 Nov., 1, 22 Dec. 1849. For the Metropolitan Trades' Delegates see also Viles, pp. 187–93, but his contention (pp. 85–7) that they had previously (from the late 1830s) constituted a recognized trades' body is misconceived.
311 *NS*, 11 Dec. 1847; 29, 15 April, 8 July 1848.
312 Charles Cochrane, as nephew of the former Lord Cochrane, possessed impressive local radical credentials and by 1847–8 was a prominent metropolitan personality. He had, most notably, instituted a 'corps of street-sweepers' and his candidature in the Westminster election of 1847 prompted dissension among Chartists as to his political merits (A Westminster Elector, *An Address to the Business-like Men of Westminster* [1847]; Frost, *Reminiscences*, pp. 29–31; *NS*, 29 May, 12, 19, 26 June 1847). Celina Fox, 'The Development of Social Reportage in English Periodical Illustration During the 1840s and Early 1850s', *P&P*, no. 74 (Feb. 1977), pp. 107–9, provides an interesting sketch of Cochrane's career, although neglecting the notoriety he acquired in 1848.
313 It should be stressed, however, that the official Chartist response to the event – and its consequences – was of entire disassociation (see *NS*, 11 March 1848).
314 I.e., Wombwell's.
315 *The Times*, 7 March 1848; *NS*, 11 March 1848; MEPO 2/64; HO 45/2412. See below, pp. 111–14.
316 The *Northern Star*, 18 March 1848, described it as adjourned from Trafalgar Square on the 6th. Cf. MEPO 2/64, report by Inspector Haynes, 6 March 1848.
317 *The Times*, 14 March 1848; *NS*, 18 March 1848; MEPO 2/63. See below, pp. 114–17.
318 See below, pp. 129–30.
319 *NS*, 18 March 1848.
320 *The Times*, 14 March 1848; *NS*, 18 March, 1 April 1848. See also *The Times*, 28 March 1848.
321 Cf. *Annual Register, 1848*, p. 36.
322 John Earl Russell, *Recollections and Suggestions, 1813–1873* (1875), pp. 252–3. Cf. Mather, in Briggs, *Chartist Studies*, pp. 395–6.
323 HO 60/5; HO 41/26; *NS*, 8 April 1848.
324 HO 79/9, Grey to Clarendon, 3 April 1848.
325 PRO, Russell Papers, PRO 30/22/7B, letter from Palmerston, 7 April 1848; HO 45/2410/Part 1. His wife finally flouted his ultra-cautious instructions (Lady Palmerston, *The Letters of Lady Palmerston*, ed. Tresham Lever (1957), p. 299). See also West, pp. 245–6. The classic example of aristocratic alarm is to be found in the Earl of Malmesbury's diary entries: *Memoirs of an Ex-Minister: An Autobiography* (2 vols., 1884), I, pp. 233–6.
326 Creighton, pp. 65–6, 73–4; PRO 30/22/7B, letter from Grey to Russell, 9 April 1848; Prest, pp. 283–5.
327 PRO, War Office Records [hereafter WO] 30/111. In 1845 rank-and-file troops stationed in Great Britain amounted to 30,000 – with a further 20,000 in Ireland (Burgoyne's assumptions concerning this matter were extraordinarily awry (*The Military Opinions of General Sir John Fox Bur-*

goyne, Bart., G. C. B., ed. George Wrottesley (1859), p. 2)) – and Wellington estimated that a mere 5,000 could be withdrawn, on the mainland, from garrison duties in an emergency, while Palmerston considered 14,000 men could be mobilized to fight an invasion south of the Thames *if* the infantry and cavalry were entirely withdrawn from London and all other inland towns. By 1848, however, the totals of rank-and-file (i.e., privates and corporals alone) in Great Britain and Ireland had been increased to 39,000 and 26,000 respectively. In both 1838 and 1842 forces of 10,000 had been assembled for the suppression of Chartist disorder, although in those years, unlike 1848, it was possible to move troops to England from Ireland (Robert A. Rizzi, 'The British Army as a Riot Control Force in Great Britain, 1811–1848' (Oxford BLitt thesis, 1975), pp. 142, 145; Mather, *Public Order*, pp. 153, 160–1, 163; Lieut.-Col. the Hon. George Wrottesley, *Life and Correspondence of Field Marshal Sir John Burgoyne, Bart.* (2 vols., 1873), I, pp. 439, 445). In March and April 1848 Ireland was supplied with extra regiments from Yorkshire and Lancashire (HO 79/9, Grey to Clarendon, 27 March 1848; Mather, *Public Order*, p. 160n).

328 See below, Tables 10 and 11.

329 *The Times*, 10 April 1848.

330 Richard Whiteing, *My Harvest* (1915), p. 14. See too *The Greville Memoirs, 1814–1860*, ed. Lytton Strachey and Roger Fulford (8 vols., 1938), VI, p. 51. Sir Edward Hertslet, *Recollections of the Old Foreign Office* (1901), pp. 67–71, gives an entertaining description of the preparations within the Foreign Office (and Board of Trade) (I owe this reference to George J. Billy).

331 HO 45/2410/Part 5, letter from Lieut.-Col. Maberly, 6 April 1848; WO 30/111, letter from Major Aldrich, 8 April 1848.

332 HO 45/2410/Parts 1 and 5.

333 *NS*, 15 April 1848; *Sun*, 10 April 1848.

334 I owe this illuminating insight to John Saville, who is currently preparing a book on the role of the British state in 1848 which will explore this and related matters at length.

335 The Lord Mayor admitted to the embarrassment of having too large a special constabulary for his control, but was content that this 'demonstration has had a fine effect' (HO 45/2410/Part 5, letter from J. K. Hooper, 4.30 p.m., 10 April 1848).

336 See below, pp. 130–3.

337 Palmerston, *Letters of Lady Palmerston*, pp. 300–1; PRO 30/22/7B, letter from C. E. Trevelyan to Russell, 4 April 1848; *Express*, 10 April 1848; *Morning Chronicle*, 11 April 1848; W. S. Dugdale's MS. diary, quoted by Norman Gash (ed.), *The Age of Peel* (1968), pp. 178–9; Asa Briggs, 'Middle-Class Consciousness in English Politics, 1780–1846', *P&P*, no. 9 (April 1956), pp. 71–2; *idem*, 'National Bearings', in Briggs, *Chartist Studies*, pp. 299–300. George R. Sims's family, however, was split, his father serving as a special whereas his maternal grandfather was a prominent Chartist (*My Life: Sixty Years' Recollections of Bohemian London* (1917), pp. 9–10) (I am indebted to George Hauger for this reference).

338 HO 45/2410/Part 1, letter from S. W. Catley, 26 April 1848.

339 MEPO 2/65, memo. by C. Yardley, 8 April 1848, and letter from George Fawler (?), 12 April 1848. Maurice would have served as constable had not his clerical status debarred him (Frederick Maurice (ed.), *The Life of*

Frederick Denison Maurice: Chiefly Told in His Own Letters (2nd edn, 2 vols., 1884), I, p. 472).

340 Rev. W. T. Henderson, 'Recollections of his Life', 1910 (MS. in possession of M. Spokes, 55 Bloxham Road, Banbury).

341 W. Holman Hunt, *Pre-Raphaelitism and the Pre-Raphaelite Brotherhood* (2 vols., 1905), I, pp. 101–2.

342 HO 45/2410/Part 5. Compare also 'the firm determination of the [Demonstration] committee that the demonstration shall be a peaceable, orderly, and moral display of the unenfranchised and toiling masses' (*The Times*, 4 April 1848). See Large, in Stevenson, *London*, pp. 186–7, and, also, Royden Harrison, *Before the Socialists: Studies in Labour and Politics, 1861–1881* (1965), pp. 78–80, for cogent refutations of the view that the Chartists proposed a revolutionary challenge on 10 April.

343 Captain G. A. Raikes, *The History of the Honourable Artillery Company* (2 vols., 1878–9), II, p. 341.

344 Mayhew, *UM*, p. 254.

345 TS 11/140/387 (Burn). See too Crowe, *Reminiscences of Robert Crowe*, p. 9.

346 Frederick Lessner, *Sixty Years in the Social-Democratic Movement: Before 1848 and After: Recollections of an Old Communist* (1907), p. 16. Cf. W. E. Adams, *Memoirs of a Social Atom* (2 vols., 1903), I, p. 183. The police reported the absence of arms – 'or even bludgeons' (HO 45/2410/Part 1).

347 Palmerston, *Letters of Lady Palmerston*, pp. 300–1; Bernard Porter, *The Refugee Question in Mid-Victorian Politics* (Cambridge, 1979), pp. 85–6; HO 45/2410/Part 1, letters from Mayne [to Grey], 10 April 1848; MEPO 2/43, report from Superintendent, H Division, 17 April 1848.

348 HO 45/2410/Part 5.

349 MEPO 2/65; MEPO 2/59; *NS*, 15 April 1848; and the press reports: for example, *Sun*, 10 April 1848. See also PRO 30/22/7B, letter from Grey to Russell, 9 April 1848, and for O'Connor's fears of carnage, Stevens, p. 44.

350 See below, pp. 146–7.

351 *Annual Register, 1848*, pp. 51, 53, is amusingly self-contradictory on this point.

352 See pp. 136–42.

353 The spectacle of the Petition being delivered at the House of Commons provided Alfred Marshall with his earliest memory (C. R. Fay, *Huskisson and His Age* (1951), p. 138).

354 HO 45/2410/Part 1 – printed, with alterations, in T. A. Critchley, *The Conquest of Violence: Order and Liberty in Britain* (1970), p. 140.

355 HO 41/19; Wellington, *Wellington and His Friends: Letters of the First Duke of Wellington to the Rt. Hon. Charles and Mrs. Arbuthnot, the Earl and Countess of Wilton, Princess Lieven, and Miss Burdett-Coutts*, ed. Seventh Duke of Wellington (1965), p. 210.

356 *Morning Chronicle*, 11 April 1848; *Sun*, 10 April 1848; *NS*, 15 April 1848.

357 *Morning Chronicle*, *Daily News* and *The Times*, 11 April 1848; *NS*, 15, 22, 29 April 1848; Frost, *Recollections*, pp. 140–1; Hunt, I, p. 102; Lessner, p. 16; HO 45/2410/Part 5, letters from Lord Mayor, 10 April 1848.

358 Wellington, *Wellington and His Friends*, p. 210. For the curious police tactics that led to this situation see *The Times*, *Morning Chronicle*, and esp. *Daily News*, 11 April 1848.

359 *Shipping and Mercantile Gazette*, 10 April 1848.

360 *Morning Chronicle*, 11 April 1848; Hunt, I, p. 102. See also Matthew Arnold, *The Letters of Matthew Arnold to Arthur Hugh Clough*, ed. Howard Foster Lowry (Oxford, 1968), p. 79.

361 Wellington, *Wellington and His Friends*, p. 210.

362 *Morning Chronicle* and *Morning Post*, 11 April 1848. For the general movement of consols: F. B. Smith, 'The View from Britain I: "Tumults Abroad, Stability at Home" ', in Eugene Kamenka and F. B. Smith (eds.), *Intellectuals and Revolution: Socialism and the Experience of 1848* (1979), p. 116.

363 HO 60/5.

364 John Vincent, 'The Oldest Profession', *New Statesman*, 5 Aug. 1966. For 10 April, in general, see also the sensible observations of Raymond Postgate, *Story of a Year: 1848* (1955), pp. 126–8. Sir Herbert Maxwell, *Sixty Years a Queen: The Story of Her Majesty's Reign* [1897], pp. 50–2, provides an example of a complacent, knock-about account.

365 Cf. Briggs, 'National Bearings', in Briggs, *Chartist Studies*, p. 299.

366 Cf. E. P. Thompson, 'Sir, Writing by Candlelight . . .', reprinted in *Writing by Candlelight* (1980), pp. 39–48.

367 *Annual Register, 1848*, p. 53.

368 Elie Halévy, *A History of the English People in the Nineteenth Century* (6 vols., 1961 edn), IV, p. 245.

369 See esp. *The Times, Morning Chronicle* and *Morning Herald*, but, above all, the evening *Standard*, 11 April 1848; and also, [Sir Arthur Helps], *A Letter from One of the Special Constables in London on the Late Occasion of Their Being Called Out to Keep the Peace* (1848), pp. 3–5, and Lady Palmerston's (less glamourized) account (*The Letters of Lady Palmerston*, pp. 299–302), both written on 14 April.

370 John Saville, 'The Christian Socialists of 1848', in John Saville (ed.), *Democracy and the Labour Movement: Essays in Honour of Dona Torr* (1954), pp. 156–7; *idem*, 'Introduction: R. G. Gammage', pp. 36–8. See Charles Kingsley, *Alton Locke, Tailor and Poet: An Autobiography* (1850; 1881 edn), chaps. 32–5, esp. p. 361. Cf. also George Jacob Holyoake, *Bygones Worth Remembering* (2 vols., n.d.), I, chap. 7.

371 Henry Vizetelly, *Glances Back Through Seventy Years: Autobiographical and Other Reminiscences* (2 vols., 1893), I, p. 334.

372 *Greville Memoirs*, VI, p. 51.

373 *Daily News*, 11 April 1848. Cf. some similar observations in the *Standard*, 11 April 1848.

374 Cf. Halévy, IV, pp. 246–7, and Jean Sigmann, *Eighteen-Fortyeight: The Romantic and Democratic Revolutions in Europe* (1973), pp. 12–13, 238. For 16 April see Georges Duveau, *1848: The Making of a Revolution* (1967), pp. 87–92.

375 For the moralizing concerning 1848 generally, see Smith, 'The View from Britain I', and J. H. Grainger, 'The View from Britain II: the Moralizing Island', in Kamenka and Smith. There is, in contrast, the pitying comment of (the anti-revolutionary) Berlioz, then living in London: Hector Berlioz, *The Memoirs of Hector Berlioz, Member of the French Institute: including his Travels in Italy, Germany, Russia and England, 1803–1865*, trans. and ed. David Cairns (1969), p. 44.

376 Donald Southgate, *'The Most English Minister . . .': The Policies and Politics of Palmerston* (1966), pp. 206–7; HO 79/9.

377 Letter to G. Cornewall Lewis, 22 April 1848, in Charles Stuart Parker,

Life and Letters of Sir James Graham: Second Baronet of Netherby, P.C., G.C.B.: *1792–1861* (2 vols., 1907), II, p. 70.

378 E.g., Gammage, p. 331.

379 See, for example, Central Criminal Court, *Sessions Papers. Minutes of Evidence, Taken in Short-hand . . .* [hereafter CCC], XXVIII, p. 962.

380 Cf. Saville, 'Introduction: R. G. Gammage', p. 33; and *idem*, 'Some Aspects of Chartism in Decline', p. 16.

381 See above, Table 5.

382 The series was started in March on waste plots or fields at New North Road, Cambridge Health Road and London Lane. Stepney Green and Hackney Field were also used (*NS*, 18 March, 1, 15, 22, 29 April, 20, 27 May 1848).

383 *Ibid.*, 11 March 1848. May, for whom see also below, pp. 89, 264 n434, was 'late candidate for the borough of St Albans' (*The Times*, 22 April 1848).

384 *NS*, 6 May 1848 *et seq.*

385 See above, Table 5.

386 *NS*, 27 May, 3 June 1848.

387 Terry M. Parssinen, 'Mesmeric Performers', *Victorian Studies*, XXI (1977–8), pp. 94–5, describes Vernon's previous, successful career as a mesmerist.

388 *NS*, 6, 13 May 1848.

389 E.g., for arming, see *The Times*, 30 May 1848; *Sun*, 12 June 1848.

390 *NS*, 29 April 1843. For Deptford and Greenwich Chartism in the 1840s: Geoffrey Crossick, *An Artisan Elite in Victorian Society: Kentish London 1840–1880* (1978), pp. 201–10.

391 *NS*, 10 June, 1 July 1848. The John Mitchel Club later met at the Crown, Gravel Lane, Southwark, and Falcon, Union Street, Southwark (*ibid.*, 1 July, 5 Aug. 1848).

392 *Ibid.*, 10 June 1848.

393 *Ibid.*, 20 May, 3, 10 June, 8 July 1848; CCC, XXVIII, p. 792. For Confederate Clubs in existence by April 1848, see above, p. 66. In the summer further Clubs were opened at Jennings' Buildings, Kensington; Victory, Deptford; Fountain and Still, Golden Lane; Denny's Coffee House, Great St Andrew's Street; Temperance Hall, Rufford's Buildings, Islington (Red Hugh O'Donnell Club); Sun Coffee House, Long Lane, Bermondsey (Charles Gavan Duffy Club); and, possibly, Farm House, Hooper Street, Waterloo Road (*NS*, 1, 8, 22 July, 5, 12 Aug. 1848). A copy of the minute-book of the Davis Club, Dean Street, 17 April–19 July 1848, is in TS 11/138/380.

394 *NS*, 6 May 1843; O'Higgins, 'Ireland and Chartism', pp. 79–80, 221. For Bryan see also Duffy, *Four Years*, p. 249n, and Treble, pp. 61–2.

395 Frost's reminiscences must, as always, be regarded with scepticism, especially his account of how Terence Bellew Macmanus (the Liverpool Confederate) visited London as an emissary, attended a meeting of the Westminster Chartists at Dean Street, thwarted the police trailing him and returned safely to Ireland – because the incident in which a detective was ejected at Dean Street and hustled down the stairs is virtually identical to one in which Michael M'Manus, a London Confederate, was concerned (Frost, *Recollections*, p. 148; *NS*, 17, 24 June 1848).

396 It seems he came from Dublin to London for 12 June (Denis Gwynn, *Young Ireland and 1848* (Cork, 1949), pp. 208–9; HO 45/2410/Part 1, report from Davis, 12 June 1848. See too below, p. 264 n439).

397 *NS*, 3, 10 June 1848.

398 Thomas Frost gives a figure of 80,000 (but is certainly incorrect in claiming that the assemblies of the 29th occurred 'without any public notification') (*Recollections*, p. 145).

399 *NS*, 27 May, 3 June 1848; *The Times*, 30 May, 1 June 1848; RA C8/17, letter from Queen to Russell, 30 May 1848; Frost, *Recollections*, pp. 145–6; CCC, XXVIII, pp. 340–56, 365–77; TS 11/136/372 (R. v. Fussell); TS 11/140/386; MEPO 2/59, letter [from John Paterson] dated (incorrectly) 6 May 1848.

400 CCC, XXVIII, pp. 370–2. See below, p. 117.

401 *The Times*, 31 May 1848; *NS*, 3 June 1848; TS 11/136/372, copy of proclamation, 30 May 1848; MEPO 7/12. Large, in Stevenson, *London*, pp. 197, 209 n118, has the events of 31 May occurring on the 30th. See also below, pp. 117–18.

402 James Elmzlie Duncan, author of the broadsides *Pe-ans for the People* (BL press mark 1871. e. 1. (232)), becaue a familiar figure in the disturbances of 1848, having been arrested at the outset during the Trafalgar Square riots on 6 March (MEPO 2/64; see also *The Times*, 6, 13 June 1848, and *NS*, 5 Aug., 16 Dec. 1848). Connected with the Concordists of Ham Common, he edited the *Sun Beam*, advocate of J. A. Etzler's Tropical Emigration Society (Frost, *Recollections*, pp. 49–50; Armytage, pp. 192–3; Dorothy Thompson, 'La Presse de la Classe Ouvrière Anglaise, 1836–1848', in Jacques Godechot (ed.), *La Presse Ouvrière, 1819–1850* (Paris, 1966), p. 39).

403 *NS*, 3 June 1848; *The Times*, 1, 2 June 1848; HO 60/5; MEPO 2/66. See below, pp. 118–19.

404 *Greville Memoirs*, VI, p. 73.

405 *The Times*, 5 June 1848; HO 45/2410/Part 1, reports from Supt. J. Johnston, 4 June 1848; MEPO 2/67, letter from J. R. D. Tyssen to Supt. Johnston, 8 June 1848; MEPO 2/59, letter from C. B. Strutfield to Commissioners, 4 June 1848; TS 11/138/376, statement by Insp. Waller.

406 *The Times* 5, 6, 7 June 1848; CCC, XXVIII, pp. 244–51. See below, p. 120.

407 *The Times*, 5 June 1848; *NS*, 10, 24 June 1848; CCC, XXVIII, pp. 216–27, 391–403, 424–31; TS 11/136/369; TS 11/138/376. See below, pp. 120–2.

408 *NS*, 10 June, 1, 8, 15 July 1848.

409 See, for example, *The Times*, 2 June 1848; *Sun*, 12 June 1848; *Greville Memoirs*, VI, p. 73.

410 Joseph Irenæus John Fussell, a Clerkenwell jeweller, had been prominent in Birmingham in 1839 as a physical-force man, urging the removal of the Convention there, but later suspected as a spy 'he was discarded by the whole of the Birmingham people' (and, back in London, a police report of 1841 reinforces this taint). On the other hand, although a prosecution jointly against Harney, Edward Brown and Fussell was dropped, it had passed into the hands of the Treasury Solicitor. In 1848 Fussell's conduct was consistent – and he experienced no leniency (Add. MSS. 34,245A, ff. 414–15, and 27,821, f. 173; HO 45/52, report of Sgt Tierney, 9 May 1841; TS 11/142/390; HO 12/81; Tholfsen, 'Chartist Crisis', pp. 465–75; Hovell, pp. 144–5, 178; Schoyen, p. 69 *et seq.*).

411 *NS*, 10, 17 June, 15 July 1848. See also TS 11/135/360; CCC, XXVIII, pp. 441–5; HO 12/81.

412 RA C8/18, letter from Queen to Russell, 31 May 1848; RA C56/84, letter from Russell to Queen, 1 June 1848; RA C56/86, letter from Grey to Queen, 4 June 1848.

413 Grey was solicitous in keeping Victoria informed of progress in the proceedings, giving details in letters of 5, 6, 7 and 8 June (RA C56/90, 91, 92 and 93) and again on 15 June (RA B10/198). Cf. John Saville's comments on the government's tactics in: 'Chartism in the Year of Revolution (1848)', *Modern Quarterly*, New Series, VIII, no. 1 (Winter 1952–3), pp. 26–7, 29–31; John Saville, 'Introduction', *The Red Republican & The Friend of the People*, I (1966), p. ix n50; *idem*, 'Introduction: R. G. Gammage', pp. 33–6; *idem*, *Ernest Jones*, pp. 31–2.

414 *NS*, 27 May, 10 June 1848; HO 45/2410/Part 1.

415 Proclamation of 10 June printed in *Sun*, 12 June 1848, and *NS*, 17 June 1848.

416 See below, pp. 142–5.

417 *NS*, 10 June 1848.

418 HO 45/2410/Part 1, report of George Davis, 10 June 1848.

419 *Ibid.*, report from Mallalieu, 2 June, and letters from Mrs A. Evans, received 9 June, and R. Palmer, received 12 June; HO 45/2410/Part 5, letter from J. W. Gutteridge, received 8 June.

420 HO 45/2410/Part 1, report of PC John Bywater, 11 June 1848.

421 Cf. *Daily News*, 7 June 1848, quoted by *NS*, 10 June 1848. Mather does not appreciate the significance of 12 June, considering the proclamation an outcome of the disorder of the beginning of the month (*Public Order*, p. 105; 'Government and the Chartists', in Briggs, *Chartist Studies*, pp. 396–7). In contrast Large, in Stevenson, *London*, pp. 199–200, interestingly detects genuine anxiety 'in the inner circles of authority' concerning 12 June as opposed to, as he considers, the pretended alarm of 10 April. Grey, however, remained as cool as ever (PRO 30/22/7C, letter to Russell, 11 June 1848).

422 *NS*, 17 June 1848; HO 41/26; HO 60/5; MEPO 7/14.

423 Quoted by *Shipping and Mercantile Gazette*, 12 June 1848, and *NS*, 17 June 1848.

424 *NS*, 17 June 1848; HO 45/2410/Part 1; MEPO 7/14; Frost, *Recollections*, p. 155.

425 HO 45/2410/Part 1, letter from T. J. Arnold, 12 June 1848.

426 The size of the crowd, since it was only a potential demonstration, is more than usually difficult to estimate. The *Northern Star*, 17 June 1848, did not commit itself to a figure, although in a digest of the morning papers' reports, referred to 'a vast concourse of persons' attracted by the soldiers when they took up position at the Gardiner's Barn end of the Fields, yet the *Morning Advertiser*, 13 June 1848, stated that 'at no period of the day did the numbers exceed three thousand'.

427 *NS*, 17 June 1848; *The Times*, 13 June 1848. See too the coverage by the *Sun*, 12 June 1848; *Nonconformist*, 14 June 1848; *Illustrated London News*, 17 June 1848; *Cause of the People*, 17 June 1848. At Ernest Jones's trial a police inspector stated that a small meeting did take place at Stepney Green on 12 June (CCC, XXVIII, p. 431).

428 MEPO 2/59; HO 60/5.

429 'Prefatory Memoir' to Charles Kingsley, p. xiii (and reprinted in [Frances E. Kingsley (ed.)], *Charles Kingsley: His Letters and Memories of His Life* (2nd edn, 2 vols., 1877), I, p. 161). Cf. the hazy reference by Edward

Stillingfleet Cayley, *The European Revolutions of 1848* (2 vols., 1856), II, p. 246.

430 Cf. the report of M'Douall's movements by *The Times,* 13 June 1848. The claim by Thomas Frost, *Recollections,* pp. 149–62, that 12 June was the first date fixed for a general rising is incorrect. See the references to Bligh belonging to 'the first conspiracy in June after the disturbance at Bonner's Fields' and to 'the Old Delegate Committee that was formed on Whit Monday' (TS 11/139/381, 'Notes relative to persons who are known to have been spd. on behalf of Prisr., as to Davis' and evidence of Davis; CCC, XXVIII, p. 934).

431 HO 45/2410/Part 1. Reading was no novice to the work of treachery. In 1839 he had given information that Beniowski and Dr Taylor had left for Newport (HO 40/52). See also HO 65/16, letter from Waddington to Mayne, 14 Oct. 1848.

432 HO 45/2410/Part 1, 1st report from Davis, 14 June 1848.

433 *Ibid.,* 2nd report from Davis, 14 June 1848.

434 *Ibid.,* reports from Davis, 12, 14 June 1848. A warrant was issued on 6 June for May's arrest (for a seditious speech at Clerkenwell Green on 25 May), but on 30 June, May having presented himself at Bow Street the previous day, Mayne wrote that there were reasons why 'It is not desirable to execute this warrant' (MEPO 2/59; *NS,* 1 July 1848). For May see above, pp. 79, 261 n383.

435 HO 45/2410/Part 1, statement of William Taylor, n.d.

436 *NS,* 22, 29 July 1848; *Lady's Newspaper,* 29 July 1848.

437 *NS,* 29 July 1848; MEPO 2/59; MEPO 7/14, 25, 28 July, 14 Aug. 1848. See too MEPO 2/62. It was not until 28 July that Clarendon informed London that Smith O'Brien was heading a rising (Nowlan, pp. 213–14). For the Irish rising – and its ignominious outcome – see Gwynn.

438 *NS,* 29 July–9 Sept., 23 Sept., 7 Oct. 1848; MEPO 2/62, communication from John Paterson, n.d. For further details: TS 11/136/368 and 373; TS 11/138/377 and 379; TS 11/1121/5785; CCC, XXVIII; TS 11/141/388, police report, 12 Aug. 1848; HO 48/40, letter from Maule to Waddington, 29 Aug. 1848; HO 12/81. Crowe, *The Reminiscences of Robert Crowe,* are naturally of considerable interest, but Crowe dwells on his prison experiences, writing very little about his political activities in 1848 (or before). Bezer's remarkable, excitingly titled 'Autobiography of One of the Chartist Rebels of 1848', published in the *Christian Socialist* in 1851 (and reprinted in Vincent), was regrettably uncompleted, never reaching 1848.

439 A warrant was issued for Daly's arrest after the inflammatory speeches of 25 May–4 June and O'Brien was told on 12 June that 'we expect that Mr. Daly will be arrested on his return to London' (RA C56/93, letter from Grey to Queen, 8 June 1848; Gwynn, pp. 208–9). His letter was published in *NS,* 21 Oct. 1848; and an informer reported on 31 July that 'Daly is in France' (MEPO 2/62). But according to Davis, he was present at a Confederate meeting in Seven Dials on 14 August, which, if true, would place him at the heart of the final insurrectionary attempt (HO 45/2410/Part 1, report of 15 Aug. 1848). His death in New York was reported early in 1849 (*NS,* 3 Feb. 1849).

440 TS 11/139/381, evidence of Davis.

441 Cf. Mather, *Public Order,* p. 214 n5.

442 In HO 45/2410/Part 1 and TS 11/142/389. This does not refer to the

June conspiracy for which Davis's reports are preserved in HO 45/2410/Part 1.

443 TS 11/138/380 (Powell); TS 11/139/381 (Powell and Davis).

444 CCC, XXVIII, p. 732.

445 *Ibid.*, p. 731.

446 Of the Chartist Executive.

447 TS 11/138/380 (Powell); TS 11/139/381 (Powell).

448 Davis's evidence, unlike Powell's, is confused concerning this matter (TS 11/139/381; CCC, XXVIII, p. 938).

449 But cf. CCC, XXVIII, p. 927.

450 *NS*, 6 May, 30 Sept. 1848; HO 45/2410/Part 1, report of Davis, June 1848; HO 45/2410/Part 5, letter from John Paterson, 20 April 1848; TS 11/141/388, unsigned note, n.d. Cf. MEPO 2/62, 26 April 1848, and *NS*, 4 Nov. 1848. Churchill had certainly been in France early in the year for he conveyed the 'sympathies' of a French 'democratic society' to the Convention (and in this connection is most fully named: as J. G. Churchill) (*NS*, 8, 22 April 1848; *Nonconformist*, 12 April 1848).

451 TS 11/138/380 (Powell); TS 11/139/381 (Powell and Davis).

452 HO 45/2410/Part 1, report from Davis, 14 Aug. 1848; TS 11/139/381 (Davis).

453 TS 11/138/380 (Powell); TS 11/139/381 (Powell and Davis); HO 45/2410/Part 1, report from Davis, 15 Aug. 1848.

454 TS 11/138/380 (Powell and Jemina Heath); TS 11/139/381 (Powell and Davis); TS 11/142/389, reports of Powell and Davis, 16 Aug. 1848.

455 HO 45/2410/Parts 3 and 4; TS 11/142/389.

456 *NS*, 28 Oct. 1848; MEPO 2/62, 28 July, 12 Aug. 1848; TS 11/141/388, 'Mayne's evidence'; TS 11/138/380 (Pearce).

457 TS 11/138/380 (Powell); TS 11/139/381 (Powell and Davis); CCC, XXVIII, pp. 738, 939.

458 See police evidence in TS 11/138/380 and TS 11/139/381. 'A Catalogue of the Arms, Ammunition &c. &c. found on the persons or at the lodgings of the several Prisoners' is contained in TS 11/138/380. Mullins was not found by the police until 18 September (*NS*, 23 Sept. 1848).

459 Cited in full above, p. 88. Cf. TS 11/139/381 (Davis); CCC, XXVIII, pp. 835, 936.

460 TS 11/142/389, reports of Powell and Davis, 16 Aug. 1848; TS 11/139/381 (Powell and Davis); TS 11/138/380 (Baldwinson).

461 CCC, XXVIII, p. 729; TS 11/138/380, copy of Davis Club minute-book.

462 They left for Australia in the *Adelaide* on 8 August 1849, were put ashore in Tasmania, with the exception of Mullins who went on to New South Wales, and all immediately obtained tickets of leave. The six received free pardons, along with Smith O'Brien and Frost, Williams and Jones, in 1856 – too late for Lacey and Ritchie who had both died in 1854 (HO 11/16; HO 10/40; HO 10/55; HO 12/81. See also HO 10/63; and, especially for Cuffay's political activities in Tasmania, Asa Briggs, 'Chartists in Tasmania: A Note', *BSSLH*, no. 3 (Autumn 1961), pp. 6–7, and George Rudé, *Protest and Punishment: The Story of the Social and Political Protesters transported to Australia, 1788–1868* (Oxford, 1978), pp. 143–4, 217–18).

463 For the lesser defendants see *NS*, 7 Oct. 1848; TS 11/138/378; TS 11/138/380; HO 45/2410/Part 1, police report, 16 Aug. 1848; HO 12/81.

464 Cf. *Illustrated London News*, 7 Oct. 1848.

465 Briggs, 'Chartists in Tasmania', p. 6; Rudé, *Protest and Punishment,* p. 144.
466 *Punch,* XIV (1848), pp. 169, 173, 176, 181–3, as well as XV (1848), pp. 154–5, 160, 168. See also *Illustrated London News,* 22 April 1848.
467 George Jacob Holyoake, *Sixty Years of an Agitator's Life* (1906 edn), Part II, p. 3. Vizetelly, I, pp. 335–7, vilifies him, extraordinarily, as 'half-witted', 'crazy' and 'shallow-pated'. Rachel O'Higgins, 'The Irish Influence in the Chartist Movement', *P&P,* no. 20 (Nov. 1961), p. 92, contributes to the confusion by suggesting that 'Cuffey' was an Irishman. For a just appreciation of Cuffay's character and career – and precise account of his origins – see the sketch in *Reynolds's Political Instructor,* 13 April 1850, written by T. M. Wheeler (Stevens, p. 53).
468 Frost, *Recollections,* p. 150. The most acceptable accounts of the insurrectionary plans are provided by Schoyen, pp. 174–6, and Mather, *Public Order,* pp. 24–6, 214–15. Reg Groves, *But We Shall Rise Again: A Narrative History of Chartism* (1938), pp. 194–201; Postgate, *Story of a Year,* pp. 166–8, 214–18; and, particularly, G. D. H. Cole and Raymond Postgate, *The Common People, 1746–1946* (1961 edn), pp. 324–5, are largely derived from Frost's memoirs and highly inaccurate. On the other hand, Postgate, *Story of a Year,* pp. 212–14, is exceptional in his appreciation that the episode marks the close of 'an epoch of the history of the working class' (one result being that it itself became completely forgotten).
469 TS 11/139/381; CCC, XXVIII, p. 937.
470 *NS,* 4 Nov. 1848.
471 Payne, Rose, Brewster and Bassett were never brought to trial. Rose, a currier, fled to Hamburg where he was joined by his family (*ibid.,* 17 March 1849; Frost, *Recollections,* p. 165).
472 CCC, XXVIII, p. 936.
473 *Ibid.,* pp. 733–4; TS 11/139/381 (Powell). Cf. CCC, XXVIII, p. 937.
474 CCC, XXVIII, pp. 735–6, 928. Figures cited in court, and totalling 1,217, covered only three of the four divisions and were found among papers taken from Rose's house on 11 August (TS 11/139/381 (Thompson, etc.); TS 11/141/388). For an intermediate aggregate: TS 11/139/381 (Davis).
475 Curiously, more accurate and comprehensively detailed for the events of 1848 as a whole than almost all works by historians is a mid-twentieth-century novel: Jack Lindsay, *Men of Forty-Eight* (1948). See esp. pp. 62–4, 118–20, 160–5, 172–83, 196–7, 274–5, 284–6, 291, 347, 382. Its general reliability is marred, though, by the conflation of the meeting of 12 June with the insurrectionary movement of July and August (pp. 384–9, 392–5, 417–18).

Part Three. Disturbance and the maintenance of order

1 Police history is an area grossly neglected by scholarly writers, although, not unnaturally, the Metropolitan Police's first ten to twenty years have received some attention: by Mather, *Public Order,* esp. pp. 96–111; Radzinowicz, IV, chap. 5; and Charles Reith, in three of his idiosyncratic, highly partisan volumes, *British Police and the Democratic Ideal* (1943), *A Short History of the British Police* (1948), chaps. 5–16, and *A New Study of Police History* (Edinburgh, 1956) (the publications of 1948 and 1956 utilize much material in that of 1943). Wilbur R. Miller has recently broken

beyond this period in his valuable comparative study, *Cops and Bobbies: Police Authority in New York and London, 1830–1870* (Chicago, 1977); but David Ascoli, *The Queen's Peace: The Origins and Development of the Metropolitan Police, 1829–1979* (1979), is an uncritical celebration.

2 It has been argued persuasively that the Chartist onslaught was responsible for the legislation of 1839 enabling the counties and several boroughs to institute police forces on the London model (J. M. Hart, *The British Police* (1951), pp. 30–1; Mather, *Public Order*, pp. 119–22, 127–30; Radzinowicz, IV, chap. 6, sects. 4, 5, and chap. 7, sects. 1, 2).

3 Rowan was knighted on 6 March 1848 and Mayne in 1851 (Reith, *New Study*, pp. 242–3; *idem, British Police and Democratic Ideal*, p. 252).

4 James Cornish, 'No. LXIII of Survivors' Tales of Great Events: London Under Arms. From the Narrative of James Cornish. As Told to Walter Wood', *Royal Magazine*, XXIII, no. 138 (April 1910) [hereafter Cornish], p. 552. For the uniform see too Ascoli, p. 90.

5 Mather, *Public Order*, p. 97; MEPO 2/26; Mayhew, *LL&LP*, II, p. 159; Briggs, *Victorian Cities*, p. 30.

6 MEPO 2/25; MEPO 5/9/41; Radzinowicz, II, pp. 425–7, 511–18; Reith, *British Police and Democratic Ideal*, pp. 39–40.

7 For the River Police: MEPO 1/45, letter to William Ballantine, 30 Aug. 1839, and MEPO 1/46, letter to G. C. Lewes, 22 March 1854.

8 MEPO 4/1; MEPO 2/26. See also Mather, *Public Order*, pp. 109–11; and, for the augmentation of 1848, MEPO 1/46, letters to Rt Hon. Lord Monteagle, 23 June 1848, and Hon. H. Fitzroy, 29 Sept. 1853, and *NS*, 8 July 1848.

9 See, particularly, MEPO 5/1/1 and MEPO 5/2/6.

10 MEPO 2/25, memo. by William Hay, 29 June 1848; Reith, *British Police and Democratic Ideal*, p. 249.

11 MEPO 5/3/10.

12 Radzinowicz, IV, pp. 162–3, 190. Until 1863 the truncheon was kept concealed in a tail pocket (Miller, p. 48).

13 But see Reith, *New Study*, pp. 136–8 *et seq.*

14 MEPO 5/1/2, letter from Maule, 14 Jan. 1840; MEPO 1/33; *NS*, 14 Sept. 1839.

15 Cf. Reith, *New Study*, pp. 145–7; and *idem, British Police and Democratic Ideal*, p. 38. Ascoli, p. 89, gives the former occupations of the 1830 constabulary.

16 For the higher ranks as well as the 1st Class of Constables although the greatest emphasis was placed upon the initiation of differentials among the Constables.

17 MEPO 1/33; MEPO 1/46, letter to Hon. H. Fitzroy, 29 Sept. 1853. Contrast the Commissioners' defeatist recommendation of 1835: Reith, *British Police and Democratic Ideal*, pp. 193–5.

18 MEPO 2/26. Mather's analysis of 'removals', 1834–8, indicates that average annual withdrawal (1,064) still remained almost as high as one-third of total strength; and also that dismissals (322.2) fell considerably to less than half the resignations (709.6) (*Public Order*, p. 97). But the causes for resignation in 1837 and 1838, specified by the Constabulary Force Commissioners, demonstrate that of an average aggregate of 745 resignations, no fewer than 316.5 were of men reported for misconduct and who either 'Resigned rather than appear' or 'Appeared and [were] allowed to resign' (Constabulary Force, *First Report of the Commissioners Appointed to Inquire as*

to the Best Means of Establishing an Efficient Constabulary Force in the Counties of England and Wales, 1839, XIX [169], para. 254). The 'Weekly State of the Metropolitan Police' (MEPO 4/1), unfortunately, does not break down the 'Number removed' for each January into resignations and dismissals, but appointments exceeded 'removals' by very small numbers throughout the thirties and forties and were sometimes negative. See too Ascoli, p. 89, and Miller, p. 41.

19 MEPO 8/2, 29 Sept., 14 Oct. 1829, 26 Nov. 1830. See also MEPO 7/5, 14 Sept. 1837, 29 Dec. 1838; MEPO 7/12, 24, 26 Dec. 1846.

20 MEPO 8/2, *Instructions, Orders*, Police Order, 21 Sept. 1830, and p. 9. See also Reith, *New Study*, pp. 140–2; Radzinowicz, IV, pp. 165–7; Miller, pp. 38–41.

21 MEPO 7/5, 15 Aug. 1837; and reinforced on 26 Aug. 1843 (MEPO 7/9). The original order is of 15 June 1830 (MEPO 8/2).

22 MEPO 7/5, 9 May 1838. Cf. MEPO 8/2, 3 Oct. 1829, 21 Aug. 1830.

23 MEPO 7/5, 8 Aug. 1838.

24 MEPO 7/14, 8 Feb. 1850. See initial order, MEPO 8/2, 19 Oct. 1830; and MEPO 7/6, 18 Feb. 1839, 11 March 1840; MEPO 7/14, 17 Jan. 1849.

25 Thomas Ainge Devyr, *The Odd Book of the Nineteenth Century, Or, 'Chivalry' in Modern Days, A Personal Record of Reform – Chiefly Land Reform, For the Last Fifty Years* (Greenpoint, NY, 1882), pp. 145–6.

26 MEPO 2/5, undated draft by Commissioners (c. 1839) and Mayne's Memorial, 30 July 1850; MEPO 2/32; Constabulary Force, *First Report of Commissioners*, para. 255. For the initial hostility to the police see Reith, *British Police and Democratic Ideal*, esp. pp. 50–3, 133–5. Miller, pp. 105–8, emphasizes the rapidity of middle-class acceptance. For the City of London Police which had an initial establishment of 500 (and no more than 627 in 1861): Mather, *Public Order*, p. 119; Radzinowicz, IV, pp. 206–7; Donald Rumbelow, *I Spy Blue: The Police and Crime in the City of London from Elizabeth I to Victoria* (1971), esp. chaps. 6, 8.

27 Charles Dickens, *Sketches by Boz: Illustrative of Every-Day Life and Every-Day People* (1837), 'Scenes', chaps. 1, 2, 3, 20; 'Characters', chaps. 1, 11; 'Tales', chaps. 6, 7. James Grant, *Sketches in London* (1838), chap. 12, gives an interesting contemporary description and evaluation of the new police.

28 For example, *Punch*, XIV (1848), p. 256; XV (1848), p. 64.

29 *Punch*, 1842–9, *passim*. The transition in assessment is revealed in Christopher Pulling, *Mr Punch and the Police* (1964), chap. 2. Cf. 'Cruel Outrage by a Policeman', *The Times*, 25 Aug. (and 6 Sept.) 1842, and Radzinowicz, IV, pp. 261–6.

30 *NS*, 15 April 1848.

31 I.e., lobsters – the comparison was with the 'cooked', redcoated soldiery.

32 *NS*, 15 Feb. 1840, 13 March 1841, 18 Oct. 1845, 21 March 1846.

33 A crescendo was reached in the *Northern Star* in 1847 (13, 27 Feb., 6 March, 22 May, 5, 12 June, 3 July, 18, 25 (2 refs.) Sept., 2, 16 (3 refs.), 30 Oct., 6, Nov. 3 (3 refs.)).

34 'Poetical Broadsides, Etc.', I, BL press mark 116221. k. 4. (321.). Cf. *Adventures of a Policeman* (broadside, n.d.), BL press mark C. 116. i. 1. (259.); Ashton, pp. 58–66. Chartist and popular hostility to the police continued unabated in the 1850s (Brian Harrison, 'The Sunday Trading Riots of 1855', *HJ*, VIII (1965), p. 229).

35 The very word 'police' was of French origin and the traditional antagonism of Englishmen to any form of the institution was derived, with jus-

tification, from the tyrannic workings of the French police under successive régimes (Radzinowcz, III, pp. 1–2 *et seq.*; App. 8. See also *ibid.*, II, pp. 405–6).

36 *Chartist,* 21 April 1839; *Charter,* 24, 31 March 1839. See too the Shoreditch resolution of 1 Oct. 1839, HO 61/24. Other important statements are to be found in the *Operative,* 3 March 1839; *Charter,* 31 March (resolution of Lambeth Political Union), 7 April 1839. Robert D. Storch, 'The Plague of the Blue Locusts: Police Reform and Popular Resistance in Northern England, 1840–57', *IRSH,* XX (1975), discusses the similar antagonism – and physical opposition – in the North.

37 MEPO 3/1 provides an indication of the impressive extent of police knowledge by the late 1830s of strictly criminal London.

38 10 Geo. 4, c. 44, sect. 7.

39 MEPO 7/7, 2 Feb. 1842; MEPO 7/8, 28 Oct. 1842 (referring to Order of 1 Feb. 1834), 24 Nov. 1842. These Police Orders conflict with Radzinowicz's judgment (IV, p. 165 – based on MEPO 8/2, *Instructions, Orders,* p. 12).

40 Devyr, p. 146. On 4 March 1840 the Commissioners prohibited the practice of examining 'the little Bundles of labouring People going to work, which Bundles generally contains [sic] their food and nothing else' (MEPO 7/6).

41 *Charter, Operative* and *Chartist,* 7 April 1839; MEPO 7/6, 28 March 1839; MEPO 7/4, 29 June 1837.

42 *NS,* 31 Aug. 1839.

43 Suppression of the fairs, over many years, is reviewed by Hugh Cunningham, 'The Metropolitan Fairs: A Case Study in the Social Control of Leisure', in A. P. Donajgrodzki (ed.), *Social Control in Nineteenth Century Britain* (1977).

44 2 & 3 Vict. c. 47, esp. sections 38–67. For a Chartist résumé of the bill see *Charter,* 10 March 1839; an enraged satire by *John Bull* was reprinted in *NS,* 5 Oct. 1839; and a Twickenham magistrate's reaction is quoted by Reith, *British Police and Democratic Ideal,* pp. 250–1.

45 Shearring, pp. 412–13; Radzinowicz, I, p. 707; John Gay, *The Beggar's Opera* (1728; 1934 edn), pp. 16, 114; Stevenson, *Popular Disturbances,* pp. 49–50.

46 Cf. Michael Ignatieff, 'Police and People: the Birth of Mr. Peel's "Blue Locusts" ', *New Society,* 30 Aug. 1979.

47 Mayhew, *LL&LP,* I, p. 10; II, p. 3. For intense hatred of hawkers, pedlars and costermongers by a parish constable: HO 44/32, letter from John Hinton, 6 July 1839; and more reasoned dislike of the 'Crushers' by the costermonger Bezer: in Vincent, pp. 156, 165.

48 2 & 3 Vict. c. 47, sect. 54 (14); Knight, I, pp. 140–2. For the Order concerning dustmen's bells see MEPO 7/6, 12 Sept. 1839. The calling of sweeps had been outlawed as early as 1834 (MEPO 7/7, 27 Jan. 1842).

49 MEPO 7/6, 4 Dec. 1839, 4, 12, 28 May 1840; MEPO 7/7, 22 Oct. 1840; MEPO 7/9, 30 Sept., 17 Oct. 1843, 23 Oct. 1844; MEPO 7/11, 20 March 1846; MEPO 7/12, 22 Oct. 1847; MEPO 7/14, 23 Nov. 1848, 11 April, 18 Oct. 1849. See also Reith, *British Police and Democratic Ideal,* p. 183.

50 MEPO 7/6, 28 May 1840; MEPO 7/12, 7 Dec. 1846.

51 MEPO 7/6, 1 April 1840.

52 This is not to say that it was not bitterly resented, nor police high-handedness widely criticized. See, for example, 'Happy Land!', 'Poetical

Broadsides', I, f. 375; Mayhew, *LL&LP*, I, p. 20. A rare study of this aspect of policing is Robert D. Storch, 'The Policeman as Domestic Missionary: Urban Discipline and Popular Culture in Northern England, 1850–1880', *Journal of Social History*, IX (1975–6).

53 *NS*, 29 Nov. 1845.

54 Radzinowicz's statement (IV, p. 184) that after the foundation of the Metropolitan Police there was never again active intervention by troops in the repression of the London populace is incorrect – 'Bloody Sunday', 1887, is perhaps the best-known exception – but this should not be allowed to detract from the most important fact that since 1829 only in a handful of highly unusual situations have the police been unable, in direct conflict, to act alone.

55 Both the size and the duration of the disorders of November 1830 (*not* September as he sometimes writes) and April and October 1831 are implicitly exaggerated by Reith, *British Police and Democratic Ideal*, chap. 11 and pp. 90–8, to whom Radzinowicz, IV, pp. 177–80, provides a useful, if sometimes derivative, corrective. (Cf., also, J. R. M. Butler, *The Passing of the Great Reform Bill* (1914); Halévy, III, Part I, chap. 1; Hamburger, pp. 139–42, 147–54, 210–11; George Rudé, 'English Rural and Urban Disturbances on the Eve of the First Reform Bill, 1830–1831', *P&P*, no. 37 (July 1967); and Brock).

56 *The Observer*, 14 Aug. 1842, quoted in *The Times*, 15 Aug. 1842, and *Evening Star*, 15 Aug. 1842.

57 *The Times*, 15 Aug. 1842; Graham Papers 52A; *NS*, 20 Aug. 1842.

58 HO 41/26; Graham Papers 52A; RA B5/52, letter from Graham to Queen, 17 Aug. 1842; MEPO 7/8; *The Times*, 17, 18, 20 Aug. 1842; *NS*, 20, 27 Aug. 1842.

59 *The Times*, 18, 19 Aug. 1842; *NS*, 20, 27 Aug. 1842; *Evening Star*, 19, 20 Aug. 1842; Graham Papers 52A; MEPO 7/8; MEPO 1/43, letters from Mayne to Sutton, 20, 31 Aug. 1842; HO 45/252, posters enclosed in letter from Merewhether to Sutton, 12 May 1843; Norman Gash, *Sir Robert Peel: The Life of Sir Robert Peel after 1830* (1972), pp. 344–5.

60 *NS*, 27 Aug. 1842; *Evening Star*, 20 Aug. 1842; *The Times*, 20, 22, 25 Aug. 1842; RA B5/60 and Graham Papers 52B, letter to Queen, 20 Aug. 1842 (published in Benson and Esher, I, p. 427); MEPO 2/59; HO 45/252; MEPO 7/8.

61 By 9.00 the police blockade was such that a fifteen-year-old boy, returning home to Islington from his father's City warehouse, 'passed quietly by a file of those men' and, crossing the Green, was ridden down by a horseman. The father and *The Times*, which took up the case, claimed the offender was one of the three mounted policemen present, while the police argued that the boy must have been knocked over by some horses coming from Smithfield Market (*The Times*, 25 Aug., 6 Sept. 1842; MEPO 1/43).

62 *NS*, 27 Aug. 1842; *The Times*, 20, 22 Aug. 1842; *Evening Star*, 20 Aug. 1842; CCC, XVI, pp. 1016–18; MEPO 7/8.

63 MEPO 7/8; Graham Papers 52B; *Evening Star*, 22 Aug. 1842; *NS*, 27 Aug. 1842.

64 *Sun*, 23 Aug. 1842, quoted in *NS*, 27 Aug. 1842.

65 *NS*, 27 Aug. 1842; *Evening Star*, 23 Aug. 1842; *The Times*, 23, 24 Aug. 1842; *Illustrated London News*, 27 Aug. 1842; Graham Papers 52B; RA B5/61, letter from Graham to Queen, 22 Aug. 1842; MEPO 7/8; CCC,

XVI, pp. 935–9. Cf. Peel to Wellington, 24 Aug. 1842, Charles Stuart Parker (ed.), *Sir Robert Peel from his Private Papers* (3 vols., 1899), II, p. 540.

66 At this time fronting the present Bishops Bridge Road, Paddington Station not being built until the early 1850s (R. J. Mitchell and M. D. R. Leys, *A History of London Life* (1958), p. 250n.).

67 *NS*, 27 Aug. 1842; *The Times*, 23, 24 Aug. 1842; CCC, XVI, pp. 1082–4.

68 Indeed, some of the police who had participated in clearing Kennington Common were then withdrawn to the riverside (*NS*, 27 Aug. 1842; *The Times*, 24 Aug. 1842; HO 45/252; MEPO 7/8).

69 But see *Evening Star*, 22 Aug. 1842.

70 *The Times*, 23, 24 Aug. 1842. The brief discussion by Mather, *Public Order*, pp. 98–9, 100, of 22 August is based entirely on *The Times's* coverage, thereby claiming that the Chartist organizers failed to appear at Kennington Common (in this he is followed by Keller, p. 84) and adopting too sanguine a view of police conduct.

71 *NS*, 30 Oct., 28 Nov. 1848; *Hansard's Parliamentary Debates*, 3rd ser., LXXXIII, 10 February 1846, pp. 718–19.

72 *The Times*, 20, 23, 24 Aug. 1842.

73 *Ibid.*, 22, 24 Aug. 1842; *Evening Star*, 20, 23 Aug., 24 Sept. 1842; *NS*, 27 Aug., 24 Sept. 1842; *Illustrated London News*, 27 Aug. 1842; CCC, XVI, pp. 937–9, 1084; HO 16/7; HO 26/48.

74 HO 45/2412; MEPO 2/64; MEPO 1/45.

75 Matthew Arnold, *Letters of Matthew Arnold, 1848–1888*, ed. George W. E. Russell (2 vols., 1895), I, p. 4; Arnold, *Letters of Matthew Arnold to Arthur Hugh Clough*, p. 74. The account by Mather, *Public Order*, pp. 99–100, is again drawn uncritically from *The Times*.

76 MEPO 2/66 (with other complaints).

77 See HO 65/16.

78 MEPO 2/65.

79 TS 11/140/386 (evidence of Jennings).

80 *The Times*, 7, 8, 9, 10, 18 March 1848; *NS*, 11 March 1848; MEPO 2/64; MEPO 7/12; PRO 30/22/7B; RA J67/107, letter from Rowan to Gen. Bowles (Master of the Household); RA J67/108, letter from Grey to Gen. Bowles, 6 March 1848. Gammage's account (pp. 293–5) is drawn from the *Northern Star*. The notice of 7 March prohibiting meetings (MEPO 2/64) is reproduced in Rodney Mace, *Trafalgar Square: Emblem of Empire* (1976), p. 136, but the accompanying pages on the riots are extraordinarily inaccurate (pp. 134–8). Keller, pp. 87–91, only discusses the first day of the riots.

81 See, for example, *The Times*, 7, 9 March 1848; *Illustrated London News*, 11 March 1848.

82 Cf. the police arrangements on 10 April below, Table 10 and p. 136.

83 *The Times*, 13, 14 March 1848; *NS*, 18 March 1848; MEPO 2/63; MEPO 7/12; HO 60/5.

84 *The Times*, 22 March 1848.

85 *Weekly Dispatch*, 16 April 1848; *The Times*, 17 March 1848.

86 MEPO 2/63; HO 45/2410/Part 1, 'Application for Legal Assistance', 29 March 1848 (*The Times*, 10 April 1848, assigns to four of the accused occupations different to those detailed in this police document) and report by Supt. Jno. Robinson, 18 May 1848; CCC, XXVII, pp. 1034–53; HO 12/81, 'A Return of Persons convicted of Political Offences in the

Years 1848 and 1849'; HO 16/9; HO 27/86. The scanty to non-existent knowledge of the occupations of the other rioters of 1842 and 1848 contrasts lamentably with the comprehensiveness of details concerning the Camberwell defendants and with the successes of George Rudé's eighteenth-century studies – see, esp., *The Crowd in the French Revolution* (1959), App. IV; *Wilkes and Liberty: A Social Study of 1763 to 1774* (Oxford, 1962), App. XI; *Paris and London in the Eighteenth Century: Studies in Popular Protest* (n.d.), pp. 282–3 (for the Gordon Rioters). Brian Harrison has experienced similar difficulty in identifying the participants in another series of mid-nineteenth-century metropolitan disturbances ('Sunday Trading Riots', pp. 224–5). Rudé discusses the variability of source material for analysis of this type and stresses the poverty of the English records in contrast with the French in *The Crowd in History: A Study of Popular Disturbances in France and England, 1730–1848* (New York, 1964), pp. 11–14, and *Paris and London*, pp. 10–12. (See also Keller, p. 30.)

87 See below, pp. 129–30.
88 Mayhew, *LL&LP*, III, p. 389; IV, pp. 376–7. Similarly, H. H. Montgomery, *The History of Kennington and Its Neighbourhood, with Chapters on Cricket Past and Present* (1889), p. 47, in writing of a baker's being broken into, almost certainly confuses 13 March with 10 April. Smith, 'The View from Britain I', in Kamenka and Smith, pp. 108–9, is exceptional in appreciating that the riot had significance (otherwise his short treatment of the day is very misleading). Only three more post-1848 references to the incident are known to me: Robert Bernard Martin, *The Dust of Combat: A Life of Charles Kingsley* (1959), pp. 78–9; Large, in Stevenson, *London*, pp. 184, 206 n49; Keller, p. 93. The transported rioters are not considered by Rudé, *Protest and Punishment*.
89 See above, pp. 81–2.
90 CCC, XXVLII, pp. 240–56, 365–77; TS 11/136/372, R. v. Fussell; TS 11/140/386.
91 Golden Lane formed part of one of early-Victorian London's major criminal areas (Tobias, pp. 152, 156–7).
92 This list suggests that Mitchel's articles on street fighting in the *United Irishman*, one reprinted in *NS*, 11 March 1848, may have been perused by the citizens of Cripplegate (cf. Gammage, pp. 296, 321).
93 CCC, XVIII, pp. 350, 367–8, 370–2; TS 11/136/372, R. v. Fussell; TS 11/140/386; HO 45/2410/Part 1, report from Rowan, 29 May 1848. For the total, large-scale police response on 29 May: MEPO 7/12.
94 *The Times*, 31 May 1848; *NS*, 3 June 1848; John Bedford Leno, *The Aftermath: With Autobiography of the Author* (1892), pp. 57–8; HO 45/2410/Part 1, reports from Rowan, 30 May 1848; RA C56/82, letter from Grey to Queen, 31 May 1848. See MEPO 7/12 for the police preparations.
95 Copies in MEPO 2/59.
96 See his report of 24 June 1848, MEPO 2/66.
97 *NS*, 3 June 1848; *The Times*, 1, 2 June 1848; HO 45/2410/Part 1; HO 60/5; MEPO 7/12; MEPO 2/66. Gammage's brief account (p. 332) of 29–31 May is a condensation of the *Northern Star*'s coverage.
98 *NS*, 3 June 1848; *The Times*, 2 June 1848; HO 45/2410/Part 1, report from Rowan to Grey; MEPO 7/12.
99 Cornish, p. 553.
100 For an indication of the ill repute of the district see Millicent Rose, *The East End of London* (1951), pp. 212–14, 256.

101 *NS*, 3, 10 June 1848; *The Times*, 5, 6, 7 June 1848; CCC, XXVIII, pp. 244–51; MEPO 2/67; HO 45/2410/Part 1, police reports, 4 June 1848. See also above, p. 83.

102 *The Times*, 5, 6, 7 June 1848; *NS*, 10, 24 June 1848; HO 45/2410/Part 1; MEPO 2/66; CCC, XXVIII, pp. 216–27, 243–4; TS 11/138/376. Mather, *Public Order*, pp. 100–1, allows that police conduct degenerated at the close of the day, while Large, in Stevenson, *London*, pp. 198–9, provides a curious, equivocal account of the evening of 4 June, but neither has read the most incriminating testimonies now filed in MEPO 2/66. MEPO 2/67, in contrast, contains seventy-seven letters expressing appreciation of the police in general and, particularly, but still for the most part abstract, in Tower Hamlets on 4 June. Many were addressed to Supt. James Johnston, N Division (who, as commander of the mounted men on the 4th, was under especial pressure to exonerate himself during the Commissioners' inquiries), and appear to have been solicited by him (cf. Keller, p. 110).

103 Even after 1848, however, police management of crowds could prove fallible: as during the Sunday Trading Riots when the police over-reacted on 1 July 1855 and when, in July 1866, they were compelled to seek military support (Harrison, 'Sunday Trading Riots'; Reith, *New Study*, p. 248; Critchley, *Conquest of Violence*, pp. 145–7 *et seq.*).

104 MEPO 8/2, *Instructions, Orders*, p. 1.

105 Quoted by Allan Silver, 'The Demand for Order in Civil Society: A Review of Some Themes in the History of Urban Crime, Police, and Riot', in David J. Bordua (ed.), *The Police: Six Sociological Essays* (New York, 1967), pp. 5, 8.

106 E.g., see MEPO 7/12, memo. by R. M., 5 June 1848.

107 MEPO 2/66, report by Supt. Lewis, n.d.

108 See, for example, MEPO 7/8, memo. by R. M., 20 Aug. 1842.

109 Evidence of Supt. George Martin, Police, *Second Report from the Select Committee on Police*, 1852–3, XXXVI [715], p. 92; also, Constabulary Force, *First Report*, para. 88. Cf. the advice in the Police Order of 20 Oct. 1847 (MEPO 7/12).

110 Rowe, *London Radicalism*, pp. 125–34; Add. MS. 27,835, ff. 51–5; Lovett, *L&S*, I, pp. 83–4; Gavin Thurston, *The Clerkenwell Riot: The Killing of Constable Culley* (1967); Reith, *British Police and Democratic Ideal*, pp. 139–55; Radzinowicz, IV, pp. 180–3; Rowe, 'Radicalism in London', pp. 106–14. Reith's assertion (pp. 139, 229) that the affray represented 'a complete victory' for the police is manifestly absurd.

111 CCC, XXVIII, pp. 219–20.

112 TS 11/140/386, evidence of Jas. Collins.

113 MEPO 7/14; *NS*, 22 July 1848. See also above, pp. 86, 89.

114 Cornish, p. 554.

115 Miller, pp. 50–1.

116 See MEPO 2/66, statement, n.d., Clerkenwell Green, 31 May 1848; and cf. Adams, II, pp. 328–9, on the Sunday Trading Riots of 1855. The originator of the baton charge was, it appears, Francis Place in 1830 (Wallas, pp. 248n–249n; Reith, *British Police and Democratic Ideal*, pp. 72–4; Radzinowicz, IV, p. 179).

117 Cornish (p. 554) specifically locates this engagement in Clerkenwell; but he possibly confused it in his old age with the aftermath of Bishop Bonner's Fields, for he did recall serving there on 4 June.

118 Cf. letter from Sir Francis Palgrave of the PRO, requesting a protective force for 10 April 1848: 'On the Continent, such Depositories have been very frequently the object of popular attack, instigated by the opinion that they contain Documents establishing aristocratic Rights and Property of Lands' (MEPO 2/65).
119 For a brief, but directly relevant, outline of London's segregation of activities and classes, see E. J. Hobsbawm, *Revolutionaries: Contemporary Essays* (1973), pp. 228–9.
120 See Hobsbawm's remarks on the trouble that demonstrations in the Square have usually occasioned (*ibid.*, p. 227).
121 Cf. Hobsbawm, *Primitive Rebels*, chap. 7, and Rudé, *Crowd in History*, chap. 12.
122 See, for example, *The Times*, 20 Aug. 1842 (first leader and 'Chartist Meeting Prevented') and 1 June 1848.
123 CCC, XXVIII, p. 222.
124 *The Times*, 9 March 1848.
125 *The Times*, 24 Aug. 1842. Cf. *ibid.*, 25 Aug. 1842; CCC, XXVIII, p. 355; HO 45/2410/Part 1, letter from 'A lover of order and a Shopkeeper'. Lucien de la Hodde comments on the high proportion of 'the people who love to stand and gawp' in the crowd which made the February Revolution (quoted in Roger Price (ed.), *1848 in France* (1975), p. 58).
126 See above, Table 7 and p. 116.
127 HO 26/54; HO 45/2410/Part 1, 'Return of Persons taken into Custody for Rioting and assaulting the Police on Sunday, the 4th June 1848'. In 1851, 25 per cent of the metropolitan male population aged ten or over were between the ages of ten and nineteen (calculated from 1851 Census, p. 1).
128 Extreme youthfulness is a common, but by no means universal, feature of riotous crowds. See Harrison, 'Sunday Trading Riots', pp. 225–6; Rudé, *Crowd in History*, pp. 208–9; *idem, Crowd in French Revolution*, App. V; and de la Hodde's remarks on the *gamins de Paris* (in Price, *1848 in France*, p. 58). Of the Irishmen arrested on 28 September 1862 (a mere five, however) the magistrate remarked, 'They were all boys' (Sheridan Gilley, 'The Garibaldi Riots of 1862', *HJ*, XVI (1973)). See also Godwin, p. 96. Cf. Tobias, pp. 68–9, for the high proportion of contemporary criminals in their teens and early twenties.
129 *The Times*, 8, 9, 10 March 1848; *Illustrated London News*, 11 March 1848; *Punch*, XIV (1848), pp. 109–16; Cayley, II, pp. 231–2; 'Poetical Broadsides', II, f. 141.
130 *The Times*, 22 Aug. 1842. Reported, however, as 'Stand together, and we'll have our rights', by the *Illustrated London News*, 27 Aug. 1842.
131 *The Times*, 1 June 1848.
132 Mayhew, *LL&LP*, III, p. 398.
133 The harsh strictures by Jones, *Outcast London*, pp. 341–3, concerning the minimal, volatile political consciousness of the unskilled and casual poor, despite their capacity for riot, are essentially correct.
134 CCC, XXVIII, pp. 225–6.
135 *NS*, 20 May 1848. The conclusion, admittedly (though necessarily) based on impressionistic evidence, that such elements formed an important component of the Chartist following at times of excitement conflicts with Rudé's portrait of the 'respectable' crowd – see *Crowd in History*, pp. 198–205, and *Paris and London*, pp. 298–302 (but also Thompson's important

reservations in *The Making of the English Working Class*, pp. 70–5). (It should be noted that the slender information concerning the 1842 rioters does suggest a more mature, artisan-based movement than that of 1848 – see above, p. 111.

136 Leno, *Aftermath*, p. 57.
137 *NS*, 3 June 1848.
138 MEPO 2/66, statement, n.d., re Clerkenwell Green, 31 May 1848.
139 See above, p. 109.
140 Cf. Saville, 'Chartism in the Year of Revolution', pp. 24–5.
141 HO 45/2410/Part 1, letter from J. W. Mason.
142 *NS*, 18 March 1848.
143 The initiative did not, as Large, in Stevenson, *London*, pp. 183–4, implies, derive from the Home Office.
144 *The Times*, 9, 10 March 1848; HO 60/5; HO 65/16; HO 45/2410/Parts 1 and 5.
145 *NS*, 18 March 1848. See also the *Nonconformist*, 15 March 1848, and *Punch*, XIV (1848), p. 121.
146 HO 45/2410/Part 3.
147 HO 60/5.
148 HO 45/2410/Parts 1 and 5. For the institution of – and legislation concerning – special constables, see Radzinowicz, II, pp. 215–24; Ronald Seth, *The Specials: The Story of the Special Constabulary in England, Wales and Scotland* (1961), pp. 46–8, 51.
149 E.g. Mather, *Public Order*, p. 84.
150 Hovell, p. 290; Halévy, IV, p. 245; *Annual Register, 1848*, p. 52. Quite recently the number has been increased to 175,000 by Jasper Ridley, *Lord Palmerston* (1970), p. 339, and to 'no fewer than 200,000' by T. A. Critchley, *A History of Police in England and Wales* (1967; 2nd edn, 1978), p. 99, a figure he repeats in *Conquest of Violence*, p. 139, and asserted too by Elizabeth Longford, *Wellington: Pillar of State* (1972), p. 379 (she appears, however, to be following Lady Palmerston's estimate of 14 April (Palmerston, *Letters of Lady Palmerston*, p. 300). But, also, Cayley, II, p. 236, plumped for 'about two hundred thousand' in 1856 and 200,000 is given in W. C. Taylor and W. H. Pinnock, *Whittaker's Improved Edition of Pinnock's Goldsmith's History of England, from the Invasion of Julius Caesar to the Close of the Abyssinian Campaign* (1873 edn), pp. 496–7 (I am indebted to Neal Rigby for the latter reference and the loan of his copy of this school text)).
151 *Express, Globe, London Telegraph*, 10 April 1848; *Standard, Sun, Morning Chronicle*, 11 April 1848; *The Times*, 10, 11 April 1848; *NS*, 15 April 1848.
152 *The Times*, 18 April 1848. One can clearly progress further than Large, in Stevenson, *London*, pp. 188, 207 n75, who has not thoroughly examined HO 45/2410/Part 5.
153 HO 45/2410/Part 1.
154 *Ibid.*; HO 45/2410/Part 5.
155 HO 45/2410/Part 1.
156 HO 45/2410/Part 5. (The figures for each ward are printed, with one error – that for Vintry should read 210 – by Wearmouth, pp. 122–3.)
157 *The Times*, 18 April 1848.
158 Even Saville, 'Chartism in the Year of Revolution', pp. 25–8.
159 *The Times*, 12 April 1848. Smith, 'The View from Britain I', in Kamenka and Smith, pp. 110–11, is refreshingly heterodox on this matter.

160 RA J68/2, letter from Rowan to Gen. Bowles, Thursday [9 March 1848].
161 HO 45/2410/Part 1, letter from Geo. Long, 25 March 1848. See the letters in the *Northern Star*, 22, 29 April, 6 May 1848, including several from men who were dismissed; and also Saville, *Ernest Jones*, p. 109.
162 HO 45/2410/Part 1, 'Return of Special Constables . . .'.
163 *NS*, 22 April 1848.
164 HO 45/2410/Part 1, letter, 8 April 1848. Cf. Wellington's findings (Longford, p. 379).
165 But see letter from J. D. Roll, Deptford, n.d., HO 45/2410/Part 1. And on 2 April Grey detected 'a good spirit of self-protection among the mass of Shopkeepers & even Workpeople which will give us a very large force of Special Constables' (HO 79/9).
166 HO 45/2410/Part 5, letter, 8 April 1848.
167 RA C56/28, letter of 11 April 1848. It is the Prince's draft letter to Russell, 10 April 1848 (RA C56/12), that is published in Benson and Esher, II, p. 168, the final version (RA C16/48) being slightly modified.
168 HO 45/2410/Part 1, letter, received 6 April 1848.
169 *Ibid.*, 'Return of Special Constables . . .'.
170 Letter from 'A Mechanic', *NS*, 29 April 1848; HO 45/2410/Part 1, letter from J. P. Ward, 19 April 1848. The circular letter of 3 April expressly instructed magistrates to enrol 'respectable Individuals'; and the appearance at his court of bodies of workmen occasioned the concern of the Clerkenwell magistrate (HO 60/5).
171 During the evening of 9 April it was decided to post three companies of the pensioners under the command of Major-General Brotherton at Blackfriars Bridge; and it would appear that this disposition involved the Chelsea reserves (WO 30/111, letter from Lieutenant-Colonel Tulloch, 7.30, n.d. [9 April 1848]). Also on the 9th the Home Secretary requested that detachments should be stationed at the Mansion House, Custom House, North Western Railway (Euston) and British Museum (these may have accounted for the reserves at the Tower) (WO 30/111, letter from Lord FitzRoy Somerset, 9 April 1848).
172 HO 45/2410/Part 1, letter from John Wray, 17 April 1848.
173 There was a total of 1,401 enrolled pensioners in the London district (WO 30/111).
174 E.g., Cayley, II, p. 238; Hovell, p. 291; Ward, *Chartism*, pp. 206–7.
175 *NS*, 15 April 1848.
176 Frost, *Recollections*, p. 139; Gammage, p. 314. See, too, letters from Thomas Plume and 'Zeta', *NS*, 22 April 1848.
177 Neil Stewart, *The Fight for the Charter* (1937), pp. 225–6, perceptively contrasts the total claimed in *The Times*'s leading article on 11 April with the eyewitness descriptions on its other pages.
178 *NS*, 22 April, 8 July, 12 Aug. 1848. Although O'Connor's statement in the *Northern Star* of 22 April 1848 is paraphrased by Gammage, pp. 321–2, this fact has otherwise been remarked by Th. Rothstein alone, who thereupon decided for 'about 150,000' (p. 343 – in contrast to p. 84). But see also Lindsay, p. 196; Groves, pp. 189–90; Éva H. Haraszti, *Chartism* (Budapest, 1978), p. 226.
179 So determined was the *Standard*, 11 April 1848, to minimize the crowd's size that it maintained the Common's area was less than a mere 2,500 sq. yds (see below, pp. 139–40).

180 Lowery, *Robert Lowery: Radical and Chartist*, p. 108, provides an interesting insight into the operations of the metropolitan press (in 1838).
181 HO 45/2410/Part 1. At 2.00 p.m. Russell assured the Queen that only 'about 12 or 15.000' had met (RA C56/19. The full letter is printed in Benson and Esher, II, pp. 168–9).
182 HO 45/2410/Part 1.
183 *Sun*, 10 April 1848. Cf. Wellington's information at 1.45 – before 1.00 he had received a report that there was 'a large body, as many as 25,000 . . . formed for a procession' (Wellington, *Wellington and His Friends*, p. 210).
184 Two other, subsidiary, meeting places were Belgrave Square and Blackheath (HO 45/2410/Part 1; *NS*, 15 April 1848. See also Figure 4).
185 Henderson MS.
186 HO 45/2410/Part 5, C. S. Butler to Marquess of Salisbury.
187 *Sun*, 10 April 1848.
188 In Stevenson, *London*, p. 192.
189 Hunt, I, p. 101.
190 *Sun*, 10 April 1848. See also *The Times*, 11 April 1848.
191 The quotations are from the *Globe* and the *London Telegraph*, 10 April 1848. The *Daily News* and the *Express*, 11 April 1848, give the most specific accounts of the inscriptions on the main van. From the description in the *London Telegraph*, 10 April 1848, there remains the possibility that O'Connor's car may be the one, at the right-hand side of Figure 11, showing 'UNIVERSAL SUFFRAGE' on its major banner. See, in general, George Perry, 'Found – The World's First Crowd Photograph', *The Sunday Times Magazine*, 5 June 1977.
192 MEPO 1/46, Rowan to Earl de Grey, 15 May 1848.
193 MEPO 2/65.
194 HO 45/2410/Parts 5 and 1.
195 The *Sun*, 12 June 1848, reported 'an immense body'.
196 MEPO 2/65; MEPO 7/14; HO 45/2410/Part 1, letter from Mayne, 11 June 1848.
197 HO 65/16, letter to John Wray, 27 June 1848.
198 See Appendices III and IV.
199 Cf. Palmerston, *Letters of Lady Palmerston*, p. 302.
200 Appendix IV; see above, pp. 86–7.
201 Appendix III; HO 45/2410/Part 5, letter to Lord Mayor, 9 April 1848; WO 30/111; HO 45/2410/Part 1. See also above, pp. 76–7.
202 See above, p. 77; Appendix III; *NS*, 15 April 1848.
203 Hovell, p. 290.
204 Reith, *New Study*, pp. 241–2; Russell, p. 253; West, p. 245; WO 30/81, memo. by Wellington, 5 April 1848; WO 30/111, memo., Horse Guards, 3 April 1848. Cf. Mather, in Briggs, *Chartist Studies*, p. 396n.
205 WO 30/81, memo. of 5 April; WO 30/81 and MEPO 2/65, memo. of 11 April; WO 30/81, memo. of 9 June. See also WO 30/111, letter to Field Marshal, The Marquess of Anglesey, 17 June 1848.
206 See Greville, *Greville Memoirs*, VI, p. 49.
207 MEPO 2/59; Burgoyne, *Military Opinions of Burgoyne*, pp. 380–8. Mace, Appendix 3, extraneously reprints the original memorandum, though relatively usefully as it suffers from remarkably few of the errors of transcription that characterize his book.

208 Burgoyne, *Military Opinions of Burgoyne*, pp. 386–7. In 1873 the views shared by Wellington and Burgoyne, as to the crucial contribution of the parks in the protection of London against internal insurrection, were continuously cited in a series of memoranda by Sir Charles Ellice, the Quarter Master General, in opposition to the proposed removal of the Hyde Park Cavalry Barracks from Knightsbridge to Millbank. Ellice's advocacy of the Wellington–Burgoyne argument was probably decisive in the ultimate rebuilding, in 1878–9, of the Barracks on the same site (WO 30/81; Nikolaus Pevsner, *The Buildings of England. London: Except the Cities of London and Westminster* (Harmondsworth, 1952), p. 250. Mace, pp. 158–9, is typically unreliable).

209 It is incorrect, as Seth, pp. 48, 60, and Ascoli, p. 101, claim, that it was the first time the new Act had been invoked in London. Three weeks after its passage 7,490 specials were sworn when the NUWC proposed to meet at White Conduit House (Hamburger, pp. 205n, 240–1).

210 MEPO 2/65, 'Suggestions for Special Constables', 8 April 1848.

211 WO 30/81; MEPO 2/65.

212 Dated 18 April 1848. Copies in MEPO 2/65; HO 45/2410/Part 5.

213 MEPO 1/46, letter from Rowan to Earl de Grey, 3 May 1848.

214 MEPO 2/65.

215 MEPO 2/59. (Cf. Burgoyne, *Military Opinions of Burgoyne*, pp. 383–5.)

216 WO 30/111, Wellington to Anglesey, 17 June 1848.

217 MEPO 2/65; MEPO 1/46.

Part Four. The trades

1 Mayhew, *UM*, p. 406.

2 Cf. the similar argument of Jones, *Outcast London*, pp. 21–3.

3 Mayhew, *UM*, p. 420.

4 *NS*, 2 Sept. 1843.

5 An admirable account by a journeyman of the workings of competition throughout shoemaking appears in Mayhew, *UM*, pp. 239–40.

6 *Operative*, 24 March, 5 May 1839.

7 Mayhew, *UM*, p. 367. For competition by apprentices in general see Mayhew, *LL&LP*, II, p. 311 *et seq.*, and Shearring, pp. 246–7.

8 Analyses of the full range of this phenomenon (and also its relationship to piecework and speeding up the job) are provided by Howell, *Conflicts*, pp. 257–68; Charles Booth, *Life and Labour of the People in London. First Series: Poverty. Vol. 4: The Trades of East London Connected with Poverty* (1904), chap. 10; Sidney and Beatrice Webb, *Industrial Democracy* (1902 edn), Part 2, chap. 5, and pp. 539–50; Hobsbawm, *Labouring Men*, pp. 297–300 and chap. 17; Duncan Bythell, *The Sweated Trades: Outwork in Nineteenth-century Britain* (1978).

9 Mayhew, *LL&LP*, III, p. 294.

10 *Trades' Societies and Strikes: Report of the Committee on Trades' Societies, Appointed by the National Association for the Promotion of Social Science, Presented at the Fourth Annual Meeting of the Association, at Glasgow, September 1860* (1860), p. 189; Keith Burgess, *The Origins of British Industrial Relations: The Nineteenth Century Experience* (1975), pp. 19–21. Though the proviso of Jefferys, *Story*, p. 63, concerning the minimal extent of piecework in London must be noted, metropolitan engineers in 1848, moving against systematic overtime, regarded piecework as a practice 'equally

injurious' and pertinent to their position (*Labour League,* 21 Oct. 1848. See also M. and J. B. Jefferys, 'The Wages, Hours and Trade Customs of the Skilled Engineer in 1861', *Econ HR,* XVII (1947)).

11 Mayhew, *LL&LP,* II, pp. 330–1; C. M. Smith, pp. 172–5; Ellic Howe (ed.), *The London Compositor: Documents relating to Wages, Working Conditions and Customs of the London Printing Trade, 1785–1900* (1947), pp. 303–4.

12 This term is suggested by Hobsbawm, *Labouring Men,* pp. 297–300.

13 Cf. *National United Trades' Association Report,* June 1848.

14 These comments were provoked by the example of the Spitalfields weavers (Add. MS. 27,828, f. 117). A pioneering survey of female labour – in all its manifestations – is provided by Sally Alexander, 'Women's Work in Nineteenth-Century London; A Study of the Years 1820–50', in Juliet Mitchell and Ann Oakley (eds.), *The Rights and Wrongs of Women* (Harmondsworth, 1976).

15 Cf. Mayhew, *LL&LP,* II, pp. 328–9.

16 George, *London Life,* pp. 174–8, 196–9.

17 *Morning Chronicle,* 18 July 1850; Mayhew, *UM,* pp. 183, 186, 200, 271–3, 350, 382. E. P. Thompson, *The Making of the English Working Class,* pp. 251–62, provides a masterly survey of these developments – to which the present writer is greatly indebted.

18 Mayhew, *UM,* pp. 373, 376, 382.

19 *Ibid.,* p. 472; Mayhew, *LL&LP,* II, pp. 232–8, 289.

20 Cf. Prothero, 'London Chartism and the Trades', pp. 215–16, who, however, exaggerates the latter aims at the expense of the former. For the parallel development of a ready-made trade and sub-contracting in France and the concomitant movement for producers' co-operatives, see Johnson, *Utopian Communism,* pp. 158–65, 175–206; and *idem,* 'Economic Change and Artisan Discontent: The Tailors' History, 1800–48', in Price, *Revolution and Reaction*; and Moss, 'Parisian Producers' Associations (1830–51): The Socialism of Skilled Workers', in Price, *Revolution and Reaction*; and *idem, Origins of French Labor Movement,* esp. pp. 32–48.

21 *Operative,* 11 Nov. 1838.

22 *Charter* and *Operative,* 31 March 1839.

23 Kiddier, pp. 85–92, 220–1; Webb TU MSS., X, f. 190; Postgate, *Builders' History,* p. 139; W. S. Hilton, p. 106.

24 *ECC,* no. 68; *NS,* 25 Nov. 1843, 21 March, 31 Oct. 1846. See also Viles, p. 48.

25 The terminology is that of the City of London Co-operative Company of Cordwainers (*NS,* 7 April 1849; *Spirit of the Age,* 16 Dec. 1848).

26 See, particularly, *NS,* 23 Feb., 18, 25 April, 2, 9, 23 May, 6, 20 June, 12 Sept., 19 Dec. 1846; *Labour League,* 11 Nov. 1848.

27 Maurice, II, chaps. 1–3, *passim*; E. P. Thompson, 'Mayhew and the *Morning Chronicle*', in Mayhew, *UM,* pp. 28–31; *Reynolds's Political Instructor,* 23 March 1850; Jefferys, *Story,* pp. 22–4, 42–4. G. D. H. Cole, *A Century of Co-operation* (n.d.), chap. 6, provides a convenient summary and Charles E. Raven, *Christian Socialism, 1848–1854* (1920), chaps. 6–10, a detailed account (see also Torben Christensen, *Origin and History of Christian Socialism, 1848–1854* (Aarhus, 1962)). Viles, pp. 201–7, discusses the Builders' Associations. Saville, 'Christian Socialists', pp. 144–56, offers an abrasive critique, while acknowledging the significance, of the movement.

28 The shoemakers' resolutions of 1842 are one example (*NS,* 2 April 1842).

29 See, for example, *ibid.,* 14 March 1846.

30 See below, pp. 188–9. Despite the cogent complaint by George L. Mosse, 'The Anti-League: 1844–1846', *Econ HR*, XVII (1947), that the Anti-League had been virtually ignored by historians only two writers – Mary Lawson-Tancred, 'The Anti-League and the Corn Law Crisis of 1846', *HJ*, III (1960), and Travis L. Crosby, *English Farmers and the Politics of Protection, 1815–1852* (Hassocks, 1977), pp. 130–9 – have since devoted significant attention to it and neither, unfortunately, develops Mosse's brief comments on the Anti-League's attempts to recruit support from the urban working class.

31 Oliver, 'Organizations', chap. 13; *NS*, 14, 28 March 1840.

32 Add. MS. 37,773, ff. 67–8; Prothero, 'Movements', p. 413.

33 *Operative*, 19 May 1839; *Charter*, 1 Dec. 1839; Lovett, *L&S*, I, pp. 162–7.

34 PC set 56, vol. I, f. 138; *NS*, 9 Nov. 1844, 21 Feb., 21 March 1846; *Operative*, 19 May 1839; *Charter*, 5 Jan. 1840.

35 See the editorial appeal by the *Operative*, 31 March 1839.

36 *Operative*, 31 March–30 June 1839; *Charter*, 27 Jan. 1839, 30 June 1839–15 March 1840; *NS*, 9 Nov. 1839–30 July 1842; *ECC*, no. 4 *et seq.*

37 For which see above, pp. 55–6.

38 *NS*, 23 May 1840; 15 Feb., 5 April 1845; 21 March 1846.

39 See, for example, *ibid.*, 14 April 1849; also above, pp. 69–70.

40 *NS*, 21 Sept. 1844.

41 *Labour League*, 5 Aug. 1848.

42 See, for example, E. J. Hobsbawm and George Rudé, *Captain Swing* (1969), pp. 63–4, 181.

43 *NS*, 5 April 1845.

44 R. A. Church, 'Labour Supply and Innovation, 1800–1860: The Boot and Shoe Industry', *Business History*, XII, no. 1 (Jan. 1970), p. 29 *et seq.*; P. G. Hall, 'The East London Footwear Industry: An Industrial Quarter in Decline', *ELP*, V, no. 1 (April 1962), pp. 17–18; Webb, *Industrial Democracy*, p. 418.

45 George, *London Life*, p. 196; John Bedford Leno, *The Art of Boot and Shoe-making: A Practical Handbook Including Measurement, Last-Fitting, Cutting-Out, Closing, and Making With a Description of the Most Approved Machinery Employed* (1885), chaps. 8–11; Alan Fox, *A History of the National Union of Boot and Shoe Operatives, 1874–1957* (Oxford, 1958), pp. 10–11; Thomas Wright, *The Romance of the Shoe: Being The History of Shoemaking in All Ages, and Especially in England and Scotland* (1922), pp. 171–2. The definitive manual of shoemaking techniques, especially in London, at the beginning of the Chartist period, is, however, provided by James Devlin, *The Guide to Trade: The Shoemaker* [I] (1839).

46 Leno, *Art*, pp. 88–9; Mayhew, *UM*, p. 253.

47 Cf. Leno, *Art*, pp. 112–13.

48 *NS*, 15 June 1844. Devlin, *Shoemaker* [I], p. 15, gives an even longer list of the different branches of the trade than that outlined above.

49 The localization index, calculated by Mounfield, falls from 13.4 in 1841 to 4.3 in 1851, despite London's gain of territory (and very many shoemakers) from Middlesex and Surrey in the 1851 Census. On the other hand, it was not until 1901 that London ceased to have a greater aggregate of shoemakers than any other county (Peter Reginald Mounfield, 'The Location of Footwear Manufacture in England and Wales' (Nottingham PhD thesis, 1962), Tables 7–13).

50 Church, 'Labour Supply', pp. 25–9; John Foster, *Class Struggle and the*

Industrial Revolution: Early Industrial Capitalism in Three English Towns (1977 edn), pp. 85–7; Bythell, pp. 106–8; Clapham I, pp. 167, 181–2; Whittock *et al.*, pp. 404–5.

51 For the 'manufacturer', see Hall, 'Footwear Industry', pp. 14–15.

52 *NS*, 1 Jan. 1848.

53 *St Crispin*, 19 June 1869; Mayhew, *UM*, pp. 234–5, 244–5 (Mayhew's second informant was almost certainly O'Neil: see *St Crispin*, 5 Feb. 1870); *National Co-operative Leader*, 8 March 1861. Cf. also Hand-Loom Weavers, *Reports from Assistant Hand-Loom Weavers' Commissioners*, Part II, 1840, XXIII (43-I), p. 282; Prothero, *Artisans and Politics*, p. 41. John Brown, *Sixty Years' Gleanings from Life's Harvest. A Genuine Autobiography* (Cambridge, 1858), pp. 43–5, provides some recollections of the 1812 strike.

54 Shearring, p. 236. See also Thompson, *Making*, p. 255.

55 William Lovett, *Twopenny Dispatch*, PC set 56, vol. I, f. 10.

56 Bezer, in Vincent, pp. 176–7.

57 Lovett, *Twopenny Dispatch*, PC set 56, vol. I, f. 10. For Mayhew on the slop trade: *UM*, pp. 254–77.

58 Devlin, *Shoemaker* [I], pp. 102–3.

59 George, *London Life*, p. 198; Whittock *et al.*, pp. 403–4; *Operative*, 25 Nov. 1838; *NS*, 11 March 1848; Devlin, *Shoemaker* [I], pp. 15, 26–9, 98–9. For the work of the shoebinder see also *Morning Chronicle*, 16 Nov. 1849, and Mayhew, *UM*, p. 259.

60 *Operative*, 25 Nov. 1838. A rand is a U-shaped strip of leather inserted between welt and upper (see Devlin, *Shoemaker* [I], pp. 87–92, and also J. Ball, 'Bespoke Bootmaking', in F. Y. Golding (ed.), *Boots and Shoes: Their Making, Manufacturing and Selling* (8 vols., 1934–5), VI, pp. 100–3).

61 Cf. Thompson, *Making*, p. 238.

62 Lovett, *Twopenny Dispatch*, PC set 56, vol. I, f. 10; *Operative*, 9 Dec. 1838. In 1839 the average wage varied from 12s. to 14s. (*NS*, 5 Oct. 1839).

63 Whittock *et al.*, p. 403.

64 *Operative*, 25 Nov. 1838 (cf. *ibid.*, 4 Nov. 1838). The survey was partially reprinted by Mayhew in the *Morning Chronicle* (*UM*, pp. 229–31).

65 *NS*, 2 April 1842. Cf. *ibid.*, 27 Aug. 1842.

66 *Ibid.*, 12 April 1845, 28 Feb. 1846.

67 *Ibid.*, 23 March 1844.

68 Mayhew, *UM*, pp. 236–7, 242–3, 249–51; *Morning Chronicle*, 7 Feb. 1850. These wage rates – and those cited in succeeding pages for other trades – do not, of course, take into consideration changes in the cost of living. They are, however, at the very least, essential data for the workers' self-perception of the deterioration in their economic position.

69 Lovett, *Twopenny Dispatch*, PC set 56, vol. I, f. 10; *Operative*, 25 Nov. 1838; *NS*, 28 Feb. 1846. On the other hand, shoemakers were notorious for the irregularity of their working habits (see, for example, Hand-Loom Weavers, *Reports*, pp. 281–2, and *St Crispin*, 10 Sept. 1870).

70 Isaac Wilson, City Man's Man, *NS*, 21 Sept. 1844. Cf. employer's testimony, Mayhew, *UM*, pp. 271–2. For all these developments see too Prothero, *Artisans and Politics*, pp. 44–5, 212–13.

71 *NS*, 29 March 1845. Cf. Webb TU MSS., XXV, f. 88.

72 Mayhew, *UM*, pp. 233–4, 246.

73 Cf. *ibid.*, pp. 233–4.

74 *Evening Star*, 25 Aug. 1842; *NS*, 27 Aug., 15 Oct. 1842.

75 Mayhew listed the fifty-six 'principal slop traders in women's boots and

shoes', overwhelmingly situated in the eastern reaches of the City and, particularly, Tower Hamlets (*Morning Chronicle*, 18 Feb. 1850).

76 *The Last*, 1 Nov. 1844; *NS*, 29 March 1845. The Borough Men's Men probably numbered around eighty (see Webb TU MSS., XXV, f. 88).

77 Devlin, *Shoemaker* [I], p. 105; *Cordwainers' Companion*, June 1844; *NS*, 26 Feb. 1848; Webb TU MSS., XXV, f. 88.

78 James Devlin, *The Guide to Trade: The Shoemaker. Part II: Being the Duties of the Shop* (1841), pp. 67–8. Cf. *Morning Chronicle*, 18 Feb. 1850. For the clickers' position *vis-à-vis* the other workers see A. Fox, pp. 20–21, and cf. *NS*, 27 April 1844. The autobiography of a shoemaker who worked at times as a clicker is Brown's (see esp. Part 3, chap. 7).

79 *Morning Chronicle*, 18 Feb. 1850.

80 *Operative*, 2, 23 Dec. 1838, 20 Jan. 1839; *Charter*, 20 Oct., 29 Dec. 1839.

81 James Dacres Devlin, a Dublinman by origin, not only wrote extensively and eruditely on shoemaking, but was an unexcelled craftsman, 'the head don closer of the day', who had worked for Hoby the Great and closed 'the celebrated shamrock tongue'. In the 1840s he belonged to the coterie which included Thomas Cooper and Harney, John Skelton and Thomas Shorter – and had earlier contributed both prose and verse to Leigh Hunt's *London Journal* (*St Crispin*, 20 March, 2 Oct. 1869; Wright, pp. 166–9; Leno, *Aftermath*, pp. 65–6; *idem, Art*, p. 72; *NS*, 8 Sept. 1849; Cooper, *Life of Thomas Cooper*, p. 313).

82 *Operative*, 4, 11, 25 Nov., 9 Dec. 1838, 31 March 1839; Mayhew, *UM*, p. 246; *Trades' Societies and Strikes*, p. 320. Devlin returned to his attack on the events of 1838 – and now hit at the *Operative* and Bronterre – in the *Cordwainers' Companion*, 10 Aug.–21 Sept. 1844.

83 *Charter*, 11 Aug. 1839; *NS*, 10 April 1841.

84 *Cordwainers' Companion*, April 1844; *NS*, 2 March 1844. For initial relations with the London men's men, see *NS*, 9 March 1844.

85 An incomplete run of the *Cordwainers' Companion*, as of *The Last*, its rival, is held by Manchester Central Library; but no surviving issues have been located of their immediate predecessor, the *Crispin*, published by the Chartist locality of the United Boot and Shoemakers and of which at least one number, in December 1843, appeared (*NS*, 9, 23 Dec. 1843).

86 *Cordwainers' Companion*, July 1844 and Supplementary Number, July 1844.

87 *NS*, 22 June, 21 Sept. 1844; *The Last*, 25 Oct., 1 Nov. 1844. On the other hand, the balance sheet for the first quarter, ending 1 Nov. 1844, gives a total of 141 societies (*The Last*, pp. 115–19 [? 31 Jan. 1845]).

88 *NS*, 31 Aug., 21 Sept., 2 Nov. 1844. *Cordwainers' Companion*, 3 Aug.–21 Sept. 1844, carried an extended polemic against these 'Lilliputians'.

89 *NS*, 26 Oct., 2, 9 Nov. 1844; *The Last*, 1, 8 Nov. 1844. A portion of the debate is also quoted by R. A. Leeson, *Travelling Brothers: The Six Centuries' Road from Craft Fellowship to Trade Unionism* (1979), p. 195. See too Alfred Hunnibell's three letters to the Philanthropic Society, *The Last*, 15, 22 Nov., 13 Dec. 1844.

90 *NS*, 5, 12 April 1845.

91 *Ibid.*, 10, 24, 31 May, 7 June 1845.

92 *Ibid.*, 21 March 1846.

93 Webb TU MSS., XXV, ff. 88–9; *The Last*, pp. 115–19 [? 31 Jan. 1845].

94 *NS*, 29 Aug., 26 Sept. 1846.

95 *Ibid.*, 28 Feb., 21 March, 18 April 1846; Webb TU MSS., XXV, f. 88.

96 *NS*, 9, 16, 23 May 1846. Devlin's centrality in this connection can probably be largely attributed to the Association's attempt to supplant the *Companion* by its official weekly, *The Last*, in the autumn of 1844 (*The Last*, 8 Nov. 1844).

97 *NS*, 16, 23 May, 6, 20 June, 11 July, 15, 29 Aug. 1846.

98 Webb TU MSS., XXV, ff. 88, 90.

99 *NS*, 26 Sept., 17 Oct. 1846, 22 May 1847.

100 *Ibid.*, 14 March, 26 Sept. 1846, 31 July 1847, 8 April 1848.

101 *Ibid.*, 1–29 Jan., 12, 26 Feb., 11 March, 8 April 1848.

102 Webb TU MSS., XXV, ff. 91, 95–8; Gary Thorn, 'The Early History of the Amalgamated Society of Boot and Shoemakers (Cordwainers)', *BSSLH*, no. 39 (Autumn 1979); A. Fox, chap. 1; Webb, *Industrial Democracy*, pp. 417–19. There is no justification for the contention by Prothero, 'London Chartism and the Trades', p. 217, that the Cordwainers' Association was absorbed, as a national union, by the NAUT.

103 *NS*, 5 Sept., 17 Oct. 1846.

104 Mayhew, *UM*, p. 181. J. W. Parker's claim of 14,000 to 15,000 is clearly derived from the 1831 aggregate and perhaps indicates that trade union estimates should be regarded with caution (*NS*, 18 Dec. 1841, 27 Jan. 1844).

105 Mayhew, *UM*, p. 216; Michael D. Avery, 'Industry in South-East London (Bermondsey and Southwark)' (London MA thesis, 1963), p. 200. Cf. Hall, *Industries*, pp. 40–2, for the distribution in 1861.

106 Barbara Drake, 'The West End Tailoring Trade', in Sidney Webb and Arnold Freeman (eds.), *Seasonal Trades* (1912), pp. 71, 73–4; S. P. Dobbs, *The Clothing Workers of Great Britain* (1928), pp. 12–13; Peter K. Newman, 'The Early London Clothing Trades', *Oxford Economic Papers*, New Series, IV (1952), pp. 243–4; Whittock *et al.*, p. 431; Mayhew, *UM*, pp. 184–6, 194; Hall, *Industries*, pp. 54–5; D. L. Munby, *Industry and Planning in Stepney* (1951), pp. 54–6.

107 [Thomas Carter], *The Guide to Trade: The Tailor* (1845), pp. 7–8; [Thomas Carter], *Memoirs of a Working Man* (1845), p. 124; Galton, pp. 126–7, 202; Mayhew, *UM*, p. 196. See also George, *London Life*, p. 204, and Newman, p. 245.

108 Cf. *The Guide to Trade: The Dress-Maker, and the Milliner* (1840), p. 5.

109 Webb TU MSS., XIV, f. 44; Whittock *et al.*, p. 432; Mayhew, *UM*, Letters VII, VIII; *Morning Chronicle*, 18 Dec. 1849. See also, for example, *Charter*, 13 Oct. 1839; *ECC*, no. 55; *NS*, 3 Feb., 14 Sept. 1844, 29 March 1845, 10 March 1849; HO 45/1821.

110 Lovett, *Twopenny Dispatch*, PC set 56, vol. I, f. 11.

111 *NS*, 2, 9 Dec. 1843; *Punch*, V, pp. viii, 203, 260. The notoriety of Elias Moses and Son was such that they were named as running a sweating shop in a broadside, 'Strike of the Journeymen Tailors' (James Klugmann Collection, Library of the Communist Party of Great Britain). Still, they remained in business; *Punch* ceased (*pace* Munby, p. 53) to regard them as an object for outrage, converting them into a favourite, amiably handled butt (e.g., *Punch*, XIV (1848), p. 127); and the firm itself, undaunted, published puffs in later years claiming to have pioneered the introduction of ready-made clothing (Hall, *Industries*, pp. 53–4. See also Mayhew, *UM*, fig. 5, p. 226).

112 E.g., *NS*, 2 Dec. 1843 (Richard Morgan's statement), 21 March 1846, 8 Dec. (Harney), 29 Dec. 1849; *Morning Chronicle*, 18 Dec. 1849 (at Hano-

ver Square Rooms meeting). The *English Chartist Circular* denunciation of 'Jew capitalists', however, dates from 1842 (no. 55). Mayhew during his enquiries spoke with several Jews (*UM*, pp. 226–7; *Morning Chronicle*, 18 Dec. 1849).

113 The 1881 edition of Kingsley, *Alton Locke*, reprints *Cheap Clothes and Nasty* as pp. lxii–lxxxvii. In the novel see pp. 108–15, 120–1, 138–9, 215, 219–26. The debt to the *Morning Chronicle* is made entirely explicit in *Cheap Clothes and Nasty* and, although he was acquainted with Walter Cooper and perhaps had some first-hand experience, Kingsley's disclaimer of his dependence on Mayhew is not convincing (letter of 13 Jan. 1851, *ibid.*, p. xxxi, and [F. E. Kingsley], I, p. 249. See also Raven, pp. 144–6, and Crowe, *Reminiscences of Robert Crowe*, p. 8. But contrast [F. E. Kingsley], I, p. 224; R. B. Martin, pp. 112–13; Thompson, 'Mayhew and the *Morning Chronicle*', Mayhew, *UM*, p. 30; Raven, pp. 168–9; Gertrude Himmelfarb, 'The Culture of Poverty', in Dyos and Wolff, II, pp. 728–9).

114 *NS*, 3 Feb. 1844.

115 Galton, pp. 150–4; [Carter], *Memoirs*, pp. 122–4.

116 *Trades' Societies and Strikes*, p. 353. A fellow unionist put the total of tailors' societies at twenty-seven in 1832 (Prothero, 'Movements', p. 33).

117 *Morning Chronicle*, 18 Dec. 1849.

118 For 1834 see Galton, pp. lxxx–xcii, 179–210, and Parssinen and Prothero. It should be noted, though, that in the 'Principles' of the Metropolitan Tailors' Protection Society the strike was described as successful (PC set 51, f. 270). The conflict between the tailors and tailoresses is discussed by Barbara Taylor, ' "The Men Are as Bad as Their Masters . . .": Socialism, Feminism, and Sexual Antagonism in the London Tailoring Trade in the Early 1830s', *Feminist Studies*, V, no. 1 (Spring 1979), pp. 23–33.

119 Galton, p. 147; Hand-Loom Weavers, *Reports*, pp. 280–1; Mayhew, *UM*, pp. 183–6, 219. The 'log' had operated before 1834, but as the 'daily task . . . fixed by the workmen themselves' ([Carter], *Memoirs*, pp. 123–4; Parssinen and Prothero, pp. 70–1).

120 Mayhew, *UM*, pp. 182, 216; *Morning Chronicle*, 11 Dec. 1849; Webb TU MSS., XIV, f. 73; Lovett, *Twopenny Dispatch*, PC set 56, vol. I, f. 11; *Charter*, 13 Oct. 1839; *ECC*, no. 55; *NS*, 21 March 1846. Parssinen and Prothero, pp. 67–70; and Prothero, *Artisans and Politics*, pp. 41, 44, 213–14, review the tailors' decline down to 1834. A denunciation describing 'the existing competition' was published in three folio pages by the London Foreman Tailors' Mutual Association in 1845 (PC set 53, ff. 307–9).

121 *NS*, 13 April 1844.

122 *Evening Star*, 24 Jan. 1843.

123 Cf. *NS*, 13 March 1847.

124 *Ibid.*, 30 Dec. 1843, 13 Jan. 1844.

125 *Ibid.*, 13 April 1844.

126 *Ibid.*, 5 March 1842, 30 Dec. 1843, 13 April 1844.

127 *Ibid.*, 11 Dec. 1841.

128 *Ibid.*, 13 April 1844, 27 March 1847; Mayhew, *UM*, p. 182; Webb TU MSS., XIV, f. 73.

129 PC set 51, ff. 269–71; *Evening Star*, 24 Jan. 1843; Galton, p. xciv.

130 *NS*, 25 Nov., 2 Dec. 1843.

131 *Ibid.*, 13 Jan. 1844. The official history of tailoring trade unionism con-

tains only two brief references to this interesting – and important – organization and both are entirely incorrect: Margaret Stewart and Leslie Hunter, *The Needle is Threaded: 'The History of an Industry'* (1964), pp. 45, 28. It has not proved possible to locate any copies of the union's weekly journal, the *Tailors' Advocate*, later *Labour's Advocate*, published between 1845 and (?) 1847 (*NS*, 19, 26 April 1845, 17 April 1847).

132 *NS*, 23 March, 13 April 1844.

133 *Ibid.*, 13, 20 April 1844.

134 *Ibid.*, 13 April, 8, 22 June, 10 Aug. 1844.

135 Another three were situated in Stratford, Tottenham and Woolwich (*ibid.*, 10, 24 Feb., 13 April 1844).

136 *Ibid.*, 13 April 1844; Galton, pp. xciv–xcv.

137 *NS*, 30 Dec. 1843.

138 *Ibid.*, 13 April 1844.

139 For the extreme seasonality of West End tailoring: Mayhew, *UM*, pp. 190–2; Parssinen and Prothero, pp. 68, 70n; Drake, esp. pp. 70–3.

140 *NS*, 10 Aug. 1844. The *Crisis* had similarly complained of 'the second book system' in 1833, contending that it divided the tailors into 'three real detachments' (Webb TU MSS., XIV, f. 60). See too Parssinen and Prothero, p. 86. (In Newcastle a system with three books operated: Lowery, *Robert Lowery: Radical and Chartist*, pp. 84–5.)

141 *NS*, 21 Sept. 1844.

142 *Ibid.*, 26 Oct. 1844.

143 *Ibid.*, 11 Jan. 1845.

144 *Ibid.*, 19, 26 April 1845.

145 *Ibid.*, 21 March, 31 Oct. 1846, 16 Jan. 1847.

146 The real desire of the London tailors for some kind of general union, albeit undemanding, is apparent from the flirtation of the houses of call with the NAUT over several years. In this the tailors' unionism in the 1840s is again remarkably similar to the cordwainers' (*ibid.*, 29 March, 26 April 1845, 13, 27 March, 26 June, 17 July 1847).

147 Although, it should be noted, Parker, a staunch Chartist, had been advocating their amalgamation with the NAUT since the 1845 Conference (*ibid.*, 26 April 1845, 17 April, 29 May 1847).

148 Richard Price, *Masters, Unions and Men: Work Control in Building and the Rise of Labour, 1830–1914* (Cambridge, 1980), pp. 22–6; Postgate, *Builders' History*, pp. 9, 72–3; Cole, *Attempts*, pp. 104–5; John Summerson, *Georgian London* (Penguin edn, 1962), pp. 75–7; Hermione Hobhouse, *Thomas Cubitt: Master Builder* (1971), pp. 4–15; Prothero, *Artisans and Politics*, pp. 45, 269; Mayhew, *UM*, p. 350. In his discussion of this development Viles, pp. 17–22, stresses that whereas in 1834 the small masters rallied to the Operative Builders' Union (OBU) in opposition to the 'gormandisers', their attitude to the contract system underwent a very sudden change following the operatives' defeat – by the late 1830s they had swung round to its support and were arrayed against their employees. See, for the business of house decoration, *The Guide to Trade: The Plumber, Painter, and Glazier* (1838), pp. 6–8.

149 For speculative building in the 18th century (and earlier): George, *London Life*, pp. 86–91; Summerson, pp. 77–9.

150 Webb TU MSS., XIII, f. 165.

151 See below, p. 180.

152 Webb TU MSS., X, f. 209. The degeneration which had resulted in the

building trades by the first years of the twentieth century, even in a small coastal town, is widely known through Robert Tressell, *The Ragged Trousered Philanthropists* (Panther edn, 1965), esp. chap. 2 and pp. 388–90, 404–5 (though the reservation expressed by Richard Price, p. 285 n9, is not surprising). For sub-contracting and its effects, see Mayhew, *LL&LP*, II, pp. 329–30; Mayhew, *UM*, pp. 336–55; Richard Price, pp. 26–32; Postgate, *Builders' History*, pp. 148–50, 267–8; Hobhouse, pp. 260–3; Viles, pp. 21–30; William Millar, *Plastering: Plain and Decorative* (3rd edn, 1905), pp. 561–2.

153 Mayhew, *UM*, p. 335; *NS*, 11 May 1844, 31 July 1847.

154 Cf. Mayhew, *UM*, p. 337.

155 *Ibid.*, pp. 338–9; Whittock *et al.*, pp. 102, 108–10; *The Guide to Trade: The Joiner and Cabinet-Maker* (1838), p. 6; Hobhouse, p. 8.

156 Mayhew, *UM*, pp. 344–5; Lovett, *Twopenny Dispatch*, PC set 56, vol. I, f. 11; Hobhouse, pp. 286–7, 490–1.

157 Mayhew, *UM*, pp. 335, 340, 345.

158 Webb TU MSS., XI, ff. 100, 173, 295; Postgate, *Builders' History*, pp. 22–3, 455. Cf. Webb TU MSS., X, f. 60.

159 *Charter*, 14 April 1839; Lovett, *Twopenny Dispatch*, PC set 56, vol. I, f. 11. In 1845 the wife of a journeyman who had attempted suicide said he had only six months' employment in two and a half years (*NS*, 14 June 1845).

160 Mayhew, *UM*, p. 355.

161 Postgate, *Builders' History*, pp. 22–3.

162 Cf. Viles, p. 45.

163 Prothero, *Artisans and Politics*, pp. 159–60, 269–70; Postgate, *Builders' History*, pp. 52–3; Webb, *History*, pp. 99, 111n.; S. Higenbottam, *Our Society's History* (Manchester, 1939), pp. 25, 28.

164 Webb, *History*, pp. 110–11; Postgate, *Builders' History*, p. 67; Prothero, *Artisans and Politics*, p. 301.

165 *NS*, 13 June 1840, 21 Aug. 1841, 16 May 1846; *Charter*, 20 Oct., 3 Nov., 15 Dec. 1839; *Operative*, 26 May 1839; Webb TU MSS., XI, ff. 95–7.

166 Prothero, 'Movements', p. 33; *NS*, 5 Dec. 1840.

167 *NS*, 10 June 1843; Viles, pp. 64, 118.

168 *NS*, 11 May, 7 Sept. 1844, 29 March 1845.

169 Webb TU MSS., XI, f. 288.

170 *Ibid.*, ff. 36, 95–7; Postgate, *Builders' History*, p. 166.

171 Webb TU MSS., XI, ff. 95–7; *NS*, 9 June 1849; *Labour League*, 21 April 1849; Viles, pp. 65, 151–3.

172 *NS*, 19 June, 31 July, 14, 21 Aug. 1847; Webb TU MSS., XI, f. 295.

173 Webb TU MSS., XIII, f. 14.

174 W. S. Hilton, pp. 26–7, 284–6; Webb, *History*, pp. 157, 195; H. A. Clegg, Alan Fox and A. F. Thompson, *A History of British Trade Unions Since 1889, vol. 1: 1889–1910* (Oxford, 1964), pp. 2–3, 8; Postgate, *Builders' History*, p. 122. For the mason's craft see Whittock *et al.*, pp. 324–5.

175 Webb TU MSS., XIII, f. 181. Cf. *ibid.*, f. 191, and *NS*, 19 June 1847. Viles, pp. 65, 142–3, gives figures for the OSM's metropolitan membership in the forties – and to these must be added the (unknown) numbers of masons in the 'Anti-Society'. See also *ibid.*, p. 38.

176 Webb TU MSS., XIII, ff. 165, 232–42; Postgate, *Builders' History*, pp. 148–50.

177 *NS*, 23 Oct. 1841.

178 *Ibid.*, 25 Sept., 9, 30 Oct. 1841; W. S. Hilton, pp. 60–1; Viles, pp. 61–2.

179 For the strike see *NS*, 25 Sept. 1841–4 June 1842; Webb TU MSS., XIII, ff. 153–7; PC set 53, Section E, ff. 7, 11–13; HO 45/297; W. S. Hilton, chap. 8; Viles, pp. 77–91; Richard Price, pp. 36–9; Postgate, *Builders' History*, pp. 129–30.

180 Postgate, *Builders' History*, p. 131; W. S. Hilton, pp. 86–9; Viles, pp. 91–3.

181 W. S. Hilton, pp. 67–72; Viles, pp. 129–33; *NS*, 27 Feb. 1841; Webb TU MSS., XIII, f. 134; Postgate, *Builders' History*, p. 128.

182 Postgate, *Builders' History*, pp. 129, 132; W. S. Hilton, pp. 73, 89; Viles, pp. 134–5; Webb TU MSS., XIII, ff. 152, 181, 183.

183 *NS*, 19, 26 June, 17, 24 July, 20 Oct. 1847: *Labour League*, 11 Nov. 1848; W. S. Hilton, pp. 102–3; Viles, pp. 160–3. The conspiracy proceedings of 1848 were ultimately dropped (for the affair: *NS*, *Spirit of the Age* and *Labour League*, Sept.–Dec. 1848; Webb TU MSS., XIII, f. 183; Postgate, *Builders' History*, pp. 159, 168; Webb, *History*, p. 166n.; Viles, pp. 163–4).

184 W. S. Hilton, pp. 26, 53; Postgate, *Builders' History*, pp. 54, 67, 116; Webb TU MSS., X, f. 190.

185 *NS*, Dec. 1840, 29 March 1845; W. S. Hilton, p. 90.

186 See Postgate, *Builders' History*, pp. 139–40, and W. S. Hilton, pp. 106, 117–19, for the financial manoeuvres which gave rise to the division.

187 Webb TU MSS., X, f. 224; cf. *ibid.*, f. 211, which cites a membership of 'nearly 2000' for 1853. See Viles, pp. 112–14; Postgate, *Builders' History*, pp. 164, 178 *et seq.*, and W. S. Hilton, pp. 123, 146 *et seq.*, for the union's subsequent development.

188 Webb TU MSS., X, ff. 209–11.

189 F. M. Leventhal, *Respectable Radical: George Howell and Victorian Working Class Politics* (1971), pp. 17–19, 29 *et seq.*

190 See Viles, pp. 41, 121, who plausibly suggests that bricklaying was overwhelmingly 'dishonourable' and that a significantly smaller proportion of men received the full artisan wage compared with the other building trades (with, it must be qualified, the exception of the painters).

191 See *ibid.*, pp. 120–1.

192 *NS*, 12 Sept. 1840, 8 Aug. 1846.

193 Dickens, *Sketches by Boz*, 'Scenes', chap. 5. Cf. Hand-Loom Weavers, *Copy of Report by Mr. Hickson on the Condition of the Hand-Loom Weavers*, 1840, XXIV (639), p. 56; George Read's remarks, *NS*, 26 Dec. 1846; John Denvir, *The Life Story of an Old Rebel* (Dublin, 1910), p. 50; Jackson, *Irish in Britain*, p. 85.

194 Webb, *History*, pp. 110–11; *idem, Industrial Democracy*, pp. 339–40; Postgate, *Builders' History*, p. 67; Oliver, 'Organizations', pp. 206–7; Prothero, 'Movements', p. 164; *idem, Artisans and Politics*, p. 301.

195 Add. MS. 27,820, f. 381; *Operative*, 31 March, 12 May 1839; *Charter*, 31 March, 22 Sept. 1839, 15 March 1840.

196 Webb TU MSS., X, f. 60; Postgate, *Builders' History*, p. 455; Hand-Loom Weavers, *Reports*, p. 279.

197 However, the opinion expressed by *Labour League*, 21 April 1849, appears more realistic. Viles, pp. 41–2, 49, contends that the plasterers' section of the OBU continued as a national union, retaining a foothold in London, but was not very powerful.

198 Webb TU MSS., X, f. 141, XII, ff. 152, 165; *NS*, 27 July 1844, 29 March 1845; Whittock *et al.*, p. 381; Millar, pp. 561–2; Hobhouse, pp. 261–2.

199 The plumbers' union did continue but did not extend much beyond the North of England (Postgate, *Builders' History*, pp. 56–7, 116–17, 122, 133; Webb, *History*, pp. 110–11, 153; J. O. French, *Plumbers in Unity: History of the Plumbing Trades Union, 1865–1965* (n.p., n.d.), pp. 7–16).

200 Whittock *et al.*, pp. 275, 360, 382–3; *Guide to Trade: Plumber*, pp. 5–6, 8–9; Webb TU MSS., XII, f. 2.

201 Webb TU MSS., X, f. 141, XII, f. 284; *NS*, 11 Dec. 1841, 18 March 1848.

202 21 April 1849.

203 *Guide to Trade: Plumber*, pp. 6–9; Postgate, *Builders' History*, pp. 150, 237; Viles, p. 37.

204 *Guide to Trade: Plumber*, pp. 81–3; *NS*, 28 Nov. 1846; Postgate, *Builders' History*, pp. 236–7; Viles, pp. 40, 121–4; Hand-Loom Weavers, *Reports*, p. 279. But cf. George, *London Life*, p. 263.

205 *Guide to Trade: Plumber*, pp. 63–5, 82–3; Whittock *et al.*, pp. 356–7, 382; Hand-Loom Weavers, *Reports*, pp. 279–80; George, *London Life*, p. 203; Viles, p. 11; Shearring, pp. 479–80; *NS*, 6 Nov. 1841, 28 Nov. 1846; Webb TU MSS., X, f. 141, XII, f. 7.

206 Winter was the period of wage-cuts and unemployment.

207 George, *London Life*, pp. 178–83, 186; Alfred Plummer, *The London Weavers' Company, 1600–1970* (1972), pp. 315–29, also chap. 14; J. H. Clapham, 'The Spitalfields Acts, 1773–1824', *Economic Journal*, XXVI (1916), pp. 459–62. For the turmoil of 1763–73 see J. L. Hammond and Barbara Hammond, *The Skilled Labourer, 1760–1832* (1919), pp. 205–9, and Rudé, *Wilkes and Liberty*, pp. 98–103.

208 Thompson, *Making*, p. 143; Mayhew, *LL&LP*, II, pp. 63–4; Mayhew, *UM*, pp. 105–6, 114; Hand-Loom Weavers, *Reports*, pp. 216–18; Hand-Loom Weavers, *Hickson's Report*, p. 79. For the Mathematical Society (and its demise in 1846), see also Rose, pp. 103–4, and Philip Howard, 'The Mathematicians of Spitalfields', *The Times*, 18 November 1978. 'The genuine Spitalfields weaver', however, even in the middle of the nineteenth century, remained 'a connoisseur in birds and flowers, under all his trials and difficulties' (Dodd, *Days*, pp. 4–5; Knight, II, pp. 386, 397; *Knight's Cyclopædia of London* (1851), p. 16; Hector Gavin, *Sanitary Ramblings: Being Sketches and Illustrations, of Bethnal Green: A Type of the Condition of the Metropolis and Other Large Towns* (1848), pp. 11–12). Place's extremely low opinion, during the 1820s, of the weavers contrasts strikingly with this evidence, both retrospective and contemporary (Add. MSS. 27,827, f. 38; 27,828, ff. 116–17).

209 And 14s. 6d. in 1824 (Mayhew, *UM*, pp. 107, 112; PC set 58, vol. I, f. 286). See also *Labour League*, 9 Dec. 1848.

210 This summary derives from Hammond and Hammond, pp. 210–20; Plummer, *Weavers' Company*, pp. 330–6; Clapham, 'Spitalfields Acts', pp. 462–71; Prothero, *Artisans and Politics*, pp. 65–6, 210–11; Hand-Loom Weavers, *Reports*, pp. 359–61, 373, 403; and develops points from E. J. Hobsbawm, *Industry and Empire: An Economic History of Britain since 1750* (1968), p. 41, and George J. Stigler, *Five Lectures on Economic Problems* (1949), p. 28. On the other hand George, *London Life*, pp. 186–96, considers that the position of weavers did not change significantly between the early-eighteenth century and the 1840s. For the highly competitive branches of the North and Midlands see Hand-Loom Weavers, *Hickson's Report*, pp. 14–17.

211 HO 44/37, letter to Marquis of Normanby, 27 April 1840.

212 James Bronterre O'Brien, *The Life and Character of Maximilian Robespierre*, I, [1838], p. 14.

213 Lovett, *L&S*, I, p. 72.

214 *NS*, 10 Feb. 1838.

215 *Charter*, 17 Nov. 1839.

216 Hand-Loom Weavers, *Reports*, pp. 239–41.

217 *NS*, 26 Dec. 1840, 11 Dec. 1841.

218 *Charter*, 3 March, 26 May 1839.

219 Hand-Loom Weavers, *Reports*, pp. 228–34, 361. Cf. O'Brien, p. 14.

220 Hand-Loom Weavers, *Reports*, pp. 236–7, 375–7; Hand-Loom Weavers, *Hickson's Report*, p. 78; George, *London Life*, p. 181 *et seq.*

221 Knight, II, pp. 395–6; Hand-Loom Weavers, *Reports*, pp. 259–60; Sir Frank Warner, *The Silk Industry of the United Kingdom: Its Origin and Development* (n.d.), pp. 101–3.

222 George, *London Life*, pp. 179–80; Clapham, 'Spitalfields Acts', pp. 459–60; Clapham I, pp. 69–70, 197–8; *NS*, 19 Aug. 1843; Mayhew, *UM*, p. 112; Add. MS. 34,245B, ff. 8–9, 18; Warner, pp. 82–3, 89; Briggs, 'Social Structure and Politics', pp. 71–2.

223 Plummer, *Weavers' Company*, pp. 162–8; Hand-Loom Weavers, *Reports*, pp. 276–7; Add. MS. 34,245B, ff. 9–10; *Charter*, 17 Nov. 1839.

224 Hand-Loom Weavers, *Reports*, p. 227. For the ingenious, delicate technique of velvet-weaving, see George Dodd, *The Textile Manufactures of Great Britain* (1844), pp. 201–4.

225 Spital Square remained 'the heart of the silk-district' for the masters continued to live there (Knight, II, p. 387; Warner, pp. 62–3, chap. 6). During the first half of the nineteenth century the rest of the parish deteriorated into a slum – for which process K. Leech, 'The Decay of Spitalfields', *ELP*, VII, no. 2 (Dec. 1964), pp. 58–60, is of some assistance.

226 The figures are from the census conducted by J. Mitchell, Assistant Hand-Loom Weavers' Commissioner, who estimated that altogether the Spitalfields weavers would number 10,500 to 11,000, pointing out that such an aggregate was markedly less than the figure customarily cited (Hand-Loom Weavers, *Reports*, pp. 218–28). Weavers informed Mayhew in 1849 there were 9,000 hands (*UM*, pp. 110, 112, but cf. p. 106). For 'Spitalfields' see also Knight, II, pp. 386–7. A. V. B. Gibson, 'Huguenot Weavers' Houses in Spitalfields', *ELP*, I, no. 1 (April 1958), pp. 8–14, links the changing architecture to the decline in the weavers' economic position, as the quarter spread to the north-east.

227 Webb, *History*, pp. 48–9, 59, 87; Plummer, *Weavers' Company*, pp. 329–30.

228 Knight, II p. 396; Hand-Loom Weavers, *Reports*, pp. 257–8; *Spitalfields Weavers' Journal*, Sept., Oct., 1837; *NS*, 10 Feb. 1838, 27 Nov. 1841, 15 Jan. 1842, 27 Feb. 1847. For the anti-Chartist orientation of the *Relief Committee* of the Broad Silk Weavers: *NS*, 5, 12 March 1842.

229 Hand-Loom Weavers, *Hickson's Report*, pp. 5, 76: Plummer, *Weavers' Company*, p. 157.

230 *NS*, 20 Feb. 1847, 13 May 1848; HO 45/1984.

231 Hammond and Hammond, p. 104; Cole, *Attempts*, pp. 8–9; Prothero, *Artisans and Politics*, pp. 274, 285; Hollis, *Pauper Press*, pp. 264–5; Oliver, 'Organizations', pp. 203, 211.

232 Hand-Loom Weavers, *Hickson's Report*, p. 78; Hammond and Ham-

mond, p. 219; Prothero, 'Movements', p. 277; *idem, Artisans and Politics*, p. 212; Charles Welch, *Modern History of the City of London: A Record of Municipal and Social Progress from 1760 to the Present Day* (1896), p. 163.

233 Warner, pp. 504–13; Webb TU MSS., XXXVI, ff. 305–8, and XL, ff. 86, 147; Prothero, *Artisans and Politics*, pp. 211–12.

234 Add. MS. 34,245B, ff. 15–16.

235 *NS*, 29 March 1845.

236 See, for example, *ibid.*, 14 March 1846. Initial involvement with the Anti-League was but fleeting (*ibid.*, 9, 12, 23 March 1844). For an interesting, sour comment on Spitalfields protectionism see Hand-Loom Weavers, *Hickson's Report*, p. 25.

237 Prothero, *Artisans and Politics*, p. 212; Hammond and Hammond, pp. 219–20; Hand-Loom Weavers, *Reports*, p. 395.

238 *NS*, 19 Aug., 4 Nov. 1843, 24 Feb. 1844.

239 *Labour League*, 16, 30 Dec. 1848. See also *NS*, 22 March 1845.

240 *NS*, 24 Aug. 1844, 1 Dec. 1849; Mayhew, *UM*, pp. 109–12.

241 J. I. Ferdinando asserted, in 1849 with the duty at 15 per cent, that 'the poor weavers of Spitalfields ... had lost sixteen shillings out of the pound by the Free Trade nostrums of Huskisson and Company' (*NS*, 10 Nov. 1849).

242 *Ibid.*, 19 Aug. 1843.

243 For Spitalfields's especial disadvantage: Clapham I, p. 499.

244 *NS*, 5 Dec. 1846, 20 Feb. 1847.

245 *Ibid.*, 8 Jan., 18 March 1848.

246 *Labour League*, 9, 16 Dec. 1848, 14, 28 April, 5, 19 May 1849; *Spirit of the Age*, 27 Jan., 10, 24 Feb., 3 March 1849.

247 HO 45/1984; *NS*, 10 March, 1 Dec. 1849; Mayhew, *UM*, pp. 107, 112; PC set 58, vol. I, f. 286; *Labour League*, 9, 16 Dec. 1848; *Spirit of the Age*, 27 Jan. 1849. But cf. Clapham II, pp. 19–20. It was the Anglo-French treaty of 1860 that virtually extinguished Spitalfields, for silk, the most favoured British manufacture of importance, was then stripped of all protection (Clapham II, pp. 1–2, 87, 244, 513–14; Plummer, *Weavers' Company*, pp. 368–71; Booth, *Poverty Series*, IV, pp. 242–4. Warner, chap. 8, recounts the death throes).

248 Letter from Francis Place, *Twopenny Dispatch*, 15 Aug. 1836, in 'Bronterre's Letters', BL press mark 8139. eee. 39.; Webb, *History*, pp. 75n., 187; Jefferys, *Story*, pp. 10–12.

249 H. J. Fyrth and Henry Collins, *The Foundry Workers: A Trade Union History* (Manchester, 1959), pp. 6–11, 29; Jefferys, *Story*, pp. 9–17, 51–2, 55–8; Webb, *Industrial Democracy*, pp. 107–8, 470–1; Clapham I, pp. 151–7, 206–8, 446–9, 550, and II, pp. 160–1; Thompson, *Making*, pp. 244–7; Burgess, pp. 1–26. Roderick Floud, *The British Machine Tool Industry, 1850–1914* (Cambridge, 1976), pp. 20–3 *et seq.*, is extremely helpful for an understanding of the range and operations of machine tools.

250 Hartridge, pp. 157, 161–3; *Charter*, 29 Dec. 1839; Jefferys, *Story*, pp. 23, 26; *NS*, 1, 27 Jan. 1844. Cf. the boilermakers' concern with helpers and 'holders-up' (*NS*, 17 Oct. 1846; J. E. Mortimer, *History of the Boilermakers' Society, vol. 1: 1834–1906* (1973), pp. 43, 205–6). One employer engaged men as 'common labourers' who might advance from 18s. to a maximum of 24s. as they gained expertise (Hand-Loom Weavers, *Reports*, p. 284. See also Burgess, pp. 12–15). London employers had taken the lead in

the repeal of the apprenticeship clauses (Prothero, *Artisans and Politics*, p. 59).

251 *NS*, 17 Oct. 1846; Mortimer, pp. 204–5; Webb, *History*, pp. 187–8; Thomas Hughes, 'Account of the Lock-Out of Engineers, &c., in 1851–2', in *Trades' Societies and Strikes*, pp. 169–205; Jefferys, *Story*, pp. 22–3, 34–42, 63–4; Burgess, pp. 13–24.

252 Clegg, Fox and Thompson, p. 4. Cf. the Boiler Makers and 'holders-up', Mortimer, p. 43.

253 Avery, pp. 202, 306; Hartridge, pp. 115, 139–40, 145, 160–1.

254 'A Day at a Copper and Lead Factory', *Penny Magazine*, June Supp., 1842; *NS*, 22 April 1848. The members of the Employers' Association of 1851 are listed in *Trades' Societies and Strikes*, p. 179.

255 Dodd, *Days*, pp. 13–14.

256 *Ibid.*, p. 14; George Dodd, *British Manufactures: Metals* (1845), p. 125, and *British Manufactures: Series VI* (1846), p. 241.

257 'Day at Copper and Lead Factory', *Penny Magazine*, June Supp., 1842. Archibald T. Kidd, *History of the Tin-Plate Workers and Sheet Metal Workers and Braziers Societies* (1949), p. 106n, describes a brazier as 'a light coppersmith'. Cf. also Charles Booth, *Life and Labour of the People in London. Second Series: Industry* (5 vols., 1903), I, p. 376. For the distinction between brazier and brassfounder see Webb TU MSS., XIX, f. 147; Whittock *et al.*, pp. 67–8.

258 *Operative*, 23 June 1839; George, *London Life*, pp. 203–4.

259 *NS*, 7, 14 Aug., 25 Sept. 1841; 'Day at Copper and Lead Factory', *Penny Magazine*, June Supp., 1842.

260 W. E. Minchinton, *The British Tinplate Industry: A History* (Oxford, 1957), chap. 1, chap. 2, sect. 1; Whittock *et al.*, pp. 443–6; Kidd, pp. 15, 36–8; Dodd, *British Manufactures: Metals*, pp. 164–5; *idem, Days*, p. 15.

261 Kidd, pp. 23–8, 37; *Charter*, 31 March 1839; *NS*, 29 March 1845.

262 Kidd, pp. 38–9; *NS*, 8 Feb., 29 March, 1, 22 Nov. 1845.

263 Kidd, pp. 32–3, 39–40, 44.

264 *NS*, 23 May 1846, 13 March, 29 May 1847; Oliver, 'Organizations', p. 123.

265 Not, it appears, in 1839, as stated by D. C. Cummings, *A Historical Survey of the Boiler Makers' and Iron and Steel Ship Builders' Society . . .* (Newcastle-on-Tyne, 1905), p. 32, and repeated by Mortimer, pp. 21, 217. See *NS*, 21 Aug. 1847.

266 *NS*, 31 Oct. 1846, 23 Jan., 6, 13 Feb., 3 April, 21 Aug. 1847.

267 *Ibid.*, 13 May 1848; and ensuing correspondence, 27 May, 10, 17 June 1848.

268 London and Scotland established district committees, empowered to pass bye-laws (Mortimer, pp. 51, 218; Cummings, p. 49).

269 Mortimer, pp. 27–9, 50–1; Philip Banbury, *Shipbuilders of the Thames and Medway* (Newton Abbot, 1971), pp. 60, 172; Jefferys, *Story*, p. 52; Clapham I, pp. 439–41; and *idem*, II, pp. 63–70; *NS*, 24 Oct. 1846; Cummings, pp. 43–4, 49–50.

270 E.g. see *NS*, 21 Aug. 1847.

271 *Ibid.*, 17, 24, 31 Oct. 1846, 3 April 1847; Cummings, pp. 42, 53; Mortimer, pp. 44, 54–5. Mortimer, App. 2, prints extracts from the prize essay competition of 1856–7 on 'the evils of piece work . . . with a suggested remedy for abolishing or remedying the same'.

272 Webb TU MSS., XV, f. 71; *NS*, 29 March 1845, 1 Aug. 1846, 2 Oct.

1847; Jefferys, *Story*, pp. 17–19, 24, 32; Webb, *History*, pp. 187–8. In addition there was the General Smiths or Derby Union (1822), which, although a 'Pioneer of Unionism' in engineering, increasingly organized the metal-workers in the building trades. For both sections of smiths: Webb TU MSS., XV, f. 75; XVII, ff. 78–87; XX, ff. 145–6, 150, 156.

273 *NS*, 5 Dec. 1840.

274 1834? In that year a transitory union, the Friendly Society of Operative Metal Workers, was formed with London as seat of government (Webb TU MSS., XV, f. 68).

275 *NS*, 1 Aug., 26 Dec. 1846.

276 *Twopenny Disptach*, 13 Aug. 1836, 'Bronterre's Letters'; Webb TU MSS., XVI, f. 33; Jefferys, *Story*, p. 21; Fyrth and Collins, pp. 30–1; Webb, *History*, p. 188.

277 Webb TU MSS., XVI, ff. 33–4; Webb, *History*, p. 188; Jefferys, *Story*, p. 26.

278 *NS*, 1 Aug., 26 Dec. 1846, 31 July 1847; *Labour League*, 21 Oct. 1848.

279 *NS*, 28 Feb., 7 March 1846.

280 *Ibid.*, 19, 26 Dec. 1846, 10, 17 April, 2 Oct. 1847; *Labour League*, 21, 28 Oct., 16 Dec. 1848; Webb, *History*, pp. 188–95; Jefferys, *Story*, pp. 26–31. Since Jefferys is unaware of the existence of the umbrella organization of 'the London Engineers' from 1844 onwards he overrates the significance of 1846–7 as far as London is concerned. For a succinct analysis of the long-term trend in engineering unionism see G. D. H. Cole, 'Some Notes on British Trade Unionism in the Third Quarter of the Nineteenth Century', reprinted in E. M. Carus-Wilson (ed.), *Essays in Economic History*, III (1962), pp. 203–4.

281 *Guide to Trade: Joiner*, pp. 6, 94–5; *Morning Chronicle*, 1 Aug. 1850.

282 *Morning Chronicle*, 8 Aug. 1850; Mayhew, *UM*, pp. 359, 364–5.

283 Mayhew, *UM*, pp. 359–60, 368–70; Mayhew, *LL&LP*, III, p. 225; Prothero, 'Movements', p. 33.

284 But cf. Webb TU MSS., XXII, ff. 12, 54.

285 J. Leonard Oliver, 'The East London Furniture Industry', *ELP*, IV, no. 2 (Oct. 1961); and J. L. Oliver, *The Development and Structure of the Furniture Industry* (Oxford, 1966), pp. 22–45. See J. E. Martin, *Greater London: An Industrial Geography* (1966), pp. 8–10, and Samuel, p. 37, for the contribution of the developments in saw-milling (which are briefly mentioned below, p. 212) to this physical movement and to the growth of the quantity production of furniture.

286 Mayhew, *UM*, pp. 367–70, 373–6; Webb TU MSS., XXII, ff. 15, 18; Lovett, *L&S*, I, pp. 24–34; *Morning Chronicle*, 8 Aug. 1850.

287 For the dishonourable trade: Lovett, *Twopenny Dispatch*, PC set 56, vol. I, f. 11; Mayhew, *UM*, Letters LXV, LXVI; Mayhew, *LL&LP*, III, pp. 221–31.

288 Oliver, 'Organizations', pp. 202–3, 211; Prothero, 'Movements', pp. 414, 417.

289 *NS*, 11, 18 March 1848.

290 Mayhew, *UM*, pp. 366, 374. See above, p. 155.

291 *NS*, 27 March, 1 May, 25 Sept. 1847; *Monthly Report*, 1 Dec. 1847.

292 Lovett, *L&S*, I, pp. 33–4; *Guide to Trade: Joiner*, p. 104; George Dodd, *British Manufactures: Series IV* (1845), pp. 216–17; Norman Robertson, 'A Study of the Development of Labour Relations in the British Furniture Trade' (Oxford BLitt thesis, 1955), p. 35.

293 Thompson, *Making*, p. 239; Prothero, 'Movements', p. 7; Whittock *et al.*, pp. 87–93; *Morning Chronicle*, 16 Nov. 1849; Robertson, p. 39; *NS*, 31 Oct. 1846, 11, 18 March 1848.

294 Viles, pp. 38–9, 128, contradicts himself on this issue.

295 Prothero, 'Movements', p. 414; Oliver, 'Organizations', p. 211; Add. MS. 37,773, f. 116; *NS*, 29 Oct. 1842, 29 March 1845, 25 March 1848.

296 Prothero, 'Movements', p. 33; *The Guide to Trade: The Carver and Gilder* (1840), p. 78; *NS*, 13 July 1844, 29 March 1845.

297 These carvers alone were considered by Mayhew: *Morning Chronicle*, 8 Aug. 1850; Mayhew, *LL&LP*, III, p. 221.

298 *Guide to Trade: Plumber*, pp. 6, 8; *Guide to Trade: Carver*, esp. pp. 5–8, 51–7, 78–9; Whittock *et al.*, pp. 114–19, 277; Booth, *Industry Series*, I, pp. 190–3.

299 Dodd, *Days*, p. 5.

300 Knight, III, pp. 30–1; Mayhew, *UM*, p. 440. It was Christy of Bermondsey Street who employed 1,500 workers (of all kinds), forbidding them to be members of the union after a strike in 1833 and 'supposed to have scruied [sic] more wealth out of his work men, than any other man in that Line of Business in england' ('A Day at a Hat-Factory', *Penny Magazine*, Jan. Supp., 1841 (from which the description in G. W. Phillips, *The History and Antiquities of the Parish of Bermondsey* (1841), pp. 105–7, is derived); [J. D. Burn], *A Glimpse at the Social Condition of the Working Classes During the Early Part of the Present Century* [1868], pp. 42, 71–2; Add. MS. 34,245A, ff. 202–3). Usually between twelve and twenty journeymen were employed by a master (Mayhew, *UM*, p. 444).

301 Mayhew, *LL&LP*, II, p. 299.

302 This would appear to account for the bitterness engendered not only in the strike of 1820 on the introduction of the 'broad yeoman crowns' but also during the 1850s when bowlers began to supplant top-hats ([Burn], *Glimpse*, pp. 39, 41; *Trades' Societies and Strikes*, p. 354; Thomas Okey, *A Basketful of Memories: An Autobiographical Sketch* (1930), p. 6).

303 Mayhew, *UM*, pp. 440–2, 445–7; *Morning Chronicle*, 7 Nov. 1850; 'Day at Hat-Factory', *Penny Magazine*, Jan. Supp., 1841; Whittock *et al.*, pp. 293–7; James Burn (The 'Beggar Boy'), *An Autobiography: Relating the Numerous Trials, Struggles, and Vicissitudes of a Strangely Chequered Life. With Glimpses of English Social, Commercial, and Political History, During Eighty Years, 1802–1882* (1882), pp. 184, 441, 508, 510; National Association of United Trades, *Report of the Central Committee* (1853).

304 *Trades' Societies and Strikes*, pp. 353–4; Mayhew, *UM*, pp. 443–7; *Morning Chronicle*, 7 Nov. 1850; *National United Trades' Association Report*, June 1848. See also Burn, *Autobiography*, pp. 184–5.

305 Booth, *Industry Series*, III, p. 39; Webb, *History*, p. 46; idem, *Industrial Democracy*, p. 11n.; Mayhew, *UM*, pp. 443, 445; *Trades' Societies and Strikes*, p. 354.

306 *NS*, 21 Aug. 1841, 4, 11 May 1844; *ECC*, no. 44; [Burn], *Glimpse*, pp. 49–50.

307 Also of hat finishers (*NS*, 4 May 1844).

308 Mayhew, *UM*, pp. 442–3; Booth, *Industry Series*, III, pp. 39–40.

309 In 1850 one-third of British leather production was centred there; and leather goods occupied second or third place in terms of output among the nation's manufacturing industries during the first half of the nineteenth century (Sheppard, *London*, p. 161; R. A. Church, 'The British

Leather Industry and Foreign Competition, 1870–1914', *Econ HR*, 2nd Ser., XXIV (1971), p. 543).

310 James Statham, 'The Location and Development of London's Leather Manufacturing Industry Since the Early Nineteenth Century' (London MA thesis, 1965), chap. 4; Knight, III, pp. 17–18, 24–5; 'A Day at a Leather-Factory', *Penny Magazine*, May Supp., 1842, p. 209; Mayhew, *UM*, pp. 451–2.

311 Knight, III, p. 27; *Morning Chronicle*, 15 Nov. 1850. See also A. Aikin, 'On Tanning and Leather-Dressing', *Transactions of the Society of Arts*, L (1836), part 1; but cf. Statham, pp. 45–6, although Booth, *Industry Series*, II, pp. 126–33, confirms that the demarcation of processes in the thirties and forties still existed at the end of the century.

312 Knight, III, p. 27; Phillips, p. 105.

313 Mayhew, *UM*, pp. 453–8; 'Day at Leather Factory', *Penny Magazine*, May Supp., 1842, p. 210; Whittock *et al.*, pp. 439–40; Hartridge, pp. 27, 56.

314 Oliver, 'Organizations', p. 211; Prothero, 'Movements', p. 415; Webb TU MSS., XXIV, ff. 44, 51.

315 On the other hand, a strike against four masters in 1836 lasted for at least seven months, costing £3,000 in the support of a weekly average of 120 men (Kiddier, p. 43).

316 'Day at Leather-Factory', *Penny Magazine*, May Supp., 1842, pp. 210–11; Whittock *et al.*, pp. 173–5; Mayhew, *UM*, pp. 458–62; Statham, pp. 111–12; Webb TU MSS., XXIV, ff. 6–7, 12–14, 19–20, 27, 61; Webb, *History*, pp. 31–2, 163.

317 Hartridge, p. 22; Statham, pp. 81–2, 124, 129; Clapham I, pp. 323–4.

318 Knight, III, pp. 29–30; 'Day at Leather-Factory', *Penny Magazine*, May Supp., 1842; *Morning Chronicle*, 15 Nov. 1850.

319 'Day at Leather-Factory', *Penny Magazine*, May Supp., 1842, pp. 211–14; *Morning Chronicle*, 15 Nov. 1850; Webb TU MSS., XXIV, ff. 67–8, 76–8.

320 *Evening Star*, 13 Sept. 1842; *NS*, 17, 24 Sept. 1842.

321 *Charter* and *Operative*, 31 March 1839; Add. MS. 35,245A, f. 246; *NS*, 8 Feb, 29 March, 2 Aug. 1845.

322 Dodd, *Days*, p. 8. B. W. E. Alford, 'Government Expenditure and the Growth of the Printing Industry in the Nineteenth Century', *Econ HR*, 2nd Ser., XVII (1964–5), pp. 96–7, has calculated that from 1831 to 1851 London accounted for more than 54 per cent of the letterpress printing industry's total output.

323 Howe, pp. 298–302; Ellic Howe and Harold E. Waite, *The London Society of Compositors (Re-Established 1848): A Centenary History* (1948), pp. 147–51; Ellic Howe and John Child, *The Society of London Bookbinders, 1780–1951* (1952), pp. 109–11.

324 Howe and Waite, chaps. 4, 5, 8, Appendix 1; Howe, chaps. 7, 8, 10, sect. 1; John Child, *Industrial Relations in the British Printing Industry: The Quest for Security* (1967), pp. 74–6, 81–3, 117–19; A. E. Musson, *The Typographical Association: Origins and History up to 1949* (1954), pp. 57–75, 264 *et seq.*; *NS*, 18, 25 Jan. 1845.

325 Howe and Waite, esp. pp. 108, 111.

326 *Operative*, 23, 30 Dec. 1838, 13, 27 Jan., 3 Feb. 1839; *Charter*, 27 Jan., 3 Feb. 1839; Howe, pp. 65, 192–200, 222–5, 241–2; Howe and Waite, pp. 93–5.

327 *NS*, 8, 15 March 1845; *Trades' Societies and Strikes*, p. 78; Howe and Waite, pp. 116, 118; Howe, pp. 241–2, 356.

328 *Trades' Societies and Strikes,* pp. 79–80; Musson, *Typographical Association,* pp. 79–80.

329 *Operative,* 23, 30 Dec. 1838; *The Guide to Trade: The Printer* (1838), pp. 35–7; Howe, pp. 60, 227–32.

330 Alford, p. 97.

331 See Howe and Waite, chap. 3 *et seq.*; and Howe, chaps. 4, 12, for the problem as it affected London; and Child, chap. 6, for a general discussion of unemployment (and also pp. 122–3, 132–3). Webb, *Industrial Democracy,* pp. 464–8, is typically illuminating on the matter.

332 1841 Census, p. 50; 1851 Census, p. 11.

333 Mayhew, *LL&LP,* II, p. 299; C. M. Smith, esp. pp. 172, 244, 312–13; Musson, *Typographical Association,* pp. 23–5; *Operative,* 23 Dec. 1838; *NS,* 9 Nov. 1839, 30 Oct. 1841, 14 Oct. 1843, 17 Oct. 1846; Howe and Waite, pp. 101–2, 104–5.

334 Ellic Howe, 'Preface', to C. M. Smith. Smith's autobiography, chaps. 8–13, vividly recounts the uncertainty of employment and the indignities to which even the most skilled compositor was subject in the 1830s (but Simon Nowell-Smith's exposure of the author as 'a romancer' must be borne in mind: 'Charles Manby Smith: His Family & Friends, His Fantasies & Fabrications', *Journal of the Printing Historical Society,* no. 7 (1971).

335 Child, p. 76; Howe, *London Compositor,* pp. 226–7.

336 *NS,* 29 March, 12 July 1845; Musson, *Typographical Association,* pp. 77–8.

337 *Operative,* 4 Nov. 1838, 24 Feb. 1839; Howe and Waite, p. 104; *NS,* 11, 18, 25 March 1848. See Musson, *Typographical Association,* pp. 24–6 and chap. 5, for a discussion of the printers' predominant political and economic moderation and of their self-consciousness as 'the aristocracy of the working classes' – and for the latter cf. Prothero, 'Movements', p. 291; and *idem,* 'London Chartism and the Trades', p. 209, who however exaggerates their isolationism.

338 *Guide to Trade: Printer,* pp. 40–42, 46–53, 67–8; Whittock *et al.,* pp. 388, 391–2; Howe, *London Compositor,* p. 308; *NS,* 7 May, 4 June 1842; Prothero, 'Movements', pp. 173, 415; Oliver, 'Organizations', p. 271; Clement J. Bundock, *The Story of the National Union of Printing Bookbinding and Paper Workers* (Oxford, 1959), pp. 258–9. There were, however, still 500 pressmen, finding 'fairly regular employment', at the time of the Booth Survey (Booth, *Industry Series,* II, p. 193).

339 *Guide to Trade: Printer,* pp. 16, 73–80; *NS,* 2, 30 Sept. 1843. The trade does not seem actually to have been as injurious as it was judged in the 1840s (Booth, *Industry Series,* I, pp. 348–52).

340 Musson, *Trade Union and Social History,* chap. 6; Child, p. 49; Thompson, *Making,* pp. 238–9, 253; Add. MS. 37,773, ff. 59–60; National Association of United Trades, *Report of Central Committee.*

341 *NS,* 19 Aug., 2, 30 Sept., 7, 28 Oct., 18 Nov., 30 Dec. 1843; 13 Jan., 24 Feb. 1844. The *Northern Star* does not record the outcome of the struggle. The type-founders appear to have experienced further difficulties in 1850 (Kiddier, p. 45).

342 *NS,* 12 June, 7 Aug., 16 Oct. 1847.

343 *Ibid.,* 21 May 1842.

344 'A Day at a Bookbinder's', *Penny Magazine,* Sept. Supp., 1842, provides an account of their imposing purpose-built bindery in Shoemaker Row.

345 Whereas the gross outputs (in London) of jobbing printing increased from £120,000 in 1831 to £170,000 in 1851 and of the government

branch from £160,000 to £230,000, that of book and periodical printing shot up from £120,000 to £400,000 (Alford, p. 97). See also Richard D. Altick, *The English Common Reader: A Social History of the Mass Reading Public 1800–1900* (Chicago, 1957), pp. 277–8.

346 *Operative*, 11 Nov. 1838–30 June 1839; *Charter*, 27 Jan.–8 Sept. 1839; *NS*, 5 Oct. 1839; T. J. Dunning, 'Some Account of the London Consolidated Society of Bookbinders', in *Trades' Societies and Strikes*, pp. 99–100; Howe and Child, chaps. 13, 14, and pp. 136–9.

347 Dunning, in *Trades' Societies and Strikes*, pp. 93–7; Howe and Child, pp. 9–11 *et seq.*, 139–45, 165; Bundock, pp. 14–16.

348 Dunning, in *Trades' Societies and Strikes*, pp. 95n., 102n. The different processes in bookbinding are fully described in 'Day at Bookbinder's', *Penny Magazine*, Sept. Supp., 1842. For a complaint by an old bookbinder as to the subdivision of labour already existing in the 1840s, see Shearring, p. 284.

349 Dunning, in *Trades' Societies and Strikes*, pp. 102–4; Howe and Child, pp. 57, 82, and chaps. 11, 17; Bundock, pp. 17–18.

350 Howe and Child, pp. 111–12, 119–20; Oliver, 'Organizations', p. 203; Prothero, 'Movements', p. 414; *Operative*, 24 Feb. 1839; Add. MS. 27,820, f. 381; *Charter*, 31 March 1839; *NS*, 8 Feb., 29 March, 2 Aug. 1845, 6 June 1846; Webb, *History*, p. 170.

351 Dodd, *Days*, p. 6.

352 Webb TU MSS., XX, ff. 2, 15, and XXIV, f. 20; Whittock *et al.*, pp. 275–8; Booth, *Industry Series*, II, pp. 14–15; Prothero, *Artisans and Politics*, p. 307; *Charter*, 8 Dec. 1839; PC set 53, f. 92; Thompson, *Making*, p. 238; *NS*, 2 Aug. 1845; Oliver, 'Organizations', pp. 209, 211; Prothero, 'Movements', p. 414.

353 Whittock *et al.*, pp. 278–83, 301–5; Booth, *Industry Series*, II, pp. 8–9; *Operative*, 4 Nov. 1838; *Charter*, 15 March 1840. From a speech by Fussell, a jeweller out of work for at least four months in 1842, it would seem wages then averaged 30s. per week, but he himself in 1848, although on arrest again unemployed, could command earnings of 50s. (*Evening Star*, 5 Oct. 1842; *The Times*, 20 June 1848).

354 Whittock *et al.*, pp. 278–83; Booth, *Industry Series*, II, pp. 11–12; *Charter*, 31 March 1839.

355 Dodd, *British Manufactures: Series IV*, p. 170; *idem, Days*, pp. 7–8; Knight, III, p. 132. The police were of the opinion that 'about 7000 Watchmakers' lived in the neighbourhood of Clerkenwell Green (letter from Rowan to Phillips, 9 Dec. 1839, MEPO 1/34 and HO 61/24). See too HO 61/23, letter from George Dugard, 16 Aug. 1839.

356 The Superintendent of G Division clearly dissociated 'Mechanics, chiefly in the watch trade' from the Chartists (HO 61/23, report, 23 Aug. 1839).

357 George, *London Life*, pp. 175–8; Knight, III, pp. 141–4; Peter Hall, 'Industrial London: A General View', in Coppock and Prince, pp. 232–3; Whittock *et al.*, pp. 469–70; Clapham I, p. 166; Booth, *Industry Series*, II, pp. 26–9, 31. On the other hand, the likelihood of clockmaking being conducted in a large unit seems to have been much greater ('Church-Clock Factory and Bell-Foundry', *Penny Magazine*, March Supp., 1842; William J. Pinks, *The History of Clerkenwell* (2nd edn, 1881), pp. 314–17. Cf. Booth, *Industry Series*, II, pp. 29–30). For a (breathless) review of the Clerkenwell trades, see J. E. Martin, pp. 13–15.

358 Cf. map in Banbury, p. 158.

359 Mayhew, *UM*, pp. 399–406; 'A Day at a Ship-Yard' and 'A Second Day at a Ship-Yard', *Penny Magazine*, May and June Supps., 1841; Dodd, *Days*, pp. 12–13; S. Pollard, 'The Decline of Shipbuilding on the Thames', *Econ HR*, 2nd Ser., III (1950–51); Hartridge, pp. 7, 19; Prothero, *Artisans and Politics*, esp. pp. 14–16, 46–50, 62–4, 163–71, 217, 304–6.

360 See above, p. 193.

361 Lovett, *L&S*, I, pp. 10–11, 20–21, 23 *et seq.*; Dodd, *British Manufactures: Series VI*, pp. 210–12; Prothero, *Artisans and Politics*, p. 215; Oliver, 'Organizations', p. 211; W. H. Fraser, 'Trade Unionism', in Ward, *Popular Movements*, p. 110; *Operative*, 17 Feb. 1839; Thompson, *Making*, pp. 426–7; National Association of United Trades, *Report of Central Committee*; 'A Day at a Rope and Sail-Cloth Factory, *Penny Magazine*, Nov. Supp., 1842.

362 Bob Gilding, *The Journeymen Coopers of East London* (Oxford, 1971), esp. pp. iii, 75, 79–82; George Pattison, 'The Coopers' Strike at the West India Dock, 1821', *Mariner's Mirror*, LV, no. 2 (1969); Mayhew, *UM*, Letter LXIX; *The Guide to Trade: The Cooper* (1842), pp. 11, 13–14, 52, 60–81; Booth, *Industry Series*, I, pp. 255–6.

363 Mayhew, *UM*, Letter LIX; Postgate, *Builders' History*, pp. 126–8; Prothero, *Artisans and Politics*, pp. 159–60, 215, 302; *idem*, 'Movements', p. 72n.; Oliver, 'Organisations', pp. 120, 123, 211; *NS*, 29 March 1845, 13 Nov. 1847.

364 *NS*, 15 Sept. 1849; *Charter*, 3 Nov. 1839; *Evening Star*, 5 Dec. 1842.

365 *The Guide to Trade: The Baker; Including Bread and Fancy Baking: With Numerous Receipts* (1841), pp. 41–2; Hand-Loom Weavers, *Reports*, p. 282; Whittock *et al.*, pp. 16–18; *Charter*, 3 Nov. 1839; Mayhew, *LL&LP*, I, p. 179.

366 Prothero, 'Movements', p. 173; *Evening Star*, 5, 13, 15 Dec. 1842; *NS*, 17 Dec. 1842.

367 And continued to enjoy, together with the absence of nightwork, in 1860 (*Trades' Societies and Strikes*, p. 295).

368 *NS*, 5, 12, 26 Dec. 1846; 30 Jan., 13, 20 March, 24 April, 1, 29 May, 5 June, 3 July, 30 Oct., 20 Nov. 1847; 13 May, 3 June 1848; 2 June 1849; *The Times*, 18 March 1848; *Labour League*, 12 Aug., 30 Dec. 1848. See too PC set 58, vol. I, f. 288.

369 Booth, *Industry Series*, III, pp. 144–57. That the baker's routine in 1862 was identical to that of the Chartist decade is familiar from Karl Marx's printing in *Capital* (Everyman edn, 2 vols., 1957), I, pp. 251–4, of a lengthy extract from Tremenheere's report, which also concluded the age of forty-two was seldom reached.

370 For drapers' shops and the competitive conduct of their business see Knight, V, pp. 391–5, 398–400, and Whittock *et al.*, pp. 310–13.

371 *Operative*, 11, 25 Nov., 2 Dec. 1838; PC set 56, vol. II, f. 314; *Charter*, 27 Oct. 1839; *NS*, 2 Nov. 1839, 5 Dec. 1846, 9 Oct. 1847; *Evening Star*, 12 Oct., 21 Nov. 1842; Wilfred B. Whitaker, *Victorian and Edwardian Shopworkers: The Struggle to Obtain Better Conditions and a Half-Holiday* (Newton Abbot, 1973), chap. 2; Christopher Kent, 'The Whittington Club: A Bohemian Experiment in Middle Class Social Reform', *Victorian Studies*, XVIII (1974–5), pp. 38–9.

372 *Operative*, 11 Nov., 9 Dec. 1838, 6 Jan., 3 Feb. 1839; PC set 56, vol. II, f. 314; Whitaker, p. 47. The derisory assessment of the skills required by

chemists and druggists in *The Guide to Trade: The Chemist and Druggist* (1838), p. 15, conflicts with the *Operative*'s view of them as 'generally, an educated class', although earning a mere £15 to £30 per annum and being confined to their premises for eighteen hours daily throughout the week (*Operative*, 9 Dec. 1838).

373 *London Democrat*, 4 May 1839 (see also *Operative*, 21 April 1839). Bank clerks, the 'aristocracy' of clerical labour, often earned as little as £50 to £70 per annum, but a strike of fleeting duration at a City bank in 1852 was unprecedented (F. D. Klingender, *The Condition of Clerical Labour in Britain* (1935), pp. 3–7. See also Sheppard, *London*, pp. 70–1).

374 M. Dorothy George, 'The London Coal-Heavers: Attempts to Regulate Waterside Labour in the Eighteenth and Nineteenth Centuries', *Economic Journal*, Economic History Series No. 2 (May 1927), pp. 229–42; George W. Hilton, *The Truck System: including a History of the British Truck Acts, 1465–1960* (Cambridge, 1960), pp. 79–85; Raymond Smith, *Sea-Coal for London: History of the Coal Factors in the London Market* (1961), pp. 166–7; Mayhew, *LL&LP*, III, pp. 235–43, 248; *Operative*, 17 Feb. 1839; PC set 53, Section B, f. 13.

375 G. W. Hilton, p. 86; Oliver, 'Organizations', pp. 206–7, 211–12; Prothero, 'Movements', pp. 314, 414; Mayhew, *LL&LP*, III, p. 240.

376 *Coal Whippers' Ready Reckoner, For One or Nine Men, at 1¼ per Ton* [1820?].

377 *Evening Star*, 16, 24 Aug., 6, 28 Oct. 1842; *The Times*, 25 Aug., 31 Oct. 1842; *NS*, 3 Sept., 8 Oct. 1842; Mayhew, *LL&LP*, III, pp. 240, 252. It is noteworthy that in 1844 one of their leaders guaranteed the whippers' (financial) support for the miners (*NS*, 29 June 1844).

378 George, 'London Coal-Heavers', pp. 242–8; G. W. Hilton, p. 86; *Knight's Cyclopædia*, pp. 495–6; R. Smith, pp. 309–10 *et seq.*; Mayhew, *LL&LP*, III, pp. 235–43, 257.

379 *Rules & Regulations of the Ballast-Heavers' Brotherhood of the Port of London* (1855), pp. 3–11. See Mayhew, *LL&LP*, pp. 272–92, for both groups of labourers.

380 James Bird, *The Geography of the Port of London* (1957), chaps. 2, 4, 5; Knight, III, pp. 65–6. In addition, both the text and illustrations of John Pudney, *London's Docks* (1975), are surprisingly informative.

381 Walter M. Stern, *The Porters of London* (1960), esp. Part 2, chaps. 1 and 4, and Part 3, chap. 1; Mayhew, *LL&LP*, III, pp. 364–7.

382 Hand-Loom Weavers, *Reports*, p. 283; Mayhew, *LL&LP*, III, p. 301 (but cf. pp. 308, 312).

383 *Charter*, 1 Sept. 1839.

384 For the strike see HO 45/5128 and George Pattison, 'Nineteenth-Century Dock Labour in the Port of London', *Mariner's Mirror*, LII, no. 3 (1966), pp. 268–9; also 'Striking Times', in 'Poetical Broadsides', II, f. 309, of which an expurgated version appears in Ashton, pp. 17–20. The *locus classicus* for details of dock labour at this period is Mayhew, *LL&LP*, III, pp. 292–312. However, Pattison persuasively suggests that the degree of casuality should not be exaggerated – there were 'permanent', 'preferable' and 'extra' labourers and even the latter were quite distinct from the mere casuals – and that it was during the third quarter of the nineteenth century that the extra labourers lost their identity as casualization intensified ('Nineteenth-Century Dock Labour', pp. 263–70. See also George Pattison, 'The East India Dock Company, 1803–1838', *ELP*,

VII, no. 1 (July 1964), pp. 34–9). This view receives support from Jones, *Outcast London*, pp. 111–25.

385 Hand-Loom Weavers, *Reports*, p. 284, gives a few details concerning two groups of the better-paid unskilled.

386 See, in particular, Dyos, pp. 63–4, and Knight, III, pp. 22–3, and V, p. 141; also Hobsbawm and Rudé, p. 174.

387 Oliver, 'Organizations', pp. 203, 211; Prothero, 'Movements', pp. 162, 414.

388 Hand-Loom Weavers, *Reports*, p. 284; Mayhew, *LL&LP*, III, p. 242; HO 45/5128.

Conclusion

1 An example is Asa Briggs, *The Age of Improvement, 1783–1867* (1979 edn), pp. 311–12.

2 *Labour League*, 2 Dec. 1848.

3 *Justice*, 24 Oct. 1885; see also 3 July 1886. Hyndman, in these two interesting leaders, was apparently referring to 1838–9, although the early Social Democrats clearly pondered over 10 April 1848 (*ibid.*, 7 March 1885 (H. W. Lee), 24 April 1886 (H. H. Champion)).

4 Gammage, pp. 46–7. See also PC set 56, vol. II, f. 117; *NS*, 20 May 1848.

5 Quoted in Stevenson, *Popular Disturbances*, p. 163.

6 *Chartist*, 30 June 1839. See also *NS*, 8 Jan. 1848.

7 For these episodes: Stevenson, *Popular Disturbances*, pp. 190–6, 199–204; Rizzi, pp. 20–5, 30–2; Thompson, *Making*, pp. 631–5; Prothero, *Artisans and Politics*, chap. 7; John Stevenson, 'The Queen Caroline Affair', in Stevenson, *London*.

8 Reith, *New Study*, pp. 121–4; Radzinowicz, IV, pp. 155–7; Miller, pp. 7–8. In contrast, John Stevenson, 'Social Control and the Prevention of Riots in England, 1789–1829', in Donajgrodzki, considers that, from the end of the eighteenth century, the policing of London was significantly improved.

9 See Peter N. Stearns, *The Revolutions of 1848* (1974), pp. 62–3.

10 Sir Lewis Namier, *1848: The Revolution of the Intellectuals* (1946), pp. 5n–6n.

11 Hobsbawm, *Revolutionaries*, pp. 227–8.

12 Quoted by Silver, p. 8.

13 Prothero, 'Chartism in London', p. 88; Harrison, 'Sunday Trading Riots', p. 238.

14 Donald Read, *The English Provinces, c. 1760–1960: A Study in Influence* (1964), p. 116.

15 His exposition is printed in full by Wallas, pp. 393–4.

16 *NS*, 21 Dec. 1850, cited by Read, pp. 116–17. See also Read, pp. 51–2, and Thompson, *Making*, pp. 20–21, 611–12.

17 *NS*, 27 Jan., 10 Aug. 1844, 30 Jan. 1847.

18 *London Democrat*, 18 May 1839.

19 *Operative*, 31 March 1839. See too HO 44/52, report of 21 Feb. 1839.

20 Mayhew, *LL&LP*, I, p. 20; II, pp. 4–5, 177, 294. In this respect Mayhew's comments about the labourers of East London, unduly coloured by the exceptional case of the coal-whippers, are misleading (*ibid.*, III, p. 233).

21 *Ibid.*, III, p. 233.

22 For implicit recognition of this: PC set 56, vol. I, f. 157.
23 Prothero, 'Chartism in London', pp. 84, 103–5; *idem,* 'London Chartism and the Trades', pp. 209–12.
24 Prothero, 'London Chartism and the Trades', pp. 216–17.
25 E.g., see *NS,* 17 April 1847.

Appendix I

1 Tucker himself observes that, of course, his index of real wages applies to the 'regularly employed London artisan', unemployment not being allowed for (p. 77).
2 Cairncross and Weber, in their Appendix, also give the number of bricks per year charged with excise duty. H. A. Shannon's index for London, 1830–48, is biennial only ('Bricks – A Trade Index, 1785–1849', reprinted in Carus-Wilson, p. 195). See also Sheppard, Belcher and Cottrell.

Bibliography

═══════════

PRIMARY SOURCES

Manuscripts

Public Record Office

Home Office Papers
HO 10   Convicts, New South Wales and Tasmania
  /40 (1849: Tasmania, Ledger Returns)
  /55 (1850–1859: New South Wales – Pardons)
  /63 (1854–1855: Tasmania – Pardons)
HO 11   Convict Transportation Registers
  /16 (1849–1850: Convicts Transported)
HO 12   Criminal Papers: Old Series
  /81 (Papers on political prisoners of 1848)
HO 16   Criminal: Old Bailey Sessions, Returns of convicted prisoners
  /7 (1839–1842)
  /9 (1847–1849)
HO 26   Criminal: Criminal Registers: Series I, Newgate, etc.
  /48 (1842)
  /54 (1848)
HO 27   Criminal: Criminal Registers: Series II, All counties
  /86 (1848 S–Y)
HO 40   Disturbances: Correspondence
  /36 (1838: Bedford – Kent)
  /44 (1839: Lancaster (Bolton), Leicester, Middlesex)
  /52 (1839: Scottish, Miscellaneous)
  /57 (1840: Yorkshire; Scottish and Welsh; Miscellaneous)
  /59 (1841–1855: Miscellaneous)
HO 41   Disturbances: Entry Books
  /15 (1839 Aug. 19–1840 July 25: Provinces)
  /16 (1840 July 25–1842 Aug. 16: Provinces)
  /19 (1848–1852: Provinces)
  /26 (1820–1848: London)
HO 44   George IV and later: Correspondence
  /32 (1839: Miscellaneous A–L)
  /35 (1840: Miscellaneous A–H)
  /36 (1840: Miscellaneous L–R)
  /37 (1840: Miscellaneous S–Z)
  /52 (1838–1850: Miscellaneous)
HO 45   Domestic: Registered Papers ('Old Series')
  /52 (Disturbances: 1841: Warwickshire)
  /102 (Disturbances: 1839 July–1841 Sept.: London)

/248 (Disturbances: 1842: Gloucestershire)
/252 (Disturbances: 1842: London)
/267 (Disturbances: 1842: Miscellaneous and Anonymous)
/297 (Secret Union of Masons)
/1821 (As to Wages of Needlewomen in 1847)
/1984 (Petition from Silkweavers of Spitalfields)
/2410 (Chartists 1848), Parts 1, 3, 4, 5
/2412 (Trafalgar Square: As to meetings in)
/5128 (Disturbances during 1853)
HO 48   Law Officers: Reports and Correspondence
/40 (1848: Cases and Reports)
HO 60   Police Courts: Entry Books
/5 (1846–1854)
HO 61   Metropolitan Police: Correspondence
/21 (1838 July–Dec.)
/22 (1839 Jan.–June)
/23 (1839 July–Sept.)
/24 (1839 Oct.–Dec.)
/25 (1840 Jan.–March)
HO 65   Police Entry Books
/13 (1839–1841: Metropolitan Police)
/16 (1847–1849: Metropolitan Police)
HO 79   Entry Books: Private and Secret
/9 (1830–1864: Ireland)

Records of the Metropolitan Police Offices
MEPO 1   Office of the Commissioner: Letter Books
/32 (1839 Mar. 16–July 5: General)
/33 (1839 July 5–Oct. 3: General)
/34 (1839 Oct. 3–Dec. 31: General)
/43 (1842 July 4–Oct. 20: General)
/45 (1836 May 25–1850 July 11: Commissioners: Confidential and Private: II)
/46 (1848 May 3–1861 Feb. 13: Commissioners: Confidential and Private: III)
MEPO 2   Office of the Commissioner: Correspondence
/5 (1836–1874: Pay)
/25 (1827–1858: Horses: Bow Street Patrol and Mounted Branch)
/26 (1830–1872: Strength and Establishment)
/32 (1835(?): Police Organization: Notes by Sir Richard Mayne)
/43 (1831–1858: Aliens Arriving in the United Kingdom)
/59 (1830–1867: Miscellaneous correspondence, Public notices, etc.)
/62 (1848 Apr.–1852 Feb.: Letters from John Paterson, informer)
/63 (1848 Mar.–April: Kennington Common)
/64 (1848 Mar.–April: Trafalgar Square)
/65 (1848 Mar.–June: Swearing in of Special Constables, protection of Public Buildings, etc.)
/66 (1848 Mar.–August: Police Conduct: complaints against)
/67 (1848 June: Police Conduct: appreciation of)
MEPO 3   Office of the Commissioner: Correspondence and Papers: Special Series
/1 (1830–1863: Miscellaneous Criminal Activities)

MEPO 4   Office of the Commissioner: Miscellaneous Books
  /1 (1829 Sept. 27–1857 Mar. 15: Weekly State of the Metropolitan Police)
MEPO 5   Office of the Receiver: Correspondence and Papers
  /1/1 (Establishment of the Metropolitan Police Force)
  /1/2 (Pay of Force)
  /2/6 (Hospital Treatment for Police: Maintenance, etc.)
  /3/10 (Premises for Metropolitan Police Service)
  /9/41 (Horse Patrol)
MEPO 7   Office of the Commissioner: Police Orders
  /4 (Nov. 1835–July 1837)
  /5 (July 1837–Jan. 1839)
  /6 (Jan. 1839–Sept. 1840)
  /7 (Oct. 1840–Jan. 1842)
  /8 (Feb. 1842–June 1843)
  /9 June 1843–Oct. 1844)
  [/10 (Oct. 1844–Feb. 1845)] *wanting*
  /11 (Feb. 1845–Sept. 1846)
  /12 (Sept. 1846–June 1848)
  [/13 (1847–June 1848)] *wanting*
  /14 (June 1848–Apr. 1850)
MEPO 8   Office of the Commissioner: Confidential Books and Instructions
  [/1 (1829 Instructions to the force)] *wanting*
  /2 (1836 Instructions, orders, etc.)

Treasury Solicitor's Records
TS 11   Papers
  /135/360 (The Queen v. Looney)
  /136/368 (The Queen v. Bryson)
  /136/369 (The Queen v. Sharpe)
  /136/371 (The Queen v. Vernon)
  /136/372 (Miscellaneous)
  /136/373 (The Queen v. Crowe)
  /138/375 (The Queen v. Williams)
  /138/376 (The Queen v. Jones)
  /138/377 (The Queen v. Shaw)
  /138/378 (The Queen v. Taylor and twelve others)
  /138/379 (Reports of Chartist Meetings)
  /138/380 (Miscellaneous)
  /139/381 (The Queen v. Mullins)
  /140/386 (The Queen v. Williams and Vernon)
  /140/387 (The Queen v. Cuffay and others)
  /141/388 (Chartist Prosecutions: Miscellaneous)
  /142/389 (Chartist Prosecutions: Miscellaneous)
  /142/390 (The Queen v. Brown, Fussell and Harney)
  /1121/5785 (The Queen v. Shell)

War Office Records
WO 30   Miscellanea–Various
  /81 (1776–1870: Miscellaneous Papers relating to Defence)
  /111 (Correspondence and Papers: *including* 'The Chartist Riots')

Russell Papers
PRO 30/22
/7B (1848 Mar.–Apr.)
/7C (1848 May–Aug.)

Royal Archives, Windsor Castle

C56 (Chartists and the Working Classes. 1848)
Letters in volumes A14, B5, B10, C8, C16, J67, J68
Daguerreotypes of the Kennington Common meeting in the Photograph
    Collection

British Library

Place Papers
Add. MS. 27,791   (Narrative of political events in England, from 1830 to
    1835. III. 8 Oct. 1831–31 Mar. 1832)
Add. MS. 27,810   (Account, letters, and printed papers of the Metropolitan
    Parliamentary Reform Association, 1842)
Add. MSS. 27,819–27,822   (Collections relating to workingmen's associa-
    tions, 4 vols.)
Add. MSS. 27,825–27,830   (Collections relating to manners and morals, 6
    vols.)
Add. MS. 27,834   (Essays for the People, 1834)
Add. MS. 27,835   (Papers, printed and manuscript, relating to working-
    men's political associations, etc., 1799–1842)

Correspondence and papers of the General Convention of the Industrious
    Classes, 1839
Add. MS. 34,245A, B

The Minutes of the Working Men's Association, established June 26th 1836
Add. MS. 37,773   (9 June 1836–30 April 1839)

The Minutes of the National Association, founded 12th Oct. 1841
Add. MS 37,774   (12 Oct. 1841–23 July 1844)

British Library of Political and Economic Science

Coll. E: Webb Trade Union Collection
Section A (Chiefly Manuscript Material)
    1–IX General history
    X–XIII Building trades
    XIV Clothing trades
    XV–XXI Engineering and metal trades
    XXII Furnishing trades
    XXIV–XXV Leather trades
    XXXIV–XL Textile trades

University Library, Cambridge

Sir James Graham's Papers (c. 1820–c. 1860): on microfilm
Bundle 52A (August 1842)

Bundle 52B (August 1842)
Bundle 53A (September 1842)

Privately held

MS. in possession of M. Spokes, 55 Bloxham Road, Banbury
Rev. W. T. Henderson, 'Recollections of his Life', 1910

Collections of newspaper cuttings, etc.

British Library

Place Collection
Set 51.   Working Men. Combinations. – Machine Breaking. – National Association for Wages, etc. 1831–1839 (ff. 269–71)
Set 53.   Working Men. Trade Clubs. – Union Strikes. – Conferences, etc. 1836–1845
Set 56.   Working Men. Reform.
  vol. I (1836–June 1838)
  vol. II (July–Dec. 1838)
Set 58.   Trades. Strikes.
  I (1846–1850)
Set 66.   Charter and Chartists. January 1839–March 1840

'Bronterre's Letters'
(volume of newspaper cuttings, including certain material additional to the
  Letters (published in 1836 in the *Twopenny Dispatch*))
[BL press mark 8139. eee. 39.]

'Poetical Broadsides, Etc.'
(2 volumes of broadsides)
[BL press marks 11621. k. 4–5.]

Birmingham Reference Library

The Lovett Collection
(2 vols. of newspaper cuttings, letters, pamphlets, leaflets, etc.)

Library of the Communist Party of Great Britain

James Klugmann Collection
(Pictorial material on the history of the labour movement)

Newspapers and periodicals

Complete runs

Cause of the People, 20 May–15 July 1848
Charter, 27 January 1839–15 March 1840
Chartist, 2 February–7 July 1839
Cordwainers' Companion, April–21 September 1844
English Chartist Circular, nos. 1–153 [? January 1841–?January 1844]

Evening Star, 25 July 1842–28 February 1843
Labour League, 5 August 1848–26 May 1849
The Last, 25 October 1844–?31 January 1845
London Democrat, 13 April–8 June 1839
Monthly Report of the National Association of United Trades for the Protection of Industry, 1 December 1847–1 March 1848
National United Trades' Association Report, 1 April–June 1848
Operative, 4 November 1838–30 June 1839
Reynolds's Political Instructor, 11 November 1849–11 May 1850
Southern Star, 19 January–12 July 1840
Spirit of the Age, 1 July 1848–3 March 1849
Spitalfields Weavers' Journal, August–December 1837

Consulted for the given dates

Annual Register, 1848
Daily News, 11 April 1848
Express, 10, 11 April 1848
Globe, 10, 11 April 1848
Illustrated London News, 1842, 1848
Justice, 1884–6
Lady's Newspaper, 1848
Lloyd's Weekly London Newspaper, 16 April 1848
London Telegraph, 10 April 1848
Morning Advertiser, 11 April, 13 June 1848
Morning Chronicle, 11 April 1848; October 1849–December 1850
Morning Herald, 11 April 1848
Morning Post, 11 April 1848
National Co-operative Leader, 16 November 1860–17 May 1861
Nonconformist, 1848
Northern Star, 6 January 1838–5 January 1850
Penny Magazine, 1841–2
Punch, 1842–9
St Crispin, 2 January 1869–31 December 1870
Shipping and Mercantile Gazette, 10, 11 April, 12 June 1848
Standard, 10, 11 April 1848
Sun, 10, 11 April, 12 June 1848
The Times, 1842; January–June 1848
Weekly Dispatch, 16 April 1848

Parliamentary Papers

Census, 1841. *Enumeration Abstract, Part I, England and Wales*, 1843, XXII [496]
Census, 1841. *Occupation Abstract, Part I, England and Wales*, 1844, XXVII [587]
Census, 1851. *Population Tables, II, Ages, Civil Condition, Occupations, and Birth-Place of the People*, 1852–3, LXXXVIII Part 1, I [1691–I]
Constabulary Force. *First Report of the Commissioners Appointed to Inquire as to the Best Means of Establishing an Efficient Constabulary Force in the Counties of England and Wales*, 1839, XIX [169]

Hand-Loom Weavers. *Reports from Assistant Hand-Loom Weavers' Commissioners,* Part II, 1840, XXIII (43-I)
Hand-Loom Weavers. *Copy of Report by Mr. Hickson, on the Condition of the Hand-Loom Weavers,* 1840, XXIV (639)
Police. *Second Report from the Select Committee on Police,* 1852–3, XXXVI [715]

Other official publications

Central Criminal Court, *Sessions Papers. Minutes of Evidence, Taken in Shorthand* . . .
   XVI: 7th Session to 12th Session, 1841–2
   XXVII: 1st Session to 6th Session, 1847–8
   XXVIII: 7th Session to 12th Session, 1847–8
A Collection of the Public General Statutes, 1829, 1839
Hansard's Parliamentary Debates, Third Series, LXXXIII, 10 February 1846

Contemporary books and pamphlets, autobiographies, correspondence, etc.

Adams, W. E., *Memoirs of a Social Atom* (2 vols., 1903).
Adventures of a Policeman. Broadside (n.d.). BL press mark C. 116. i.1. (259.).
Aikin, A., 'On Tanning and Leather-Dressing', *Transactions of the Society of Arts,* L (1836), part 1.
Arnold, Matthew. *The Letters of Matthew Arnold to Arthur Hugh Clough,* ed. Howard Foster Lowry (Oxford, 1968).
Arnold, Matthew. *Letters of Matthew Arnold, 1848–1888,* ed. George W. E. Russell (2 vols., 1895).
Ashton, John, *Modern Street Ballads* (1888).
Benson, Arthur Christopher, and Esher, Viscount (eds.), *The Letters of Queen Victoria: A Selection from Her Majesty's Correspondence Between the Years 1837 and 1861* (3 vols., 1908).
Berlioz, Hector. *The Memoirs of Hector Berlioz, Member of the French Institute: including his Travels in Italy, Germany, Russia and England, 1803–1865,* trans. and ed. David Cairns (1969).
Black, Frank Gees, and Black, Renee Métivier (eds.), *The Harney Papers* (Assen, 1969).
Brooke, James Williamson, *The Democrats of Marylebone* (1839).
Brown, John, *Sixty Years' Gleanings from Life's Harvest. A Genuine Autobiography* (Cambridge, 1858).
Burgoyne. *The Military Opinions of General Sir John Fox Burgoyne, Bart.; G.C.B.,* ed. George Wrottesley (1859).
Burn, James (The 'Beggar Boy'), *An Autobiography: Relating the Numerous Trials, Struggles, and Vicissitudes of a Strangely Chequered Life. With Glimpses of English Social, Commercial, and Political History, During Eighty Years, 1802–1882* (1882).
[Burn, J. D.], *A Glimpse at the Social Condition of the Working Classes During the Early Part of the Present Century. Trade Strikes and Their Consequences to the People Who May be Immediately Connected With Them. With Reflections Upon Trades' Unions and Their Management* [1868].
[Carter, Thomas], *The Guide to Trade: The Tailor* (1845).
[Carter, Thomas], *Memoirs of a Working Man* (1845).
Cayley, Edward Stillingfleet, *The European Revolutions of 1848* (2 vols., 1856).

Coal Whippers' Ready Reckoner, For One or Nine Men, at 1¼ per Ton [1820?]. BL press mark 1881.a.3.(79.).

Cooper, Thomas. *The Life of Thomas Cooper: Written by Himself* (2nd edn, 1872).

Cooper, Thomas, *The Purgatory of Suicides: A Prison-Rhyme. In Ten Books* (1845; 3rd edn, 1853).

Cornish, James. 'No. LXIII of Survivors' Tales of Great Events: London Under Arms. From the Narrative of James Cornish. As Told to Walter Wood', *Royal Magazine*, XXIII, no. 138 (April 1910).

Crowe, Robert, 'The Reminiscences of a Chartist Tailor', *Outlook* (New York), 9 August 1902.

Crowe, Robert, *The Reminiscences of Robert Crowe, The Octogenerian Tailor*[sic] ([New York], n.d.).

Denvir, John, *The Life Story of an Old Rebel* (Dublin, 1910).

Devlin, James, *The Guide to Trade: The Shoemaker* [I] (1839).

Devlin, James, *The Guide to Trade: The Shoemaker, Part II: Being the Duties of the Shop* (1841).

Devyr, Thomas Ainge, *The Odd Book of the Nineteenth Century, Or, 'Chivalry' in Modern Days, A Personal Record of Reform – Chiefly Land Reform, For the Last Fifty Years* (Greenpoint, NY, 1882).

Dickens, Charles, *Sketches by Boz: Illustrative of Every-Day Life and Every-Day People* (1837).

Dodd, George, *British Manufactures: Metals* (1845).

Dodd, George, *British Manufactures: Series IV* (1845).

Dodd, George, *British Manufactures: Series VI* (1846).

Dodd, George, *Days at the Factories; Or, The Manufacturing Industry of Great Britain Described, and Illustrated by Numerous Engravings of Machines and Processes. Series 1. – London* (1843).

Dodd, George, *The Textile Manufactures of Great Britain* (1844).

Duffy, Sir Charles Gavan, *Four Years of Irish History, 1845–1849: A Sequel to 'Young Ireland'* (1883).

Duffy, Sir Charles Gavan, *Young Ireland: A Fragment of Irish History, 1840–1850* (1880).

Duncan, James Elmzlie, *Pe-ans for the People* [1848]. BL press mark 1871.e.1. (232.).

Evans, D. Morier, *The Commercial Crisis, 1847–1848; Being Facts and Figures Illustrative of the Events of That Important Period, Considered in Relation to the Three Epochs of the Railway Mania, The Food and Money Panic, and The French Revolution* (1849; Newton Abbot, 1969 edn).

FitzPatrick, W. J. (ed.), *Correspondence of Daniel O'Connell, The Liberator* (2 vols., 1888).

Frost, Thomas, *Forty Years' Recollections: Literary and Political* (1880).

Frost, Thomas, *Reminiscences of a Country Journalist* (1886).

Gammage, R. G., *History of the Chartist Movement, 1837–1854* (Newcastle-on-Tyne and London, 2nd edn, 1894).

Garratt, Rev. Samuel, 'The Irish in London: A Lecture Delivered on Monday, Dec. 6th, 1852, at the Music Hall, Store Street', in *Motives for Missions: A Series of Six Lectures Delivered Before the Church of England Young Men's Society in the Autumn of 1852* (1853).

Gavin, Hector, *Sanitary Ramblings: Being Sketches and Illustrations, of Bethnal Green: A Type of the Condition of the Metropolis and Other Large Towns* (1848).

Gay, John, *The Beggar's Opera* (1728; 1934 edn).

Godwin, George, *Town Swamps and Social Bridges* (1859; Leicester, 1972 edn).
Grant, James, *Sketches in London* (1838).
The Greville Memoirs, 1814–1860, ed. Lytton Strachey and Roger Fulford (8 vols., 1938).
The Guide to Trade: The Baker; Including Bread and Fancy Baking: With Numerous Receipts (1841).
The Guide to Trade: The Carver and Gilder (1840).
The Guide to Trade: The Chemist and Druggist (1838).
The Guide to Trade: The Cooper (1842).
The Guide to Trade: The Dress-Maker, and the Milliner (1840).
The Guide to Trade: The Joiner and Cabinet-Maker (1839).
The Guide to Trade: The Plumber, Painter, and Glazier (1838).
The Guide to Trade: The Printer (1838).
[Helps, Sir Arthur], *A Letter from One of the Special Constables in London on the Late Occasion of Their Being Called Out to Keep the Peace* (1848).
Hertslet, Sir Edward, *Recollections of the Old Foreign Office* (1901).
Hogg, John, *London as it is; Being a Series of Observations on the Health, Habits, and Amusements of the People* (1837).
Holyoake, George Jacob, *Bygones Worth Remembering* (2 vols., n.d.).
Holyoake, George Jacob (ed.), *The Life and Character of Henry Hetherington, From the Éloge, by T. Cooper, Author of the 'Purgatory of Suicides': The Oration at Kensal Green Cemetery, By G. J. Holyoake, Editor of the 'Reasoner': The Speech of James Watson: A Tribute, by W. J. Linton: with Hetherington's 'Last Will and Testament'* (1849).
Holyoake, George Jacob, *Sixty Years of an Agitator's Life* (1906 edn).
Hunt, W. Holman, *Pre-Raphaelitism and the Pre-Raphaelite Brotherhood* (2 vols., 1905).
Kingsley, Charles, *Alton Locke, Tailor and Poet: An Autobiography . . . With a Prefatory Memoir by Thomas Hughes, Esq., Q.C.* (1850; 1881 edn).
Knight, Charles (ed.), *London* (6 vols., 1841–4).
Knight's Cyclopædia of London (1851).
Leno, John Bedford, *The Aftermath: With Autobiography of the Author* (1892).
Leno, John Bedford, *The Art of Boot and Shoemaking: A Practical Handbook Including Measurement, Last-Fitting, Cutting-Out, Closing, and Making With a Description of the Most Approved Machinery Employed* (1885).
Lessner, Frederick, *Sixty Years in the Social-Democratic Movement: Before 1848 and After: Recollections of an Old Communist* (1907).
Linton, W. J., *James Watson: A Memoir of the Days of the Fight for a Free Press in England and of the Agitation for the People's Charter* (Manchester, 1880).
Linton, W. J., *Memories* (1895).
Lovett, William. *Life & Struggles of William Lovett in His Pursuit of Bread, Knowledge, and Freedom: With some Short Account Of the Different Associations He Belonged To and of the Opinions He Entertained* (1876; 2 vols., 1920 edn).
Lovett, William, and Collins, John, *Chartism: A New Organization of the People* (1840; Leicester, 1969 edn).
Lowery, Robert. *Robert Lowery: Radical and Chartist*, ed. Brian Harrison and Patricia Hollis (1979).
Mackay, Charles, *Forty Years' Recollections of Life, Literature, and Public Affairs: From 1830 to 1870* (2 vols., 1877).
Malmesbury, The Right Hon. the Earl of, *Memoirs of an Ex-Minister: An Autobiography* (2 vols., 1884).

Mayhew, Henry, *London Labour and the London Poor; A Cyclopædia of the Condition and Earnings of Those That* Will *Work, Those That* Cannot *Work, and Those That* Will Not *Work* (4 vols., 1861–2).

Mayhew, Henry. *The Unknown Mayhew: Selections from the 'Morning Chronicle', 1849–1850,* ed. E. P. Thompson and Eileen Yeo (1971).

National Association of United Trades. *Arbitration of Disputes Between Employers and Employed* (1854).

National Association of United Trades. *Report of the Central Committee of United Trades on the Proceedings Connected with the 'Combination of Workmen Bill' in the Parliamentary Session, 1853* (1853).

O'Brien, James Bronterre, *The Life and Character of Maximilian Robespierre,* I [1838].

O'Connell, Maurice R. (ed.), *The Correspondence of Daniel O'Connell* (Shannon and Dublin, 8 vols., 1972–).

Okey, Thomas, *A Basketful of Memories: An Autobiographical Sketch* (1930).

Palmerston, Lady. *The Letters of Lady Palmerston,* ed. Tresham Lever (1957).

Parker, Charles Stuart, *Life and Letters of Sir James Graham: Second Baronet of Netherby, P.C., G.C.B.: 1792–1861* (2 vols., 1907).

Parker, Charles Stuart (ed.), *Sir Robert Peel from his Private Papers* (3 vols., 1899).

Phillips, G. W., *The History and Antiquities of the Parish of Bermondsey* (1841).

Place, Francis. *The Autobiography of Francis Place (1771–1854),* ed. Mary Thale (Cambridge, 1972).

Richardson, Rev. J., *Recollections, Political, Literary, Dramatic, and Miscellaneous, of the Last Half-Century, Containing Anecdotes and Notes of Persons of Various Ranks Prominent in Their Vocations, With Whom the Writer Was Personally Acquainted* (2 vols., 1856).

Rowe, D. J. (ed.), *London Radicalism, 1830–1843: A Selection from the Papers of Francis Place* (1970).

Rules & Regulations of the Ballast-Heavers' Brotherhood of the Port of London. (Originated August 18th, 1854.) With Some Introductory Observations, By J. Dacres Devlin (1855).

Russell, John Earl, *Recollections and Suggestions, 1813–1873* (1875).

Sims, George R., *My Life: Sixty Years' Recollections of Bohemian London* (1917).

Smith, Charles Manby, *The Working Man's Way in the World* (1853; 1967 edn).

Stevens, William, *A Memoir of Thomas Martin Wheeler, Founder of the Friend-in-Need Life and Sick Assurance Society, Domestic, Political, and Industrial, with Extracts from His Letters, Speeches, and Writings* (1862).

Trades' Societies and Strikes: Report of the Committee on Trades' Societies, Appointed by the National Association for the Promotion of Social Science, Presented at the Fourth Annual Meeting of the Association, at Glasgow, September, 1860 (1860).

Vincent, David (ed.), *Testaments of Radicalism: Memoirs of Working Class Politicians 1790–1885* (1977).

Vizetelly, Henry, *Glances Back Through Seventy Years: Autobiographical and Other Reminiscences* (2 vols., 1893).

Weerth, Georg. *A Young Revolutionary in Nineteenth-Century England: Selected Writings of Georg Weerth,* ed. Ingrid and Peter Kuczynski (Berlin, 1971).

Wellington. *Wellington and His Friends: Letters of the First Duke of Wellington to the Rt. Hon. Charles and Mrs. Arbuthnot, the Earl and Countess of Wilton, Princess Lieven, and Miss Burdett-Coutts,* ed. Seventh Duke of Wellington (1965).

A Westminster Elector, *An Address to the Business-like Men of Westminster. On*

Their Present Candidates. With a Review of Mr. Cochrane's Work 'Juan de Vega' [1847].

Whiteing, Richard, *My Harvest* (1915).

Whittock, N., Bennett, J., Badcock, J., Newton, C., and Others, *The Complete Book of Trades, Or the Parents' Guide and Youths' Instructor; Forming a Popular Encyclopædia of Trades, Manufactures, and Commerce, As at Present Pursued in England; With a More Particular Regard to Its State In and Near the Metropolis . . .* (1837).

Maps

Collins' Illustrated Atlas of London (1854; Leicester, 1973 edn).
Smith's New Map of London and Environs (1848), Guildhall Library.
A Survey of the Parliamentary Borough of St. Marylebone, engraved by B. R. Davies (1834; 1962–3 edn).

SECONDARY SOURCES

Unpublished theses

Avery, Michael D., 'Industry in South-East London (Bermondsey and Southwark)' (London MA, 1963).

Bennett, J. A., 'A Study in London Radicalism: The Democratic Association, 1837–1841' (Sussex MA, 1968).

Dyos, H. J., 'The Suburban Development of Greater London South of the Thames, 1836–1914' (London PhD, 1952).

Epstein, James A., 'Feargus O'Connor and the English Working-Class Radical Movement, 1832–1841; A Study in National Chartist Leadership (Birmingham PhD, 1977).

Hartridge, R. J., 'The Development of Industries in London South of the Thames, 1750 to 1850' (London MSc (Econ.), 1955).

Keller, Lisa, 'Public Order in Victorian London: The Interaction Between the Metropolitan Police, the Government, the Urban Crowd, and the Law' (Cambridge PhD, 1977).

Mounfield, Peter Reginald, 'The Location of Footwear Manufacture in England and Wales' (Nottingham PhD, 1962).

O'Higgins, Rachel, 'Ireland and Chartism: A Study of the Influence of Irishmen and the Irish Question on the Chartist Movement' (Trinity College, Dublin PhD, 1959).

Oliver, W. H., 'Organizations and Ideas behind the Efforts to Achieve a General Union of the Working Classes in the Early 1830s' (Oxford DPhil, 1954).

Prothero, Iorwerth J., 'London Working-Class Movements, 1825–1848' (Cambridge PhD, 1967).

Rizzi, Robert A., 'The British Army as a Riot Control Force in Great Britain, 1811–1848' (Oxford BLitt, 1975).

Robertson, Norman, 'A Study of the Development of Labour Relations in the British Furniture Trade' (Oxford BLitt, 1955).

Rowe, D. J., 'Radicalism in London, 1829–1841: With Special Reference to its Middle- and Working-Class Components' (Southampton MA, 1965).

Shearring, H. A., 'The Social Structure and Development of London, circa 1800–1830' (Oxford DPhil, 1955).

Statham, James, 'The Location and Development of London's Leather Manufacturing Industry Since the Early Nineteenth Century' (London MA, 1965).

Viles, David Brian, 'The Building Trade Workers of London, 1835–1860' (London MPhil, 1975).

Books and articles

Alexander, Sally, 'Women's Work in Nineteenth-Century London; A Study of the Years 1820–50', in Juliet Mitchell and Ann Oakley (eds.), *The Rights and Wrongs of Women* (Harmondsworth, 1976).

Alford, B. W. E., 'Government Expenditure and the Growth of the Printing Industry in the Nineteenth Century', *Economic History Review*, Second Series, XVII (1964–5).

Altick, Richard D., *The English Common Reader: A Social History of the Mass Reading Public 1800–1900* (Chicago, 1957).

Armytage, W. H. G., *Heavens Below: Utopian Experiments in England, 1560–1960* (1961).

Ascoli, David, *The Queen's Peace: The Origins and Development of the Metropolitan Police, 1829–1979* (1979).

Ashforth, David, 'The Urban Poor Law', in Derek Fraser (ed.), *The New Poor Law in the Nineteenth Century* (1976).

Banbury, Philip, *Shipbuilders of the Thames and Medway* (Newton Abbot, 1971).

Barker, Ambrose G., *Henry Hetherington, 1792–1849: Pioneer in the Freethought and Working Class Struggles of a Hundred Years Ago for the Freedom of the Press* (n.d.).

Barker, Theo, 'The Early Railway Age', in Theo Barker (ed.), *The Long March of Everyman, 1750–1960* (Penguin edn, 1978).

Baxter, John L., 'Early Chartism and Labour Class Struggle: South Yorkshire 1837–1840', in Sidney Pollard and Colin Holmes (eds.), *Essays in the Economic and Social History of South Yorkshire* (Sheffield, 1976).

Bédarida, François, 'Londres au Milieu du XIXe Siècle: une Analyse de Structure Sociale', *Annales: Economies-Sociétés-Civilisations*, XXIII (1968).

Bédarida, François, *A Social History of England, 1851–1975* (1979).

Behagg, Clive, 'Custom, Class and Change: the Trade Societies of Birmingham', *Social History*, IV (1979).

Bird, James, *The Geography of the Port of London* (1957).

Booth, Charles, *Life and Labour of the People in London. First Series: Poverty. Vol. 4: The Trades of East London Connected with Poverty* (1904).

Booth, Charles, *Life and Labour of the People in London. Second Series: Industry* (5 vols., 1903).

Briggs, Asa, *The Age of Improvement, 1783–1867* (1979 edn).

Briggs, Asa, 'The Background of the Parliamentary Reform Movement in Three English Cities (1830–2)', *Cambridge Historical Journal*, X, no. 3 (1952).

Briggs, Asa (ed.), *Chartist Studies* (1959).

Briggs, Asa, 'Chartists in Tasmania: A Note', *Bulletin of the Society for the Study of Labour History*, no. 3 (Autumn 1961).

Briggs, Asa, 'Middle-Class Consciousness in English Politics, 1780–1846', *Past and Present*, no. 9 (April 1956).

Briggs, Asa, 'Open Questions of Labour History', *Bulletin of the Society for the Study of Labour History*, no. 1 (Autumn 1960).

Briggs, Asa, 'Social Structure and Politics in Birmingham and Lyons (1825–1848)', *British Journal of Sociology,* I (1950).

Briggs, Asa, 'Thomas Attwood and the Economic Background of the Birmingham Political Union', *Cambridge Historical Journal,* IX, no. 2 (1948).

Briggs, Asa, *Victorian Cities* (Penguin edn, 1968).

Brock, Michael, *The Great Reform Act* (1973).

Bundock, Clement J., *The Story of The National Union of Printing Bookbinding and Paper Workers* (Oxford, 1959).

Burgess, Keith, *The Origins of British Industrial Relations: The Nineteenth Century Experience* (1975).

Butler, J. R. M., *The Passing of the Great Reform Bill* (1914).

Bythell, Duncan, *The Sweated Trades: Outwork in Nineteenth-century Britain* (1978).

Carus-Wilson, E. M. (ed.), *Essays in Economic History,* III (1962).

Centre for Urban Studies, *London: Aspects of Change* (1964).

Challinor, Raymond, and Ripley, Brian, *The Miners' Association: A Trade Union in the Age of the Chartists* (1968).

Child, John, *Industrial Relations in the British Printing Industry: The Quest for Security* (1967).

Christensen, Torben, *Origin and History of Christian Socialism, 1848–54* (Aarhus, 1962).

Church, R. A., 'The British Leather Industry and Foreign Competition, 1870–1914', *Economic History Review,* Second Series, XXIV (1971).

Church, R. A., 'Labour Supply and Innovation, 1800–1860: The Boot and Shoe Industry', *Business History,* XII, no. 1 (January 1970).

Clapham, J. H., *An Economic History of Modern Britain: The Early Railway Age, 1820–1850* (Cambridge, 2nd edn, 1930).

Clapham, J. H., *An Economic History of Modern Britain: Free Trade and Steel, 1850–1886* (Cambridge, 1932).

Clapham, J. H., 'The Spitalfields Acts, 1773–1824', *Economic Journal,* XXVI (1916).

Clegg, H. A., Fox, Alan, and Thompson, A. F., *A History of British Trade Unions Since 1889, vol. 1: 1889–1910* (Oxford, 1964).

Cole, G. D. H., *Attempts at General Union: A Study in British Trade Union History, 1818–1834* (1953).

Cole, G. D. H., *A Century of Co-operation* (n.d.).

Cole, G. D. H., *Chartist Portraits* (1965 edn).

Cole, G. D. H., *Studies in Class Structure* (1955).

Cole, G. D. H., and Filson, A. W., *British Working Class Movements: Select Documents, 1789–1875* (1965 edn).

Cole, G. D. H., and Postgate, Raymond, *The Common People, 1746–1946* (1961 edn).

Conklin, Robert J., *Thomas Cooper the Chartist (1805–1892)* (Manila, 1935).

Coppock, J. T., and Prince, Hugh C. (eds.), *Greater London* (1964).

Creighton, M., *Memoir of Sir George Grey, Bart., G.C.B.* (Newcastle-upon-Tyne, 1884).

Critchley, T. A., *The Conquest of Violence: Order and Liberty in Britain* (1970).

Critchley, T. A., *A History of Police in England and Wales* (2nd edn, 1978).

Crosby, Travis L., *English Farmers and the Politics of Protection, 1815–1852* (Hassocks, 1977).

Crossick, Geoffrey, *An Artisan Elite in Victorian Society: Kentish London 1840–1880* (1978).

Cummings, D. C., *A Historical Survey of the Boiler Makers' and Iron and Steel Ship Builders' Society from August, 1834, to August, 1904, With a Brief Sketch of the Life and Work of its Leading Officials: Comparisons between Boilermaking, Shipbuilding, and Bridgebuilding in the Early Days of its History and of Modern Times: and Interesting Arbitration Awards and Agreements* (Newcastle-on-Tyne, 1905).

Denvir, John, *The Irish in Britain from the Earliest Times to the Fall and Death of Parnell* (1892).

Dobbs, S. P., *The Clothing Workers of Great Britain* (1928).

Donajgrodzki, A. P. (ed.), *Social Control in Nineteenth Century Britain* (1977).

Drake, Barbara, 'The West End Tailoring Trade', in Sidney Webb and Arnold Freeman (eds.), *Seasonal Trades* (1912).

Duncombe, Thomas H. (ed.), *The Life and Correspondence of Thomas Slingsby Duncombe, Late MP for Finsbury* (2 vols., 1868).

Duveau, Georges, *1848: The Making of A Revolution* (1967).

Dyos, H. J., and Wolff, Michael (eds.), *The Victorian City: Images and Realities* (2 vols., 1973).

Edsall, Nicholas C., *The Anti-Poor Law Movement, 1834–44* (Manchester, 1971).

Edwards, R. Dudley, and Williams, T. Desmond (eds.), *The Great Famine: Studies in Irish History 1845–52* (Dublin, 1956).

Epstein, J. A., 'Feargus O'Connor and the *Northern Star*', *International Review of Social History*, XXI (1976).

Falkus, M. E., 'The British Gas Industry before 1850', *Economic History Review*, Second Series, XX (1967).

Fay, C. R., *Huskisson and His Age* (1951).

Floud, Roderick, *The British Machine Tool Industry, 1850–1914* (Cambridge, 1976).

Foster, John, *Class Struggle and the Industrial Revolution: Early Industrial Capitalism in Three English Towns* (1977 edn.).

Fox, Alan, *A History of the National Union of Boot and Shoe Operatives, 1874–1957* (Oxford, 1958).

Fox, Celina, 'The Development of Social Reportage in English Periodical Illustration During the 1840s and Early 1850s', *Past and Present*, no. 74 (February 1977).

Fraser, W. H., 'The Glasgow Cotton Spinners, 1837', in John Butt & J. T. Ward (eds.), *Scottish Themes: Essays in Honour of Professor S. G. E. Lythe* (Edinburgh, 1976).

French, J. O., *Plumbers in Unity: History of the Plumbing Trades Union, 1865–1965* (n.p., n.d.).

Fyrth, H. J., and Collins, Henry, *The Foundry Workers: A Trade Union History* (Manchester, 1959).

Galton, F. W. (ed.), *Select Documents Illustrating the History of Trade Unionism: 1. The Tailoring Trade* (1896).

Gash, Norman (ed.), *The Age of Peel* (1968).

Gash, Norman, *Sir Robert Peel: The Life of Sir Robert Peel after 1830* (1972).

George, M. Dorothy, 'The London Coal-Heavers: Attempts to Regulate Waterside Labour in the Eighteenth and Nineteenth Centuries', *Economic Journal*, Economic History Series No. 2 (May 1927).

George, M. Dorothy, *London Life in the Eighteenth Century* (Penguin edn, 1966).

Gibson, A. V. B., 'Huguenot Weavers' Houses in Spitalfields', *East London Papers*, I, no. 1 (April 1958).

Gilboy, Elizabeth W., *Wages in Eighteenth Century England* (Cambridge, Mass., 1934).

Gilding, Bob, *The Journeymen Coopers of East London. Workers' Control in an Old London Trade: with Historical Documents and Personal Reminiscences by one who has worked at the Block, and an account of Unofficial Practices down the Wine Vaults of the London Dock* (Oxford, 1971).

Gill, Conrad, *History of Birmingham, vol. 1: Manor and Borough to 1865* (1952).

Gilley, Sheridan, 'The Garibaldi Riots of 1862', *Historical Journal*, XVI (1973).

Golding, F. Y. (ed.), *Boots and Shoes: Their Making, Manufacturing and Selling* (8 vols., 1934–5).

Goodway, David, 'Chartism in London', *Bulletin of the Society for the Study of Labour History*, no. 20 (Spring 1970).

Grady, A. D., 'The Lower Lea Valley: A Barrier in East London', *East London Papers*, II, no. 1 (April 1959).

Groves, Reg, *But We Shall Rise Again: A Narrative History of Chartism* (1938).

Gurr, Ted Robert, Grabosky, Peter N., and Hula, Richard C., *The Politics of Crime and Conflict: A Comparative History of Four Cities* (Beverly Hills, 1977).

Gwynn, Denis, *Young Ireland and 1848* (Cork, 1949).

Hadfield, Alice Mary, *The Chartist Land Company* (Newton Abbot, 1970).

Halévy, Elie, *A History of the English People in the Nineteenth Century* (6 vols., 1961 edn).

Hall, P. G., 'The East London Footwear Industry: An Industrial Quarter in Decline', *East London Papers*, V, no. 1 (April 1962).

Hall, P. G., *The Industries of London: Since 1861* (1962).

Hamburger, Joseph, *James Mill and the Art of Revolution* (New Haven, Conn., 1963).

Hammond, J. L., and Hammond, Barbara, *The Skilled Labourer, 1760–1832* (1919).

Haraszti, Éva H., *Chartism* (Budapest, 1978).

Hardy, Dennis, *Alternative Communities in Nineteenth Century England* (1979).

Harrison, Brian, 'The Sunday Trading Riots of 1855', *Historical Journal*, VIII (1965).

Harrison, Brian, 'Teetotal Chartism', *History*, LVIII (1973).

Harrison, J. F. C., *Robert Owen and the Owenites in Britain and America: The Quest for the New Moral World* (1969).

Harrison, Royden, *Before the Socialists: Studies in Labour and Politics, 1861–1881* (1965).

Hart, J. M., *The British Police* (1951).

Higenbottam, S., *Our Society's History* (Manchester, 1939).

Hill, Christopher, *Puritanism and Revolution: Studies in Interpretation of the English Revolution of the 17th Century* (Panther edn, 1968).

Hilton, George W., *The Truck System: including a History of the British Truck Acts, 1465–1960* (Cambridge, 1960).

Hilton, W. S., *Foes to Tyranny: A History of the Amalgamated Union of Building Trade Workers* (1963).

Hobhouse, Hermione, *Thomas Cubitt: Master Builder* (1971).

Hobsbawm, E. J., *Industry and Empire: An Economic History of Britain since 1750* (1968).

Hobsbawm, E. J., *Labouring Men: Studies in the History of Labour* (1964).

Hobsbawm, E. J., *Primitive Rebels: Studies in Archaic Forms of Social Movement in the 19th and 20th Centuries* (Manchester, 1959).

Hobsbawm, E. J., *Revolutionaries: Contemporary Essays* (1973).

Hobsbawm, E. J., and Rudé, George, *Captain Swing* (1969).

Hollis, Patricia, 'Introduction', *The Poor Man's Guardian, 1831–1835*, I (1969).

Hollis, Patricia, *The Pauper Press: A Study in Working-Class Radicalism of the 1830s* (1970).

Hovell, Mark, *The Chartist Movement* (Manchester, 2nd edn, 1925).

Howard, Philip, 'The Mathematicians of Spitalfields', *The Times*, 18 November 1978.

Howe, Ellic (ed.), *The London Compositor: Documents relating to Wages, Working Conditions and Customs of the London Printing Trade, 1785–1900* (1947).

Howe, Ellic, and Child, John, *The Society of London Bookbinders, 1780–1951* (1952).

Howe, Ellic, and Waite, Harold E., *The London Society of Compositors (Re-Established 1848): A Centenary History* (1948).

Howell, George, *The Conflicts of Capital and Labour: Historically and Economically Considered. Being a History and Review of the Trades Unions of Great Britain, Showing Their Origins, Progress, Constitution, and Objects, in Their Varied Political, Social, Economical, and Industrial Aspects* (2nd edn, 1890).

Howell, George, *A History of the Working Men's Association from 1836 to 1850* (Newcastle upon Tyne, n.d.).

Howell, George, *Labour Legislation, Labour Movements, and Labour Leaders* (1902).

Ignatieff, Michael, 'Police and People: the Birth of Mr Peel's "Blue Locusts" ', *New Society*, 30 August 1979.

Jackson, John Archer, *The Irish in Britain* (1963).

Jackson, John A., 'The Irish in East London', *East London Papers*, VI, no. 2 (December 1963).

James, Louis, *Fiction for the Working Man, 1830–50: A Study of the Literature produced for the Working Classes in Early Victorian Urban England* (Penguin edn, 1974).

Jefferys, James B., *The Story of the Engineers, 1800–1945* (1945).

Jefferys, M. and J. B., 'The Wages, Hours and Trade Customs of the Skilled Engineer in 1861', *Economic History Review*, XVII (1947).

Jenkin, Alfred, 'Chartism and the Trade Unions', in Lionel M. Munby (ed.), *The Luddites and Other Essays* (Edgware, 1971).

Jenkins, Mick, *The General Strike of 1842* (1980).

Johnson, Christopher H., *Utopian Communism in France: Cabet and the Icarians, 1839–1851* (Ithaca, NY, 1974).

Jones, David, *Chartism and the Chartists* (1975).

Jones, Gareth Stedman, *Outcast London: A Study in the Relationship Between Classes in Victorian Society* (Oxford, 1971).

Jones, Gareth Stedman, 'Working-Class Culture and Working-Class Politics in London, 1870–1900; Notes on the Remaking of a Working Class', *Journal of Social History*, VII (1973–4).

Judge, Kenneth, 'Early Chartist Organization and the Convention of 1839', *International Review of Social History*, XX (1975).

Kamenka, Eugene, and Smith, F. B. (eds.), *Intellectuals and Revolution: Socialism and the Experience of 1848* (1979).

Kent, Christopher, 'The Whittington Club: A Bohemian Experiment in Middle Class Social Reform', *Victorian Studies*, XVIII (1974–5).

Kidd, Archibald T., *History of the Tin-Plate Workers and Sheet Metal Workers and Braziers Societies* (1949).

Kiddier, William, *The Old Trade Unions: From Unprinted Records of the Brushmakers* (2nd edn, 1931).

[Kingsley, Frances E. (ed.)], *Charles Kingsley: His Letters and Memories of His Life* (2nd edn, 2 vols., 1877).

Kirby, R. G., and Musson, A. E., *The Voice of the People: John Doherty, 1798–1854: Trade Unionist, Radical and Factory Reformer* (Manchester, 1975).

Klingender, F. D., *The Condition of Clerical Labour in Britain* (1935).

Large, David, 'William Lovett', in Patricia Hollis (ed.), *Pressure from Without: in Early Victorian England* (1974).

Laughton, James Knox, *Memoirs of the Life and Correspondence of Henry Reeve, C.B., D.C.L.* (2 vols., 1898).

Lawson-Tancred, Mary, 'The Anti-League and the Corn Law Crisis of 1846', *Historical Journal,* III (1960).

Leech, K., 'The Decay of Spitalfields', *East London Papers,* VII, no. 2 (December 1964).

Lees, Lynn Hollen, *Exiles of Erin: Irish Migrants in Victorian London* (Manchester, 1979).

Lees, Lynn H., 'Patterns of Lower-Class Life: Irish Slum Communities in Nineteenth-Century London', in Stephan Thernstrom and Richard Sennett (eds.), *Nineteenth-Century Cities: Essays in the New Urban History* (New Haven, 1969).

Leeson, R. A., *Travelling Brothers: The Six Centuries' Road from Craft Fellowship to Trade Unionism* (1979).

Leventhal, F. M., *Respectable Radical: George Howell and Victorian Working Class Politics* (1971).

Lindsay, Jack, *Men of Forty-Eight* (1948).

Longford, Elizabeth, *Wellington: Pillar of State* (1972).

McCord, Norman, *The Anti-Corn Law League, 1838–1846* (2nd edn, 1968).

Mace, Rodney, *Trafalgar Square: Emblem of Empire* (1976).

Macintyre, Angus, *The Liberator: Daniel O'Connell and the Irish Party, 1830–1847* (1965).

Marlow, Joyce, *The Tolpuddle Martyrs* (1971).

Martin, J. E., *Greater London: An Industrial Geography* (1966).

Martin, Robert Bernard, *The Dust of Combat: A Life of Charles Kingsley* (1959).

Marx, Karl, *Capital* (Everyman edn, 2 vols., 1957).

Mather, F. C., *Chartism* (1972 edn).

Mather, F. C., *Public Order in the Age of the Chartists* (Manchester, 1966 edn).

Matthews, R. C. O., *A Study in Trade-Cycle History: Economic Fluctuations in Great Britain, 1833–1842* (Cambridge, 1954).

Maurice, Frederick (ed.), *The Life of Frederick Denison Maurice: Chiefly Told in His Own Letters* (2nd edn, 2 vols., 1884).

Maxwell, Sir Herbert, *Sixty Years a Queen: The Story of Her Majesty's Reign* [1897].

Millar, William, *Plastering: Plain and Decorative. A Practical Treatise on the Art and Craft of Plastering and Modelling: Including Full Descriptions of the Various Tools, Materials, Processes, and Appliances Employed: Also of Moulded or 'Fine' Concrete as Used for Fire-Resisting Stairs and Floors, Paving, Architectural Dressing, &c., and of Reinforced or Steel Concrete; Together with an Account of Historical Plastering in England, Scotland and Ireland, Accompanied by Numerous Examples* (3rd edn, 1905).

Miller, Wilbur R., *Cops and Bobbies: Police Authority in New York and London, 1830–1870* (Chicago, 1977).

Minchinton, W. E., *The British Tinplate Industry: A History* (Oxford, 1957).

Mitchell, R. J., and Leys, M. D. R., *A History of London Life* (1958).

Montgomery, H. H., *The History of Kennington and Its Neighbourhood, with Chapters on Cricket Past and Present* (1889).

Mortimer, J. E., *History of the Boilermakers' Society, vol. 1: 1834–1906* (1973).

Moss, Bernard H., *The Origins of the French Labor Movement, 1830–1914: The Socialism of Skilled Workers* (Berkeley and Los Angeles, 1976).

Moss, D. J., 'A Study in Failure: Thomas Attwood, MP for Birmingham, 1832–1839', *Historical Journal*, XXI (1978).

Mosse, George L., 'The Anti-League: 1844–1846', *Economic History Review*, XVII (1947).

Munby, D. L., *Industry and Planning in Stepney* (1951).

Musson, A. E., *British Trade Unions, 1800–1875* (1972).

Musson, A. E., *Trade Union and Social History* (1974).

Musson, A. E., *The Typographical Association: Origins and History up to 1949* (1954).

Namier, Sir Lewis, *1848: The Revolution of the Intellectuals* (1946).

Neale, R. S., *Class and Ideology in the Nineteenth Century* (1972).

Newens, Stan, 'Thomas Edward Bowkett: Nineteenth Century Pioneer of the Working-Class Movement in East London', *History Workshop Journal*, no. 9 (Spring 1980).

Newman, Peter K., 'The Early London Clothing Trades', *Oxford Economic Papers*, New Series, IV (1952).

Nowell-Smith, Simon, 'Charles Manby Smith: His Family & Friends, His Fantasies & Fabrications', *Journal of the Printing Historical Society*, no. 7 (1971).

Nowlan, Kevin B., *The Politics of Repeal: A Study in the Relations between Great Britain and Ireland, 1841–50* (1965).

O'Higgins, Rachel, 'The Irish Influence in the Chartist Movement', *Past and Present*, no. 20 (November 1961).

O'Higgins, Rachel, 'Irish Trade Unions and Politics, 1830–50', *Historical Journal*, IV (1961).

Oliver, J. L., *The Development and Structure of the Furniture Industry* (Oxford, 1966).

Oliver, J. Leonard, 'The East London Furniture Industry', *East London Papers*, IV, no. 2 (October 1961).

Oliver, W. H., 'The Consolidated Trades' Union of 1834', *Economic History Review*, Second Series, XVII (1964–5).

Oliver, W. H., 'The Labour Exchange Phase of the Co-operative Movement', *Oxford Economic Papers*, New Series, X (1958).

Olsen, Donald J., *The Growth of Victorian London* (1976).

Parssinen, T. M., 'Association, Convention and Anti-parliament in British Radical Politics, 1771–1848', *English Historical Review*, LXXXVIII (1973).

Parssinen, Terry M., 'Mesmeric Performers', *Victorian Studies*, XXI (1977–8).

Parssinen, T. M., and Prothero, I. J., 'The London Tailors' Strike of 1834 and the Collapse of the Grand National Consolidated Trades' Union: A Police Spy's Report', *International Review of Social History*, XXII (1977).

Pattison, George, 'The Coopers' Strike at the West India Dock, 1821', *Mariner's Mirror*, LV, no. 2 (1969).

Pattison, George, 'The East India Dock Company, 1803–1838', *East London Papers*, VII, no. 1 (July 1964).

Pattison, George, 'Nineteenth-Century Dock Labour in the Port of London', *Mariner's Mirror*, LII, no. 3 (August 1966).

Peacock, A. J., *Bradford Chartism, 1838–1840* (York, 1969).

Perry, George, 'Found – The World's First Crowd Photograph', *The Sunday Times Magazine*, 5 June 1977.

Pinks, William J., *The History of Clerkenwell . . . With Additions by the Editor, Edward J. Wood* (2nd edn, 1881).

Plummer, Alfred, *Bronterre: A Political Biography of Bronterre O'Brien 1804–1864* (1971).

Plummer, Alfred, *The London Weavers' Company, 1600–1970* (1972).

Pollard, S., 'The Decline of Shipbuilding on the Thames', *Economic History Review,* Second Series, III (1950–1).

Pollard, Sidney, *A History of Labour in Sheffield* (Liverpool, 1959).

Porter, Bernard, *The Refugee Question in Mid-Victorian Politics* (Cambridge, 1979).

Postgate, R. W., *The Builders' History* (n.d.).

Postgate, Raymond, *Story of a Year: 1848* (1955).

Prest, John, *Lord John Russell* (1972).

Price, Richard, *Masters, Unions and Men: Work Control in Building and the Rise of Labour, 1830–1914* (Cambridge, 1980).

Price, Roger (ed.), *1848 in France* (1975).

Price, Roger (ed.), *Revolution and Reaction: 1848 and the Second French Republic* (1975).

Prothero, I. J., *Artisans and Politics in Early Nineteenth-Century London: John Gast and his Times* (Folkestone, 1979).

Prothero, Iorwerth, 'Chartism in London', *Past and Present,* no. 44 (August 1969).

Prothero, I. J., 'London Chartism and the Trades', *Economic History Review,* Second Series, XXIV (1971).

Prothero, Iorwerth, 'The London Working Men's Association and the "People's Charter" ', *Past and Present,* no. 38 (December 1967).

Prothero, Iorwerth, 'William Benbow and the Concept of the "General Strike" ', *Past and Present,* no. 63 (May 1974).

Pudney, John, *London's Docks* (1975).

Pulling, Christopher, *Mr Punch and the Police* (1964).

Radzinowicz, Leon, *A History of English Criminal Law and its Administration from 1750* (4 vols., 1948–68).

Raikes, Captain G. A., *The History of the Honourable Artillery Company* (2 vols., 1878–9).

Raven, Charles E., *Christian Socialism, 1848–1854* (1920).

Read, Donald, *The English Provinces, c. 1760–1960: A Study in Influence* (1964).

Read, Donald, and Glasgow, Eric, *Feargus O'Connor: Irishman and Chartist* (1961).

Reeder, D. A., 'A Theatre of Suburbs: Some Patterns of Development in West London, 1801–1911', in H. J. Dyos (ed.), *The Study of Urban History: The Proceedings of an International Round-table Conference of the Urban History Group at Gilbert Murray Hall, University of Leicester on 23–26 September 1966* (1968).

Reid, Douglas A., 'The Decline of Saint Monday, 1766–1876', *Past and Present,* no. 71 (May 1976).

Reith, Charles, *British Police and the Democratic Ideal* (1943).

Reith, Charles, *A New Study of Police History* (Edinburgh, 1956).

Reith, Charles, *A Short History of the British Police* (1948).

Ridley, Jasper, *Lord Palmerston* (1970).

Roebuck, Janet, *Urban Development in 19th-Century London: Lambeth, Battersea & Wandsworth, 1838–1888* (Chichester, 1979).

Rose, Millicent, *The East End of London* (1951).

Rosenblatt, Frank F., *The Chartist Movement: In Its Social and Economic Aspects* (New York, 1916).

Rothstein, Th., *From Chartism to Labourism: Historical Sketches of the English Working Class Movement* (New York, 1929).

Rowe, D. J., 'Chartism and the Spitalfields Silk-weavers', *Economic History Review*, Second Series, XX (1967).

Rowe, D. J., 'Class and Political Radicalism in London, 1831–2', *Historical Journal*, XIII (1970).

Rowe, D. J., 'The Failure of London Chartism', *Historical Journal*, XI (1968).

Rowe, D. J., 'Francis Place and the Historian', *Historical Journal*, XVI (1973).

Rowe, D. J., 'The London Working Men's Association and the "People's Charter" ', *Past and Present*, no. 36 (April 1967).

Rowe, D. J., 'The London Working Men's Association and the "People's Charter": Rejoinder', *Past and Present*, no. 38 (December 1967).

Royle, Edward, *Victorian Infidels: The Origins of the British Secularist Movement, 1791–1866* (Manchester, 1974).

Rudé, George, *The Crowd in the French Revolution* (1959).

Rudé, George, *The Crowd in History: A Study of Popular Disturbances in France and England, 1730–1848* (New York, 1964).

Rudé, George, 'English Rural and Urban Disturbances on the Eve of the First Reform Bill, 1830–1831', *Past and Present*, no. 37 (July 1967).

Rudé, George, *Hanoverian London, 1714–1808* (1971).

Rudé, George, *Paris and London in the Eighteenth Century: Studies in Popular Protest* (n.d.).

Rudé, George, *Protest and Punishment: The Story of the Social and Political Protesters transported to Australia, 1788–1868* (Oxford, 1978).

Rudé, George, *Wilkes and Liberty: A Social Study of 1763 to 1774* (Oxford, 1962).

Rumbelow, Donald, *I Spy Blue: The Police and Crime in the City of London from Elizabeth I to Victoria* (1971).

Samuel, Raphael, 'Workshop of the World: Steam Power and Hand Technology in mid-Victorian Britain', *History Workshop Journal*, no. 3 (Spring 1977).

Saville, John, 'The Background to the Revival of Socialism in England', *Bulletin of the Society for the Study of Labour History*, no. 11 (Autumn 1965).

Saville, John, 'Chartism in the Year of Revolution (1848)', *Modern Quarterly*, New Series, VIII, no. 1 (Winter 1952–3).

Saville, John, 'The Chartist Land Plan', *Bulletin of the Society for the Study of Labour History*, no. 3 (Autumn 1961).

Saville, John, 'The Christian Socialists of 1848', in John Saville (ed.), *Democracy and the Labour Movement: Essays in Honour of Dona Torr* (1954).

Saville, John, *Ernest Jones: Chartist. Selections from the Writings and Speeches of Ernest Jones with Introduction and Notes* (1952).

Saville, John, 'Introduction', *The Red Republican & The Friend of the People*, I (1966).

Saville, John, 'Introduction: R. G. Gammage and the Chartist Movement' to R. G. Gammage, *History of the Chartist Movement, 1837–1854* (New York, 1969 edn).

Saville, John, 'Some Aspects of Chartism in Decline', *Bulletin of the Society for the Study of Labour History*, no. 20 (Spring 1970).

Schoyen, A. R., *The Chartist Challenge: A Portrait of George Julian Harney* (1958).

Schwartz, L. D., 'Income Distribution and Social Structure in London in the

Late Eighteenth Century', *Economic History Review*, Second Series, XXXII (1979).

Seth, Ronald, *The Specials: The Story of the Special Constabulary in England, Wales and Scotland* (1961).

Shepherd, Michael A., 'The Origins and Incidence of the Term "Labour Aristocracy" ', *Bulletin of the Society for the Study of Labour History*, no. 37 (Autumn 1978).

Sheppard, F. H. W., *Local Government in St Marylebone 1688–1835: A Study of the Vestry and the Turnpike Trust* (1958).

Sheppard, Francis, *London, 1808–1870: The Infernal Wen* (1971).

Sheppard, Francis, Belcher, Victor, and Cottrell, Philip, 'The Middlesex and Yorkshire Deeds Registries and the Study of Building Fluctuations', *London Journal*, V, no. 2 (November 1979).

Shipley, Stan, *Club Life and Socialism in Mid-Victorian London* (Oxford, 1971).

Sigmann, Jean, *Eighteen-Fortyeight: The Romantic and Democratic Revolutions in Europe* (1973).

Silver, Allan, 'The Demand for Order in Civil Society: A Review of Some Themes in the History of Urban Crime, Police, and Riot', in David J. Bordua (ed.), *The Police: Six Sociological Essays* (New York, 1967).

Slosson, Preston William, *The Decline of the Chartist Movement* (New York, 1916).

Smith, F. B., 'Mayhew's Convict', *Victorian Studies*, XXII (1978–9).

Smith, F. B., *Radical Artisan: William James Linton 1812–97* (Manchester, 1973).

Smith, Raymond, *Sea-Coal for London: History of the Coal Factors in the London Market* (1961).

Southgate, Donald, *'The Most English Minister . . .': The Policies and Politics of Palmerston* (1966).

Stearns, Peter N., *The Revolutions of 1848* (1974).

Stern, Walter M., *The Porters of London* (1960).

Stevenson, John (ed.), *London in the Age of Reform* (Oxford, 1977).

Stevenson, John, *Popular Disturbances in England, 1700–1870* (1979).

Stewart, Margaret, and Hunter, Leslie, *The Needle is Threaded: 'The History of an Industry'* (1964).

Stewart, Neil, *The Fight for the Charter* (1937).

Stigler, George J., *Five Lectures on Economic Problems: Five Lectures delivered at the London School of Economics and Political Science on the Invitation of the Senate of the University of London* (1949).

Storch, Robert D., 'The Plague of the Blue Locusts: Police Reform and Popular Resistance in Northern England, 1840–57', *International Review of Social History*, XX (1975).

Storch, Robert D., 'The Policeman as Domestic Missionary: Urban Discipline and Popular Culture in Northern England, 1850–1880', *Journal of Social History*, IX (1975–6).

Strauss, E., *Irish Nationalism and British Democracy* (1951).

Summerson, John, *Georgian London* (Penguin edn, 1962).

Taylor, Barbara, ' "The Men Are as Bad as Their Masters . . .".: Socialism, Feminism, and Sexual Antagonism in the London Tailoring Trade in the Early 1830s', *Feminist Studies*, V, no. 1 (Spring 1979).

Taylor, W. C., and Pinnock, W. H., *Whittaker's Improved Edition of Pinnock's Goldsmith's History of England, from the Invasion of Julius Caesar to the Close of the Abyssinian Campaign* (1873 edn).

Tholfsen, Trygve R., 'The Artisan and the Culture of Early Victorian Birmingham', *University of Birmingham Historical Journal*, IV, no. 2 (1954).

Tholfsen, Trygve R., 'The Chartist Crisis in Birmingham', *International Review of Social History*, III (1958).

Tholfsen, Trygve R., 'The Origins of the Birmingham Caucus', *Historical Journal*, II (1959).

Tholfsen, Trygve R., *Working Class Radicalism in Mid-Victorian England* (1976).

Thomas, W. E. S., 'Francis Place and Working Class History', *Historical Journal*, V (1962).

Thompson, Dorothy, *The Early Chartists* (1971).

Thompson, Dorothy, 'Notes on Aspects of Chartist Leadership', *Bulletin of the Society for the Study of Labour History*, no. 15 (Autumn 1967).

Thompson, Dorothy, 'La Presse de la Classe Ouvrière Anglaise, 1836–1848', in Jacques Godechot (ed.), *La Presse Ouvrière, 1819–1850* (Paris, 1966).

Thompson, E. P., *The Making of the English Working Class* (1963).

Thompson, E. P., *Writing by Candlelight* (1980).

Thompson, Paul, *Socialists, Liberals and Labour: The Struggle for London, 1885–1914* (1967).

Thorn, Gary, 'The Early History of the Amalgamated Society of Boot and Shoemakers (Cordwainers)', *Bulletin of the Society for the Study of Labour History*, no. 39 (Autumn 1979).

Thurston, Gavin, *The Clerkenwell Riot: The Killing of Constable Culley* (1967).

Tobias, J. J., *Crime and Industrial Society in the Nineteenth Century* (Penguin edn, 1972).

Trades Union Congress, *The Book of The Martyrs of Tolpuddle, 1834–1934: The Story of the Dorsetshire Labourers Who Were Convicted and Sentenced to Seven Years' Transportation for Forming a Trade Union* (1934).

Treble, J. H., 'O'Connor, O'Connell and the Attitudes of Irish Immigrants towards Chartism in the North of England 1838–1848', in J. Butt and I. F. Clarke (eds.), *The Victorian and Social Protest: A Symposium* (Newton Abbot, 1973).

Tressell, Robert, *The Ragged Trousered Philanthropists* (Panther edn, 1965).

Tucker, Rufus S., 'Real Wages of Artisans in London, 1729–1935', *Journal of the American Statistical Association*, XXI (1936).

Vincent, John, 'The Oldest Profession', *New Statesman*, 5 August 1966.

Wallas, Graham, *The Life of Francis Place, 1771–1854* (4th edn, 1925).

Ward, J. T., *Chartism* (1973).

Ward, J. T. (ed.), *Popular Movements, c. 1830–1850* (1970).

Warner, Sir Frank, *The Silk Industry of the United Kingdom: Its Origin and Development* (n.d.).

Wearmouth, Robert F., *Some Working-Class Movements of the Nineteenth Century* (1948).

Webb, Sidney and Beatrice, *The History of Trade Unionism* (1894).

Webb, Sidney and Beatrice, *Industrial Democracy* (1902 edn).

Weisser, Henry, *British Working-class Movements and Europe, 1815–48* (Manchester, 1975).

Welch, Charles, *Modern History of the City of London: A Record of Municipal and Social Progress from 1760 to the Present Day* (1896).

West, Julius, *A History of the Chartist Movement* (1920).

Whitaker, Wilfred B., *Victorian and Edwardian Shopworkers: The Struggle to Obtain Better Conditions and a Half-Holiday* (Newton Abbot, 1973).

Wiener, Joel H., *The War of the Unstamped: The Movement to Repeal the British Newspaper Tax, 1830–1836* (Ithaca, NY, 1969).

Wright, Thomas, *The Romance of the Shoe: Being The History of Shoemaking in All Ages, and Especially in England and Scotland* (1922).

Wrottesley, Lieut.-Col. the Hon. George, *Life and Correspondence of Field Marshal Sir John Burgoyne, Bart.* (2 vols., 1873).

Works of reference

Dictionary of National Biography

Harrison, J. F. C., and Thompson, Dorothy, *Bibliography of the Chartist Movement, 1837–1976* (Hassocks, 1978).

Harrison, Royden, Woolven, Gillian B., and Duncan, Robert, *The Warwick Guide to British Labour Periodicals 1790–1970: A Check List* (Hassocks, 1977).

Kent, William (ed.), *An Encyclopaedia of London* (1937).

Pevsner, Nikolaus, *The Buildings of England. London: Except the Cities of London and Westminster* (Harmondsworth, 1952).

Pevsner, Nikolaus, *The Buildings of England. London: The Cities of London and Westminster* (Harmondsworth, 2nd edn, 1962).

Index